YALE UNIVERSITY PUBLICATIONS
IN ANTHROPOLOGY
NUMBER 73

FENGPITOU, TAPENKENG,
AND THE PREHISTORY OF TAIWAN

KWANG-CHIH CHANG

with the collaboration of
Ch'ao-ch'i Lin, Minze Stuiver, Hsin-yüan Tu,
Matsuo Tsukada, Richard J. Pearson, and Tse-min Hsü

NEW HAVEN
PUBLISHED BY THE
DEPARTMENT OF ANTHROPOLOGY
YALE UNIVERSITY

1969

LIBRARY OF CONGRESS CATALOG CARD NUMBER: 69–11698

IRVING ROUSE
Acting Editor
ANNE F. WILDE
Assistant Editor

PRINTED IN THE UNITED STATES OF AMERICA

Preface

THE results of archeological excavations at two prehistoric sites in Taiwan and their significance in the prehistory of Taiwan and adjacent areas in the Far East are the subjects of this monograph. The pertinent field, laboratory, and library research was carried out during 1964–66 under the joint auspices of the Department of Anthropology and the Peabody Museum of Natural History, Yale University, and the Department of Archaeology and Anthropology, National Taiwan University (Taita). Excavations at Fengpitou and Tapenkeng, in Taiwan, the Republic of China, were undertaken in July–October 1964, and January–February 1965. From July 1, 1964, through June 30, 1965, the author and his collaborators carried out museum, laboratory, and library research and reconnaissance in Taiwan, and extensive laboratory and library studies continued after July 1, 1965, at the Peabody Museum.

In both conception and execution the Yale–Taita work done in 1964–66 has been teamwork. As Principal Investigator the author was responsible for the general organization and coordination of the various phases of research; he was assisted throughout the project by Dr. Richard J. Pearson, formerly a graduate student in anthropology at Yale and now on the faculty of the University of Hawaii. Dr. Matsuo Tsukada, Research Associate in Biology at Yale, was associate investigator in palynology, in charge of the palynological research in Taiwan, an independent phase of the project. The results of his research are being published separately. The radiocarbon determinations were undertaken by Dr. Minze Stuiver, Director of the Radiocarbon Laboratory at Yale University.

Professor Lin Ch'ao-ch'i, of the Department of Geology, National Taiwan University, rendered invaluable collaboration by serving as the expedition's geological consultant. He was an active participant in the fieldwork, provided information on the geological aspects of the prehistoric sites, identified all the mollusk shells at the Fengpitou site (Appendix 3) and the rock materials of all the stone artifacts, and served as liaison man between the expedition and the service laboratories in Taiwan that processed many soil and sherd samples.

Dr. Hsin-yüan Tu of the U.S. Mineralogy Laboratory at Beltsville, Maryland, analyzed the thin sections of pottery prepared by the Rock Preparation Laboratory of Yale University. Mr. Tse-min Hsü, formerly of the Laboratory of Physical Anthropology, Institute of History and Philology, Academia Sinica (Taipei, Taiwan, China), and now a graduate student in anthropology at the University of Wisconsin, studied the human bones unearthed from Fengpitou. Their papers appear as Appendices 1 and 2 of this volume.

Although his collaborators provided invaluable assistance and were responsible for much of the results that are worthwhile, the basic approach to the expedition's work and the methodological orientation guiding the interpretation of the findings are the author's own responsibility.

Acknowledgments

The Yale–Taita expedition to Taiwan was made possible through a grant (GS-410) awarded by the National Science Foundation, Washington, D.C. Publication was supported by the Information Services Program of the National Science Foundation, Washington, D.C. (GN 308), and a supplementary subsidy from the Harvard-Yenching Institute, Cambridge, Mass.

The entire collection of prehistoric artifacts resulting from this work is now permanently deposited at the Department of Archaeology and Anthropology, National Taiwan University, Taipei. While in Taiwan during 1964–65, the author held a visiting professorial title established at the Department of Archaeology and Anthropology, National Taiwan University at Taipei, by the National Council of Scientific Development of the Republic of China. The privileges afforded by this position and the active support and cooperation rendered by the department are the two important factors that enabled him to acquire the information published herein. For this the author gratefully acknowledges his indebtedness to Dr. Ch'ien Ssu-liang, President of National Taiwan University; Professor Shen Kang-po, Dean of the College of Arts; Dr. Ling Shun-sheng, Acting Chairman of the department during 1964–65; and many officers of the university who directly or indirectly gave invaluable assistance and support. Thanks are due especially to Mr. Chou Ch'ung-teh, departmental secretary, and Miss K'o Huan-yüeh, departmental librarian. We found indispensable the assistance given in the field and in the laboratory by many students and teaching assistants of the department, especially Mr. Lin Tsung-yüan, Mrs. Hu Hung Hsiu-kui, Miss Lü Ch'eng-jui, Miss Ch'en Ching-yüan, Mr. Huang Shih-ch'iang, Miss P'an Hsiu-ying, Mr. Hsü Tse-min, and Miss Chang Ch'eng-mei.

To Professor Sung Wen-hsün, who throughout the year shared with us the joys and the worries, the decisions and the responsibilities, in every phase of the expedition, we owe everything worthwhile that is contained in this volume.

We are indebted to many local officials, police officers, and landlords of our lodgings and sites, who in one way or another did their warm best to make our excavations possible and our lives comfortable and pleasant. We are especially thankful to the Commission for Historic Research of Taipei Perfecture and Mr. Wu Chi-jui, its chief field investigator; the Farmers' Association of Pa-li Hsiang; Mr. Tung P'eng-nien, formerly public relations officer of the Chinese Youth Corps; Mr. Hsiao Yen-hsi, Chief of Police of Lin-yüan Hsiang; and Mr. Chin Chen-kuan, superintendent of the Hsiao-kang sugar factory, Mr. Fu Meng-pi, deputy superintendent, Mr. Lü Yü-lin, business manager, and Mr. Chu Shih-chün, plant manager.

Last, but positively not least, the author deeply appreciates the able assistance given by Jonathan H. Kress, a graduate student at Yale. Mr. Stephen MacKinnon, former graduate student in history at Yale, and Miss Canta Pian, then a student at the Connecticut College for Women in New London, Connecticut, delighted us by joining the expedition in the summer of 1964 which they could have spent otherwise, perhaps more pleasurably.

Mrs. Mary Ling Tobing of Albany, New York, and Miss Ward Whittington of the Peabody Museum, Yale, were responsible for the drawings contained in the volume. The author is indebted to Mrs. Anne F. Wilde for her editorial assistance, and to Mrs. Marcia Ezra, who patiently typed the various drafts of the manuscript time and again. The photographic prints were prepared by the Audio-Visual Center, Yale University. There are perhaps more photographs here than are ordinarily included in such monographs; Chinese archeological publications usually do not contain large numbers of photographs of good quality, and the author wishes to provide enough of them here for comparative use.

Portions of Chapters 10, 11, and 12 have been included in the author's papers on the "Prehistory of Formosa" (presented at the sixty-fifth annual meeting of the American Anthropological Association on November 18, 1966), which will be published in *Asian Perspectives* (vol. 11, in preparation by Social Science Research Institute, University of Hawaii). Portions of these chapters also were included in "Neolithic Cultures in the Coastal Areas of Southeast China" (presented at the Symposium on Early Chinese Art and Its Possible Influence in the Pacific Basin, under the joint auspices of Columbia University and the Sackler Foundation, New York City), to be published in the proceedings of the symposium. Thanks are due to *Asian Perspectives* and the Sackler Foundation for permission to reprint them here as integral parts of a monograph dealing with the whole scope of the problem of Formosan prehistory in the context of southeast China.

Kwang-chih Chang

New Haven, Connecticut
October 1967

Contents

PART III. COMPARATIVE STUDIES

Text Figures

Plates

xiv

Tables

Introduction

The Island

THE island of Taiwan, or Formosa, is sometimes compared in shape to a sweet potato or to a tobacco leaf, two of its major crops; 300 km long and 120 across at its widest part, Taiwan is some 110 km off the southwest coast of Fukien Province of mainland China and about 300 km north of the Philippine island of Luzon. Small islands off Taiwan further serve as stepping-stones between Taiwan and mainland China on the west, and the Philippines on the south—the Pescadores in the former case and Botel Tobago and the Bataan and Babuyan islands in the latter (Fig. 1).

The location of the island—the Tropic of Cancer cuts across it about five-ninths from the northern end—puts it in the tropical–subtropical category, and the annual precipitation ranges for the most part from 1,500 to 4,000 mm, accounted for during the summer months by thunderstorms and cyclones and during the spring and fall by monsoons (Fig. 2). Tropical and subtropical vegetations abound, and rice is the main crop—planted and harvested twice a year in the north and thrice in the south.

The climate and vegetation, however, vary greatly within the island because of topography (Fig. 3). Dominating the landscape is the central mountain range, varying in altitude from 250 to 3,000 m. The highest peak, Yüshan (Jade Mountain), or Mount Morrison, at the heart of the island, is 3,997 m above the sea, the highest peak on the eastern coast of Asia. Along the coasts, surrounding the central mountain range and between it and the eastern coastal range, are arable plains. From the coastal plains upward, the temperature drops from an annual average of 24°C to 16°, and the vegetation changes from tropical to alpine (Fig. 4). While the coastal plains yield enough rice to sustain 80 per cent of the island's population, the inhabitants of the high elevations have to rely heavily on dry farming—dry paddy, millet, and sweet potatoes, and forests take over from fields at higher altitudes. Land over 2,000 m is practically uninhabited.

The present population of some 12 million is a stratification of at least three groups of people: the Malayopolynesian-speaking natives, numbering about 170,000, who live in the mountainous areas and the east coast; the sinicized aborigines, of unknown numbers, found along the west coast for the most part; and the Han Chinese, of Fukienese and Hakka descent. After 1950, the Han Chinese population was greatly augmented by immigrants from the mainland.

The documented history of Taiwan is for all practical purposes the history of Chinese settlement (C. Y. Chang 1953). The name Yi Chou had already appeared in a Chinese book early in the third century B.C., and it has been convincingly identified with the modern island of Taiwan (Ling 1951). From then on the island

1

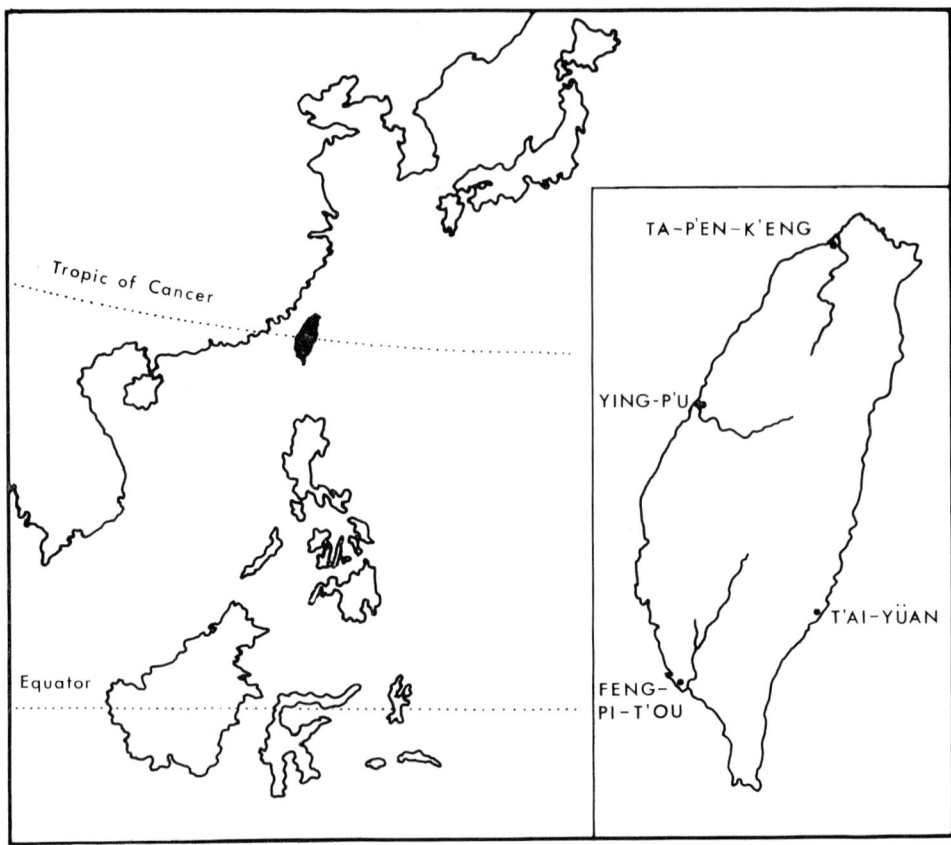

Fig. 1. Location of Taiwan in East Asia and the Location of the Prehistoric Sites Excavated by the Yale–Taita Expedition.

and its inhabitants were mentioned intermittently in Chinese historic annals, apparently through the accounts of occasional traders and travelers (Kokubu 1962b).

The colonization of Taiwan by the Chinese (Fig. 5) began at the Pescadores, which were invaded during the Sui Dynasty by General Ch'en Ling in A.D. 610. In the Sung Dynasty, Ch'üan-chou of Fukien became a major port of overseas trade; trade centers were established at the Pescadores and the port of Pei-kang in midwestern Taiwan, and Chinese settlers began to immigrate into the southern part of Taiwan. The city of An-p'ing was built in 1624. At the same time, several Western colonial powers also attempted entry. Portuguese sailors first encountered the island in 1590. They called it *Ilha Formosa* (The Beautiful Island) and close on their heels came the Dutch and the Spaniards. The Spaniards ruled the northern part of Taiwan between 1626 and 1646; the Dutch ruled the south and then the north as well, after the Spaniards left, between 1624 and 1661. But Chinese immigrants kept pouring in, the first wave of mass immigration occurring in 1628 when a severe

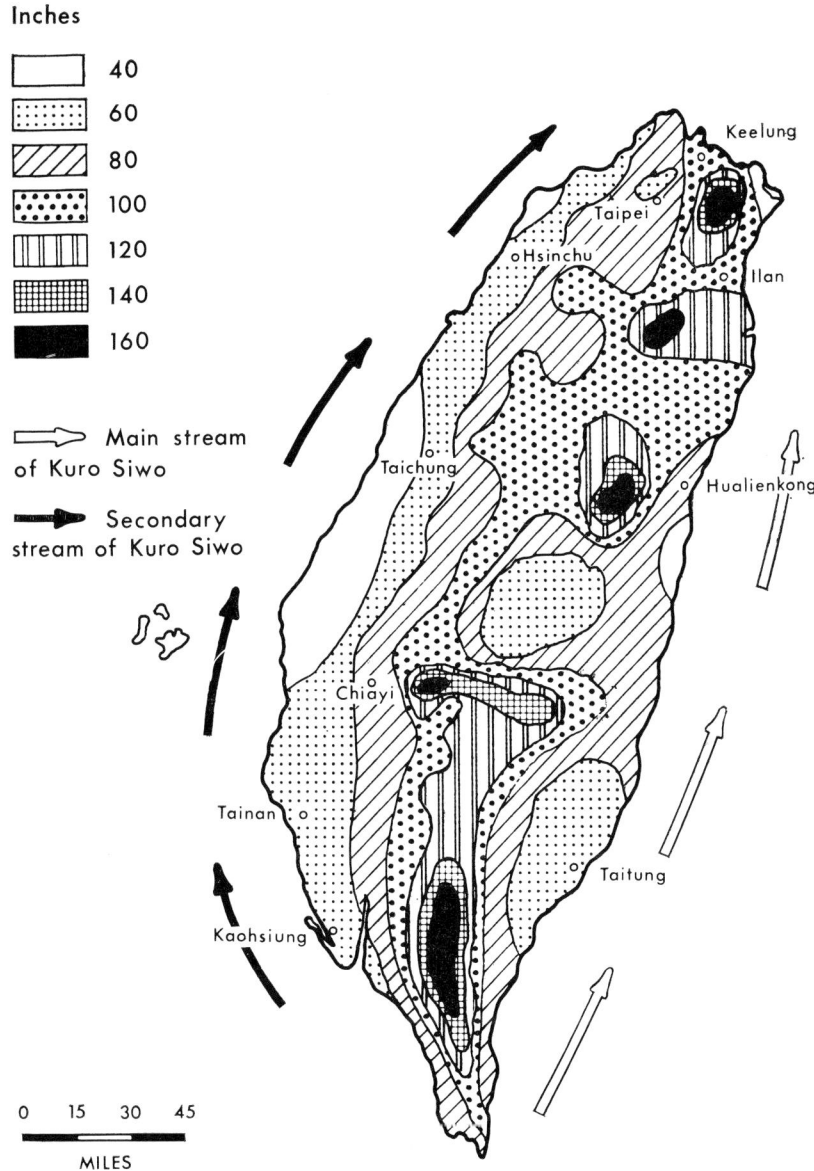

Inches

☐ 40

▦ 60

▨ 80

▨ 100

▥ 120

▦ 140

■ 160

⇨ Main stream
of Kuro Siwo

➤ Secondary
stream of Kuro Siwo

Keelung

Taipei

oHsinchu

Ilan

Taichung

Hualienkong

Chiayi

Tainan

Taitung

Kaohsiung

0   15   30   45

MILES

FIG. 2. Average Annual Rainfall of Taiwan (*after* Hsieh 1964).

drought in Fukien forced thousands to seek refuge on the island. In 1661, with a force of 25,000 troops from Amoy, General Cheng Ch'eng-kung (Koxinga) invaded the Pescadores and then finally drove the Dutch out of the island. The Cheng family reigned here from 1661 until 1683 when Taiwan fell to the Manchus. It has

Altitude in feet

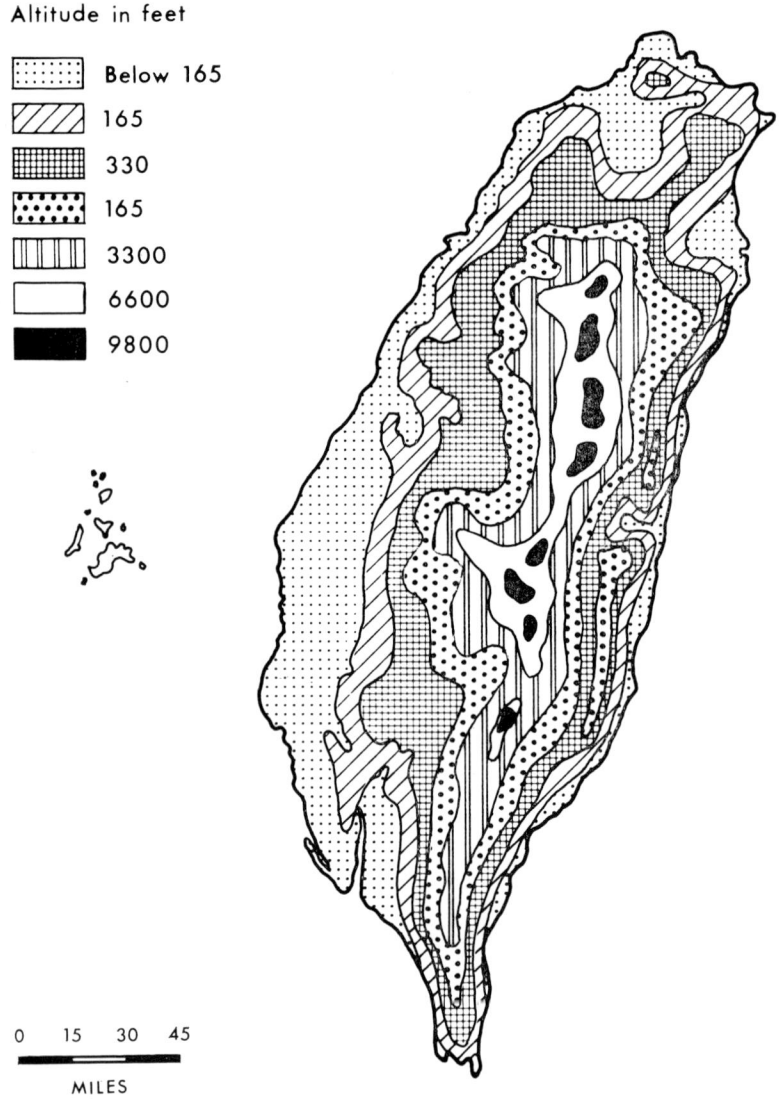

	Altitude
⬚	Below 165
▨	165
▦	330
⠿	165
⦀	3300
⬜	6600
■	9800

0   15   30   45

MILES

FIG. 3. Relief Map of Taiwan (*after* Hsieh 1964).

remained under Chinese rule ever since except for the interval between 1895 and 1945 when the island was occupied by the Japanese.

The Prehistory

Although the Chinese and other literate peoples first set foot on Taiwan and made brief accounts of the island and its inhabitants as early as the third century B.C., it

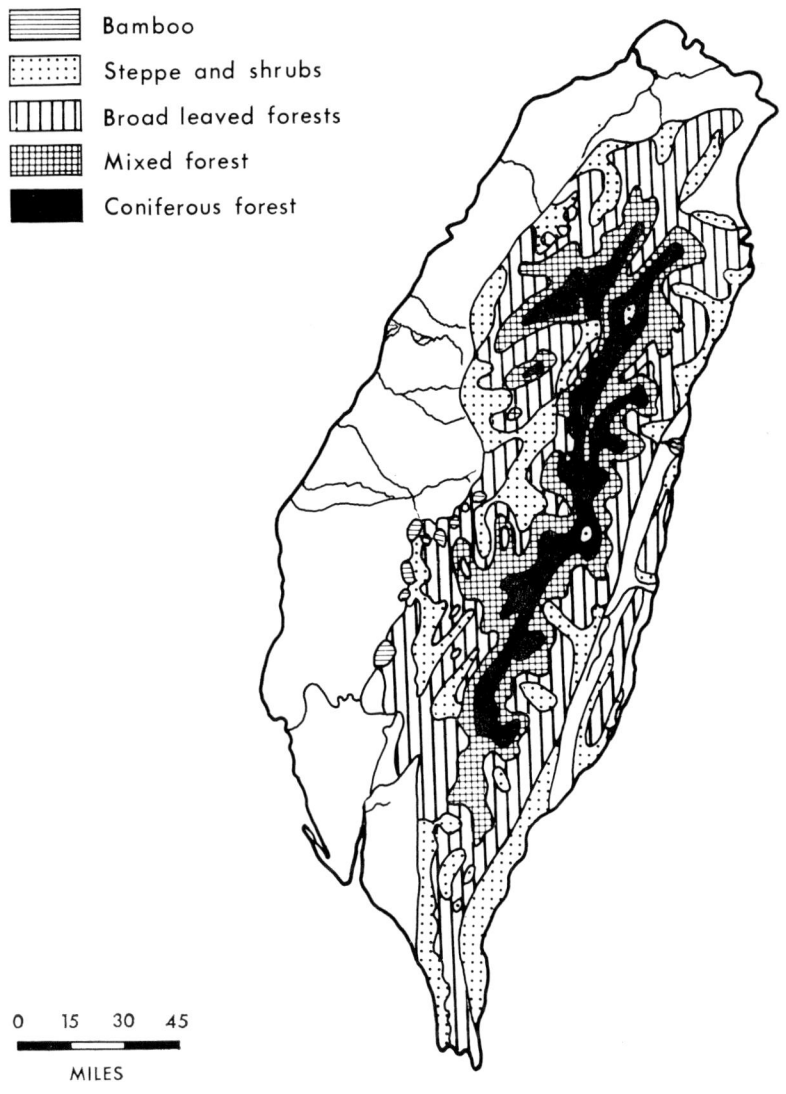

Bamboo

Steppe and shrubs

Broad leaved forests

Mixed forest

Coniferous forest

0   15   30   45

MILES

FIG. 4. Natural Vegetation of Taiwan (*after* Hsieh 1964).

was not until around A.D. 1600, when large numbers of immigrants entered Taiwan, that significant historical accounts became available. These settlers at first centered in the southern ports of the island and only gradually expanded north, east, and up into the highlands. Thus the historic period of Taiwan spans no more than three hundred years for the most part, and the investigation of the island's history of human settlement and culture before the short historic period must be left to the archeologists (Kanaseki and Kobuku 1950).

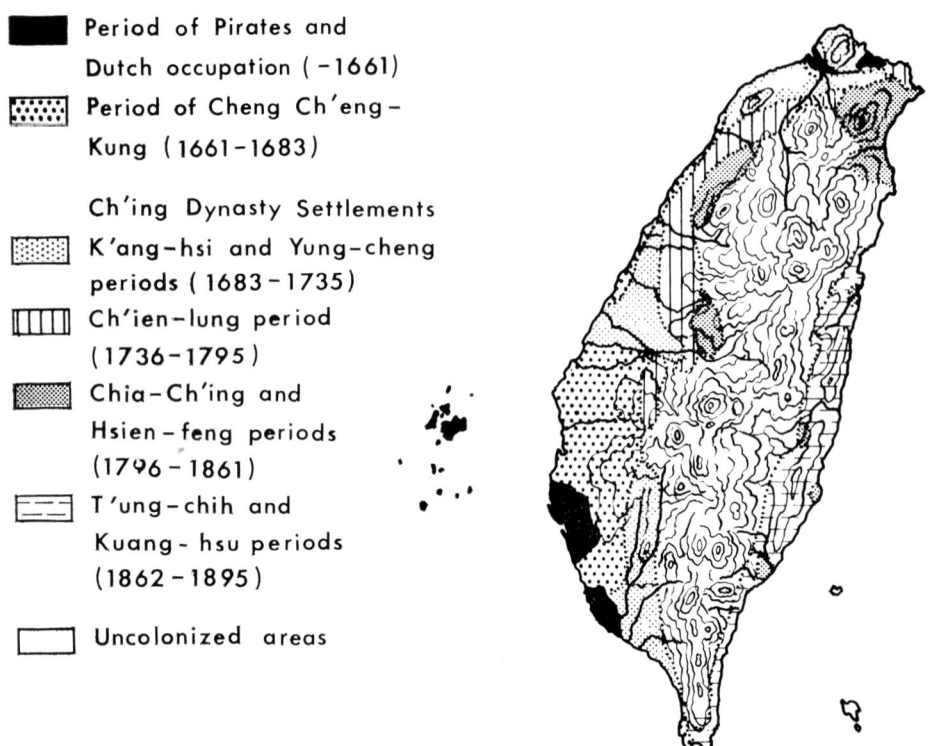

Period of Pirates and
Dutch occupation (–1661)

Period of Cheng Ch'eng –
Kung (1661–1683)

Ch'ing Dynasty Settlements
K'ang–hsi and Yung–cheng
periods (1683–1735)

Ch'ien–lung period
(1736–1795)

Chia–Ch'ing and
Hsien – feng periods
(1796 – 1861)

T'ung–chih and
Kuang – hsu periods
(1862 –1895)

Uncolonized areas

FIG. 5. Major Periods of Chinese Colonization in Taiwan (*after* Mabuchi 1953b).

The first prehistoric stone implements were discovered in 1896 by a Japanese schoolteacher at Chih-shan-yen, in the northern end of the city of Taipei; this led to the discovery of the first prehistoric site in Taiwan in March 1897, at the nearby Yüan-shan shellmound. In the same year the famous Japanese anthropologist, Torii Ryuzō, came to visit the site and began to speculate upon the cultural affinities of the early inhabitants of the island:

> I have not been able to determine the relationship between the Stone Age remains of Taiwan and the Stone Age remains of Japan proper. The Taiwanese Stone Age remains are certainly prehistoric, but the problem is who left them? Were these people Malays? Negritos? Or Papuans? This should be further studied [Torii 1897].

In subsequent years, more and more prehistoric sites became known, first in the mountainous areas but later extensively on the coastal plains. The first major excavation was carried out in 1930 at the stone-cist site of K'en-ting in southern Taiwan by Professor Utsurikawa Nenozō and other members of the staff of the Taihoku Imperial University (Utsurikawa 1936), and beginning in 1939 a large number of sites found in the central and southern parts of the west coast began to yield black and painted pottery that brought attention to the cultural relationship of Taiwan with the eastern coastal regions of China (see Sung 1953/54).

In fact, ever since the first speculations by Torii, archeologists working in Taiwan had paid very close attention to the outside affinities of the prehistoric remains. In 1925 Torii compared the Taiwan remains with South China, Annam, and the Philippines, and concluded that "the Miao people and the Philippine people had cultural contacts in Formosa" (Torii 1925; also 1900). Professor Utsurikawa published his study of the *Patu*-type of stone artifact in Taiwan in 1934 and first pointed out the Pacific affinities of the prehistoric culture on the island. Kokubu in 1941 (Kokubu 1943) and Kanaseki in 1943 drew attention to the similarity of prehistoric stone implements and black pottery in Taiwan to those in the prehistoric cultures of North, Central, and South China. These speculations eventually led Kano Tadao to conclude in 1943:

> The substratum of the prehistoric cultures in Taiwan is the mainland culture of China, which was introduced into Taiwan in several waves. Subsequent to this is the Eneolithic culture of Indochina, which contains bronze and iron artifacts. Finally, there is the Iron Age culture (without bronzes) introduced from the Philippines [Kano 1955: 115-6].

More specifically, Kano distinguishes seven strata of prehistoric cultures in Taiwan: (1) cord-marked pottery, probably introduced from the Asian mainland; (2) check-impressed pottery, introduced from Central China; (3) black pottery, introduced from the eastern coastal regions of China; (4) stepped adz, introduced possibly from Fukien; (5) Proto-Dongsonian stratum, introduced from Indochina before the Chinese influence; (6) Megalithic Culture stratum, probably related to the Megalithic culture of French Indochina, especially of Cambodia; and (7) Philippine Iron Age Culture stratum, confined to the east coast.

Kano's chronological study in fact also served as the first attempt to group the prehistoric remains in Taiwan into cultural classes; he postulated that these prehistoric cultures in Taiwan were introduced from the outside and continued to maintain their respective identities. Some of these groups at least, according to Kano (1955) and Miyamoto (1956), were directly ancestral to some of the modern aboriginal populations.

Kano's cultural grouping and chronological studies, however brilliant, were primarily based on single items of material culture and on the pattern of their distribution outside Formosa. Toward the close of World War II, several Japanese archeologists, outstanding among them being Kanaseki and Kokubu (e.g. Kanaseki and Kokubu 1953), began to identify and test-dig a number of stratified sites, results from which are only now gradually appearing in print. After the war, a series of excavations at important sites was carried out by the staff of the newly established Department of Archaeology and Anthropology, National Taiwan University (K. C. Chang 1964c). In 1954 the present author was able to formulate a cultural grouping and stratigraphy of the prehistoric cultures in Taiwan accord-

ing to excavated materials. My conclusions, in a 1956 version (K. C. Chang 1956:
379–80), were:

> On the basis of surface finds and excavated materials found to date in Formosa, assem-
> blages can be very tentatively grouped into the following seven cultures:
>
> 1. The Cord-Impressed Pottery Culture. (Type sites: Yüan-shan I, Shui-yüan-ti I, Fu-
> ting-chin A, K'en-ting.) The complete inventory of this culture has not been worked out
> yet, although it is very widespread in the island. It is represented by reddish or brown
> potsherds bearing cord impressions. The sherds are coarse, ill-fired, fine-sand tempered,
> and of varying thicknesses. The associated traits include Hoabinhian axes, necked axes,
> certain kinds of polished flat axes, and tapa beaters.
>
> 2. The Yüan-shan culture. (Type sites: Yüan-shan II, Chiang-t'ou AI, Chih-shan-yen
> II, Chien-shan.) This seems to have been the dominant influence in the northern part of
> the west coast of Formosa during prehistoric times. Pottery is coarse and crude, frequently
> sand-tempered, predominantly brown in color, often brushed with reddish paint, round-
> bottomed or ring-footed, sometimes with a lid, and poorly decorated with impressed de-
> signs of net, rings, and parallel dots. Stone implements include shouldered axes, stepped
> axes, Tembeling knives, *Patu*-type implements, triangular arrowheads, and chisels. It is
> also remarkable for jade implements and bone tools. The members of this culture were
> hunters, fishermen, collectors of molluscan shells, and probably horticulturalists and
> stock-breeders. They buried their dead in kitchen middens, and they practiced the extrac-
> tion of four upper teeth; very probably they were head-hunters.
>
> 3. The Brown Impressed Checker Design Pottery Culture. (Type sites: Shu-lin, Ta-yüan.)
> Scattered side by side with the Yüan-shan complex, the stone inventory of this culture in-
> cludes chipped axes and knives, sinkers, manos and metates, and many Yüan-shan type
> items.
>
> 4. The Black and Gray Pottery Culture. This prevailed in the middle of the west coast
> of Formosa, diffused later to the south, and persisted a very long time. The pottery is soft,
> coarse, and dark in the early period (type sites: Shui-yüan-ti II, Ma-t'ou-lu, Ta-ma-lin),
> later becoming harder, finer, and lighter (type sites: Pa-kua-shan, Yüan-li,Ying-p'u, Ta-
> hu). The decoration is mainly impressed checker and incised and combed parallel and wavy
> designs. The stone inventory includes rectangular stone axes, arrowheads, knives, hal-
> berds, chipped axes, knives made on flakes struck from pebbles, Tembeling knives, etc.
> These people did not practice extraction of the teeth and, at least in some cases, they
> buried their dead in prone posture in unlined pits. Cist coffins occur at Ta-ma-lin.
>
> 5. The Red Polished Pottery Culture. (Type sites: K'en-ting, Feng-pi-t'ou I, T'ao-tse-
> yüan.) This culture obtained in the southern part of the west coast. The pottery is pre-
> dominantly red, often polished, occasionally painted with designs; the stone inventory
> covers a wide range of objects. Stone cists were used to bury the dead.
>
> 6. The Gray and Brown Impressed Checker Design Pottery Culture. This culture pre-
> vailed in the Taipei basin during a later period. It is known to represent the Ketangalan
> group of the living plains aborigines. Potsherds are usually associated with implements of
> modern Peipohuan tribes and the Formosan Chinese.
>
> 7. The Red Unpolished Pottery Culture. This is scattered along the east coast of For-
> mosa and is often associated with Megalithic structures.
>
> Deferring consideration of the Megalithic monuments of the east coast for the moment,
> the cultural history of the island can be reconstructed on the basis of the stratigraphic
> correlation of the major culture groups as shown in Table 1.

That this resumé contained some errors of fact and was somewhat naive in theory
is now clear, but it was nevertheless the first attempt of its kind and it served as the
preliminary basis on which the investigations described herein proceeded.

TABLE 1. SEQUENCE OF PREHISTORIC CULTURES OF THE WEST
COAST OF FORMOSA—VERSION OF 1956

Chronology		Northern Area	Central Area	Southern Area
Historic Times	ca. 1600–	The Modern Chinese Culture		
Late Neolithic or Eneolithic	1700 A.D.	Ketangalan culture	Black and gray pottery culture	Black and gray pottery culture and persisting cord-impressed and red polished pottery culture
		_____ A.D.? _____		_____ A.D.? _____
	Yüan-shan culture	Brown impressed checker design pottery culture	Black pottery culture	Red polished pottery culture and persisting cord-impressed pottery culture
	ca. 1000–			
Middle Neolithic	1600 B.C.	The cord-impressed pottery culture		

Problems

During the sixty years from 1896 when the first stone tools were collected in Formosa, to 1956 when the above synthesis of Formosan prehistory appeared in print, archeologists had indeed begun to fill the vacuum that is the island's culture prehistory. Several prehistoric culture groups were distinguished in the island's Stone Age remains, and close relationships had been recognized between the island in prehistory and some other areas of East Asia and the western Pacific Islands. In the late 1950s and the early 1960s, however, when archeological theory, method, and technique made remarkable strides in elucidating world prehistory, and when archeological materials began to accumulate in South China, Southeast Asia, and the Pacific Islands, new demands began to be made on the prehistoric archeology of the island of Taiwan. It was being realized gradually that Taiwan holds the key to many culture-historical problems of the larger cultural sphere, by virtue of its strategic location, and that more vigorous methods and a wider perspective must be applied to its archeology. More specifically, the following areas of problem awaited attack and solution.

—For any further understanding of Formosan prehistory a prerequisite is a classification of cultures according to excavated data from *sites*, as against one based upon single cultural traits dissociated from archeological contexts. At least six or seven hundred archeological localities were known on the island, but too few had been excavated and too little was known of the excavated sites for any characterization of culture groups as groups of assemblages. For any sophisticated picture of the prehistoric cultures on the island, information about the association of cultural traits and about the natural environment must first be sought. The latter calls for vigorous collaboration with natural and physical scientists.

—Owing to the small number of excavated sites, the island-wide time–space framework of prehistoric cultures had been very loose, particularly in view of the late start of historic documentation of the island. With the exception of Japan and a small number of sites in Southeast Asia, East Asia archeology in general remains a pre-carbon-14 stage insofar as chronological assessment of data is concerned, and as a result the absolute chronology of Taiwan prehistory must be built up independently.

—Despite its small size, the island of Taiwan could serve as a significant laboratory for the study of the processes of culture growth. It is at the crossroads between the Asian mainland and the insular area of the western Pacific, and its culture history presumably illuminates problems of migration and diffusion of peoples and cultures over a wide area of East Asia. Furthermore, because of its topographical complexity, the island is a microcosm for the study of cultural variations vis-à-vis environmental factors. The abundance of ethnographical material and the demonstrated beginning in the archeological period of some of the modern ethnic groups make the island's culture history a treasure chest for the direct historic approach. In short, as soon as the archeological remains of the island can be put into some kind of order, the archeologist will have plenty of problems concerning cultural continuity, stability, change, and dynamics.

—Moreover, precisely because of its strategical location, outside comparisons would necessarily form a substantial part of the archeological study, and it is apparent that the archeologist must eventually bring the prehistoric information here to bear on problems in the archeology of South China, Southeast Asia, the Ryukyus, and the Pacific Islands. These may be exemplified by the following specific topics.

1. Insofar as the available evidence is concerned, there are in East Asia two or possibly three early centers for the development—interrelated or independent—of the cord-marked pottery: the Japanese islands; southwestern China and scattered areas of Southeast Asia, both peninsular and insular; and, possibly, North China. If, as assumed by Kano (1955) before the war, on distributional grounds, and reaffirmed by the author (1954a) according to his own observations in the field during 1952–53, the cord-marked pottery constitutes the basic substratum of prehistoric culture on the island, this cultural horizon potentially can give information on the interrelationship of these divers distributional centers of the same ceramic complex. Furthermore, it is important to know for the early history of agriculture in East Asia whether the culture with cord-marked pottery in Southeast Asia was one with at least incipient agriculture, and an intensive research of this cultural stratum on Formosa may shed light on the larger picture.

2. On the basis of a number of prehistoric sites on the eastern and southern coasts of the Chinese mainland, the author, in a series of articles (K. C. Chang 1959, 1963, 1964b, d) has proposed the "Lungshanoid" concept as a category of the cultures of

pioneer farmers migrating downward along the coast from North China at the end of the Yang-shao stage of primary village farmers in that area, as a result of a number of interrelated factors, among which the growing population pressure and an advanced agricultural technology are paramount. An intensive search at the Formosan sites that have been and can be attributed to this Lungshanoid horizon would undoubtedly further clarify and amplify the pertinent issues relative to the Lungshanoid. Any absolute dates that could be obtained from the Lungshanoid sites on Formosa would contribute to the chronology of this horizon in general.

3. Subsequent to the Lungshanoid horizon on the mainland coast is another extensive and well-defined cultural horizon that has been characterized as the Geometric, and its formation has been attributed to influence from Bronze Age North China. Geometric ceramic remains have been uncovered widely on Taiwan along the west coast, and similar pottery has continued to be manufactured in the ethnographic present by some of the mountain-dwelling aborigines. The pertinence of the Geometric phases in Taiwan to the coastal cultures of South China cannot be overstated.

4. Largely because of Wilhelm G. Solheim's work in the Philippines, several ceramic complexes have been recognized in Southeast Asia, such as the Sa-Huynh-Kalanay, the Bau-Malay, and the Navaliches "traditions" (Solheim 1964a). Their similarity to both the Lungshanoid and the Geometric ceramic horizons in Southeast China have been generally realized, but a finer time–space framework for these ceramic complexes must wait until many more excavations are undertaken in that area. In view of Taiwan's proximity to the Philippine Islands, the cultural stratigraphy—containing many of the major ceramic varieties seen to its south—has obvious bearing upon the ceramic history of Southeast Asia as a whole.

5. Very few bronze artifacts have been recovered on the island, but those rare finds are of the utmost interest. Some dagger handles in the form of plastic human figures are thought to recall the Dongsonian style of Indochina, and a bronze arrowhead is said to be of the Hsiao-t'un type of the Shang Dynasty. In addition to contacts across the strait with the mainland and to the south with Luzon, Formosa seems to have had intimate contacts with peninsular Southeast Asia by way of the northern shores of the South China Sea.

6. Another allegedly Indochinese affinity in Taiwan is the so-called Megalithic Culture, found mainly along the east coast, which is the least known area of Taiwan's prehistoric period. It is not only interesting from the Indochinese point of view but presumably also offers information pertaining to both the Philippines and the Ryukyus.

7. Finally, Formosa has a unique bearing upon the early history of the Malayopolynesians. In an Introduction to the Special Taiwan Section of *Asian Perspectives* (vol. 7, 1963), the author made the following observation:

> A primary reason for the interest in Taiwan among the prehistorians of the Far East (enough to warrant a special section on Formosa in *Asian Perspectives*) is that Taiwan is archaeologically of great importance for data on the historic relationships between the

mainland of East Asia and the islands of the Western Pacific. It is unique in that it is probably the only place where studies of such relationships can be undertaken both archaeologically and ethnologically. In other words, it is the only existent link of significant substance between the ethnology of the Pacific and the archaeology of the mainland mass. It is close enough to the mainland to have close historic ties with it, but isolated enough from it so that remnants of the ancient ties are still found ethnologically today, whereas the entire southeastern coastal area of South China has long since become totally sinicized. Finally, Taiwan is the only outpost of the Western Pacific cultures along the entire southeastern Asiatic island arc that is close enough to the mainland to have served as a most convenient stepping-stone of ethnic and cultural movements in both directions—as long as such movements are postulated [K. C. Chang 1964a: 197].

As long as one searches into Formosan prehistory along these lines, some interesting findings must result. If the Lungshanoid and Geometric cultures on the island came from across the Formosa Strait, and if the modern aboriginal population constitutes a substantial or even appreciable part of the descendants of the prehistoric inhabitants, the traditional theory attributing the modern peoples and cultures of the Pacific Islands to a homeland in the coastal regions of Southeast China would appear to be validated. This surely would not please the linguists. In the first place, they would have to explain how an ancestral Chinese culture—presumably Sino-Tibetan speaking—gave rise to the modern Malayopolynesian linguistic group. In the second place, they would have to reconcile this archeological picture with the fashionable hypothesis that the Malayopolynesian family originated in Melanesia rather than in mainland Asia. No matter how these conflicts are to be resolved, it is clear that "The problem of Malayo-Polynesian migrations demands careful thinking in the realms of culture, race, and language. Any sweeping conclusions reached by archaeology alone, no matter how satisfactory they may appear, cannot be accepted with complacency. The same remark applies to physical anthropological, ethnological, and linguistic studies" (Chang 1964a: 201).

These problems dealing with Formosan prehistory call for vigorous and competent work with an interdisciplinary approach, and archeologists have no illusions that answers can be found with a single expedition. But these questions must be a consideration in any archeological project on the island, and the Yale–Taita expedition of 1964–65 was no exception.

The Yale–Taita Expedition, 1964–1965

The Yale–Taita expedition to Formosa was in the field from the end of June 1964 to the middle of August 1965, and on the Yale side consisted of four members of Yale University: the present author, Principal Investigator; Matsuo Tsukada, Associate Investigator in palynology; and Richard J. Pearson and Jonathan H. Kress, research assistants. The major considerations that guided the fieldwork and the actions taken accordingly were as follows.

1. In view of the fact that the Department of Archaeology and Anthropology, National Taiwan University (Taita), had been active in the island's archeological investigations for a decade and a half, largely through the personal efforts of Pro-

fessor Sung Wen-hsün, the expedition was necessarily a joint affair between the Yale staff and the Taita personnel. The department gave consent to this arrangement, and Professor Sung and Mr. Huang Shih-ch'iang, Research Assistant, joined the expedition as permanent members, and several teaching assistants and students in the department participated as part-time excavators. It was further agreed that the excavated materials were to be permanently housed at the University's Archaeological and Anthropological Museum when study was completed, and the reports of the excavations in the Chinese language were to be published by Taita.

2. The research was to be as interdisciplinary as the available personnel permitted. In addition to Tsukada, who was to spend two to three months in Taiwan to collect samples for a series of pollen profiles in lake deposits and Pleistocene outcrops as well as from the archeological sites, Professor Lin Ch'ao-ch'i of the Department of Geology, Taita, distinguished authority on the geomorphology and paleontology of the Pleistocene period in Taiwan, was invited to join the expedition as a consultant. Professor Lin was in the field during most of the field season and has been responsible for obtaining expert analysis and identification of soil, pottery, stone, and animal bone samples.

3. The expedition expected to obtain a maximum of information by way of excavation and reconnaissance at a minimum of carefully selected sites that were expected to yield representative cross sections at different parts of Taiwan. As a result, four sites were selected: (1) Ta-p'en-k'eng, at Pa-li Hsiang, in Taipei Prefecture, a site that was known to contain a long prehistoric sequence covering the whole range of the prehistoric period in the Taipei basin. (2) Ying-p'u, at Ta-tu Hsiang, Taichung Prefecture, in central Taiwan. This site was known to have a black pottery culture, an important culture in that part of the island, and was selected by Professor Sung for his own project, which was supported by a grant from the China Council for East Asia Studies for 1964–65. It was agreed that the Yale staff would give him maximum support and that Professor Sung was to be responsible for the research and publication of his findings. (3) Feng-pi-t'ou, at Lin-yüan Hsiang, in Kao-hsiüng Prefecture, in southwestern Taiwan, a site that was reported to have yielded both painted and black pottery in stratified relationship. (4) T'ai-yüan, in T'aitung Prefecture, a site near a Megalithic complex known to yield abundantly a variety of pottery. The responsibility for the excavation and publication of this site fell on Richard Pearson. It was expected that with the information obtained at these four sites, plus the pollen profiles from a number of locations all over the island and the carbon-14 determinations for a number of key sites as well as the above four, the prehistoric research of the island could be placed on firmer ground and that future potentials could be evaluated and guide lines for further work formulated.

4. Since the purpose of the expedition was to obtain a maximum of information at a minimum of sites within the span of a single year and in view of the necessity as well as advisability of processing the bulk of the remains in Taiwan within the same period, it was decided that various and flexible techniques were to be applied

to each particular site to take advantage of its specific potentials according to its underground situation. At Ta-p'en-k'eng, therefore, where remains were scattered over a very uneven terrain and stratigraphy varied from spot to spot, a combined natural–artificial stratification was employed at a selected portion of the site, and both vertical and horizontal controls of a very fine degree were stressed. Feng-pi-t'ou, on the other hand, was relatively flat and few barriers were in the way; the excavated area was therefore much larger, and natural stratification was stressed for a more extensive horizontal analysis.

Method of Analysis

The methods of and perspectives for the excavation, and the interpretation of the remains, that the author has adopted throughout the present research, have been described in detail in *Rethinking Archaeology* (Chang 1967a), to which the interested reader is referred.

From a methodological perspective, the archeological study may be characterized as a classificatory process. The smallest empirical unit for our study is the minimal attribute of an artifact, and the largest empirical unit in field operations is usually the archeological site in its entirety. Between these two extremes, different conceptual levels serve as operative foci for the contrastive and hierarchical organization of the archeological variations. Two of these levels are of paramount importance: the *settlement* and the *culture*.

A settlement is an empirical entity—or an approximation thereof—with empirically defined temporal and spatial boundaries within which the prehistoric remains exhibit features of a single "stationary state." Within the settlement the archeological variations have identical values with reference to the characterization of the prehistoric culture; the settlement is a "synchronic" unit, no matter what its actual span of scientific time, and a spatial locus where a communal group of people engaged in interrelated and mutually complementary activities. When cultural and social variations obtain, with reference to time or to space, to the extent and of a degree that force a reassessment by the archeologist of their overall alignment and result in reorganization of their structural order, a different settlement unit must be conceptualized. Classifications must then go beyond the settlement level, resulting in classes of settlements grouped according to a number of different criteria. When the criterion is one of historical relationship to be recognized on the basis of stylistic characters, the resultant group of settlements is referred to as an archeological culture.

Settlements can be formulated at single sites, whereas cultures are always derived comparatively. A settlement can be studied as a totality, but a culture is manifest mainly through its stylistic aspects. An archeologist could formulate a settlement even if he knows only a single site, but he could never properly grasp the characters of a culture without comparative knowledge. Since, however, competence and such knowledge on the part of the archeologist should always be assumable, settlement formulation and cultural characterization are always simultaneous operations. In his analysis and description, the archeologist operatively formulates his synchronic structural units and compares them within a larger sphere of reference at the same time, but he must always keep these two levels conceptually distinct.

In this monograph the sites of Feng-pi-t'ou and Ta-p'en-k'eng will be analyzed and described in the manner characterized above. The data from each site will first be presented—history of past investigations, aims of our investigations, tactics and techniques of our excavations, and summary of observations in the field in connection with cultural distribution and stratification. Then the history of the site's occupation by Neolithic inhabitants will be traced, and major occupational categories will be formulated with reference to the temporal locus. Settlements and cultures will be recognized for each site's total occupation. Descriptions and cultural–social articulations will then be attempted within each major culture at the sites; special attention will be given to the variations of archeological remains in regard to area and through different time periods, so that interpretations of cultural–social distribution and change can be made. The author attempts to present all the essential data brought to light by our investigations, but at the same time to present them in such a way that all the information will be organized according to its relevance to an interpretation of the prehistoric cultures and their histories.

Part I. Fengpitou

Chapter 1. The Site

THE site of Fengpitou[1] is located in Lin-yüan District (*Hsiang*), Kao-hsiung County (*Hsien*), in southwestern Formosa, about 1 km north of the Chung-k'eng-men section of Kang-p'u village (Lin-yüan District, Kao-hsiung County) and about 1 km east of Feng-ming (or Feng-pi-t'ou) village (Hsiao-kang District, Kao-hsiung County) (Figs. 1, 6), lat. 22°31'45"N, long. 120°21'38"E, geographic coordinates 2114-I-SW, L 892-TQ-51Q-28509195. It is a small terrace above the 25-m contour line, about 400 m north of the Kaohsiung–Linyüan main road (Pl. 1, *A*). Between the site and the road are vegetable and sugarcane fields, but a small dirt road leads from the main road northward to the foot of the hill and then turns east uphill all the way to the top of the terrace. It is mainly used by cattle carts that transport sugarcane down from the fields on the slopes and on top of the hill. In addition to sugarcane, small vegetable patches and sweet-potato fields dot the terrace, and tombs of the villagers nearby are scattered all over. The whole hill belongs to a Mr. Lu Teng-fu of Tung-shan District of Tainan County, about three hours north of the hill by bus. He has planted sisal (*Agave sisalana* Perrine) all over the hill—making our reconnaissance rather difficult at times—and has a profitable business selling sisal leaves for cordage, and tomb plots, allegedly at $25.00 per plot.

The top of the hill is exactly 39 m above the main road. Standing at the top and facing south (Pl. 1, *B*), one first sees the paved Kaohsiung-Linyüan road about 500 m beyond; the beach lies 600 or 700 m farther south. The islet of Hsaio-liu-ch'iu, clearly visible unless the sky is extremely foggy, is 13 km directly to the south. The coastal strip—approximately 1.5 km wide at this part but extending around the Fengshan tableland at both east and west—is a rather flat, raised coastal and alluvial plain; the soil is said to be highly saline near the beach. When the site was occupied by Neolithic inhabitants the shoreline must have been much farther inland, and seawater probably reached the foot of the hill at high tide in all directions except northeast where the elevation is higher (see Chapter 9). Marine resources were at hand, and mollusk shells and fishbones are found at the site in large quantities.

Looking north, one faces the arc-shaped Fengshan tableland, which has a total north–south length of about 13 km; the Fengpitou site is at its very southern end (Fig. 6). Topographically the tableland is dissected into three main parts: Shih-shang-shan at the north, P'ing-ting-shan at the center, and T'an-t'ou-shan at the

[1] Simplified from the correct spelling, Feng-pi-t'ou. The name means Nose of the Phoenix and refers to the complex of small hills at the southern end of the Fengshan Mountains. The site is on one of the hills, and this is referred to by local farmers as Ta-p'u, or the Big Slope. In archeological literature the site has been referred to either as Feng-pi-t'ou or Chung-k'eng-men, a village nearby.

19

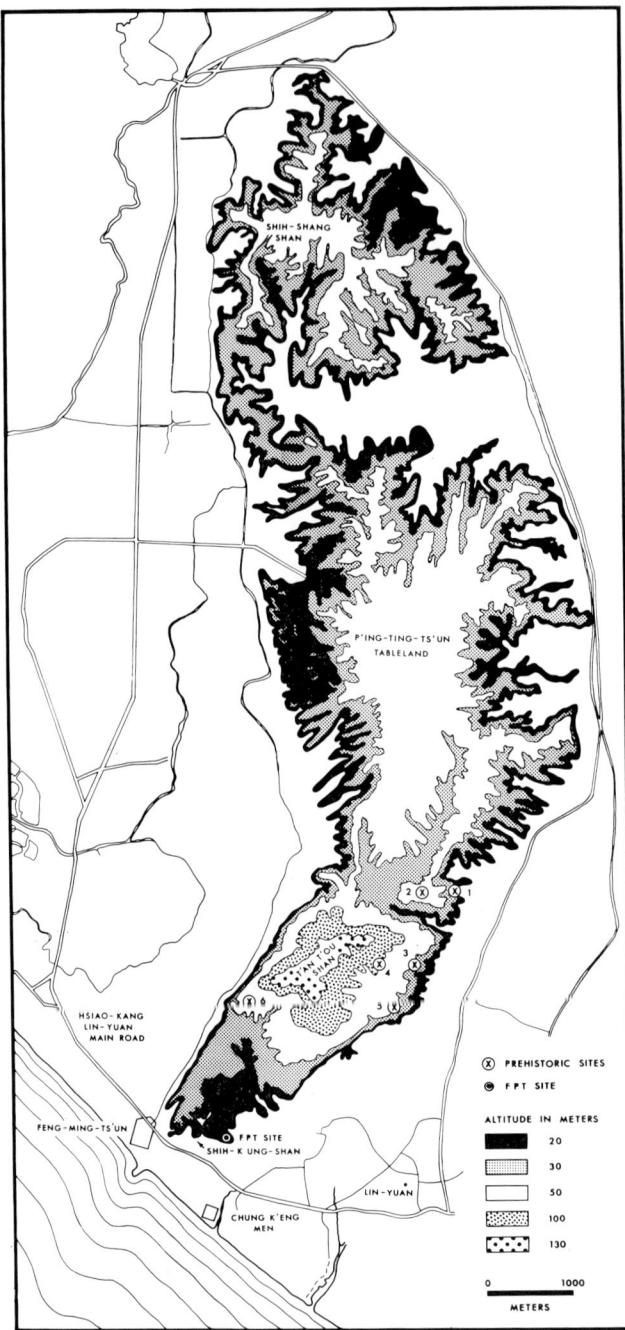

Fɪɢ. 6. The Fengshan Tableland and Prehistoric Sites.

south. The foundation rocks of the entire area consist of massive, bluish-gray, sandy shale or mudstone, in which are found fossils of mollusks and foraminifers. Lying on a surface of disconformity of the foundation rocks in the southern part of the Fengshan tableland is a layer of raised coral limestones of the Pleistocene period, at times attaining a thickness of over 60 m (Figs. 7, 8). A dome-shaped structure with an elevation of over 140 m above sea level is formed of white-grayish chunky coral limestones, some of which have been weathered to a yellowish-brownish color; in the limestones are found a great variety of mollusk-shell fossils. Irregular fissures abound, and many caves have been formed by the erosion of underground water. Fossilized bones and teeth of deer and wild cattle have been collected from the clay deposits in some of the fissures and caves, and at least two or three caves contain evidence of human occupation in prehistoric times.

Terrace deposits cover the top of the raised coral limestone structure, and three terrace levels can be distinguished. The Higher Terrace deposits, probably the oldest, constitute the original surface of the tableland, between 100 and 145 m in elevation, and consist of over 2 m of lateritic soil. Round gravels of sandstone sometimes separate the lateritic soil from the coral limestone base. The Middle Terrace deposits, probably somewhat younger in age, are between the 70-m and the 25-m contour lines. The lower part of the deposits—no more than 1 m thick—consists of gravels, overlain by 1 to 2 m of lateritic soil. The gravels are mostly of sandstone but include a few quartz pebbles, and the lateritic soil is occasionally sandy. The Lower Terrace deposits, the youngest and below the 25-m contour line, consist of a granular bed at the lower part and a grayish-brownish surface soil at the upper; these are the layers in which the Fengpitou prehistoric remains occur.

Although a large cluster of prehistoric sites has been located in the plains area of Tainan and Kaohsiung, only two sites had been reported on the Fengshan tableland, one of which is the site of Fengpitou we selected for excavation. During the course of our excavations an extensive reconnaissance brought to light six more prehistoric locations, all on the slopes of the T'ant'oushan tableland, both east and west (Fig. 6).

The site of Fengpitou remains, however, the most important. Prehistoric remains are located over the entire hill in an area about 500 m east–west and 300 m north–south. Whole sections of cultural debris are exposed by the building of the cattle-cart road and by the removal of dirt in the construction of tombs; and farmers turn up stones, bones, and potsherds as they cultivate. A communication ditch, moreover, about 1 m wide and 1.5 to 2 m deep, was dug around and across the hill by Japanese troops during the last stage of the Pacific War, and very clear soil and cultural profiles are available on the trench walls after some grass-cutting and sweeping. It is almost incredible that this enormously rich, exposed, and easily accessible site was not discovered by archeologists until the end of the war and had never been explored except by brief and casual surface collecting. Apparently Kaneko first discovered the site, and Kobuku visited it in the summer of 1943. It

SEDIMENTARY FORMATIONS

Recent clay, sand, and gravel

Pleistocene coral reefs

Pleistocene clay and sand

Tertiary shale and sandstone

Paleozoic sandstone, slate, and limestone

Jurassic shale and sandstone

Precarboniferous limestone

CRYSTALLINE FORMATIONS

Precarboniferous schist

Andesite tuff

Diabase, gabbro, peridolite

Shistose granite

Basalt

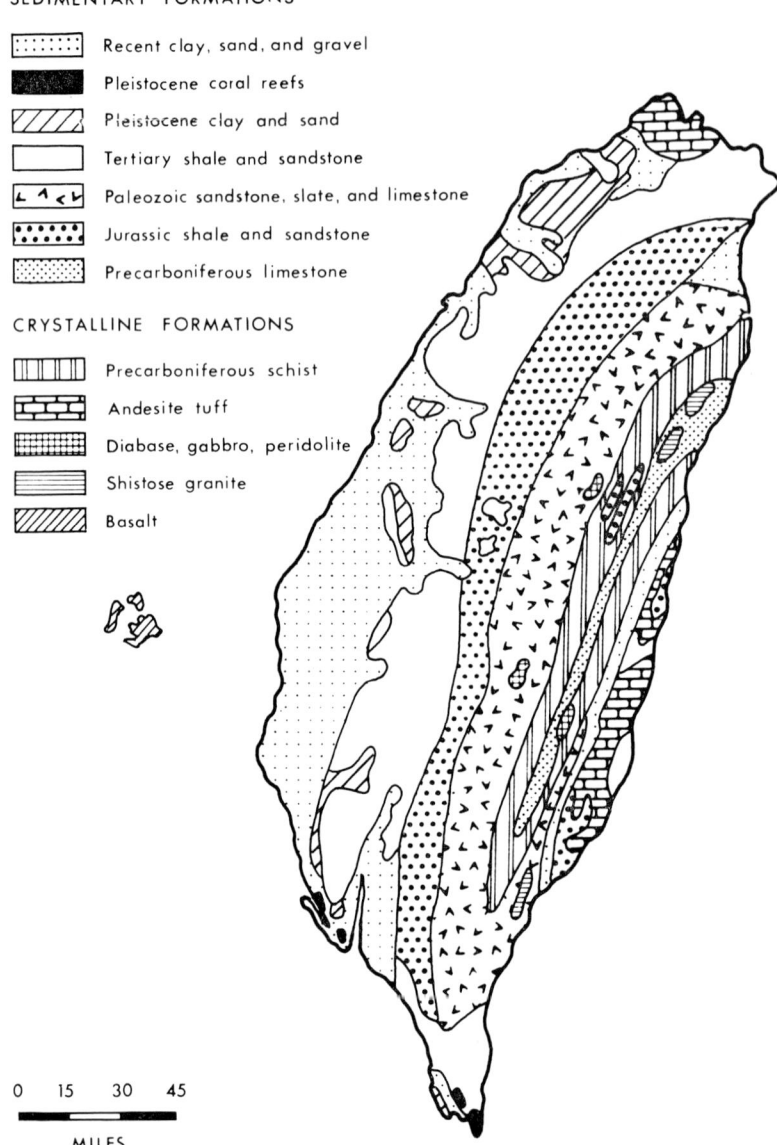

0   15   30   45

MILES

FIG. 7. Geology of Taiwan (*after* Hsieh 1964).

was reported for the first time by Tsuboi Kiyotari in 1953, who described his investigations as follows (1956: 277–9):

> I was sent to Formosa as a private in the early fall of 1944, and . . . in January, 1945, I was moved to the town of Ping-tung and happened to be favored with the opportunity of

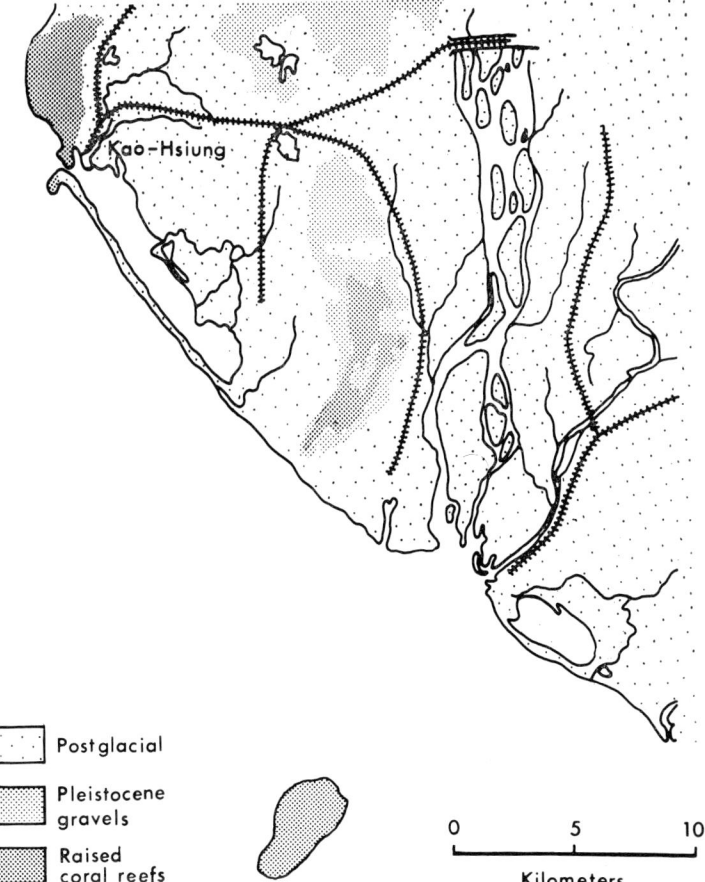

Postglacial

Pleistocene
gravels

Raised
coral reefs

0   5   10

Kilometers

FIG. 8. Geology of the Environs of Fengpitou (*after* C. C. Lin 1957).

becoming friendly with Mr. Kaneko, who accidentally worked in the unit to which I was attached. He was very kind to furnish me with first-hand information about the finds he possessed. In May, I was again moved to the aerodrome of Lin-yüan village . . . The following is a report of one of those sites which I frequented during the leisure hours of my military service. . . .

When you look towards the south-east from the city of Kao-hsiung, you will see a series of undulating hills of upheaved limestone, running N–S. The southern end of these "Feng-shan" hills looks like a camel's hump and [abruptly terminates at] the sea. This hump is called "Feng-pi-t'ou" whose eastern slope is made of fan-shaped terraces, 15 to 20 metres high. A neolithic site is situated on one of these terraces that slopes towards the south, and pot-sherds and other objects are scattered over an area about 100 metres long from west to east. There are six spots where the prehistoric relics were discovered in shell-mounds or in cultural layers, three of which are situated on the terrace—named consecutively from west to east, "A," "B," and "C" and the remaining three, named likewise "D," "E," and "F," on the slopes or under the cliff. Mr. Kaneko first discovered the spot "D," and the rest were discovered during the war by digging trenches.

Spot A. Situated at the westernmost part of the top of the terrace and incidentally the highest point of the hill. There is a cultural layer, 30 to 40 cm. deep, below the surface of the ground . . . Only the potsherds of the "red pottery" and the stone implements are discovered.

Spot B. Situated at the centre of the terrace. There is a cultural layer 40 to 50 cm. deep under the present ground surface. The layer is more extensively spread than at any other spot in the site and there are two shell deposits at the centre. There are also some smaller heaps of ashes and charcoal, and also small spots where pot-sherds are densely accumulated. Only pot-sherds of the "black pottery" and stone implements are found.

Spot C. Situated at the eastern side of the terrace. . . . The cultural layer is here found rather deep, 70 to 100 cm. below the ground surface, and belongs to the "red pottery" culture.

Spot D. The western half of the southern slope of the terrace. Here a shell layer, 15 to 20 metres long, is exposed on the northern side of a road and is the conspicuous shell-mound of the site. It is said that a great quantity of animal bones and also a stone axe 40 cm. long were discovered from under a rock beneath a cliff at its western end. From the shell-mound and a trench south of it, only remains of the "black pottery" culture were collected, but from a field between them many axe-heads made of quartzite have been found.

Spot E. Along the southeastern end of the terrace, there is a steep cliff several metres high. Under this cliff, a thick cultural layer was found. Removal of a part of this layer has revealed an abundant deposit of pot-sherds and other artifacts. The layer is about 20 metres long but it is exceptionally thick, measuring more than 2.5 metres. Here the lower bed of the layer yields only the pot-sherds and stone implements of the "painted pottery" culture and the upper bed yields those of the "black pottery" culture.

Spot F. There are two cultural layers extending over the eastern slope of the terrace. The upper layer lies 30 to 50 cm. below the present ground surface, and the lower layer about 1 metre below the present surface. From the upper layer, only the grey coarse pottery sherds are found and the lower layer produces only sherds and stone implements belonging to the "red pottery."

It is apparent that on this terrace and its slope, a prehistoric village of extensive scale was built at least more than two times—and I am of [the] opinion that in the abundance and variety of the artifacts, the site ranks perhaps among the leading sites in the southern part of Formosa.

Tsuboi groups the pottery of the site into four classes—painted, red, black, and brown. The first two are "contemporary and kindred," and so are the last two, and each group is accompanied by its peculiar stone implements. After describing the inventories of these two groups, Tsuboi comes to the following conclusions (pp. 290–2):

> The significance of Feng-pi-t'ou site in the prehistory of Formosa—although the foregoing description is based on incomplete observation made during the leisure hours of my military service—lies in clarifying to some extent the mutual relation between the two distinctive cultures represented by the two respective ceramic groups—the "painted and red pottery" group and the "black and brown pottery" group.
>
> The painted pottery has never been found independently. It has always been found with the red pottery, although the red pottery has been found without the accompanying painted wares . . . And the stratigraphical condition at Spot E of Feng-pi-t'ou revealed that they antedated the black and brown pottery. The relation of the black pottery to the brown pottery is strikingly similar . . . The black pottery does not exist alone. It exists side by side with the brown pottery and the latter represents only the coarser ware almost without decoration. . . .

From the foregoing it is at once noticed that in both groups of potteries, there are two kinds of vessels different in function and fabrication. One, represented by pots . . . bowls, and fruit-stands, is a vessel or receptacle used for storing or for serving, while the other, represented by larger bowls and jars . . . is a vessel used for cooking. . . .

But such a combination of two functionally different types of pottery is not a phenomenon peculiar to Formosa. . . . For in the painted pottery culture of China proper . . . the same combination of two types of pottery does exist . . . The black pottery in China is also accompanied with the rough pottery to make a set. . . .

That each phase of prehistoric culture has its own combination of fine and coarse pottery, and that each also has the stone implements with distinctive features, are facts common to Formosa and China proper. And these facts are more than the mere analogy of the shape and fabrication of the artifacts between these two regions . . . They rather indicate the fundamental coincidence of the cultural phenomena in both regions which could not have been realized unless the substantial culture was transplanted from the Chinese mainland and settled in the field district of Southwestern Formosa which became incidentally the "painted and black pottery" civilization.

Tsuboi's report brought wide attention to the Fengpitou site for two important reasons. This was the first site reported in southern Formosa that indicated a long and stratified prehistoric sequence; and the "painted" and "black" pottery furnished fresh evidence for the historical relationship between Taiwan and mainland China that was beginning to be seriously discussed by archeologists, who had hitherto taken for granted that the early inhabitants of the island were Proto-Indonesians who presumably had come from the south. A surface collection was made in the late 1950s at the site by Mr. Chiang Chia-chin of the Commission for Historic Research of Tainan City and his son, Dr. Chiang Chin-p'ei of the Kaohsiung Medical College, where it is now deposited. Professor Lin Ch'ao-ch'i of the Department of Geology, National Taiwan University, visited the site in 1960 and identified three cultural spots, two of which were shellmounds.

The Yale–Taita excavation of Fengpitou occurred from 8 January–27 February, 1965, for a total of six working weeks. During this period the weather was extremely fine; not a single day was spoiled by rain. Crops were being harvested, leaving a fresh, loose, and clean surface that was ideal for reconnaissance. The permanent staff consisted of Chang, Lin, Sung, Pearson, Kress, Huang, and Hsü; and student excavators—Lü, P'an, Ch'en, and Mrs. J. L. Chang—took part at various times for one to three weeks. On average, eight laborers were employed from the Lin-chia village on the plains. The management of the Hsiao-kang sugar factory, of the Taiwan Sugar Company, graciously provided a house which the staff used for living quarters and a laboratory. A station-wagon taxi took us daily from Hsiao-kang to the site—a twenty-minute ride—and back, and each day's find was washed and sun-dried the next day at the house with the help of two additional laborers. Part of the crew stayed at the house to process the collection, and we were able to classify, count, weigh, sketch, and photograph a substantial portion of the artifacts before they were packed and transported back to the Taipei laboratory on 27 February. The rest of the finds were similarly treated, and the total collection was gone over in greater detail in Taipei during the months of March, April, and May.

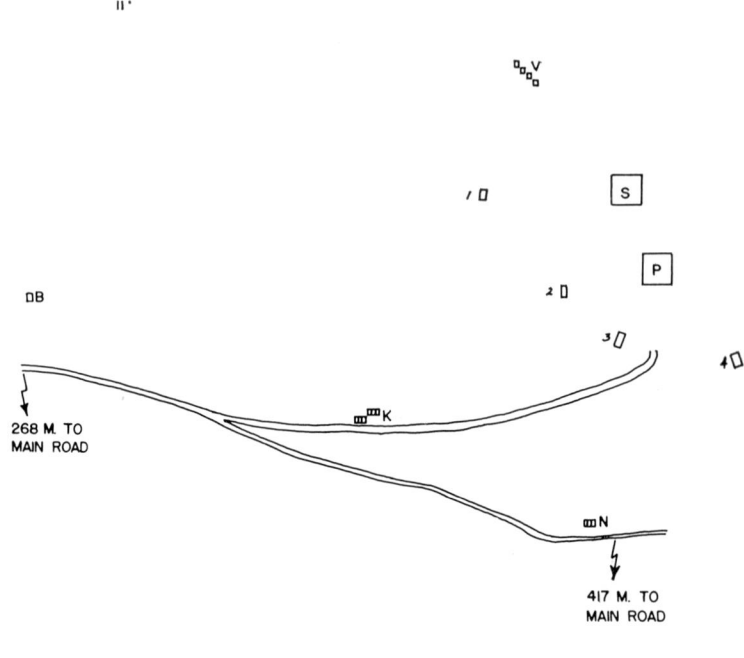

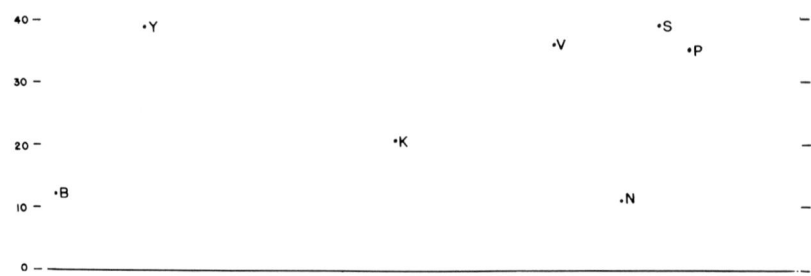

FIG. 9. Excavations at Fengpitou. (Plan in upper half of figure indicates the distribution of the various loci in relation to the cart road and to the four concrete structures. In lower part of figure the loci are placed in relation to each other according to elevation from the Kaohsiung–Linyüan main road. Scale of elevation in meters at left is also the scale of the plan.)

We decided at the beginning to sample the entire site to the extent necessary to get the whole picture within two months, and we expected to achieve this by a combination of excavations at selected loci and intensive surface collecting over the whole hill. Except for tombs, which were numerous, little else stood in the way for the selection of areas to excavate. Each of the loci, either excavated or where intensive collection was made on the surface and from the exposed profile, was designated by a letter, and letters were arranged alphabetically counterclockwise around the hill, starting from the southwestern corner, the first spot in from the main road. Six loci were excavated: B, K, N, P, S, and V; and seven loci saw intensive reconnaissance: E, M, Q, R, T, U, and Y (Fig. 9). (The surface samples for the most part belong to the upper level of the site, according to stratigraphical evidence, indicating that the surface disturbances did not alter the stratigraphical picture.) Since Tsuboi did not include a map in the report of his investigation, definite correlations are difficult to make between his designations and ours. But the correspondence probably was his B to our S; his C to our P; his D to our K, and his E to our N.

Where excavations were carried out, an arbitrary grid unit, 10 × 10 m, was lined up on the ground; it was further subdivided into twenty-five squares, each 2 × 2 m, forming five columns of five squares each. A base line was placed 4 m from the east (Fig. 10). Each square was further divided into four quarters, referred to as A1, A2, B1, and B2, from left to right and upper to lower quarters. Thus, potsherds and stone fragments are horizontally identified by one of a hundred small grids within each excavation unit; for all remarkable finds, however, the exact coordinates were taken. For vertical control, surface contours were first taken, and these were used for depth measurements. One of the twenty-five squares was first excavated as a master square, and a natural stratigraphy was devised. Within each natural stratum, artifacts were recorded in 20-cm artificial levels. Thus, except for remarkable finds, for

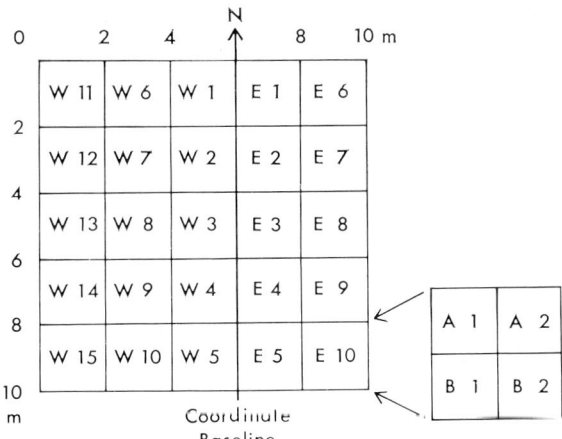

Fig. 10. Grid Designation at Locus of Excavation at Fengpitou.

which a three-dimensional measurement was recorded, all potsherds and stone fragments within a dimension 100 × 100 × 20 cm were placed together in one bag and stayed there permanently as the basic unit for analysis. The entire excavation unit in each locus was not dug; excavation commenced with an arbitrary first square and then was extended lengthwise or sidewise—after the rock base was reached, and the four walls drawn, and special features left in place—as dictated by the underground situation. Each of the squares was excavated by two persons—one of the staff or a student, and one laborer—but sometimes one staff member and two laborers excavated two adjoining squares at the same time. Each excavation locus was in the charge of a senior assistant, and the author coordinated the whole site. Hand trowels and small picks (including the convertible pick-spade used by army personnel) were the principal tools, and dirt was piled up around the entire excavation unit. The dirt was not sifted, but every lump of earth was crushed and carefully felt by hand.

A description of the thirteen loci follows.

Locus B

The cart road begins to climb the hill at the southwest corner and goes up and eastward to the top. At the southwest corner to the north of the road a section of the ground was cut into by the road and a profile about 2 m deep was exposed, exhibiting potsherds, fish vertebrae, and pebbles in a layer about 1.4 m thick, lying above the coral limestone base.

A pit, 2 m north–south and 1 m east–west, was excavated on top of the bank along the road to a depth of 80 cm before the coral limestone base was reached. The ground surface was barren except for the sisal, and the earth, mixed with a large amount of granules and pebbles, was extremely hard and dry. The cultural deposits were apparently secondary, and artificial layers of 10 cm were distinguished. Sandy red and gray potsherds with check, basket, and cord impressions predominated throughout (Fig. 20), and long (over 10 cm) bracelets of clay were found all the way to the bottom. Charcoals, tiny bone fragments, large and small pieces of pottery, and stone implements (arrowheads with stems and with straight bases, polished adzes) were found scattered here and there.

This locus is not represented among Tsuboi's finds. Although the finds were mixed with granules and pebbles, in the same condition as those from the earliest cultural phases at the site (see below), the pottery is of late types, and the deposits were secondary, probably washed down from higher slopes that were now exposed to the bare rock bottom.

Locus E

Fifty meters east of Locus B on the north side of the road was a sweet-potato plot, about 20 × 20 m. Potsherds and stone implements were scattered over the freshly harvested field but, to judge from exposed banks, the cultural deposits were apparently too heavily disturbed to warrant excavation. Incised and impressed gray pottery predominated in the surface collection, which included stone arrowheads and fragments of very large, polished, flat hoes made of sandy slate.

Locus K (Figs. 11, 12; Pl. 3)

Farther up the road and at the center of the southern slope of the hill, "the conspicuous shell-mound" mentioned by Tsuboi was exposed by the road banks and by a section of the communication trench. Tsuboi's *Spot D* and Lin's shellmounds were both in this area. We selected a bean and sweet-potato field between the road and a concentrated burial area to the north for excavation; three pits, 2 × 2 m, aligned east–west, were excavated, designated from west to east as K-1, K-2, and K-3. Both K-1 and K-3 were excavated clear to the bottom, but only a column 50 × 50 cm was dug in K-2 for a sampling of shell and soil; K turned out to be the most important locus at the site in cultural stratigraphy.

The total depth of cultural deposits in K-1 was 320 cm, and that in K-3 370 cm, the greatest depth ever reached at a prehistoric site on Formosa. Five layers were distinguished in each pit according to condition of deposition, and were designated as Cultivated Layer, Layer 1, Layer 2, Layer 3, and Layer 4. Artificial layers within the natural layers were designated by small letters:

K-1 (Fig. 11)   Cultivated Layer: 0–15 cm
     Layer 1a: 15–60 cm
       1b: 60–100 cm
       1c: 100–135 cm

    Layer 2a: 135–160 cm
       2b: 160–175 cm

    Layer 3a: 175–225 cm
       3b: 225–240 cm along north wall, and
         225–280 cm along south wall
       3c: 280–320 cm

    Layer 4:   A thin layer over the bottom

K-2 (Pl. 3, *B*) Cultivated Layer a: 0–15 cm
           b: 15–35 cm
    Layer 1a: 35–55 cm
       1b· 55–75 cm
       1c: 75–95 cm
       1d: 95–115 cm
       1e: 115–135 cm
       1f: 135–145 cm

    Layer 2a: 145–165 cm
       2b: 165–185 cm
       2c: 185–205 cm

Layer 3a: 205–225 cm
       3b: 225-245 cm
       3c: 245-265 cm
       3d: 265-285 cm

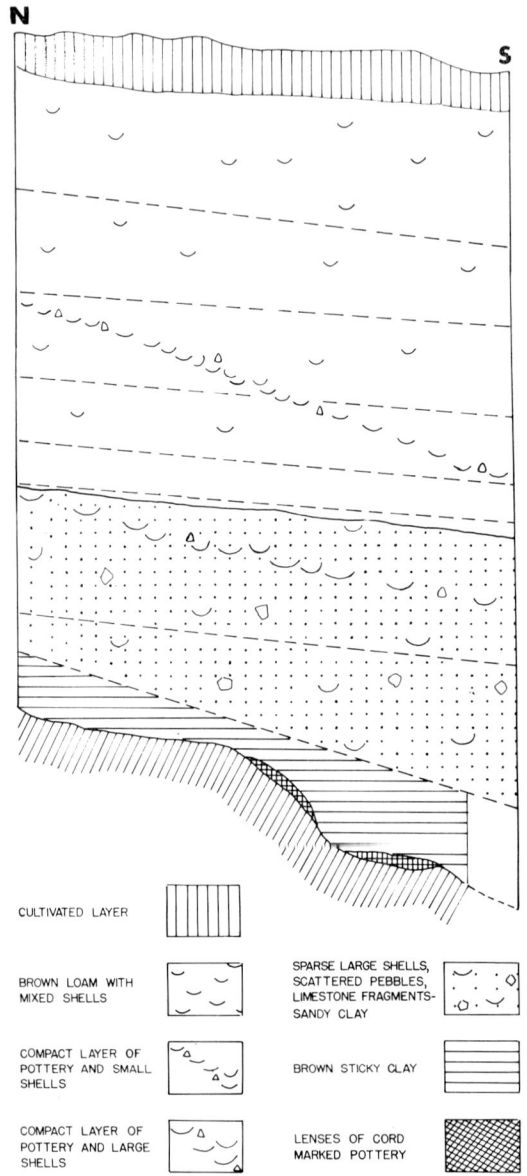

Fɪɢ. 11. North–South Section of Locus K, Pit 1, Fengpitou (north–south length: 2 m).

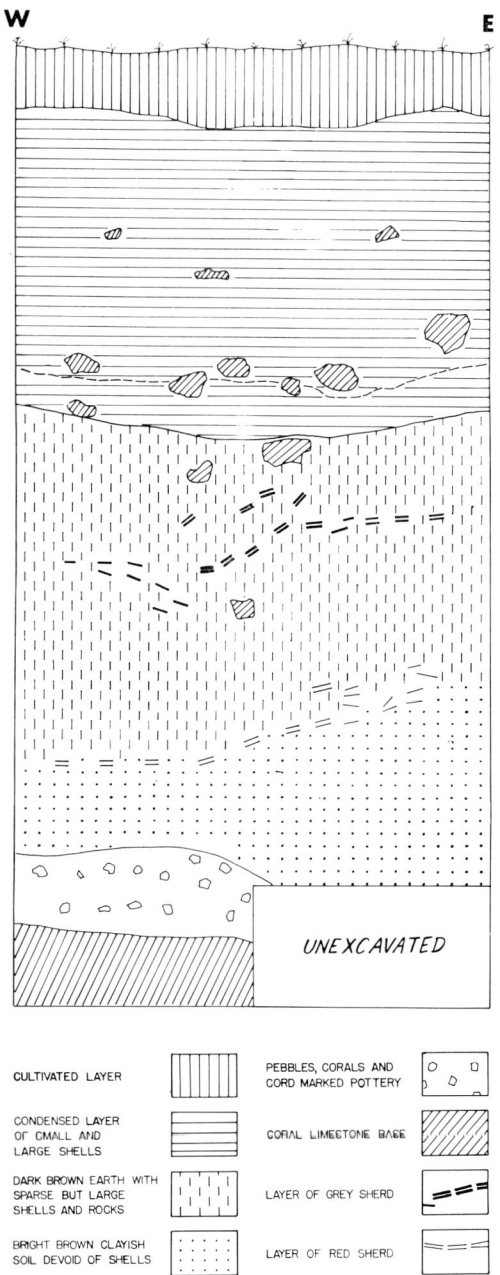

FIG. 12. East–West Section of Locus K, Pit 3, Fengpitou (east west width: 2 m).

K-3 (Fig 12;   Cultivated Layer: 0–20 cm
  Pl. 3, *A*)   Layer 1a: 20–40 cm
                          1b: 40–70 cm
                          1c: 70–90 cm
                          1d: 90–110 cm
                          1e: 110–130 cm

                Layer 2:   130–160 cm

                Layer 3a: 160–180 cm
                          3b: 180–200 cm
                          3c: 200–220 cm
                          3d: 220–240 cm
                          3e: 240–265 cm
                          3f: 265–285 cm
                          3g: 285–305 cm
                          3h: 305–325 cm
                          3i: 325–335 cm

                Layer 4:   335–370 cm

Excavated layers are relative to ground level, which was a slight slope down from north to south. Cultural layers were always in a similar slope, indicating that Locus K was probably a shellmound area for a habitation center to the north on more level ground near or at the top. This center, unfortunately, was completely covered with tombs, and excavation was out of the question.

The Cultivated Layer was undoubtedly secondarily deposited, probably mostly by fill from the communication trench that lay immediately south of the excavated area. The trench was about 1 m deep, and the fill presumably contained artifacts from no deeper than Layer 1.

The distinctive features of Layer 1 were relatively hard soil (light buff in color), limestone fragments, and numerous shells of small size and great variety. Layer 2 appeared to be transitional between Layers 1 and 3, somewhat loose and softer in texture, light brown in color, with somewhat fewer shells.

Layer 3 contained softer, rather sandy soil, becoming harder in the lower part. The earth was dark brown in the upper part, and bright brown and yellowish in the lower. The upper part contained scattered shells of large size and less variety; the lower part was devoid of shells. Potsherds formed distinctive layers on the walls; gray pottery predominated in the upper layers, but the lower layers contained red sherds almost exclusively. Smooth, large cobblestones were seen throughout Layer 3. The coral limestone bottom was reached sooner in the north than in the south, and the lowermost layers occurred only in pockets along the south wall.

Layer 4 had sparse occurrence of cord-marked pottery in reddish gritty soil, together with limestone fragments and mixed river pebbles. The granular pebbles in the corresponding cultural horizon in Locus P (see below) were not present here.

The four layers in K-1 and K-3 represent all the known ceramic phases in this part of Formosa in one stratified sequence, beginning with cord-marked pottery, through polished red pottery, to impressed sandy red and gray wares. Painted and polished jet-black pottery occurred throughout Layers 1 and 2 and the upper portions of 3, and there was no stratified relationship between them. Tsuboi's observation that the painted pottery preceded the black pottery at this site was not supported by our data.

Locus M

A side trail branched out near Locus K toward the southeast, downhill from the cart road going to the top, and ran parallel to the cliffs at the southeastern part of the hill. To the north of the trail, not far from Locus K, was a cement machine-gun position and a maze of communication trenches. From the ground surface and from the exposed profiles in the trenches, large numbers of stone tools and pottery were collected. The ground surface, about 20 to 40 cm deep, was very hard and consisted of large and small pieces of limestone rock presumably fallen from the cliff. A layer of cultural debris, at least 1.5 m thick, lay between the surface layer and the coral limestone base. Most of the potsherds were plain and sandy, corresponding in general to Layer 1 ceramics of Locus K.

Locus N (Fig. 13; Pl. 4, *B*)

East of M and directly below an overhanging cliff at the southeastern corner of the hill were sweet-potato fields and sisal plots, immediately south of which was an irrigation ditch bordering on the north a vast sugarcane field. At one place there was a cut into the fill below the cliff, about 15 m long (east–west) and 3 m high, which had a smooth and flat vertical surface about 8 m long. A very good cultural profile occurred on the surface, and we believe this was probably cut by Tsuboi and designated as his *Spot E*. We cut a space into the wall, 3 m long (east–west) and 1 m wide (north–south), and designated the three 1 × 1 columns as N-A, N-B, and N-C, from west to east.

The stratification of Locus N was very confused, owing mainly to the fact that the southern portions of the deposits were apparently talus formations which had slid down from the upslope at the north. An arbitrary base line was placed on the northern wall 120 cm down from the highest point of the ground surface, and the deposits above the line were designated as Layer 1 and those to a depth of 1 m below the line as Layer 2. Layer 1 had four subdivisions: 1a, 0–40 cm; 1b, 40–70 cm; 1c, 70–100 cm; and 1d, 100–120 cm. Layer 2 had five subdivisions of 20 cm each: 2a, 2b, 2c, 2d, and 2e. In the southern portions of the pit Layer 2 went deeper, and 2f, 2g, and 2h were distinguished. Layer 3 included 3a and 3b, 20 cm each, but the bottom of Layer 3 was 123 cm below the base line in the northern part and 185 cm in the southern part.

Three natural strata were chiefly represented here: secondary deposits, probably washed down from the top of the cliff; a compact layer of yellow earth, with a few

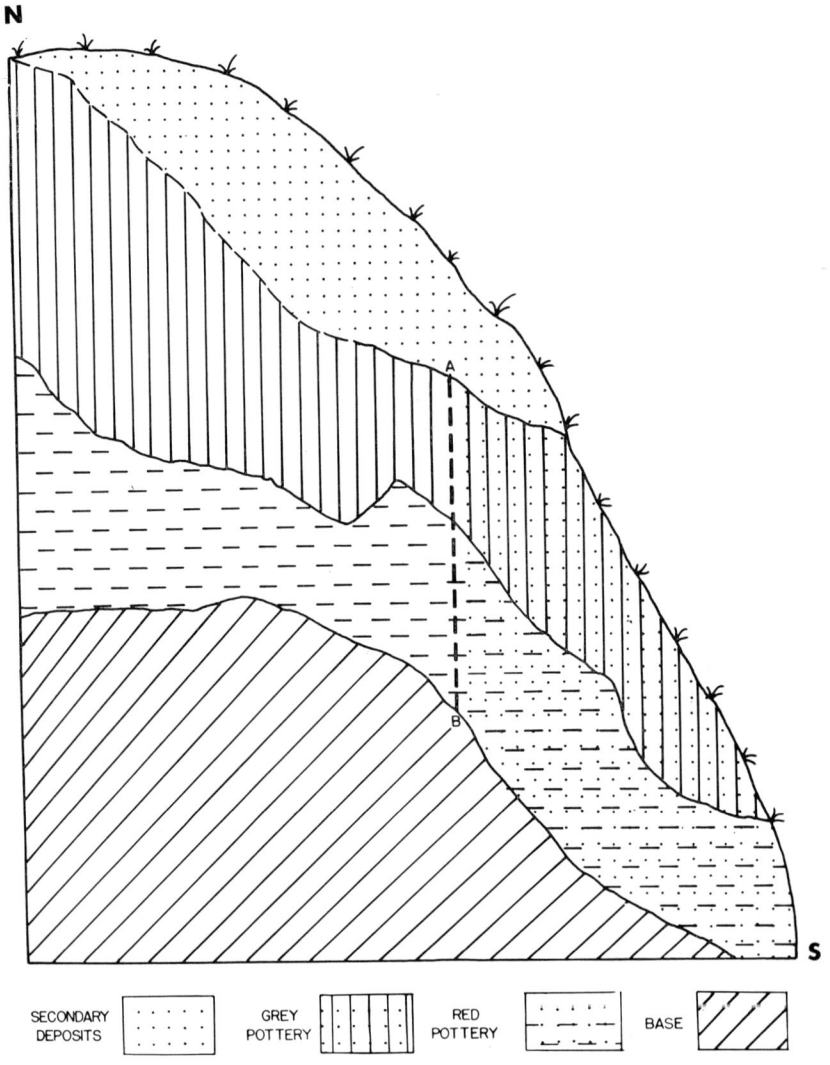

FIG. 13. North–South Section of Locus N, Fengpitou. (North–south length at base of pit: 2.86 m. Layers to the right of the dotted A–B line were secondarily deposited.)

large shells, and sandy red and gray pottery with impressions and paintings; and loose yellow clay, without shells and mixed with limestone rocks and polished red pottery (Pl. 4, *B*). The second cultural stratum corresponds to Layers 1 and 2, and the third cultural stratum to Layer 3. Compared with K Locus, Layer 4 of K was not present, and Layer 3 of K was divided into Layers 2 and 3 of N. If it is assumed that this area is identical with Tsuboi's *Spot E*, we are in agreement with him that red pottery underlies gray pottery, but in complete disagreement that painted pottery underlies black pottery. This discrepancy occurs throughout the site. It is probable that Tsuboi, not being able to excavate to great depth and seeing that painted pottery was red in base color, assumed that painted pottery was originally from the red pottery bed, which does lie beneath the gray pottery bed. Actually, both the painted and the black pottery occur in the same layer above the polished red pottery stratum (for details see Chapter 2).

Locus P (Fig. 14; Pls. 2; 5, *C*; 6; 7)

If one takes the road at Locus K all the way to the top of the hill, one comes to the eastern part of the top of the terrace and finds many more trenches and a row of four cement structures left by the Japanese troops. We selected a level area in a sweet-potato field, immediately west of a trench, and designated it Locus P (Pl. 2, *A*). According to the farmers, the top of the terrace once was not nearly so flat as it is today, because the higher spots have been leveled and the fill moved to pave the lower spots and fill the slopes. Hence there was considerable disturbance in this part of the site, not to mention the Japanese military activities.

Locus P was the most extensively excavated. Within the 10 × 10 unit, nine 2 × 2 squares were dug to the bottom: W1, W3, W7, W13, E3, E4, E5, E8, and E9; the eastern half of W4 (quadrants A2 and B2) was also excavated to the base; and the southern half of E2 (quandrants B1 and B2) was excavated to the bottom of the second cultural layer. The underground condition of the entire unit is known even though the rest of the squares were not touched.

The ground surface before occupation in Locus P was a slope from west to east (Fig. 14). In W13 the coral limestone base was reached at a depth of 50 cm from the present ground surface, but in E8 and E9 the base did not appear until 230 cm below the surface. The bottom in north–south cross section is like a gently sloping pit; it occurs at about 40 cm at both ends (W1 and E5) but reaches a depth of 2 m at the center (E3, E4, E8, E9). Immediately to the east of the excavated area was the trench, which must have cut into and disturbed the spot where the deepest cultural deposits occur.

Three natural strata were easily recognizable. Layer 1 was sandy yellowish clay, loosely deposited, mixed with a huge amount of limestone rock, and yielding such items as iron nails. This was possibly made up of earth transported to level the ground. Layer 2 consisted of brownish, hard, sticky clay with an enormous amount of pottery, sometimes occurring in distinctive horizons. Most of the pottery was pure red ware, but sandier red and gray potsherds occurred in the upper layers toward the eastern part of the locus. Seven post molds, making up the southwestern corner of a rectangular house plan, were uncovered from this layer, at about 70 cm below the ground surface, under a layer of very compactly placed potsherds (Pls. 6, 7). Layer 3 consisted of cord marked pottery mixed with granules and small pebbles lying on the surface of the coral limestone base (24.3% sand, 26.1% silt, 49.6%

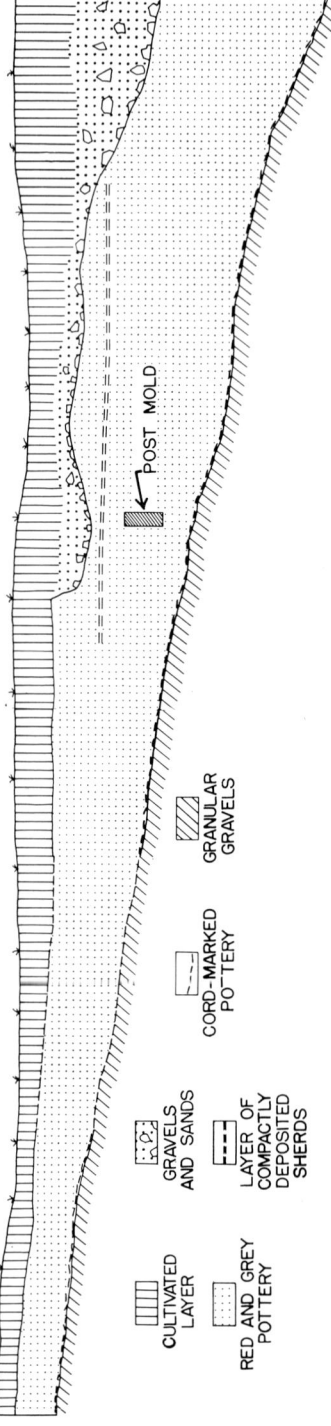

POST MOLD

CULTIVATED
LAYER

RED AND GREY
POTTERY

GRAVELS
AND SANDS

LAYER OF
COMPACTLY
DEPOSITED
SHERDS

CORD-MARKED
POTTERY

GRANULAR
GRAVELS

Fig. 14. East–West Section of Locus P, Fengpitou (east–west width: 10 m).

clay). In E3, E4, E8, and E9, fragments of human long bones were scattered, mixed with cord-marked potsherds, but no clear burial patterns were recognizable (Fig. 27). Layer 3 corresponds to Layer 4 of K, and Layer 2 of P to Layer 3 of K.

The thickness of each of the layers varied from square to square because of the sloping base, and the artificial layer divisions vary accordingly. Where each natural layer exceeded 20 cm in depth, a second artificial layer was distinguished, designated by a letter. In the eastern part of the unit, Layer 2 was broken up into 2a through 2f, and Layer 3 included 3a and 3b.

Loci Q and R

The trench east of Locus P marks the eastern margin of the terrace top, and a gentle slope leads from there down all the way to the valley floor. The farmers apparently leveled the slope into successive terraces for sweet potatoes and sugarcane, and on two of these levels on the eastern slope, designated Q and R respectively from west to east, we collected a large amount of potsherds, stone implements, and animal bones. Disturbance was, however, too extensive to warrant excavating at this time.

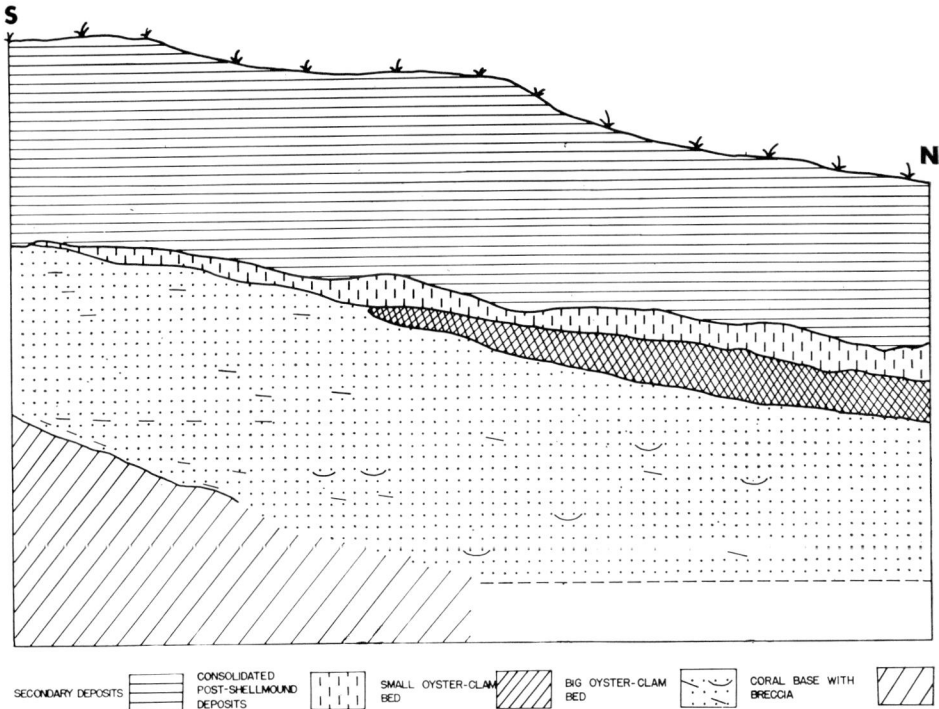

SECONDARY DEPOSITS | CONSOLIDATED POST-SHELLMOUND DEPOSITS | SMALL OYSTER-CLAM BED | BIG OYSTER-CLAM BED | CORAL BASE WITH BRECCIA

FIG. 15. V-section, South–North, Exposed on the West Wall of the Trench East of Locus V, Fengpitou (total north–south length: 4 m).

Locus S

Thirty meters northwest of Locus P was the highest ground on the eastern part of the hilltop, currently a sugarcane plot. An excavation unit, designated as S, was outlined, and four squares were excavated down to the bottom—W2, W6, E1, and E7. After the surface layer (designated as Layer 1) came a layer of shellmound, ranging in depth from 20 to 80 cm from the ground level. Beneath the shell layer (Layer 2) was the coral limestone base, exhibiting many pockets filled with shell-less deposits (Layer 3) with a maximum depth of 120 cm from the surface. This area was apparently one of the higher grounds leveled by the farmers, and the upper part of the cultural debris was probably completely removed. The excavation was discontinued after the four squares were dug to the bottom, but the cultural inventory from the thin shell layer was rather rich and roughly corresponds to Layers 1 and 2 of Locus K.

Loci T and U

The hill slopes down northward beyond Locus S, and in the sugarcane and sweet-potato fields north and northeast of Locus S large numbers of potsherds and stone

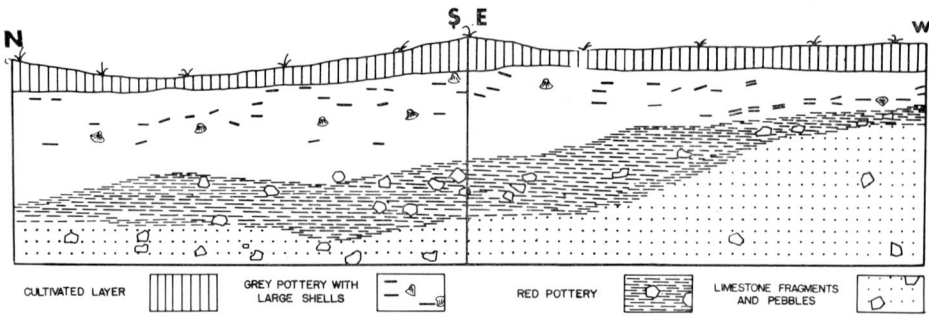

| CULTIVATED LAYER | | GREY POTTERY WITH LARGE SHELLS | | RED POTTERY | | LIMESTONE FRAGMENTS AND PEBBLES | |

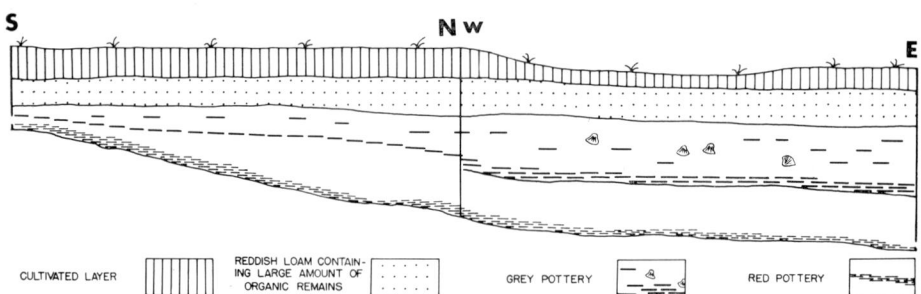

| CULTIVATED LAYER | | REDDISH LOAM CONTAINING LARGE AMOUNT OF ORGANIC REMAINS | | GREY POTTERY | | RED POTTERY | |

FIG. 16. East–West and North–South Sections of Pits E-10 (*upper*) and E-4 (*lower*), Locus V, Fengpitou (north–south and east–west length: each 2 m).

implements were scattered on the surface. A sweet-potato field northeast of S was designated Locus T, and the sweet-cane terraces north of S were designated Locus U. Extensive collections were made from both loci.

Locus V (Figs. 15, 16; Pls. 4, *A*; 5, *A,B*)

At the center of the northern slope of the terrace was a communication trench running north–south, its western wall exhibiting a clear cross section of the underground deposits (Fig. 15). The bottom of coral limestones sloped down to the south, and the top of the section was redeposited dirt. In between were two clearly distinguished layers of shellmounds, the bottom one consisting of large and sparse shells, the top one of smaller and more concentrated shells, a condition closely parallel to Locus K. An excavation area, designated as V (Pl. 5, *B*), was set up in the sweet-potato field immediately west of the trench section, and squares W3, W7,

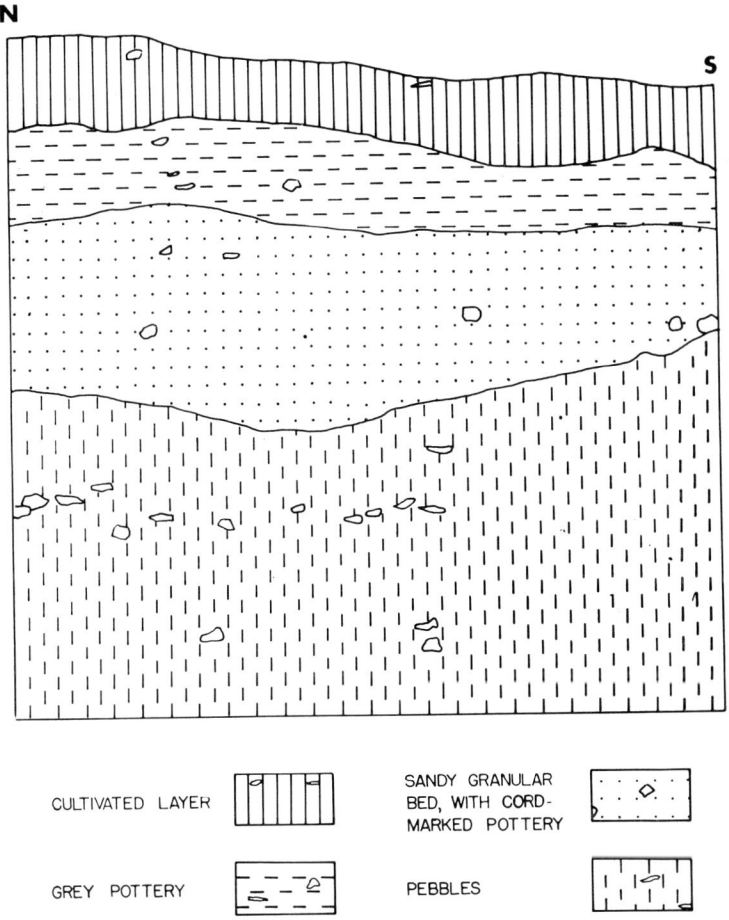

CULTIVATED LAYER		SANDY GRANULAR BED, WITH CORD-MARKED POTTERY
GREY POTTERY		PEBBLES

FIG. 17. North–South Section of Locus Y, Fengpitou (north–south length: 2 m).

W9, E4, the quadrant A2 of E5, the western half of E9 (quadrants A1 and B1), and E10 were excavated to the coral limestone base. Apparently the upper portions of the original deposits were leveled off, removing the entire small-shell portion seen on the V section.

The stratification of Locus V (Fig. 16) closely paralleled N and the lower part of K. Layer 1, some 20 cm in depth, consisted of disturbed surface soil. Layer 2, containing a few large shells, was characterized by thin levels of gray potsherds and a large amount of bone implements. Layer 3, 60 to 80 cm below the ground surface, was devoid of shells and characterized by very rich deposits of polished red pottery. At some places there were more potsherds than earth. From Layer 2 a human burial was found in squares E4, E5, E9, and E10 (Fig. 67; Pl. 5, *A*). Fragments of human long bones were collected in Locus V, and a molar was excavated from Layer 2 (Pl. 66). In all likelihood the cemetery of the folk associated with the gray and red painted and the black pottery was nearby, in the northern part of the village on the shady side of the hill.

Locus Y (Fig. 17)

The areas described thus far were along the southern, eastern, and northern slopes of the hill and at the eastern end of the terrace top. Very careful reconnaissance undertaken in the remaining part of the hill failed to identify any other deposit of noteworthy richness and depth. At the center of the top of the hill, bare bedrock was exposed or very shallowly covered, probably a combined result of artificial leveling of the hilltop and intensive weathering. At the western end of the top and along the western slopes, there were extensive layers of potsherds mixed with granules and pebbles lying above the coral limestone base 1 to 1.5 m below ground level. The condition of deposition was similar to the cord-marked pottery stratum in Locus P, but the finds appear to be of a much later origin. It is possible that these were mostly secondary deposits, as in Locus B. A section at the western end of the hilltop in the trench was investigated and designated Y.

Chapter 2. History of Neolithic Settlement

THE artifactual variations reflected by the data of Fengpitou can truly be called enormous and numerous; they provide a highly valuable source of information for the study of culture characterization, distribution, and change. Before their meaning can be recognized, however, efforts must be made to localize the variations both spatially and temporally. I will first delineate the units at the site of Fengpitou in which the archeological changes can be recognized and characterized universally and macrotypologically, and minute studies of distribution and change will then be undertaken within each of the units that have resulted.

It is obvious that the terrace deposits at Fengpitou over the Pleistocene coral limestone base were left during the postglacial period, but the different parts of the site were also obviously deposited at various time intervals and sometimes under different environmental conditions. Moreover, the various areas of human occupation underwent diverse subsequent disturbances. It is therefore necessary as a first step toward an interpretation of the culture history to synchronize the various parts of the site into a broad sequence of natural and cultural events that took place from the beginning of human occupation to the end. Only after a variety of extensive analyses can such problems as cultural ecology, the horizontal layout of cultural variations, and culture change be discussed. But these analyses cannot always be complete, and the archeologist must use whatever information is available. Fortunately, a synchronization of the various components of the site need only be broad and general for culture-historical discussions, and for this purpose the following information and interpretation appear to suffice.

Ceramic Seriation

The most abundant find at the site is the pottery, and it is unusually abundant compared with other sites in this area. In some layers potsherds are much more plentiful than earth, and throughout the occupational stratum huge quantities of sherds form distinctive, compact layers. Moreover, in variety of types and modes this is also one of the richest sites in East Asia, and probably the richest on the island thus far. It includes most of the shapes, pastes, and decorations known on the island, thereby affording an excellent laboratory for the study of temporal and horizontal variations of ceramics.

Problems of ceramic typology of Fengpitou will be discussed in other parts of this volume. Here, broad categories of pottery will be used for chronological purposes. The assumption is that the *major trends* of ceramic development and change are site-wide and that *at any one time* the percentages of these major categories were identical throughout the site. In particular, if at one part of the site there is a complete sequence of percentages of the major ceramic categories and if these percentages form distinct patterns through time, then these percentages at other parts

41

of the site, less complete perhaps, can be considered as chronological segments and be matched against the master sequence. The technique is much like dendrochronology, varve analysis, and the matching of pollen profiles, except that the time unit to be matched must be much broader. For this purpose the following ceramic categories have been made.

Corded. First identified in an excavated assemblage at Tapenkeng, to be described in Part II of this volume, this ware is characterized by coarse sand temper; relatively thick wall (5–8 mm average); heterogeneous color spectrum, ranging from light buff to dark brown; coarse-stranded cord impression; combed lines on the vessel rim and shoulder; a ridged neck; low neck that thins out toward the rim; globular body with occasional lug handles; low ring foot with occasional cut-out holes near the top.

Painted. Fine-sand temper or very fine paste; orange, red, or dark buff color; as a rule hard; often burnished before painting; painted designs in dark red pigment on the exterior of body and both the exterior and the interior of the rim; bowl and beaker with ring foot; absence of decorative designs other than painting. This is made a distinctive category for two reasons: painted pottery carries significant historical information in East and Southeast Asia; and painting as a means of design execution is exclusive, even though the paste and firing are not uniform within the category.

Fine red. Very fine paste; relatively hard; often polished on the exterior; often wheel-touched inside the rim and the ring foot; shapes of bowl, cup, jar, and fruit stand are characteristic; cord impression on the lower part of the body very frequent, these being thinner-stranded and deeper than the cord impression of the corded ware; very occasional incision near the neck. Two main subdivisions can be made: one highly burnished, the other very porous and softer.

Sandy red. Coarse sand temper; rather hard; color ranging from light buff to dark brown; shapes are bowls and jars; incised rim and neck; body often impressed with cord mark, mat mark, or basket mark.

Sandy gray. Same as sandy red, except that the color ranges from light to very dark gray.

Fine gray. Fine paste; rather hard; gray color; incised and combed patterns; bowl and cup are leading shapes.

Polished black. Very fine paste; very hard; color ranging from dark yellow to jet black; very thin body (thinnest sherds being no more than 1.5 mm); incised, engraved, and combed decoration; several shapes, mostly smaller than the others; wheel marks distinctive.

More precise descriptions of these wares will be made elsewhere, but these are the preliminary categories we employed in the laboratory as a first step. The percentages of the different wares by levels in K-3 are indicated in the accompanying graphs, one according to number of sherds (Fig. 18) and the other to their weight (Fig. 19). These two graphs by number and by weight are in broad agreement in indicating the following major trends of ceramic change.

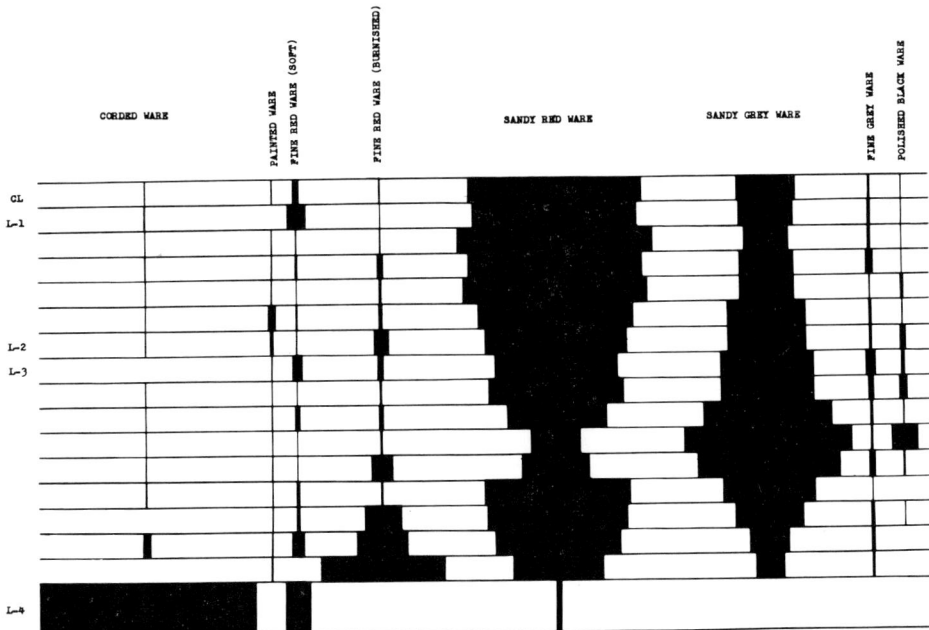

FIG. 18. Percentage Graphs of the Occurrence of Various Wares According to Vertical Strata at Locus K, Pit 3, Fengpitou (by number of potsherds).

1. Layer 4 is distinctive, characterized by corded ware. Very little of this ware continues into the layers above, and very little of the other wares was initiated in this layer. During the excavations the distinction between the corded ware stratum and the next ceramic layer was even more conspicuously observable than the graph indicates for this area.

2. Layer 3i is largely dominated by the fine red ware, but the sandy wares have already begun.

3. The layers above contain mainly sandy wares; each of the other wares (painted, fine gray, black, and fine red) has a small percentage. According to the distribution of the gray against the red, three levels are apparent. The lowermost are Layers 3f, 3g, and 3h, where fine red lingers on but sandy red predominates, and sandy gray begins to show.

4. In Layers 3d and 3e, sandy red is minimal but sandy gray is at the peak. This is also the peak of the polished black.

5. From Layer 3c on upward there is a steady growth of sandy red and a proportionate decline of sandy gray.

With this graph from K-3 as a master sequence and matching the other areas against it, the sequence in Figure 20 results.

Purely from these graphs it is possible to synchronize the excavated profiles in the following way:

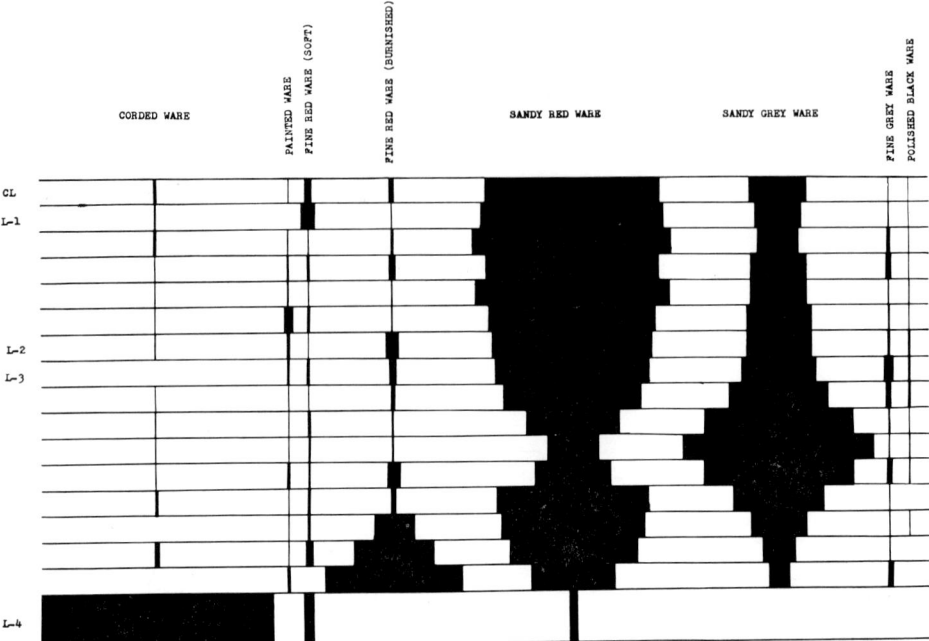

Fig. 19. Percentage of the Occurrence of Various Wares According to Vertical Strata at Locus K, Pit 3, Fengpitou (by weight of potsherds).

1. Corded ware strata: P-L3; K-L4
2. Fine red ware strata: P-L2c–f; K-L3i; N-L3; V-L3
3. Sandy red predominant: K-L3f–h; P-L2a, b
4. Sandy gray predominant: K-L3c–e; N-L2; V-L2
5. Sandy red predominant: K-L1 and 2; N-L1; B

Distribution of Mollusk Shells

Collecting mollusk shellfish was an important means of subsistence during much of the Neolithic occupation of Fengpitou, as shown by the huge quantities of shells—shellmounds—at most of the excavated areas. Thirty-two species of mollusks have been identified (see Appendix 3 and Pls. 105–107), and the most common are *Terebralia semistriata*, *Ostrea gigas*, *O. vitrefacta*, *Gafrarium tumidum*, *Meretrix petechialis*, *Chione* (*Anomalodiscus*) *squamosa*, *C. isabelina*, *Ketelysia virginea*, *Telescopium telescopium*, and *Placuna placenta*. These are all marine species which clearly belong to the shellfish assemblage common throughout this part of Formosa in prehistoric periods. Aside from its environmental and subsistence significance, the mollusk shell at the site is important in providing chronological clues through its distributional patterns.

In the first place, mollusk shells were absent in the strata at the lowest levels where cord-marked pottery and burnished red pottery predominated. These were

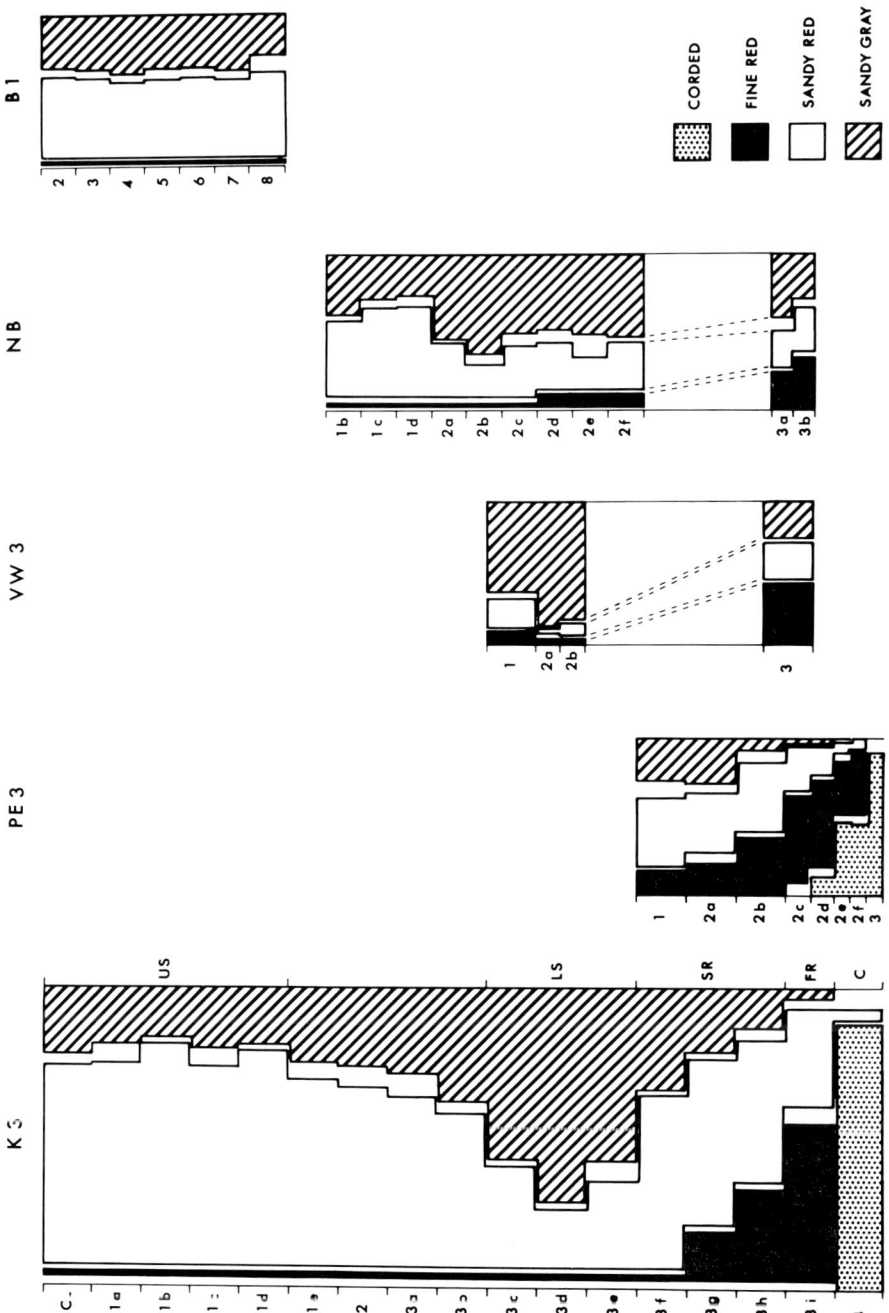

Fig. 20. Matching the Ceramic Graphs of P-E3, V-W3, N-B, and B-1 Against the K-3 Sequence.

Layer 4 and lower levels of Layer 3 in Locus K, Layer 3 in N, Layer 3 and most of Layer 2 in P, and Layer 3 in V. As far as the shellmound phenomenon is concerned, these layers predate the shellmounds chronologically.

The longest shellmound sequence was from Locus K; here it lasted from the upper levels of Layer 3 to Layers 2 and 1 and finally to the Cultivated Layer. A small number of large shells was found in Layer 3, and small and abundant shells occurred in Layers 2 and 1. On the basis of this a tentative division was made in the field: the shellmounds in N and the excavated portions of V were designated "big oyster and clam layers," and the shellmounds in S and in the upper part of the V section "small oyster and clam layers." Roughly speaking, the assumption made in the field was that Layer 3 (upper levels) of K, Layer 2 (and lower part of Layer 1) of N, and the lower levels of V section (and Layer 2 of the excavated unit V) were largely contemporary, whereas Layers 1 and 2 of K, Layer 2 of S, and the upper part of V section were probably contemporary. Thus a broad synchronization of the various parts of the site according to the distribution of shells is as follows:

1. Pre-shellmound: Layer 4 and lower levels of Layer 3 in K, Layer 3 in N, Layer 3 and most of Layer 2 in P, Layer 3 in V.
2. Big oyster and clam layers: Middle levels of Layer 3 in K, Layer 2 and part of Layer 1 in N, uppermost levels in P, possibly Layer 3 in S, lower part of V section and Layers 1 and 2 in V unit.
3. Small oyster and clam layers: Layers 1 and 2 and uppermost 3 in K, Layer 2 in S, upper part of V section.

A more refined synchronization of the parts of the site can be made according to the distributional pattern of the species of mollusk shells, but the general tendency remains the same. The longest shell sequence being in Locus K, we made a detailed count of the numbers of shells of all species in the column (50 × 50 cm) in K2, and the percentages of species by level are shown (Fig. 21).

This graph indicates the following chronologically significant phenomena. (1) Shells were absent in the lower levels of Layer 3 as well as the entire Layer 4. (2) The shellmound sequence has three apparent points of significance. The first is in the middle levels of Layer 3 and is characterized by a small number of species of individuals of large sizes. These earliest species include *Anomalocardia producta*, *Ostrea gigas*, and *Meretrix petechialis*, among others. It is possible that at this time the occupants of the site were only beginning to utilize the marine resources and, since the pressure on this means of subsistence was not yet heavy, they chose only a small number of species of large size. The second point centers in uppermost Layer 3, Layer 2, and the lower levels of Layer 1, and is characterized by the predominance of *Chione squamosa*. The third point was reached in mid-Layer 1 and was marked by the great abundance of *Ostrea vitrefacta*. Both the second and the third points are characterized by a greatly increased variety of species and the smaller size of the individual shells. It is possible that this means of subsistence was then relied upon more heavily than before—possibly because of population pressure and a greater familiarity with the marine resources—and the collection of mollusks was therefore less discriminating and the shellfish had less chance to grow to full size.

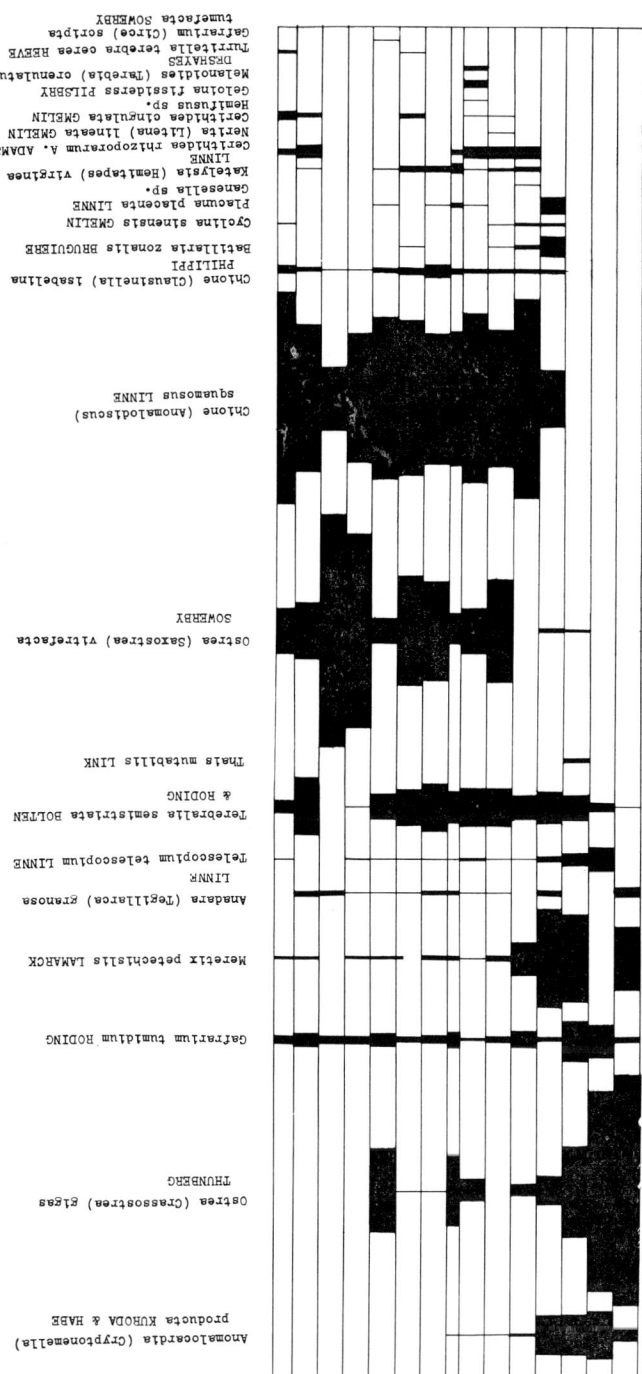

47

Fig. 21. Percentage Graphs of the Occurrence of Various Mollusk Species According to Vertical Strata at Locus K, Pit 2, Feng-pitou (by number of individuals).

With the K-2 sequence as a guide, the distribution of the shellfish species in other localities can be assessed chronologically.

Locus E. The following species of shells were collected on the surface: *Terebralia semistriata, Ostrea gigas, Gafrarium tumidum, Meretrix petechialis,* and *Chione squamosa.* Since these were not excavated, the chronological significance is not conclusive, but it is likely that the chronological segment corresponding to the second stage of K (Layer 2 and lower 1) was present in this area.

Locus N. Most of the mollusk shells collected here came from Layer 2 and were of large size. The predominant species are: *Ostrea gigas, Placuna placenta, Meretrix petechialis, Gafrarium tumidum,* and *Anadara granosa. Anomalocardia producta* is seen in one case from Layer 2b, and the only shells from Layer 1 (1d) were all *Ostrea gigas.* Only one individual of *O. vitrefacta* (L2e), and none of *Chione squamosa,* was found in the undisturbed layers. It is probable that the entire N sequence with shells can be placed within the shellmound part of Layer 3 of K, and that Layers 1 and 2 of K are not represented by undisturbed N strata.

Locus P. The bulk of shells collected in this locus came from Layer 1, the secondary deposits. Either the entire Layer 2 must be placed within the pre-shellmound period of the site, or the area was not utilized as a shell midden during the entire occupation. The few shells found *in situ* in Layer 2 (*Ostrea gigas, O. vitrefacta, Gafrarium tumidum, Chione squamosa*) were near the top and could be intrusive.

Locus S. The species found in Layer 2 (shellmound layer) include *Turritella terebra cerea, Melanoides crenulatus, Telescopium telescopium, Terebralia semistriata, Anadara granosa, A. ehrenbergi, Placuna placenta, Ostrea gigas, O. vitrefacta, Geloina fissidens, Gafrarium tumidum, G. scripta tumefacta, Meretrix petechialis, Chione squamosa, C. isabelina,* and *Anomalocardia producta.* The predominant species is the small oyster *Ostrea vitrefacta,* and there is little question that this segment is comparable to Layer 1 of Locus K. Shells from Layer 3 are few but include more *Chione squamosa* than anything else.

Locus V. Shells from the excavated unit (Layer 2 primarily) are mainly of two species: *Ostrea gigas* and *Meretrix petechialis.* There is no question that this is comparable to Layer 3 shellmound layers of K and to N. From the upper levels of the V section, *Ostrea vitrefacta* and *Chione squamosa* were collected, but this layer was presumably completely removed in the excavated portions of the locus.

Soil Analysis

Samples of soil collected from the K-2 column at 20-cm intervals were processed by Professor Lin with the Tyler standard sieves, with the result shown in Table 2. The top layers, to a depth of slightly less than 1 m, consist of soil of very fine texture, whereas the transition from the fine soil of samples 2 and 4 to the coarse soil of samples 6–14 is obvious and conspicuous, clearly indicating the possibility that the deposits below were accumulated without major intervals of exposure. In other words, the deposition of the layers at Locus K containing the sandy wares and the

TABLE 2. SIEVE ANALYSIS OF SOIL SAMPLES FROM LOCUS K, PIT 2, FENGPITOU*

Sieve / Sample	24 Mesh (%)	28 Mesh (%)	48 Mesh (%)	65 Mesh (%)	100 Mesh (%)	150 Mesh (%)	−150 Mesh (%)
2(L1a)	2.67	1.78	23.50	14.50	10.80	10.55	36.20
4(L1c)	7.85	1.95	26.40	13.70	9.80	10.50	29.80
6(L1e)	21.00	1.97	20.60	10.90	11.90	9.40	24.23
8(L2a)	16.40	1.44	20.30	12.30	9.75	10.30	29.51
10(L2c)	22.40	1.36	18.50	10.90	9.64	13.40	23.80
12(L3)	27.60	1.52	17.80	8.71	7.70	7.40	29.20
14(L3a)	29.40	1.55	17.80	9.41	5.60	7.70	28.55

* By C. C. Lin.

TABLE 3. CHEMICAL ANALYSIS OF SOIL SAMPLES FROM LOCUS K, PIT 2, FENGPITOU*

	Loss of Ignition	SiO_2	Al_2O_3	Fe_2O_3	TiO_2	CaO	MgO	$Na_2O + K_2O$ by Diff.
1(LCL)	6.63	67.30	13.80	4.70	0.56	3.48	1.13	2.40
3(L1b)	7.62	59.31	17.18	5.27	0.53	7.02	1.68	1.39
5(L1d)	7.51	60.86	15.44	4.56	0.48	7.14	1.55	2.46
7(L1g)	*12.42*	*52.63*	*11.95*	*4.16*	*0.42*	*14.14*	*1.39*	*2.89*
9(L2b)	9.92	60.96	12.95	4.42	0.49	7.59	1.62	2.05
11(L3a)	9.04	61.89	12.70	5.15	0.50	7.75	1.62	1.35
13(L3e)	7.54	64.17	14.26	4.04	0.47	6.79	1.01	1.72

* By C. C. Lin.

shell middens were likely a continuous process. It must be pointed out, however, that sample 8 is of a conspicuously finer texture than all the other samples in the lower layers. The meaning of this may be suggested by the results of a chemical analysis of the K-2 soil samples shown in Table 3. The loss of ignition in sample 7 is extraordinarily high (12.42% vs. 7.54–9.92% below and 6.63–7.51% above). Since the source of the ignition loss principally comes from decomposed organic matters, the likelihood that sample 7 was exposed for a prolonged period in a heavily vegetated environment is strongly suggested. This is further borne out by the low content of SiO_2 in sample 7.

Microscopic examination of the coarse silt fraction (20–50 μ) of the soil samples from Locus P from −70 cm (gray pottery), −130 cm (red pottery), −200 cm (granular soil), and −220 cm (bottom of culture layer) below ground level, respectively, shows that the content of plant opal increases from a very small amount at the bottom to very abundant in the sample from −130 cm, suggesting a post-red pottery interval in which abundant grass grew at the locus. The fine texture of this red pottery layer sample (56.6% clay), in contrast to the coarse texture of the sample from the bottom of the cultural layer (49.6% clay), also indicates an interval of exposure and weathering.

Carbon-14 Dates

From the Radiocarbon Laboratory of Yale University came the following carbon-14 determinations for the Fengpitou site. All are B.P. dates (before 1950).

Y-1580	Shells, from lower part of V section	$3{,}310 \pm 80$
Y-1581	Shells, from upper part of V section	$2{,}910 \pm 80$
Y-1649	Shells, from N-A-L2e	$2{,}900 \pm 120$
Y-1578	Shells, from S-E7-L3a	$2{,}780 \pm 80$
Y-1648	Shells, from K-3-L3d	$2{,}670 \pm 60$
Y-1584	Shells, from K-1-L3	$2{,}670 \pm 80$
Y-1577	Shells, from K-1-L2	$2{,}440 \pm 100$
Y-1600	Charcoal, from V-W3-L2	$1{,}380 \pm 160$

All dates derived from shell samples have been corrected. The $1{,}380 \pm 160$ date of Y-1600 is not in agreement with the rest, because Layer 2 of Locus V should correspond, according to its shell content and its ceramics, to the upper levels of Layer 3 of Locus K, and the sample was either contaminated or intrusive. Thus the entire cultural sequence of Fengpitou can be broken down as follows according to the carbon-14 data (Fig. 22).

1. Cord-marked pottery; no C-14 dates available, but obviously earlier than 2.

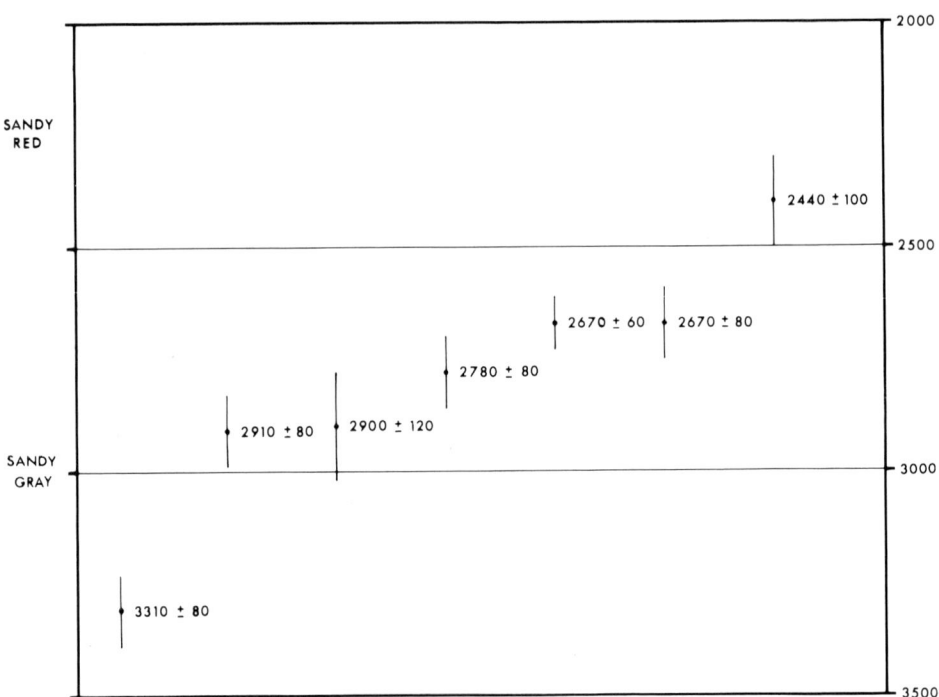

Fig. 22. Carbon-14 Dates from Fengpitou.

2. Red fine and sandy pottery layers without shells; no C-14 dates available, but obviously later than 1 but earlier than 3.

3. Shellmound layers with big oysters and clams, namely, middle levels of Layer 3 of K, Layer 2 of N, and Layer 2 of V: Y-1580, Y-1581, Y-1649, Y-1578, Y-1648, and Y-1584, which give a series of C-14 dates (B.P.) as follows: 3,310, 2,910; 2,900; 2,780; and 2,670. An average of 1400 to 900 B.C. can be used for this layer.

4. Shellmound layers with small oysters and clams, i.e. the uppermost Layer 3 and Layers 1 and 2 of K, Layers 2 and 3 of S, and Layer 1 of V: Y-1577, which gives a single C-14 date of 2,400 B.P. A rough date of 900 to 400 B.C. can be used for this segment.

Summary

On the basis of the above analysis, the different cultural strata at the various loci at the site of Fengpitou can be synchronized into the master sequence of Table 4.

Many other changes and variations in the salient attributes of the prehistoric remains are manifest, but their detailed study will not be undertaken in the present context. As stated in the Introduction and at the beginning of this chapter, in studying cultural change one is faced with a number of different problems which can, nevertheless, be characterized under two distinct levels: those that concern the site as a whole and have reference to the characterization and subdivision of the

TABLE 4. SYNCHRONIZED SEQUENCE OF CULTURE DEPOSITS AT THE VARIOUS ARCHEOLOGICAL LOCI OF THE FENGPITOU SITE

B.C.		B	K	N	P	S	V
400							
	Sandy Red *Small shells*	L1–8	L1 L2[2440] L3a b	L1		L2	L1
900							
	Sandy Gray *Large shells*		L3c d[2670] e	L2a b c d e[2900]		L3a[2780] b	L2a[2910] b[3310]
1400							
	Sandy Red *No shells*		L3f g h		L2a b		
1900							
	Fine Red *No shells*		L3i	L3	L2c d e f		L3
2400							
	Corded		L4		L3		

site's total body of artifactual and scientific data, and those that concern the external contrasts and the internal articulations of the various subdividions. Under the former area of investigation one seeks to isolate clusters of variations and to characterize the major cultural types at the site, and under the latter to articulate the variations within each of the culture types and to trace the major trends of change from one cultural type to another.

At the level of macrotypology, then, the site of Fengpitou can be said to be the seat of no fewer than five major cultural segments. These segments are recognizable through the temporal pattern of ceramic change, the distribution of mollusk shells, soil alteration, stratigraphical observations (described in the previous chapter), and carbon-14 synchronization. Furthermore, the ceramic seriations indicate that at a higher level of contrast the earliest segment forms a unit by itself, clearly characterized by the cord-marked pottery and separated from the subsequent segments which form a distinct cluster by themselves characterized by several related though slightly different wares. It is thus clearly indicated by the above analysis that at the site one can formulate the occupation of no fewer than five settlements and, further, that the four later settlements form a separate cluster at a higher level of contrast.

The contrasts between the earliest settlement and the later four settlements, and among the later four settlements themselves, are further illustrated by artifacts other than pottery and by ceramic features other than those considered above, which will be described in some detail in the following chapters. I shall refer to the first settlement as the Corded Ware culture, because cord-marked pottery is its most distinctive feature, and to the later cluster of four settlements as the Lungshanoid culture, adopting this name from the Neolithic archeology of southeastern China. These cultural definitions cannot be justified until after comparative studies have been undertaken in Part III of this monograph, but the terms will be used from the beginning for the sake of convenience.

Chapter 3. The Corded Ware Culture

THE finds within the corded ware strata at Fengpitou are insufficient for the characterization of a whole culture, but they clearly and decisively indicate affiliation with a culture different from the Lungshanoid that followed it at the site. The important things about this culture that we do *not* know are its absolute dating, its subsistence pattern, its settlement pattern, its complete stone inventory, and its range of industrial activities—to mention only a few that are ordinarily expected of archeological sites. We do know that this is a local component of a widespread Corded Ware horizon on the island, and that inference can be made concerning this culture at Fengpitou according to our knowledge of it elsewhere in Taiwan. These studies will be described in Part III of this volume.

Finds of this culture are found in occupational layers at loci K and P of Fengpitou. At both loci the corded ware sherds were excavated from the lowermost strata above the coral limestone base, mixed with limestone fragments at K and with granular pebbles at P. Sherds of the same category have been found at other excavated loci near the bottom, but always mixed with, and as a minority element among, the Lungshanoid sherds. Therefore it is possible to say only that the Corded Ware culture occupation at the site was probably confined to the southern slope and the eastern end of the terrace top. If the extent of artifact distribution and the amount of artifacts are any indication of population density, then the Corded Ware culture settlement at the site was considerably smaller than the Lungshanoid settlements, and the population was possibly less dense.

Neither shells nor charcoals have been found from this layer, and the human bones from Locus P have a carbon content of less than 0.5 per cent and have proved inadequate for dating. The problem of dating this cultural horizon on Formosa will be discussed later. As far as Fengpitou is concerned, the Corded Ware culture must be at least as early as the fourth millennium B.C. The Lungshanoid culture, as will be discussed later, began here around 2500 B.C. at the latest, and an interval of at least 500 years must have intervened between the Corded Ware and the Lungshanoid cultures to explain the depositional disconformity as well as the cultural discontinuity.

Implements

Five stone implements were discovered in this cultural stratum:

1. A medium-grained sandstone pebble with vein belts, approximately 9 cm long, 7 cm wide, and 1.2 cm thick (Fig. 23, *1*; Pl. 16, *A*). There is no sharpened edge nor evidence of pounding at the ends, but two notches were flaked at the opposite sides at the waist. It came from P-W4-A2-L3a, in indisputable association with corded sherds. The only possible inference is that it was a net sinker.

2. An elongated, polished arrowhead of black slate, from K-3-L4, broken at both

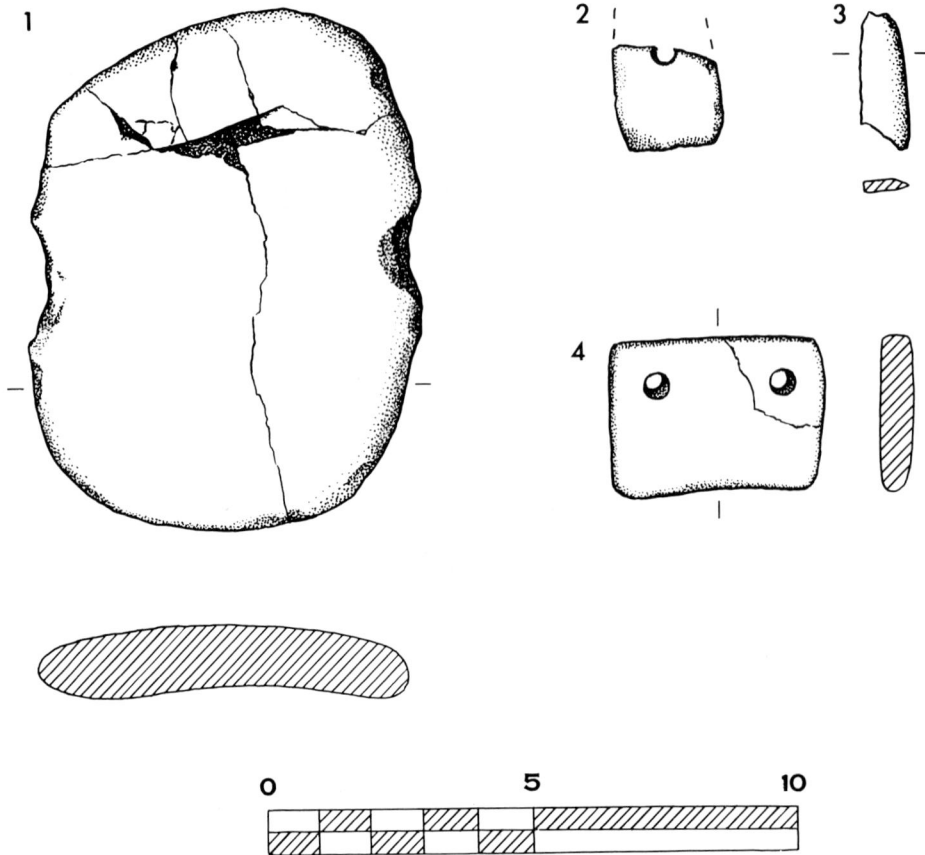

FIG. 23. Stone and Clay Artifacts from the Corded Ware Culture Stratum at Fengpitou. (*1*, Net sinker of pebble with chipped notches; *2* and *3*, slate arrowheads; *4*, clay object of unknown use.)

tip and base, with a remaining length of 25 mm, width of 9 mm, and thickness of 1.5 mm. It is flat, and its original shape was probably that of a willow leaf (Pl. 16, *C*; Fig. 23, *3*).

3. A triangular, polished arrowhead of gray-greenish slate, from P-E8-B1-L3. It has a straight base, about 19 mm wide, and a perforation at the center, about 12 mm from the base and 5 mm in diameter. The upper (tip) part of the point is broken at the perforation (Fig. 23, *2*; Pl. 16, *D*).

4 and 5. Two fragments of sandstone pebbles, too incomplete to indicate original shape and use; both show evidence of polishing, and one has a remaining section of a cutting edge. Both came from P-E4-B2-L3 (Pl. 16, *B,E*).

In addition, there is a fragment of a long bone, about 50 mm long (Pl. 16, *G*). Evidence of cutting with a blunt instrument is observed at both ends. There is also

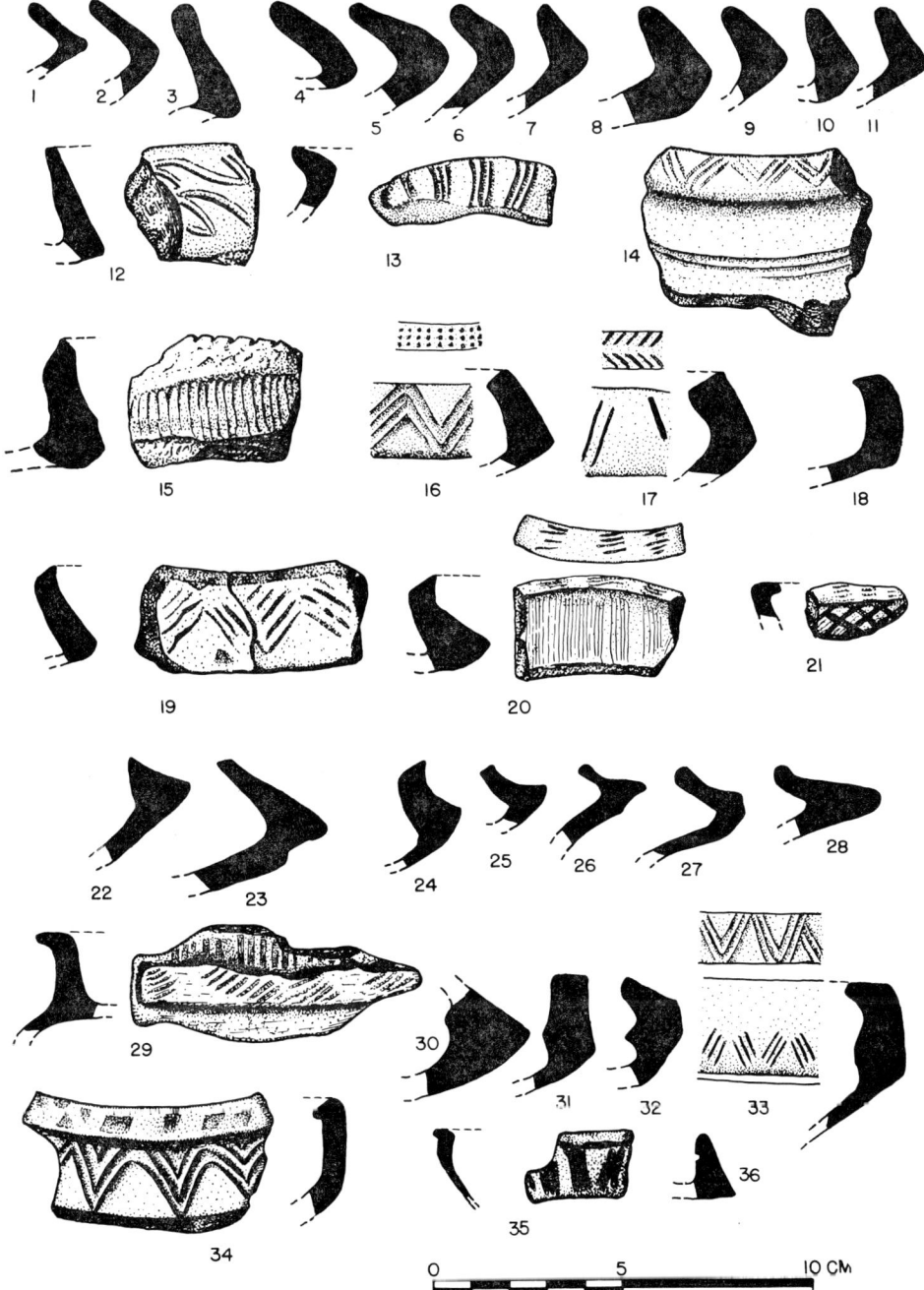

FIG. 24. Corded Ware Sherds, Fengpitou: Rim Shapes and Decorations of Pots and Jars.

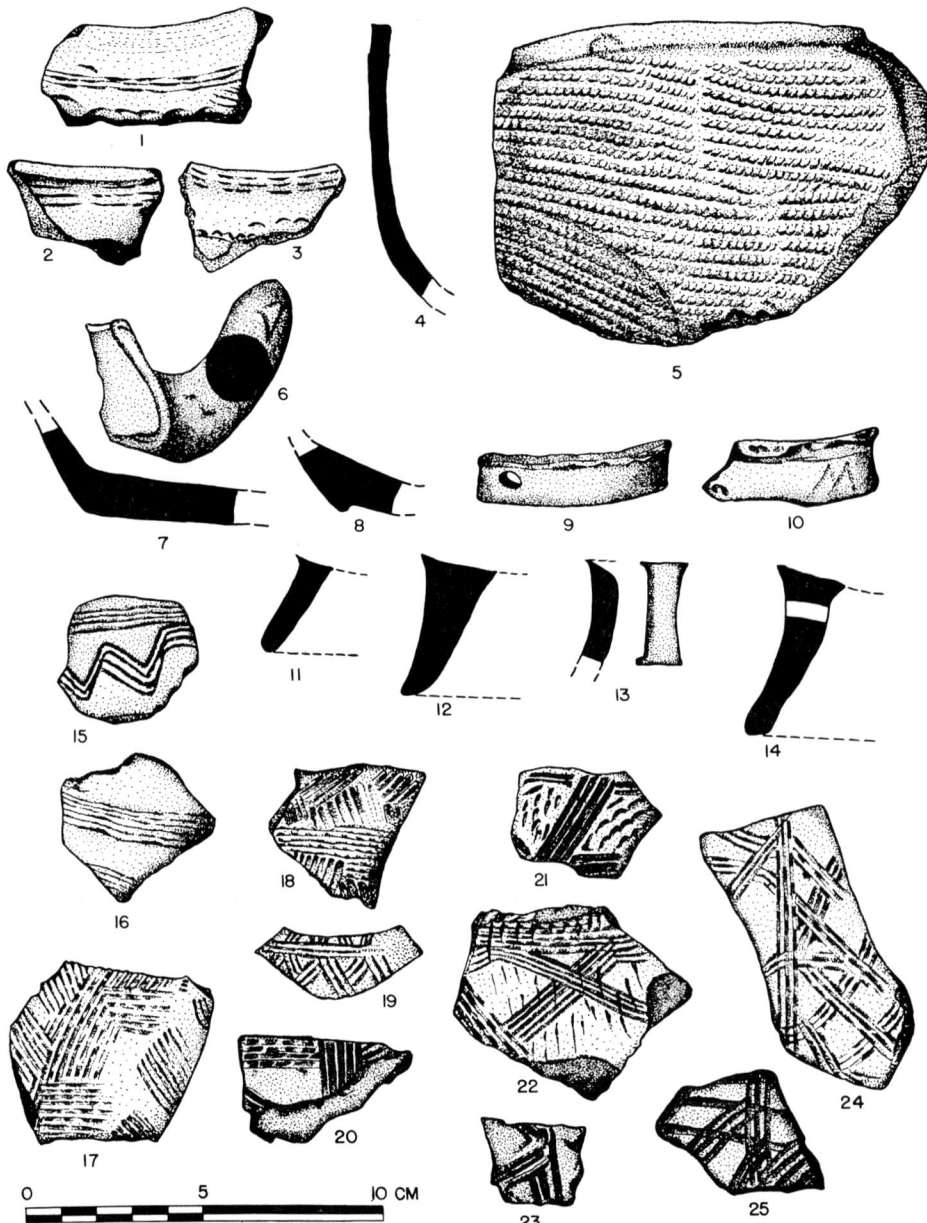

FIG. 25. Corded Ware Sherds, Fengpitou: Bowls, Lugs, Ring Feet, and Body Sherds.

a clay plate with two holes along one side (Fig. 23, *4*; Pl. 16, *F*). This type of artifact is also found in the Lungshanoid layers, but the paste of this particular specimen and its context (P-E9-L3) both suggest a Corded Ware culture association. Its use is unclear.

Pottery

Corded pottery (Figs. 24–26; Pls. 14, 15) characterizes the Corded Ware culture at Fengpitou. It is the only ware and is relatively homogeneous. The demarcation between the corded ware and the Lungshanoid wares is both physically and stratigraphically clear-cut; the classifiers have had no difficulty in distinguishing these sherds.

Paste. The corded ware sherds are grouped into three kinds: rims, body sherds, and others (ring-foot sherds and one lug). The rim sherds, invariably broken at the neck, are relatively heavy, the thickest part often reaching 10 to 20 mm. With rare exceptions they are short segments, and the complete diameter is difficult to restore. The body sherds, which constitute the majority, average between 20 and 50 mm long and 5 to 8 mm thick. There is no evidence of wheel-making or touching, but

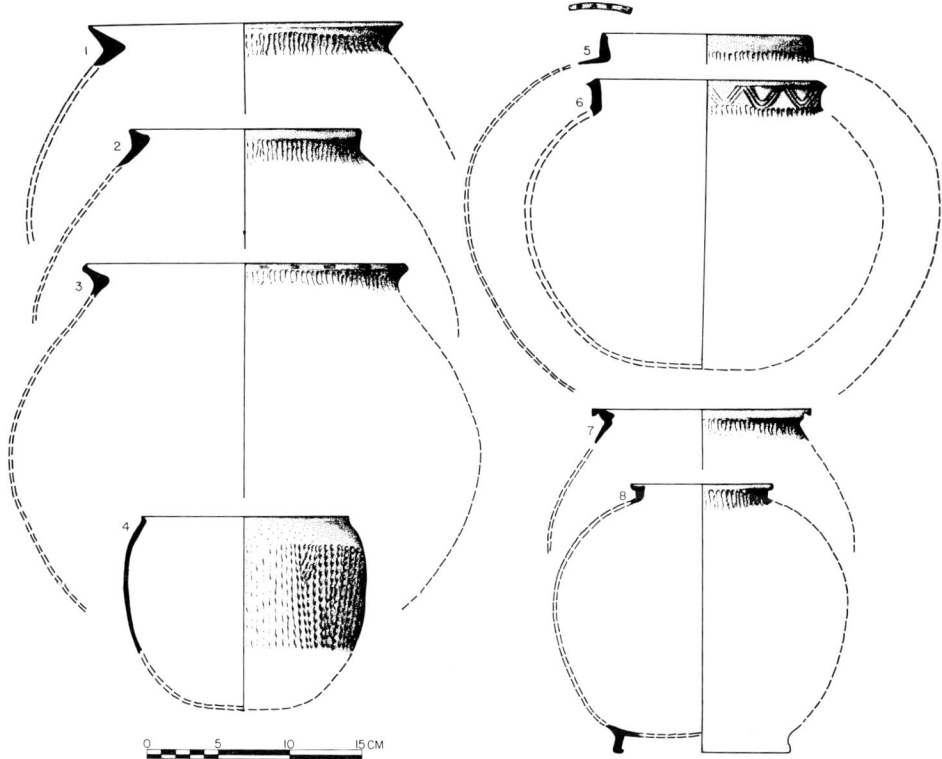

FIG. 26. Corded Ware Pottery, Fengpitou: Reconstructed Shapes of Pots and Jars.

the lip and the interior of the rim were in many cases smoothed by fingers. As far as can be determined, the body was usually made first, and the rim, ring foot, and/or lug was attached to the body subsequently.

The paste is relatively fine but contains a considerable amount of sand temper; the sand grains range greatly in size but average 0.5 to 1 mm. Analyses of two thin sections reveal 5 per cent quartz and traces of feldspar and mica in one, and 25 per cent quartz, 6 per cent feldspar, and traces of mica in the other. The firing was not thorough; in the majority of sherds the core is dark gray or black, and the color of the exterior is pale reddish-orange (Munsell scale: 9.0R6.2/4.2) or light brownish-gray (Munsell scale: 7.5YR6.1/0.6). The firing temperature is estimated at 450–500°C for a reddish sherd and at 500–550°C for a gray sherd. The hardness is on average 2.5° (on a scale of 10). Firing with wood or straw fuel in open kilns is indicated.

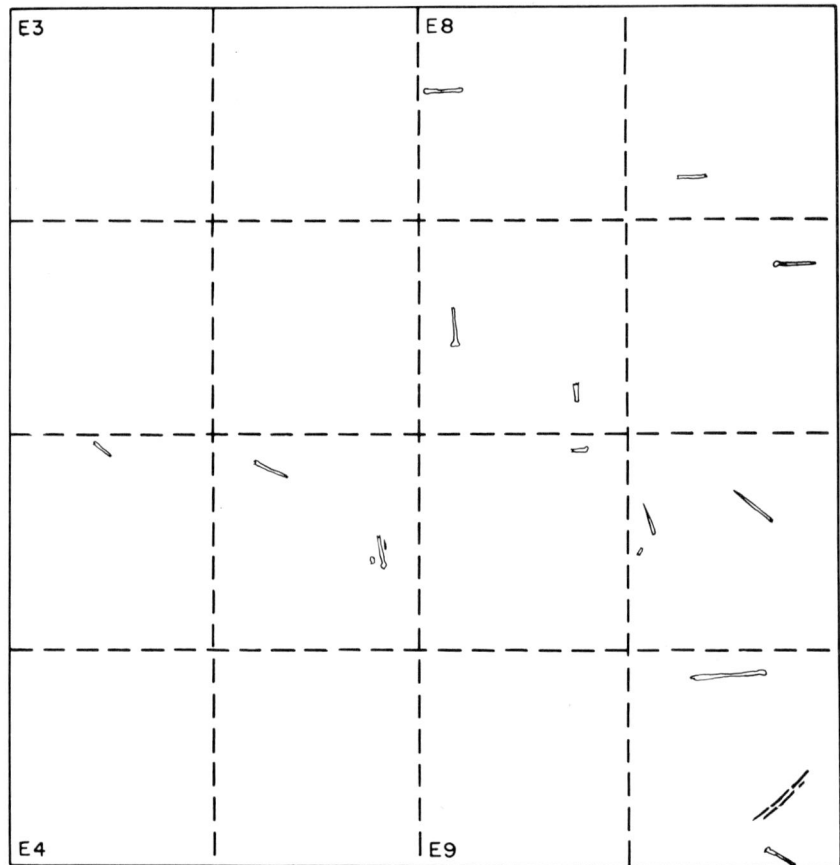

Fig. 27. Human Bones in the Corded Ware Stratum at Locus P, Pits E3, E4, E8, and E9, Fengpitou. (Upper side of figure is north; each square is 1 m.)

Form. Bowl and jar are distinguishable in this ware. Bowl sherds (Fig. 25, *1–5*) are few and are invariably large; the height of the bowl can be placed at 10–12 cm, and the diameter possibly 13–15 cm. The jar has basically a wide mouth and short neck, globular body, flat or roundish bottom, with or without a ring foot (Fig. 26). There are two major types of rims: flat, with width greater than height (Fig. 24, *22–28*), and regular, with height greater than width (Fig. 24, *1–21*). Among the regular rims, some thin out toward the lip, and some have a wide lip. A very characteristic feature of the rims of this ware is the presence, in many cases, of a ring or ridge below the lip and above the shoulder (Fig. 24, *30–33*).

Only one lug was found; it is round in section and pointed at the end, attached perpendicularly to the upper part of the body of (possibly) a bowl (Fig. 25, *6*). The ring foot is invariably low, in no case exceeding 30 mm in height. Holes and cut-out squares are present in some, near the top where the foot is attached to the bottom of the jar (Fig. 25, *9–14*; Pl. 15, *Q,R*).

Surface treatment and decoration. In a few cases a light red slip was applied after smoothing and before the cord impression, but in the majority of sherds such slip is not in evidence. The whole jar, including the bottom, was always impressed with cord marks, covering the entire body from the neck down. The rim, however, was never so impressed. The impression was probably made in two ways—the first by using a cord-carved paddle (the cord strands are thin and wide apart, making negative impressions on the body); the second by a cord-wrapped paddle (the negative cord impressions are thicker and closer between the strands).

Thin incisions were very often made on the rim, on the exterior and on the interior. Long parallel lines are seen in many cases on the shoulder, just below the neck, made by incising with a comb-like instrument. The designs are illustrated in Figures 24–26 and Plates 14, 15.

Human Bones

Many fragments of human long bones are found in the east-central part of Locus P (Fig. 27), in direct association with corded ware sherds. Possibly these were the remains of a burial site of the Corded Ware culture but, if so, they were heavily intruded into by the Lungshanoid occupational deposits, and no burial patterns can be recognized.

Chapter 4. The Lungshanoid Culture

EXCEPT for the corded ware layers, and despite internal variations, the artifacts excavated from the entire Fengpitou site can be said to belong to the same culture—the Lungshanoid. The name is derived from the Lungshanoid horizon that has been characterized for the Neolithic cultures on the eastern and southeastern coasts of mainland China, for the culture at the Fengpitou site agrees in the main with the Lungshanoid definition. Both agreements and deviations will be further discussed in Part III. Insofar as the site of Fengpitou is concerned, the Lungshanoid culture has the following characteristics. (1) Cultivation of plants on a rather intensive scale as the principal mode of subsistence, supplemented more or less by fishing, hunting, and gathering mollusks. (2) Extensive settlement of apparently permanent nature, with considerable population density. (3) A stone inventory including the following diagnostic stylistic features: rectangular adz, stemmed arrowhead, slate implements, semilunar and rectangular stone knives, slate halberd, rudimentary stepped adz, and jade and serpentine artifacts. These are basically Lungshanoid types, and contrast sharply with the contemporary Yüan-shan tradition to the north on the island. (4) Extensive use of bone and shell artifacts. (5) The pottery exhibits the following characteristics: use of potter's wheel; impression and incision-engraving as two principal decorative techniques; use of paddle and pad; coiling; modeling; *ting* tripod feet and *tou* pedestals with cut-out holes as principal supporting devices; painted designs; thin, lustrous, black pottery; mat, basket, and cord marks; popularity of lids. These are again diagnostic features of the Lungshanoid horizon.

Settlement Patterns and Microenvironment

During the interval from approximately 2400 to 400 B.C., when there were Lungshanoid settlements on the hill of Fengpitou, the landscape was quite different. The time period falls within the range of the hypsithermal interval, according to the Jih-yüeh-t'an sequence (see Chapter 9), when a somewhat warmer and more moist climate than the present probably obtained. The coastline was probably farther inland, and the southern slope of the hill was much closer to the shoreline than it is today. This is not only suggested by our general understanding of the shoreline change of western Taiwan during the postglacial period but is directly indicated by the contents of the shellmounds. Of the three dozen mollusks mentioned, *Melanoides crenulatus* is a freshwater species found in areas where the river flows into the sea, and *Ganesella* is a land snail. Most of the other varieties lived in very shallow intertidal waters where estuarine conditions prevailed. Sandy mud and mangroves dominated the habitat of most of these species. Also, the bones and shells that abound in the shellmounds must have derived from fish, crabs, and turtles from these waters.

On the hill itself and on the other hills to the north that are parts of the Fengshan tableland where one now sees cultivated fields, barren areas, and grasses and shrubs, forests must have flourished during the Lungshanoid occupation. In the shell-mounds are found large numbers of bones, antlers, and tusks of deer and wild boar—animals that were not likely to occur unless there were nearby forests of consider-able proportions. Soil analysis of the K-2 column has disclosed a significant con-trast in the amount of ignition loss between the surface accumulation and the layers of the shellmound: the former amount is between 6.63 and 7.62 per cent, and the latter between 7.54 and 12.42 per cent, apparently indicating a thicker vegeta-tional cover during the prehistoric period. Soil samples collected throughout the site yield a high clay content, providing good soil for agricultural purposes.

Thus the ecological components of the Lungshanoid settlements at Fengpitou consisted at least of the terraces and slopes of the hills where agricultural activities were presumably carried out; the small rivers to the east and west of the site; woods to the north with wild animal resources; and the estuary and sea waters from which mollusks, fish, and other aquatic creatures were taken. Not all of these ecological components were utilized equally throughout the occupation, for the nature of the deposits and the patterns of settlement seem to suggest a differential pattern of ecological exploitation through time.

At the beginning, when the fine red ware predominated in pottery making, the marine resources had apparently not yet been tapped to any significant extent, for the shellmound was conspicuously absent. Occupation was significant on the top of the hill where house remains were found, and trash heaps occur on both the northern and southern slopes. The same pattern of settlement appears to continue into the second stage, when the sandy red ware replaced the fine red ware, although the area of significant occupation might have been more restricted. Greater activities, how-ever, are indicated along the southern, seaward slope of the hill during the shell-mound settlements where the marine resources were evidently fully utilized, as indicated by the mollusk shells and aquatic residue. Remains are much fewer on the hilltop, and it is quite likely that habitation was concentrated along the slopes of the hill. An increasing use of the marine resources and a population increase are sug-gested by the changing pattern of distribution of the molluscan species. In short, during the Lungshanoid occupation one observes a trend from a more specialized subsistence pattern—farming and hunting—toward a more balanced and diversified pattern that took advantage of the various resources of the microenvironment—farming, hunting, fishing, and shellfish collecting, all of increasing sophistication and efficiency. This observation gains strong support from a study of the artifactual variations through time, as is discussed later in the chapter.

The accelerated intensity of cultural activities in the area during the Lungshanoid occupations is signified by the changing ratio of the number and weight of sherds relative to the area of occupation. The excavated areas were carefully selected according to surface remains, the profiles of the many communication trenches at the site, and knowledge from previous investigations; and it is my belief that the sherd counts from these pits suffice as samples of the total. If it is assumed that the total inhabited area of the site (at various times) was 60,000 square meters, we can use each of the six carefully selected excavation loci to represent one sixth of the site, or 10,000 square meters. The total sherd volume of each region can be calculated by multiplying the actual sherd numbers of the sample pits by the ratio of the total region to the actual excavated area. No great accuracy is claimed for the method, and the results may tend to be inflated because some of the spots may never have been occupied intensively, but the relative trend can be considered to be grossly indicative.

1. The Fine Red Ware Settlement. The estimated total of sherds of this settlement is 46 million, and the area covered is 40,000 square meters.

2. The Sandy Red Ware Settlement. The estimated total of sherds is 44 million, a slight decrease from the previous 46, but the area inhabited was only 20,000 square meters.

3. The Lower Shellmound Settlement. The estimated total of sherds is 111 million, a drastic increase, and the area of occupation is placed at 40,000 square meters.

4. The Upper Shellmound Settlement. The estimated total of sherds is 196 million, and the area of occupation is 50,000 square meters.

In evaluating these figures we must bear in mind that the time factor is, in this case, constant—500 years for each settlement; therefore, unless we are to compare the Fengpitou settlements with settlements of other areas, this factor need not enter into consideration. On the basis of restoration experience, one could estimate that approximately one hundred sherds equal one complete vessel. In other words, the number of pottery vessels that were broken and thrown into the rubbish heaps can be determined, as can the number of pots broken each year. Table 5 shows a steady increase in the number of pots that were broken—and presumably replaced—at the site each year, which in turn must indicate a steady increase of population and/or cultural activities.

The House

In view of the fact that the slope on the south was abundant in shellmounds and that burials occupied at least a part of the northern slope, the houses of the

TABLE 5. VOLUME INCREASE IN NUMBER OF POTTERY VESSELS MANUFACTURED AT THE FOUR LUNGSHANOID SETTLEMENTS AT FENGPITOU

	Total, 500 Years	Each Year	Increase* (%)
Upper shellmound	1,960,000	3,800	253
Lower shellmound	1,100,000	2,200	222
Sandy red ware	440,000	900	180
Fine red ware	460,000	1,000	100

* Calculated by using the volume of fine red ware settlement as 100%, and correcting the area discrepancy by taking 40,000 square meters as the base.

Lungshanoid village at Fengpitou were presumably constructed around and on the top of the terrace. Unfortunately, the southeastern part of the hilltop serves as a cemetery for modern villagers from the valley and its excavation is out of the question. The center of the hilltop was bare almost to the bedrock, probably because of weathering and cultivation. The northwestern part has been so heavily cultivated that excavation was not considered worthwhile. Only a small area along the eastern edge of the terrace top has the remains of habitation, and a house was discovered there in Locus P.

What is left of a rectangular house, oriented west–northwest to east–southeast lengthwise consists of seven post molds at its southwestern corner (Fig. 28; Pl. 6). Five of the molds form the western segment of the south wall; the other two, together with the corner post, form the west wall. Each of the molds is 15 to 16 cm in diameter, and is about 40 cm deep. The distance between each pair is about 90 cm, except for 180 cm between the second and the third molds of the west wall. The molds consist of solidly packed clay, mixed with a small amount of potsherds, and are apparently the matrices of decomposed wooden posts (Pl. 7). The upper ends of the molds are on an approximate plane, and a layer of concentrated deposit of potsherds of fine red ware is seen immediately above the molds (Fig. 14). Some

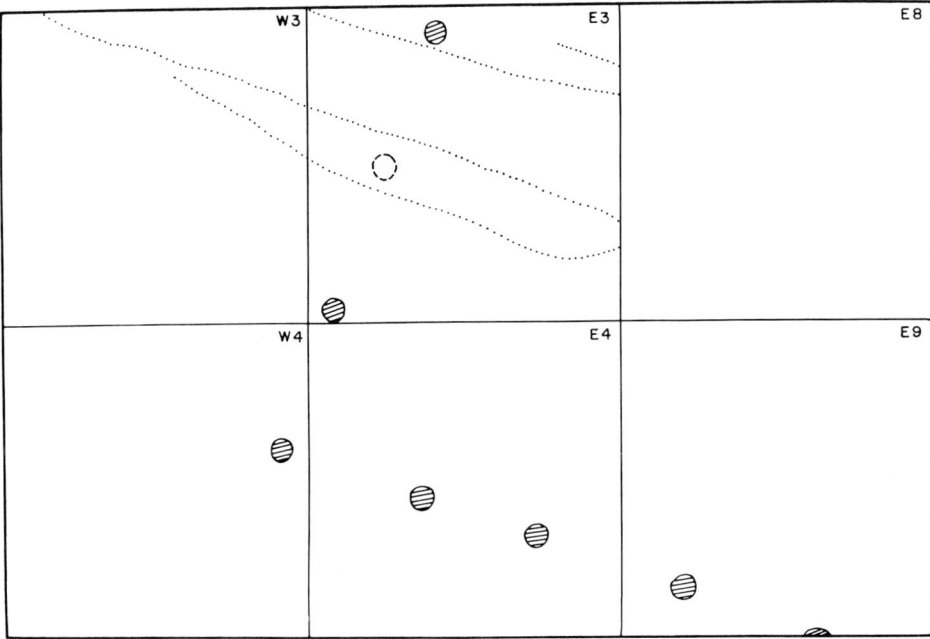

FIG. 28. The Seven Post Molds of a Lungshanoid House in Locus P, Fengpitou. (Upper side of figure is north. The side of each square is 2 m. The dotted circle indicates the spot where a post should have been; possibly a door was located there. The dotted areas indicate two troughs at the bottom of the Lungshanoid layer; their significance is unclear.)

of the molds are still covered with a thin layer of asphalt. No floor was recognized, and no superstructure can be identified. The length of the house is not known because the area immediately to the east of the excavated area of Locus P was cut by the communication trench. The area immediately north of the molds was disturbed by a deep ditch, presumably destroying the northern wall and its posts, and no molds have been identified north of the ditch; it is thus possible to restore the western end of the house to a width of about 4.5 meters.

Although these are the only data we have on the house, we note the following clues. The house was probably rectangular in shape, with long northern and southern walls and short (4.5 m) eastern and western walls. The middle of the western wall was without a post, suggesting that the entrances to the house were probably at the shorter ends. About 40 to 50 cm of the posts was buried in the ground, and the concentrated potsherd layer is immediately above the top of the molds. This probably means that the surface on which the pottery layer began to accumulate and which is also the molds' plane was the original ground surface. No wall foundations were found, nor was there any evidence of floor. Very careful observation failed to distinguish any depositional demarcation of the sides of the wall, suggesting the possibility of a raised floor. A rectangular house with a raised floor and doors at the ends suggests the pile buildings common in the Pacific areas and Southeast Asia, and remains of this type of dwelling have been found in Lungshanoid sites on the southeast China coast. It is also interesting to note that asphalt was used to coat the posts before they were driven into the ground. Natural gas and asphalt wells have been reported from Lin-yüan, a few kilometers southeast of the site, and it is probable that the Lungshanoid inhabitants were able to collect the natural asphalts—carried ashore by seawater?—for constructional use, that is, to waterproof their houseposts. Natural asphalt was used in America by prehistoric man, but this is the first such instance found in this part of the world.

Subsistence Implements

The Lungshanoid inhabitants at Fengpitou were primarily tillers of the soil. The shellmounds make the site conspicuous, and the animal and fish bones contained in them indicate that animals, fish, and mollusks constituted an important part of the Lungshanoid diet, but in the inventory of implements, those related to agriculture—wood cutting, earth moving, and grass cutting—are an overwhelming majority over those probably used for hunting and collecting. More than 108 stone axes, hoes, and adzes and at least 30 stone knives have been recovered, and 47 stone points, 16 bone points, and 1 stone net sinker are among the finds directly related to hunting and fishing activities.

THE AX–ADZ–HOE GROUP

Many stone implements with cutting edges at the ends are found at the site; they clearly fall within the ax–adz–hoe category related to agricultural activities (Figs. 29–34; Pls. 69–72). They are always rectangular on the broad side, relatively flat (never cylindrical or square), and the cutting edge is either symmetrical or asymmetrical, but there are obviously several types. In view of their cutting edge, general size, and shafting, the implements were without question used as axes for cutting trees, adzes for woodworking, and/or hoes for moving earth. For the purpose of cultural reconstruction, they should be classified according to use, but their uses cannot be specifically known, and any classification according to what we might think to be their specific uses is likely to be misleading. It is nevertheless self-evident that form follows use, and a *meaningful* description of form contains implicit categorization according to use. Formal and physical variations are considered meaningful when they are consistent and contrastive; in short, when they indicate *patterns*. Thus, the following hierarchical and contrastive arrangement is made for this broad category.

1. *Thin, with rounded edge.* Implements of this category invariably have a cutting edge that is rounded on the broad side, in contrast to implements in the next category which have a straight and angular cutting edge on the broad side. These are also thin, compared with the next category; the thickness–breadth index (thickness × 100/breadth) is without exception below 30, and the overwhelming majority is below 20. The leading materials are black slate and basalt, and a few are of sandstone. These implements are generally large and heavy; with a couple of exceptions their total length is greater than 70 mm, and in most it is over 100 mm. In view of the size and the shape of the cutting edge and the cross section, these are possibly earth-moving (cultivating) implements.

a. Flat, trapezoidal (Figs. 29, 30; Pls. 71, 72). Highly polished and in general beautifully made of basalt and black slate. The length ranges from 90 to 140 mm, and the thickness–breadth index centers between 10 and 15. The two major divisions within this category are the straight rounded edge (Fig. 29; Pls. 71, *B,E–H; 72, E–H*) and the oblique rounded edge (Fig. 30; Pl. 71, *A,C,D,* 72, *A–D*). This distinction in edge shape cannot be related to stratigraphy, size, material, or overall form, but must be relevant to use.

b. Spatula-shaped (Fig. 31, Pl. 69). Between 100 and 150 mm long, and extremely thin (index centers within 10 and 15), implements of this type are highly polished and lustrous slate and have a flat surface and a slightly convex back. They coincide with the peak of the sandy gray ware, but are also seen slightly earlier and later.

c. Large, polished (Pl. 70, *A*). Implements of this class are large (probably more than 200 mm long as a minimum), highly polished, and of sandstone. The thickness–breadth index is between 5 and 25. They occur relatively late.

d. Chipped, elongated (Pl. 70, *E,F*). Mostly of slate, this type is characterized by relatively long (110–170 mm) and thin (10–30) chipped edged implements. Relatively late occurrence.

e. Perforated (Fig. 32; Pl. 70, *B–D*). These are invariably made of slate, chipped, and have a perforation at the center. One or two notches can sometimes be observed at the end, presumably for hatting.

2. *Thick, with straight edge* (Figs. 33, 34; Pls. 74, 75). In contrast to the former

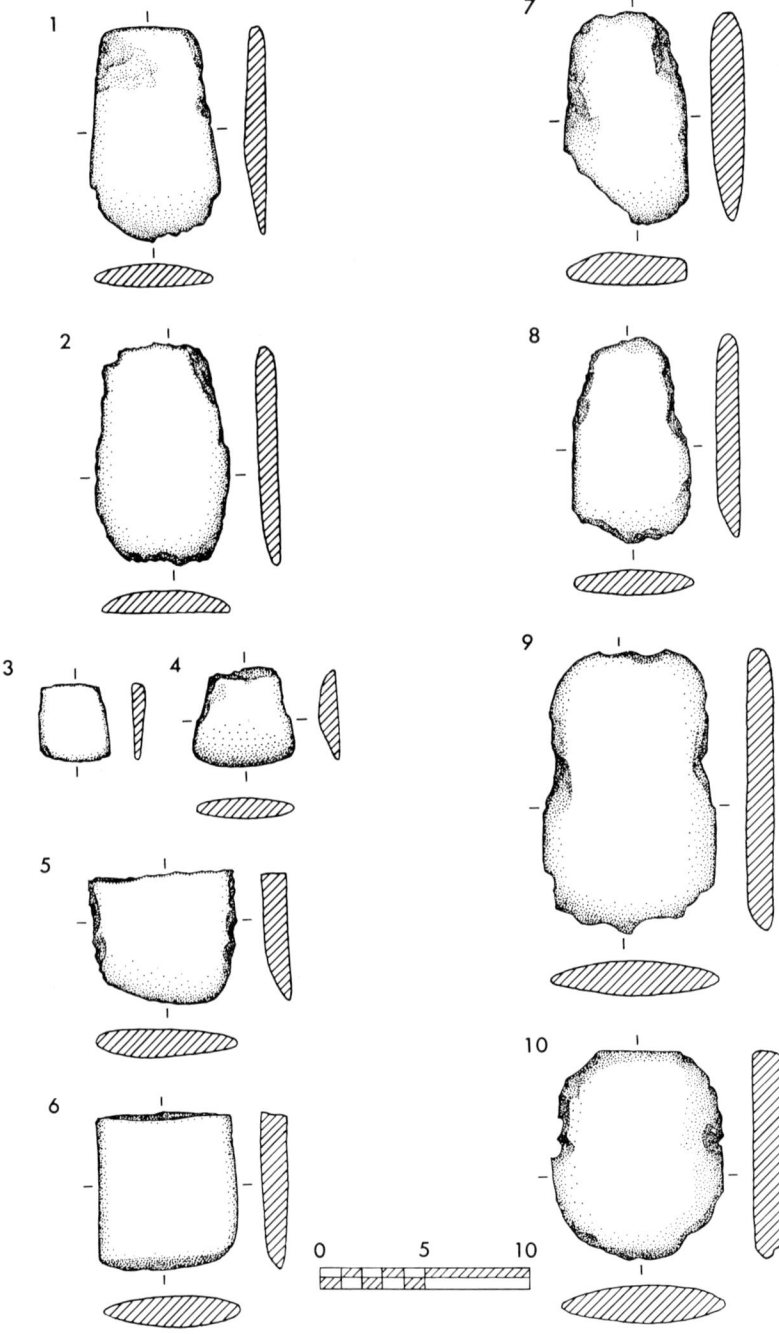

Fɪɢ. 29. Flat Stone Hoe-Axes, Straight Rounded Edge, Fengpitou.

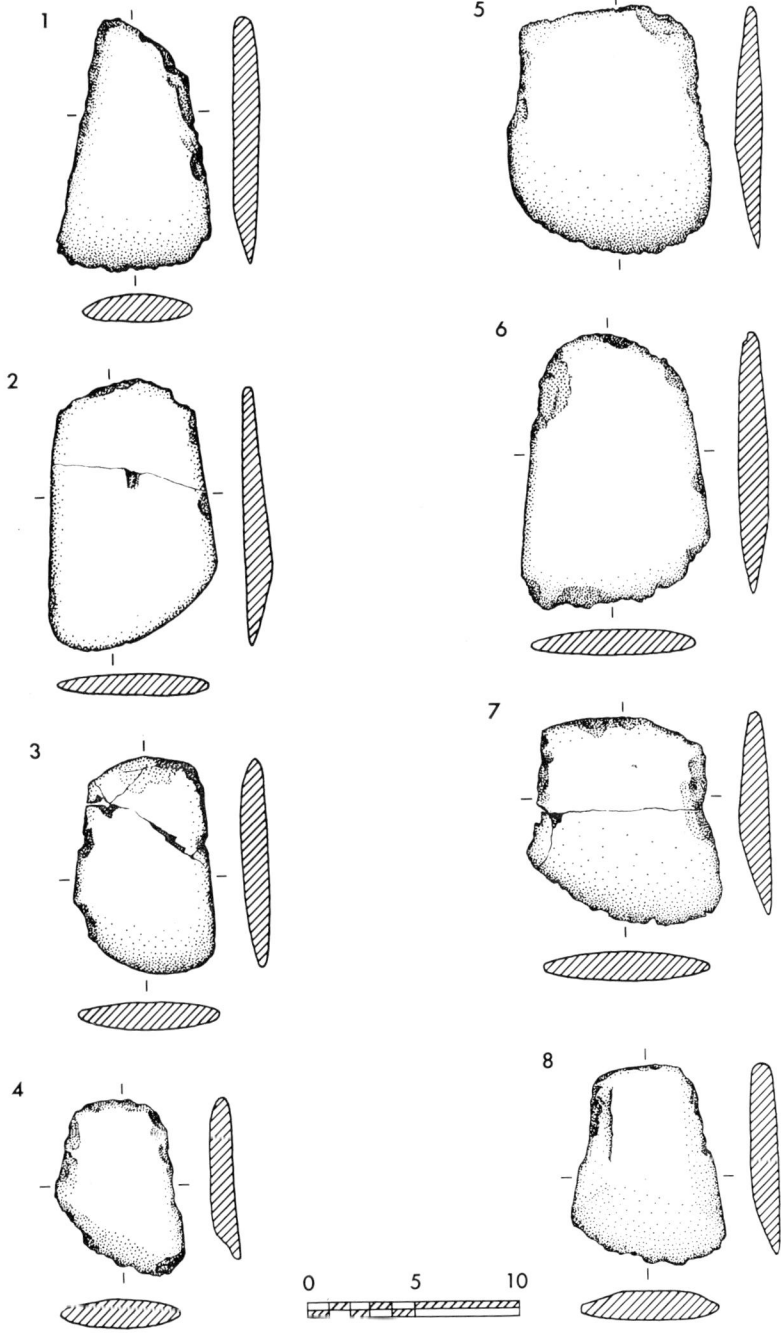

F_{IG}. 30. Flat Stone Hoe-Axes, Oblique Rounded Edge, Fengpitou.

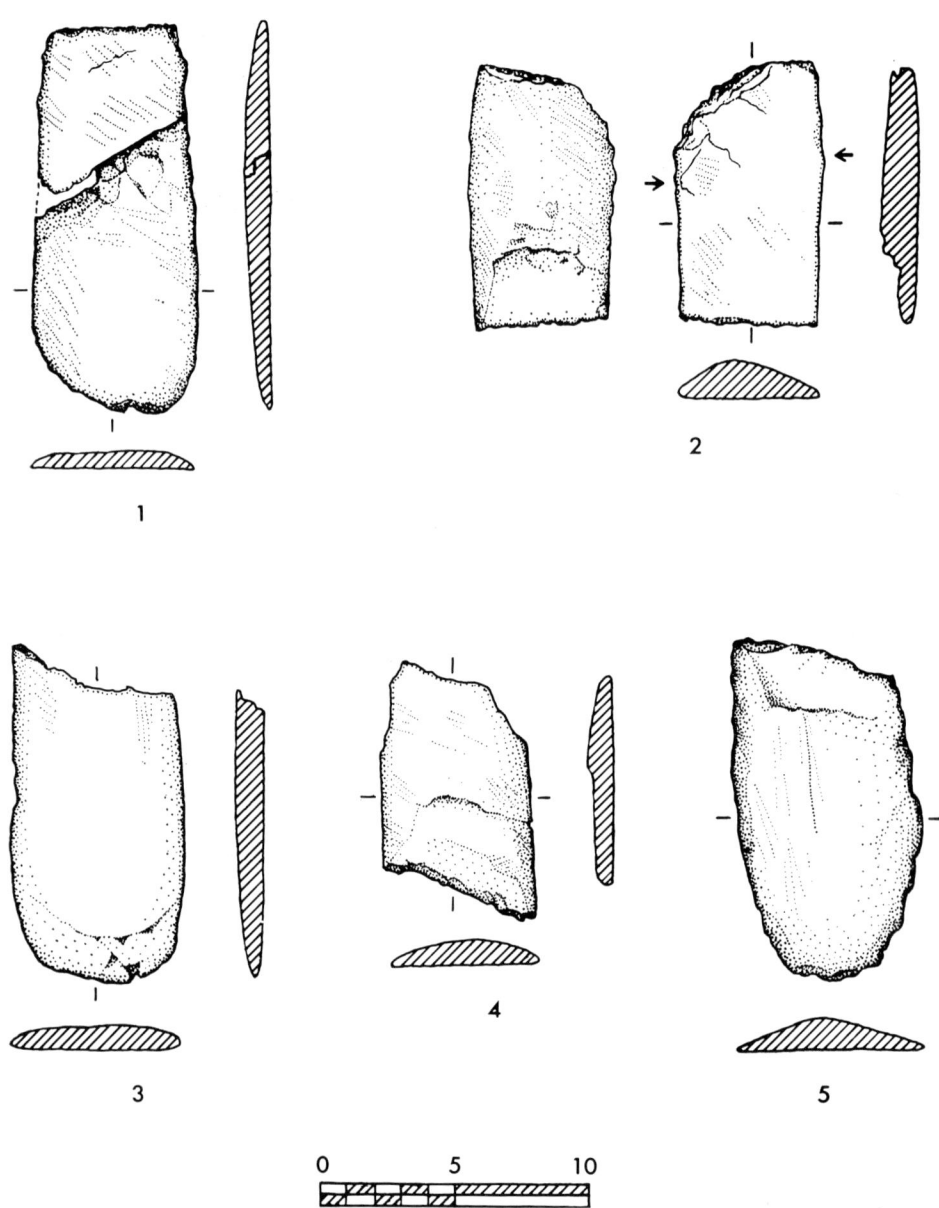

FIG. 31. Spatula-shaped Stone Hoe-Axes, Fengpitou.

class, this one is characterized by implements with a straight cutting edge. On the broad side the edge is a straight line, with one or both ends forming angles rather than curves. These tools are also thick; the thickness–breadth index ranges from 20 to over 50. Compared with the first category, these implements are also smaller;

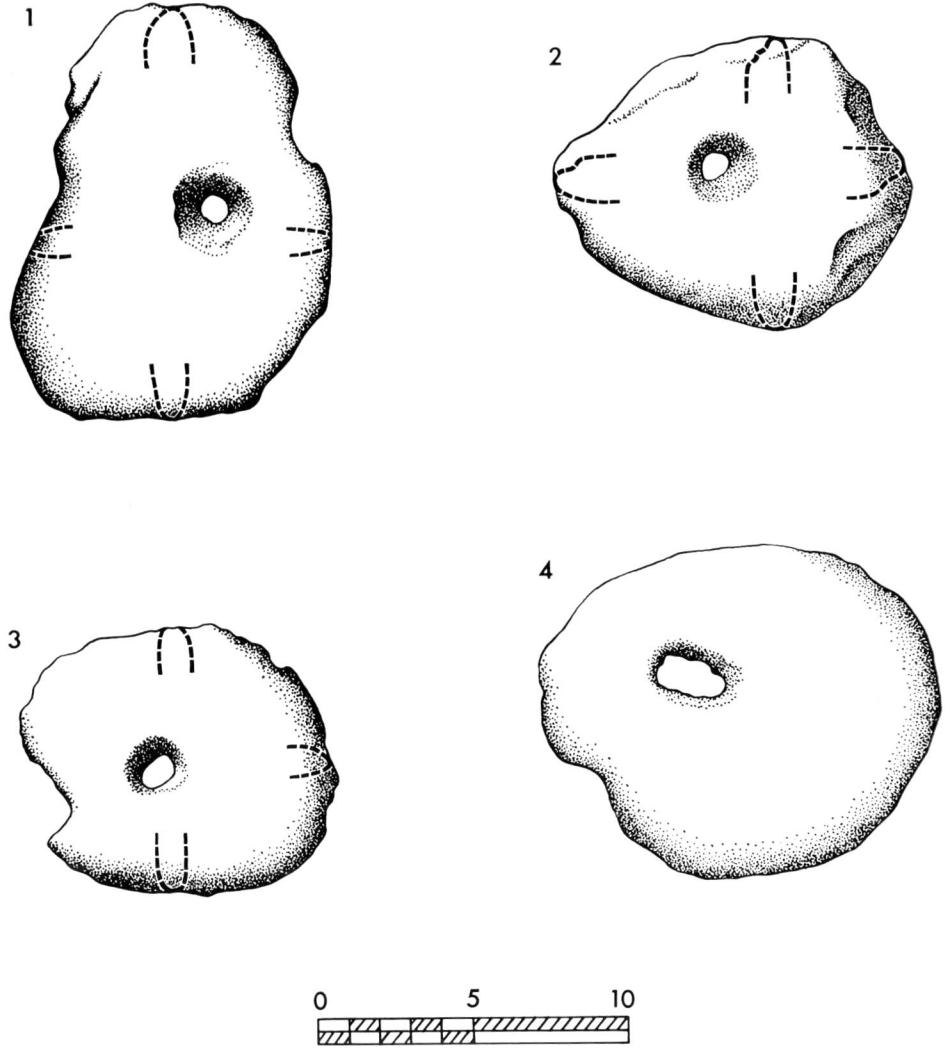

FIG. 32. Perforated Stone Hoe-Axes, Fengpitou.

the length ranges from 20 to 90 mm in practically all cases. In cross section, at least two corners (usually four) are angular. All these features suggest that these implements are more suited to work with wood than earth. Four subdivisions can be made: adz (Pl. 74), flat adz (Pl. 75, *A–I*), small adz (Pl. 75, *L,M*), and chisel (Pl. 75, *J,K*). The criteria for these are self-evident.

As provisional substitutes for this cumbersome system, the following shorthand terms will be employed:

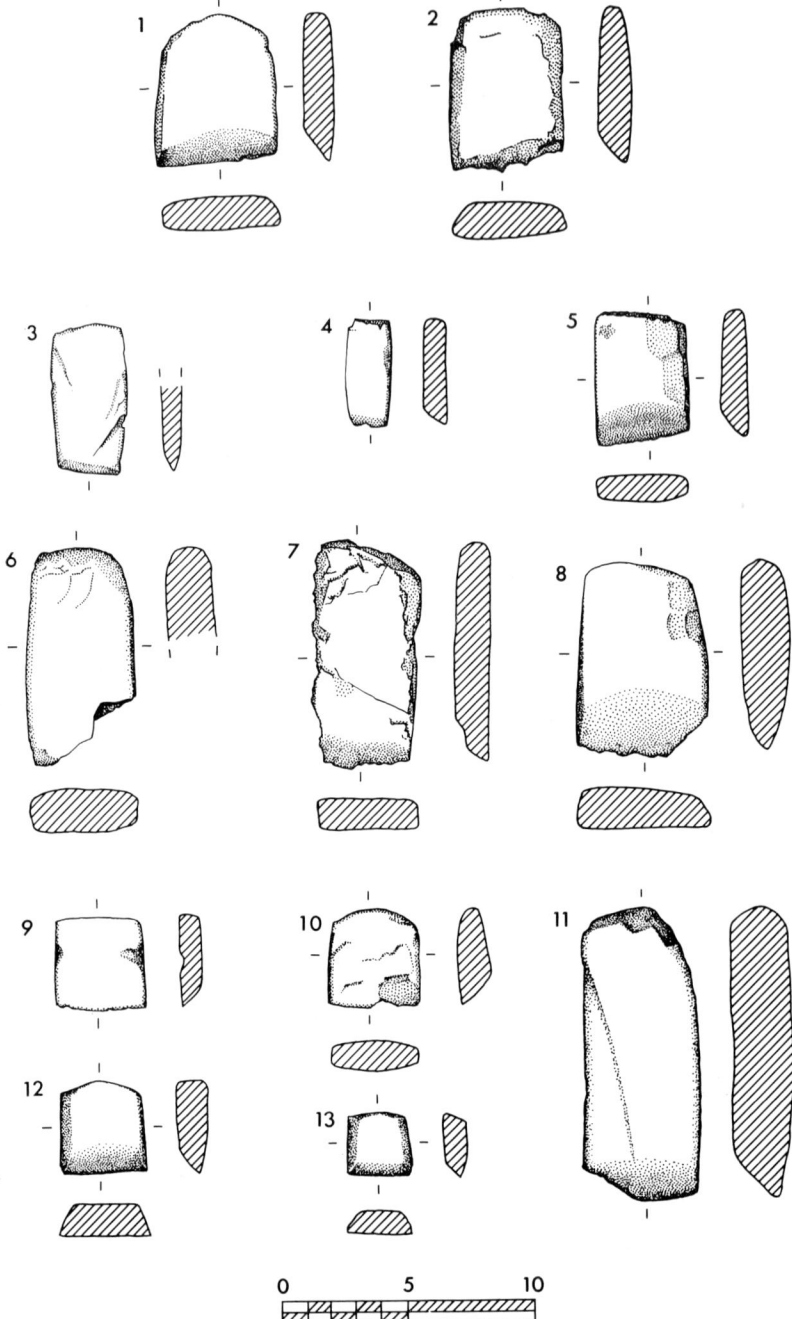

FIG. 33. Stone Adz-Axes with Angular Corners, Fengpitou.

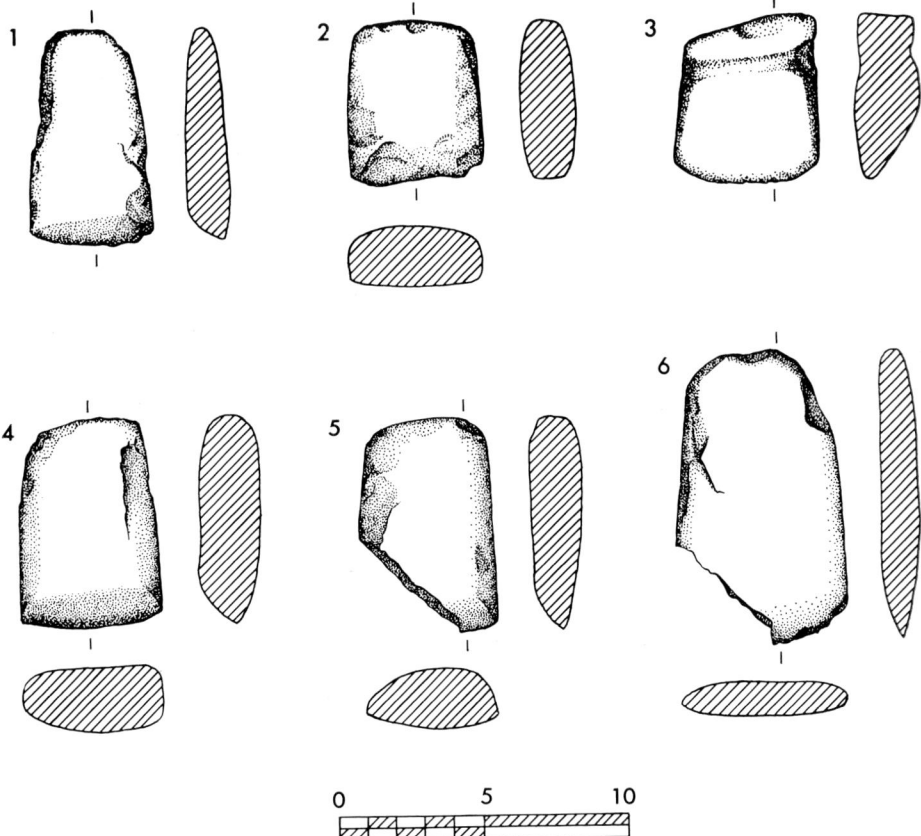

Fig. 34. Stone Adz-Axes with Round Corners, Fengpitou.

Hoe-axes	*Adz-axes*
a. Flat hoe-ax	a. Adz-ax
b. Spatula-shaped hoe-ax	b. Flat adz-ax
c. Large hoe-ax	c. Small adz-ax
d. Chipped hoe-ax	d. Chisel
e. Perforated hoe-ax	

KNIVES

Among the stone knives (a thin blade with the cutting edge on the long side) excavated from the Fengpitou site, there are one boot-shaped, eleven rectangular, and eighteen semilunar. All have an asymmetrical edge, all are made of slate, and most have a perforation or two at the center near the back edge.

Boot-shaped (Fig. 35; Pl. 73). Made of dark gray, muscovite-bearing arenaceous slate with quartz veinlets and beautifully polished, this boot-shaped knife (*hache pédiforme*) is the most complete and best-made specimen of its class on the island

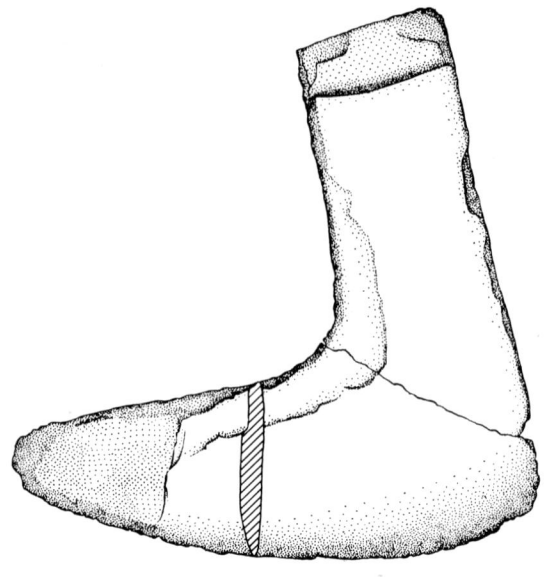

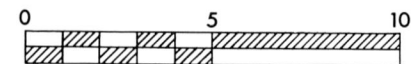

Fɪɢ. 35. Stone Boot-shaped Knife, Fengpitou.

and perhaps even in Southeast Asia. The hafting part, from ankle to sole, is 140 mm long and 42 mm wide, and the blade, from sole to toe, is 141 mm long and 45 wide in the middle. One broad side is flat, the other slightly convex, and the thickest portion is about 6 mm deep. It was broken in the middle into two parts, one found in P-E5(A2)L2c, and the other in P-E4(B2)L2b, in association with fine red ware sherds. The cutting edge bears signs of wear.

Rectangular (Fig. 36; Pl. 76, *A–E*). These knives are made of black or gray slate and are about 7 or 8 cm long, 4 cm wide, and 0.5 cm thick. A small hole occurs often at the center near the back; in a few cases two perforations were made. By definition, the edge and the back are parallel, more or less straight lines, and the edge is invariably asymmetrical. One specimen has a curved back, recalling the so-called saddle-shaped knife of central Formosa and the winged knives of North China (Fig. 36, *6;* Pl. 76, *A*).

Semilunar (Fig. 37; Pl. 76, *F–Q*). In size, material, and manufacture, these are identical with the rectangular variety, but either the back or the cutting edge, or

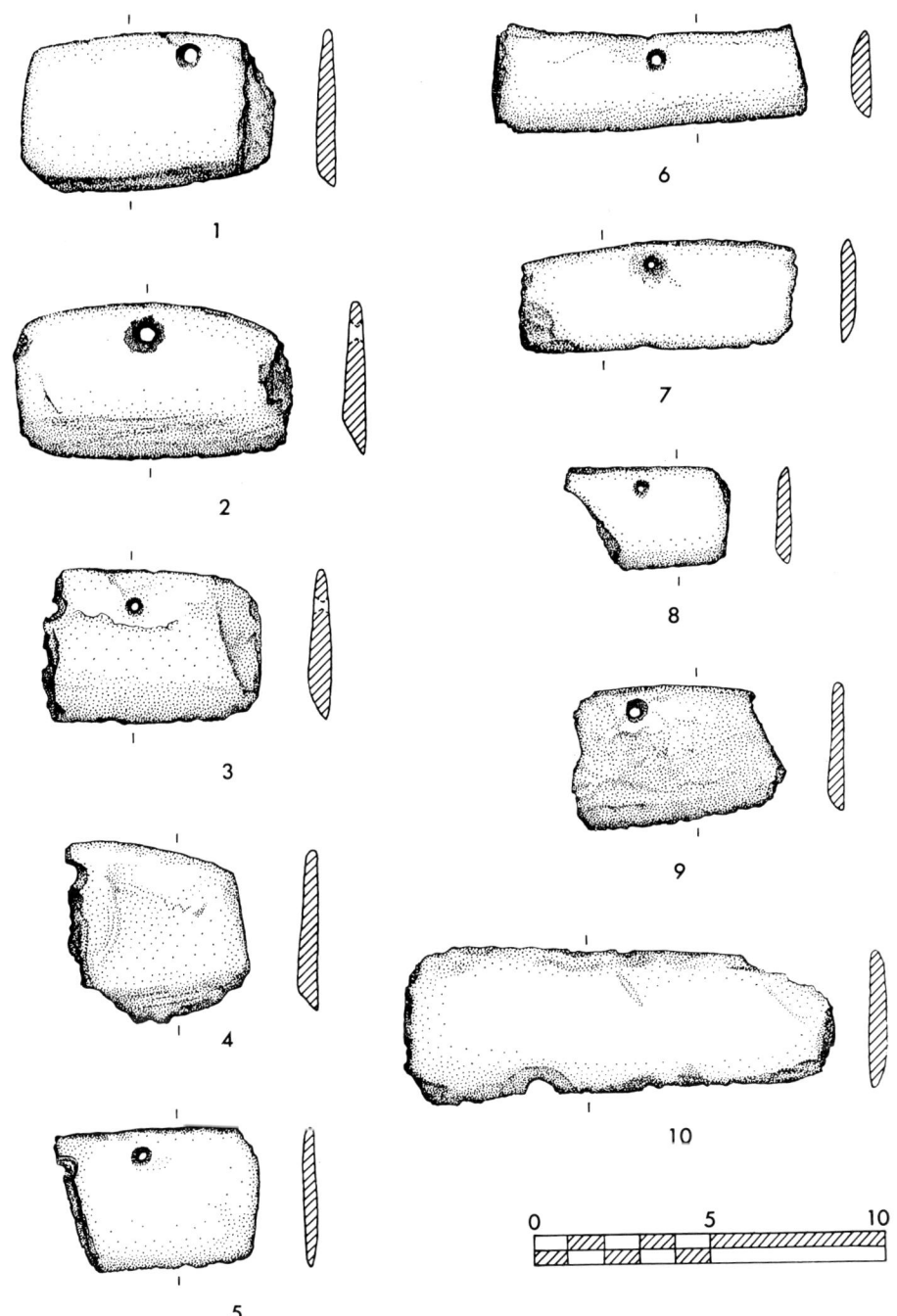

FIG. 36. Rectangular Stone Knives, Fengpitou.

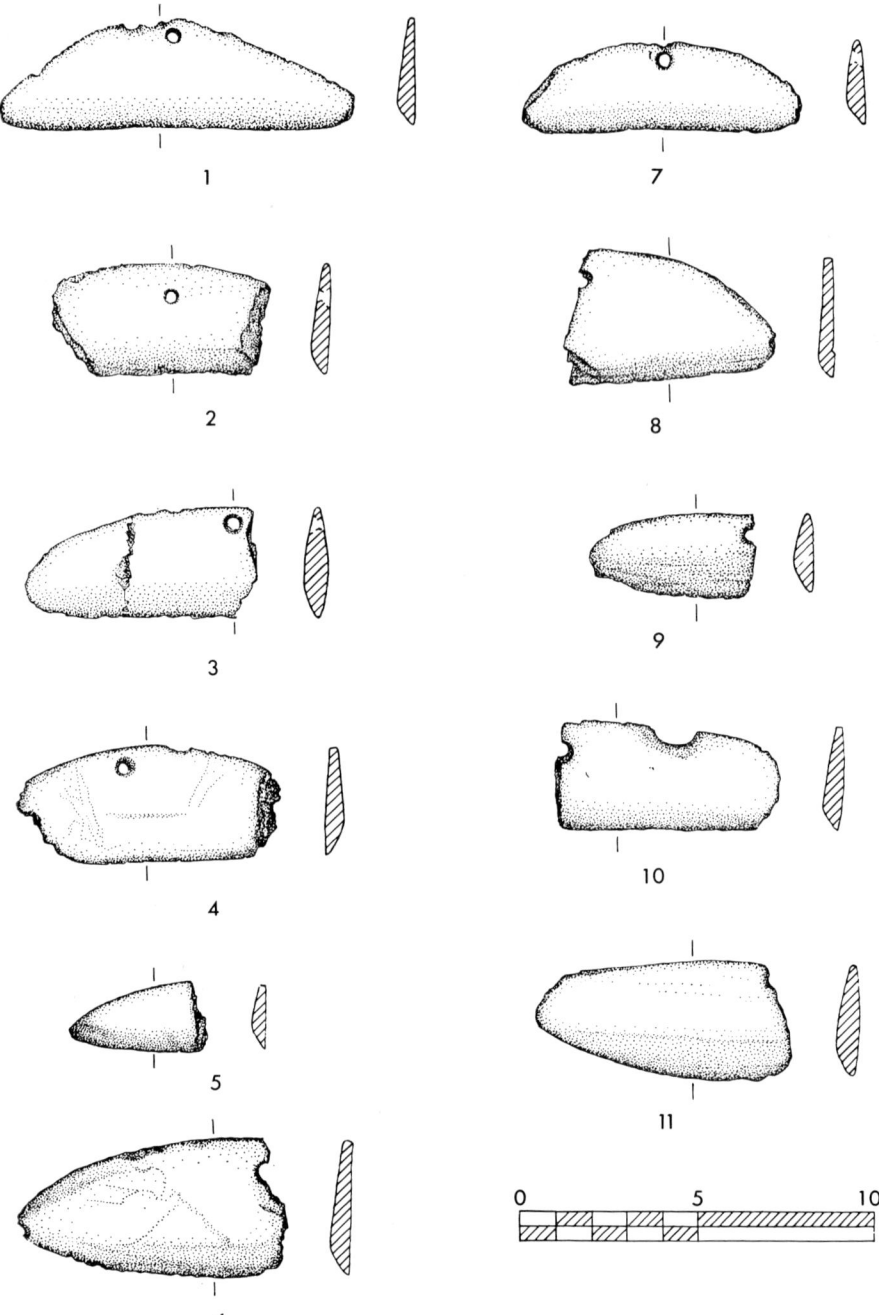

FIG. 37. Semilunar Stone Knives, Fengpitou.

even both, is curved instead of straight. A further distinction may be made between semilunar knives with straight edges (Pl. 76, *F–O*), and leaf-shaped knives with curved edges (*P,Q*).

It has been suggested that the *hache pédiforme* was used for weeding (Kanaseki and Kokubu 1949b) and that the slate knives in the Chinese Neolithic context were cutting and harvesting implements (Andersson 1945: 223–9). Kokubu (1964b: 231–3) is of the opinion that bamboo knives were associated with millet cultivation and slate knives with rice (see also Kaneko 1953).

HUNTING IMPLEMENTS

During the occupation of Fengpitou by the Lungshanoid inhabitants, forests abounded on the higher terraces of Fengshan, and it can be presumed that the people relied on wild animals for a considerable amount of their food. Large amounts of wild animal bones have been found in the shell middens, most belonging to the deer family and a few from wild boars. A few bird bones are also found. Many of the implements recovered were made of bones and antlers. Of the hunting gear, only projectile points are recognized. These points could of course have been used for both hunting and warfare.

Stone points. Projectile points of stone, invariably of black or gray slate, can be grouped into four types: perforated, triangular, stemmed, and willow-leaf-shaped. The order in which they are listed has some chronological significance, but there is considerable overlap.

Perforated. Only two were found, one from P-E4(B1)L2c (Fig. 38, *4;* Pl. 77, *A*), and the other from N-B-L3b (Fig. 38, *5;* Pl. 77, *B*), both strata of the fine red ware level. There is a central ridge on each face and a perforation at the center. Both points are broken at the perforation, leaving only the point end. The length from the hole to the point is 45 mm in one case and 35 in the other. To judge from the length, these were probably arrowheads. No representative of this class has been found from the upper levels, and it appears to carry on in form the Corded Ware culture tradition. It also resembles the Yüan-shan culture points of about the same age, or slightly later, in the northern part of the island, but the Yüan-shan type has more characteristically a flat face than a ridged face.

Triangular (Fig. 38, *1–3;* Pl. 77, *C–F*). The triangular points have a broad and probably rounded base and a central ridge on each side, but no perforation at the center. The length (about 50 mm) again suggests the arrowhead. Their stratigraphical occurrence is not conclusive, since many of this type came from the surface. But the occurrence of a typical triangular point in P-E4(B2)-L2c (Fig. 38, *2;* Pl. 77, *E*) suggests that it was concurrent with or slightly later than the perforated variety. These two types are similar in broad outline and cross section, and differ mainly in the presence or absence of the central perforation.

Stemmed (Fig. 39; Pl. 77, *R–Z, a–e;* 79, *G–K*). These points have well-shaped stems, some broad and short, others narrower and longer. Some stems are so broad that they are wider than the blade, separated from the latter by notches. Some of

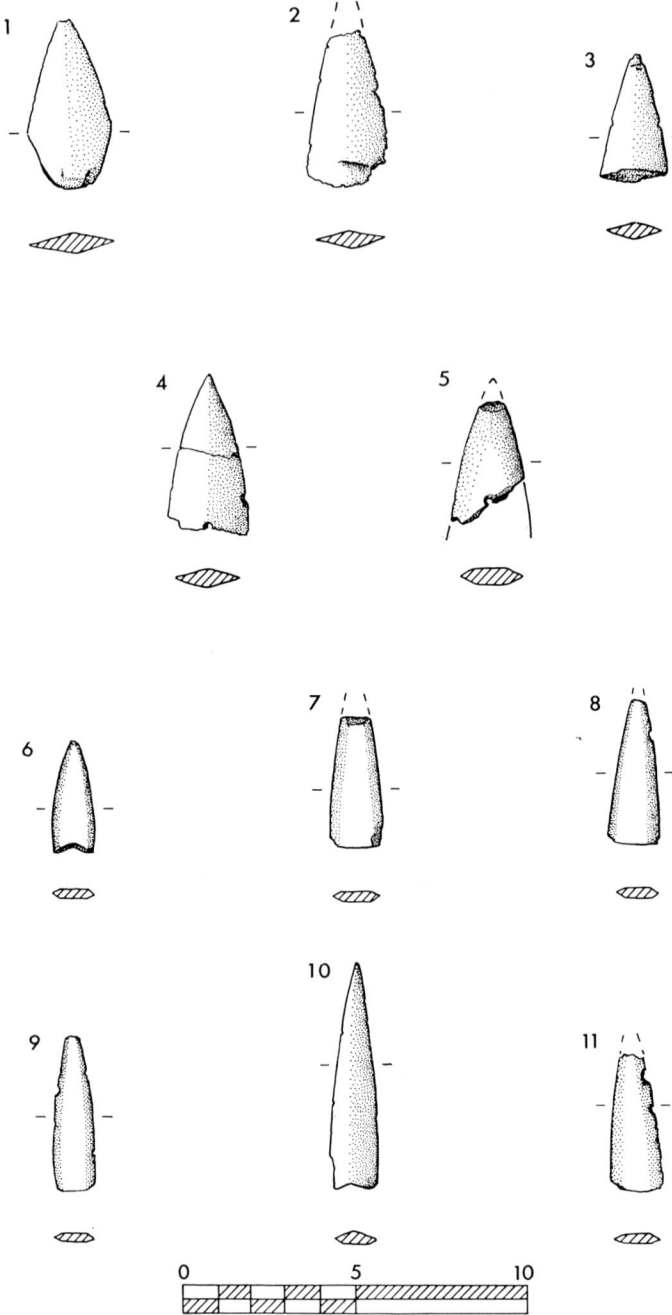

FIG. 38. Stone Points of Fengpitou: Triangular, Perforated, and Leaf-shaped Types.

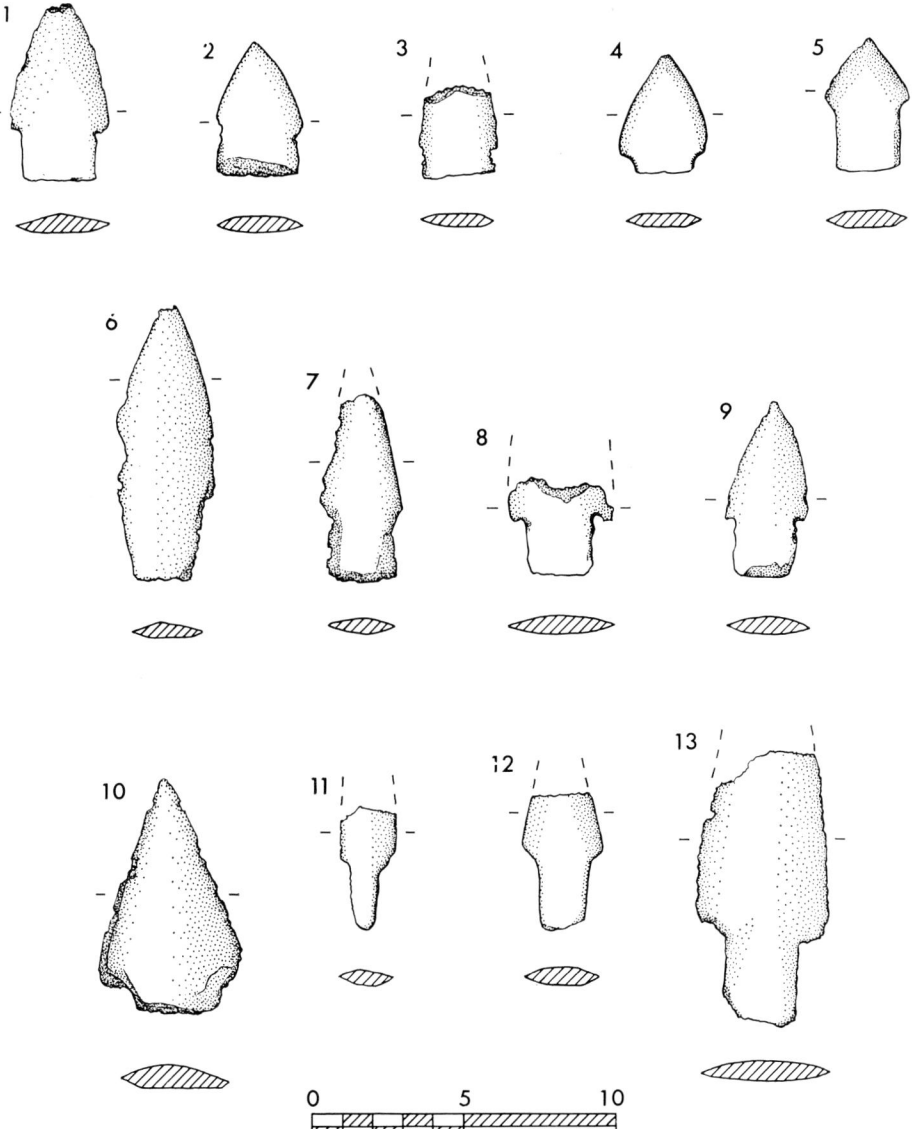

FIG. 39. Stone Points of Fengpitou: Stemmed Types.

the stems have saw-teeth on the sides, and a few have notches at the root of the stem, presumably to secure hafting. Central ridges are present in a few cases, but most of the faces are ground flat. The length ranges from a little over 40 to well above 100 mm; possibly the larger ones were lanceheads rather than arrowheads. Stratigraphically, members of this class occur from fine red ware strata in Locus P

(P-W1-B1-L2c) to throughout Layer 1 of Locus K, and most of those collected on the surface are assignable to this type. The earlier ones have broader stems, distinguished from the triangular points mainly by the notches and (occasionally) by the absence of the central ridge, whereas later specimens have narrower and longer stems.

Willow-leaf-shaped (Fig. 38, *6–11;* Pl. 77, *K–Q*). These are thin (1–2) mm, narrow (8–12 mm), elongated (5–8 cm), and well-polished specimens, with flat faces, parallel or slowly converging sides, and straight bases. They came from K-L1, P-L2a, N-L1, and V-L1 levels, obviously of later date than the other three types. They are also the most numerous (23, vs. 2 perforated, 5 triangular, and 17 stemmed).

Bone points. Bone, antler, and shell artifacts are found only in the shellmounds in Loci K, S, and V. Many bone and antler implements are pointed, but definite projectile points are few—totaling eighteen in the entire site. Seven of these are possibly harpoon points and will be described in relation to fishing. The other eleven can be grouped into three types: triangular (Pl. 67, *F–J*), stemmed (*K–N*), and leaf-shaped (*O,P*). All the triangular points (five) are made of turtleshell, and the rest of animal long bones. Three points (Pl. 67, *B,P,R*) are jet-black, smooth, and lustrous. The cause of this condition is not clear, but probably they were made from charred bones.

Fishing Implements

There are many fish vertebrae in the shellmounds, but neither other fishbones nor fish scales are noted. In view of the fact that these Lungshanoid inhabitants reached Fengpitou at all—presumably from across the Formosa Strait—they were apparently capable of taking good advantage of the marine resources far from shore. The evidence that they actually did this must, however, remain for further investigation. Two artifactual items apparently pertain to this phase of their subsistence activities: harpoon heads and net sinkers.

Bone harpoon heads. There are seven of these points, all stemmed, all coming from upper levels at the site (Pl. 67, *A–E,Q,R*). The only characteristic feature distinguishing them from the arrowheads are one or two grooves near the base of the stem or notches presumably for wrapping on the toggle lines. No device other than the toggle action can explain why these notches were needed for hafting. The points have no barbs, and admittedly they could have been used for hunting land animals as well as for spearing such large fishes as sharks whose vertebrae are found at the site.

Net sinker. Only a single specimen of this type was found, in Locus P from disturbed surface layers. It is a small sandstone pebble with two notches on the long sides (Fig. 40; Pl. 79, *F*).

Remains of Shellfish Gathering

As indicated by the stratigraphical profile in Locus K, there is no evidence that shellfish gathering began until after the fine red ware strata were laid down at the site. In the beginning, only a few varieties of shellfish were collected, and the indi-

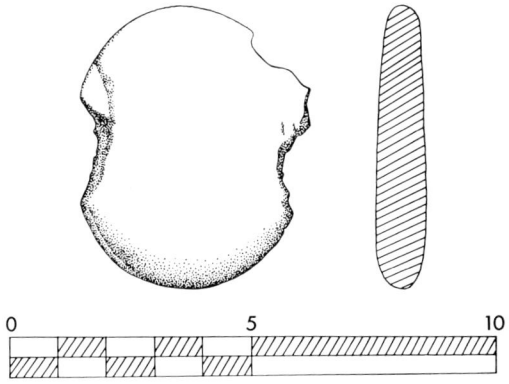

FIG. 40. Stone Net Sinker, Fengpitou.

viduals were large in size. In upper levels the variety of species increased as the size of the individuals decreased, apparently indicating a growing dependence upon this means of subsistence and a growing population pressure. Over thirty species (see Appendix 3) are recognized in the shellmounds at the site. Shells were also utilized for making artifacts (Pls. 63, *F,G;* 64, *D;* 65, *A,B,E,F;* 66, *A–E,F*), especially the window shell and *Anadara granosa*, but oysters and clams were apparently the major sources of food.

Four sandstone pebbles from the shellmound layers at the site bear evidence of knocking at the ends and at the center of the broad sides (Pl. 79, *A–D*). Sung (1958) has suggested that the pebbles with central depressions commonly found in pre-historic sites on Formosa were probably used for knocking open the mollusk shells. The pebbles found here could have served this purpose, but no shells at the site ex-hibit any damage that could be said to have been inflicted by any such implement.

Technology and Industry

According to the generally accepted usage of technological classification, industry of the Fengpitou site of the Lungshanoid culture is Neolithic of an advanced level. The artifacts uncovered here illustrate the technological aspects of stone, wood, bone, antler, shell, fabric, and ceramic manufacture.

STONE MANUFACTURE

Different rocks were selected for making specific types of stone implements. The most commonly used were sandstone (dark gray or yellowish, fine- or coarse-grained, occasionally schistose) for hammerstones and grinding stones, sinkers, and large, polished hoe-axes; basalt for flat hoe-axes and adz-axes; black and gray slate (often arenaceous or with veinlets) for weapons, hoe-adz-axes, and knives; silicified green-rock for adz-axes; and serpentine and jade for ornaments and small adz-axes. Aside from sandstones, which are locally available at the bottom of the valleys, all the other materials came from a distance. Of particular interest are serpentine and jade, which are produced mostly on the east coast of Taiwan, and basalt, which is said to be of an olivine variety that is seen only on the Pescadores (Hayasaka and Rin 1934). These suggest the sphere of cultural contacts of Lungshanoid inhabitants, and the origin of the basalt in the Pescadores is of some significance in indicating the interrelationship of Formosan and mainland Chinese Lungshanoid cultures (see Chapter 9).

Very few stone implements are found that can be regarded as blanks or half finished, and stone-making areas are not indicated at the site. The rule in making a stone implement appears to be grinding and polishing after a rough shape was formed by flaking and sawing. Flaked implements belong to specific categories such as chipped hoe-axes and pitted pebbles.

Ten hammerstones and five grinding stones (Pl. 79, *E*) were found at the site. Perforations occur on perforated hoe-axes, some arrowheads, and stone knives, presumably accomplished by a perforator made of material other than stone, with the aid of abrasives. No evidence of cutting stones by seriating perforations or of the tubular boring technique—common in the Yüan-shan culture in the north and in the prehistoric east coast—is noted at this site.

WOODWORKING

Many of the adz-axes described earlier were probably used for such woodworking as house construction and canoe or boat building. To supplement the stone chisels, which are few in number, bone and antler wedges and chisels were made (Pl. 68, *A–I*).

BONE, ANTLER, AND SHELL ARTIFACTS

Awls, points, gravers, needles, and chisels were made of bone, antler, or shell (Pls. 66, 68), and ornaments of mollusk shells (Pls. 63–65). Long bones and antlers (Pl. 64, *E, F*) were sawed into segments, which were then ground, grooved, and notched into final shape. Holes in the shells were probably ground. Grinding marks are visible on most, probably produced by small stone polishers and large abrasive stones. Metapodial bones of deer had been frequently selected, presumably because of their tight texture. A few arrowheads were made from charred long bones—probably charred to harden them.

GARMENT MAKING AND BASKETRY

Garments were probably sewn of animal skins and plant fabrics. Antler and bone awls and needle points are discovered, and some of the edged stone implements could have served to cut and scrape animal skins as well as for cultivation.

There is no evidence to indicate the kind of plants used for fabrics, but the cord marks on pottery suggest the cultivation of hemp, and a cloth impression on a pottery cover shows a fabric of fine strands, presumably woven on a loom. Many spindle whorls were found throughout all levels, but more in the lower levels than in the upper. These are made of clay, highly polished, and are sometimes incised with decorative designs (Fig. 65, *4–7;* Pls. 63, *A–D;* 64, *C*).

Impressions on pottery indicate wide use of cordage (Pl. 25, *A,B*) and basketry; the latter includes mat (Pl. 25, *D*) and basket designs.

CERAMICS

Pottery kilns have not been located at the site, but an area in Locus V has a cluster of burned clay fragments and a huge amount of sandy gray potsherds. So far as is known, no roofed kiln has ever been found in prehistoric Formosa, and bonfire kilns were presumably used, with wood and/or straw fuels. The paste is tempered with sand (quartz, feldspar, and mica) of varying amounts ranging from 5 to 35 per cent. The firing temperatures are estimated between 550 and 740°C.

The body of the pots was apparently molded by hand, many being constructed from coils (Pl. 25, *C*). Paddle and anvil were used to shape and to press. Rim, lug, and foot were then attached to the body. A jar with a long neck and a small mouth (into which fingers could not be inserted to press the rim onto the upper rim of the body) was built in two sections, a lower one with a larger opening, and an upper one constructed on top after the attachment to the body was secure (Pl. 30, *C*).

The lid was sometimes made by spreading paste on a flat board carved with designs (Pls. 25, *E;* 58, *B*), and the ring foot was sometimes modeled over a core, as is indicated by the impressions on the interior surface of the ring foot (Pl. 25, *G*). Circular or rectangular openings were frequently cut into the ring foot. After the rim and foot were attached to the body, a wheel was frequently used to smooth out interior and exterior.

Burnishing and polishing of the surface followed, often producing a very lustrous exterior, and vertical burnishing marks are often observed on the exterior. Then painting, incision, or stamping of designs was executed on the polished surface.

Pottery

The approximately 320,000 potsherds constitute the single most abundant category of finds at the site. The sherds range in size from under 1 cm to over 30 cm in diameter or length (sherds much less than 1 cm long were not collected unless they exhibited special features). They were placed in paper bags keyed to the $100 \times 100 \times 20$ cm excavation units, and bags from selected pits were classified, counted, and weighed at the field headquarters at Hsiao-kang. Then the sherds were returned to the bags and all bags were crated and transported to the laboratory at Taipei where the sherds were gone over again for quantitative study of shape and decoration, and some restoration work was done. Most of the sherds are now stored at the Department of Archaeology and Anthropology, National Taiwan University, and only a small sample collection was brought back to Yale, mainly for paste analysis. Because of limited time, relatively little restoration was accomplished, although the shapes of the various portions of the major pottery vessels were ascertained. The entire sherd collection from Fengpitou should be studied more intensively and completely in the future. What is reported below is the result of the paste analysis undertaken at Yale and the shape, decoration, and quantification analyses carried out largely in the field.

Both for analysis and presentation, the following categories of ware have been found meaningful and significant: Painted, Fine Red, Sandy Red, Sandy Gray, and Black. The binomial nomenclature of wares, commonly employed in American archeology, will not be used at this time. Since the characterization of most of these wares, all of which have a wide distribution in southeast China and Southeast Asia, starts with the Fengpitou site, scholars doing comparative work may simply add FPT to the terms adopted here should they find it convenient; e.g. FPT Painted, FPT Fine Red, FPT Black.

Painted Ware

Paste. The principal characteristic of the sherds of this category is the exclusively painted decoration. Their paste is not homogeneous; at one end of the range are sherds of a very fine texture similar to the fine red ware to be described below; at the other are sherds of a coarse texture with a more noticeable amount of sand inclusions which makes them feel like the sandy red. In general, however, the texture is finer than the sandy red and coarser than the fine red, the body is thinner (1.5–6 mm, averaging about 3 mm), and some forms are exclusive. Two painted sherds analyzed in the laboratory have shown the same amount of quartz (10%), feldspar (4%), and mica (some). Estimated firing temperature is 550–600°C. The core and the surface are generally of the same dull reddish-orange color (9.3R4.8/7.6), but a few have gray cores. The average hardness is 4°.

Construction from coils is manifest in many painted sherds. Rims and appendages were attached to the body and the edges were folded over. The line of attachment was smoothed over by fingers which left prints in various directions on the interior of many sherds. The exterior underwent various degrees of burnishing and polishing, and many samples exhibit a red or orange slip. Reddish-brown (7.1R3.6/5.5) patterns were painted on the surface; the pigment used for painting was red ocher (hematite) or limonite.

Form. Complete and completely restorable vessels of the painted ware are rare, but rim and body sherds can usually be classified into one of the following three basic shapes (Fig. 41). (1) *Bowls* and *dishes* (Fig. 42, *1–8;* Pl. 31). These are shallow (ca. 4–7 cm deep) and wide (diameter 20–30 cm), with thick lips (8–10 mm). The shape of the bottom is unknown, but it was presumably flat or gently rounded. Some vessels were probably supported on ring feet. The lip is usually thickened and forms a bevel higher along the outer edge. The edges are angular or roundish. Painted decorative patterns occur on the flat surface of the lip or on the upper edge of the interior surface just below the rim. (2) *Beakers* (Figs. 42, *9,10;* 45, *4;* Pl. 32). Thin (2–4 mm), with a wide and slightly flaring mouth (7–12 cm diameter), the beakers are of two kinds. One has an almost cylindrical body and probably a flat bottom; the other has a body that bulges around the waist, below which is a round-

FIG. 41. Painted Pottery, Fengpitou: Principal Shapes of Vessels.

ish lower body-bottom. Both types of beakers are 7–12 cm high. Painted patterns occur on the entire exterior surface. (3) *Jars* (Figs. 43–45; Pls. 33–40). The most common form, the jar, has a collar distinctive from the body. From 10 to 22 cm in diameter and 3 to 6 mm thick, the collar ranges in height from 2.5 to 7.5 cm. Mean heights appear to cluster in two groups, high (>4 cm) and low (<3 cm). The wall of the collar is vertical or slightly flaring, with an angular, roundish, or slightly thickened lip. The collar is generally applied to the upper part of the body (shoulder), at a 90–135° angle, and the line of attachment is either sharply angular or roundish. The body has a maximum diameter of 14 to 40 cm and a height of 8 to 30 cm. A ridge was applied to some pots around the circumference of the body (Pl. 39, *A,C,H*). The base is roundish flat or slightly concave. To many, ring feet were attached. Painted decorations occur on various parts of the exterior and on the interior of the collar.

Isolated ring-foot fragments occur in large numbers (Fig. 46; Pls. 41–43). Ranging in height from 3 to 10 cm and in diameter from 7 to 15 cm, these ring feet are never perforated and are very often painted with decorative patterns. The bottom is usually larger than the top, and the wall is straight, although a few samples have slightly bent walls. These were applied to the bottoms of the bowl-dishes and jars.

Decoration. The dull reddish-orange exterior of the painted ware is decorated with dark red or brown patterns. No other methods of decoration are used in association. Two rim sherds show both painted patterns and incised signs (Fig. 57, *1,3;* Pl. 34, *A*), but the latter are apparently not decorative.

The painting was executed with a brush; in many cases it is apparent that two or more brushes were bound together to form a group instrument for painting parallel

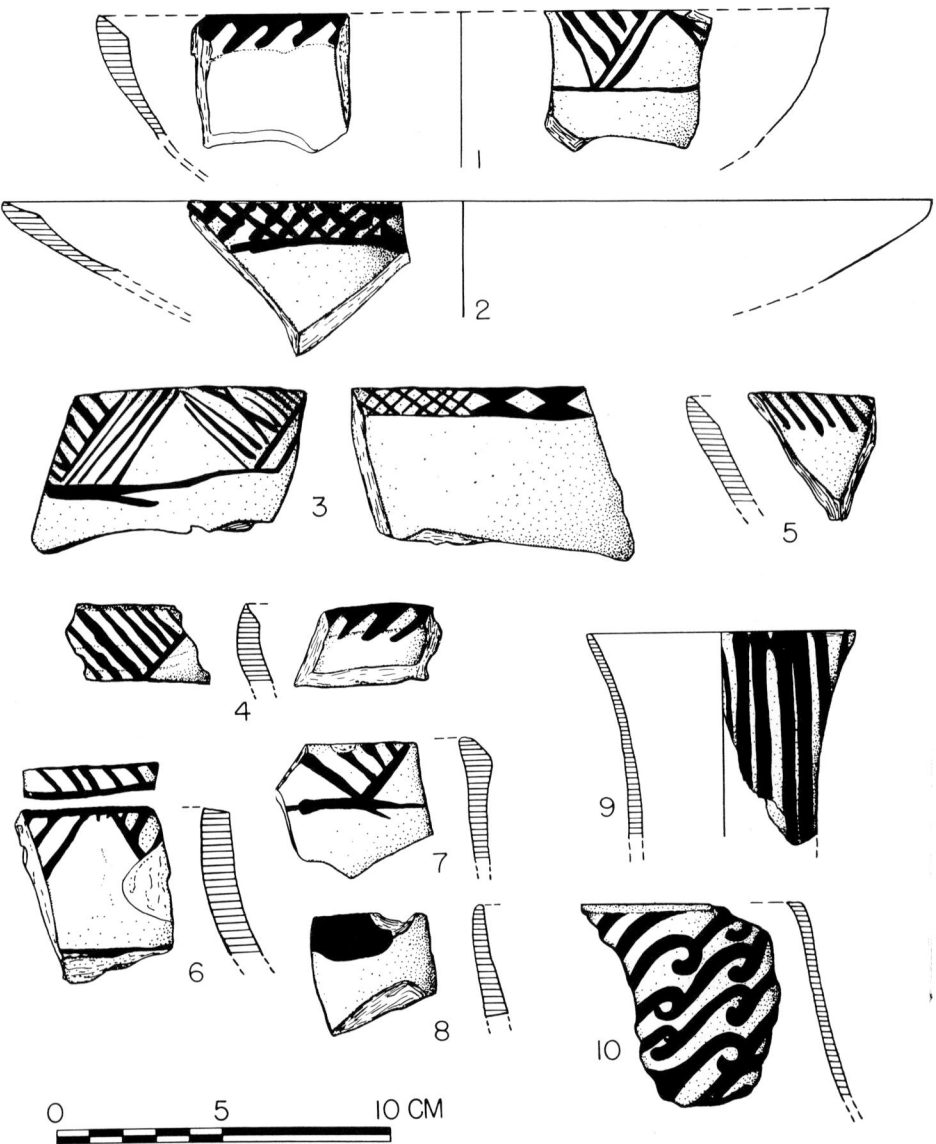

FIG. 42. Painted Pottery, Fengpitou: Bowls and Beakers.

lines and dots. A group instrument was also used for incision in the other wares. Decorative patterns were placed on the lips, the interior surface of bowls, dishes, and collars just below the rim, the exterior surface of the collars, the upper part of the body and occasionally the lower part of the body also, and the exterior surface of the ring foot.

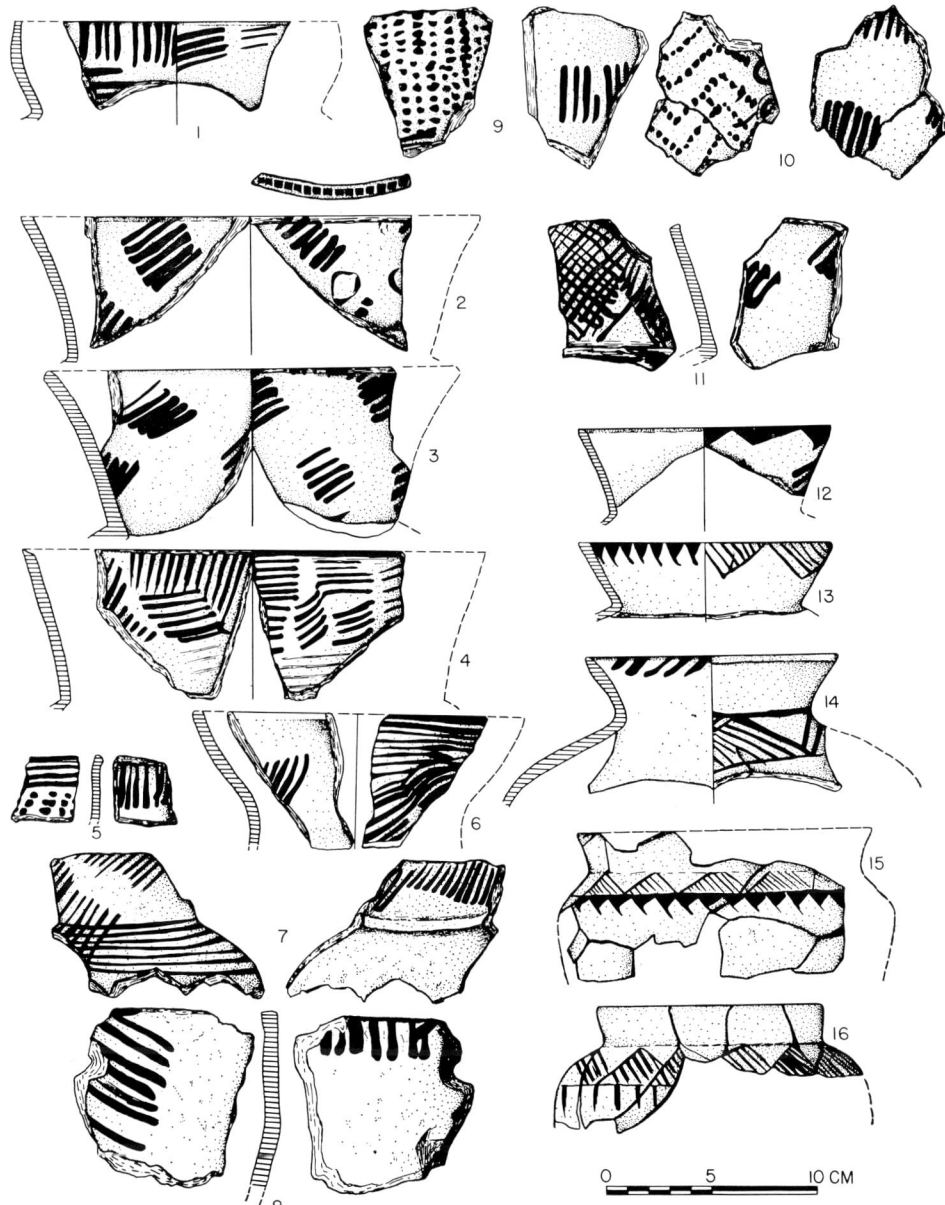

Fɪɢ. 43. Painted Pottery, Fengpitou: Rim Sherds of Pots and Jars.

FIG. 44. Painted Pottery, Fengpitou: Body Sherds.

There is a large variety of design elements and composition (Figs. 42–46; Pls. 31–43). Basic elements are solid dots, small rings, hooks, commas, short strokes, wavy lines, solid stripes, solid triangles, solid lozenges, and negative lozenges enclosed in solid triangles. These basic elements make up bands or zones to encircle the rims, the shoulders, and the ring feet. The composition is usually guided by the

FIG. 45. Painted Pottery, Fengpitou: Body Sherds.

FIG. 46. Painted Pottery, Fengpitou: Ring Feet.

principles of repetition and horizontal symmetry. Choice of basic elements for the composition of designs is to a large extent determined by the part of the vessel to be decorated and by the form of the vessel.

FINE RED WARE

Paste. Potsherds from Fengpitou can easily be sorted according to color, and two major color categories are conspicuous: red and gray. Within the red sherds there is a large variety of paste with reference to the size and amount of inclusions, but in the wide spectrum two clusters are evident. On one hand are red sherds of a fine texture whose inclusions can hardly be seen by the naked eye, and on the other are those with sands of easily observable amounts and sizes. These two types are designated Fine Red and Sandy Red.

Two varieties of sherds can further be distinguished within the fine red category. One is harder (3°) and is dark rose in color (3.5R4.8/5.9). Two thin sections have shown a higher percentage of inclusions (quartz, 10%; feldspar, 4%; and some mica) and are estimated to have been fired at a temperature of 550–600°C. Sherds of this variety are better preserved, exhibiting well-burnished surfaces. Sherds of the second variety are softer (1.5–2°) and porous, and a powdery residue comes off on the fingers with a not very heavy touch. Its color is coral or light reddish-orange (8.9R6.3/8.4). The texture is even finer: two thin sections show only 5 per cent quartz and some feldspar and mica. One is estimated to have been fired at a temperature of 550 to 600°C, but the other seems to have been fired at 700 to 740°C.

Since the surfaces of the softer variety are not so well preserved as the harder kind, it cannot be determined whether these two varieties of fine red ware underwent different surface treatment. In shape, recognized decoration, and manufacturing techniques, there do not appear to be meaningful differences between the two. For analytic purposes the fine red ware is treated as one category. The distinction should nevertheless be noted for possible comparative significance.

Small bowls were apparently molded by hand; a bowl has impressions of basketry at the bottom (Pls. 25, *F*; 30, *A*). A core was used for making some ring feet, for impressions of mats occur on some pieces of ring feet on the interior surface (Pl. 25, *G*). The body of vessels was probably built from coils (Pl. 25, *C*) and then smoothed over. Feet and other appendages were attached to the body and smoothed by hand. Long necks of bottles were attached to the body in two sections (Pl. 30, *B,C*). In average the body is 4 to 5 mm thick. The hard variety of sherds exhibits clear evidence of careful polishing and burnishing. Wheel marks and finger marks are shown on the rims (Pl. 26, *D*) and ring feet; probably vessels were placed on a turntable for retouch.

Form. Rim, body, and foot sherds of this ware are classifiable into five basic types of vessels: basins, bowls, and dishes; the same, with ring feet; jars; long-neck bottles; and tripods (Fig. 47).

FIG. 47. Fine Red Ware, Fengpitou: Principal Shapes of Vessels.

(a) *Basins, bowls, and dishes* (Figs. 48, 51; Pl. 26). These are relatively shallow, with a wide mouth and a large diameter relative to height. The maximum diameter ranges from 9 to 35 cm, and the height from 2.5 to 15 cm or more. The most common forms are: small bowls (Fig. 48, *14,15;* Pl. 30, *A*); flat-base mugs (Fig. 48, *16*);

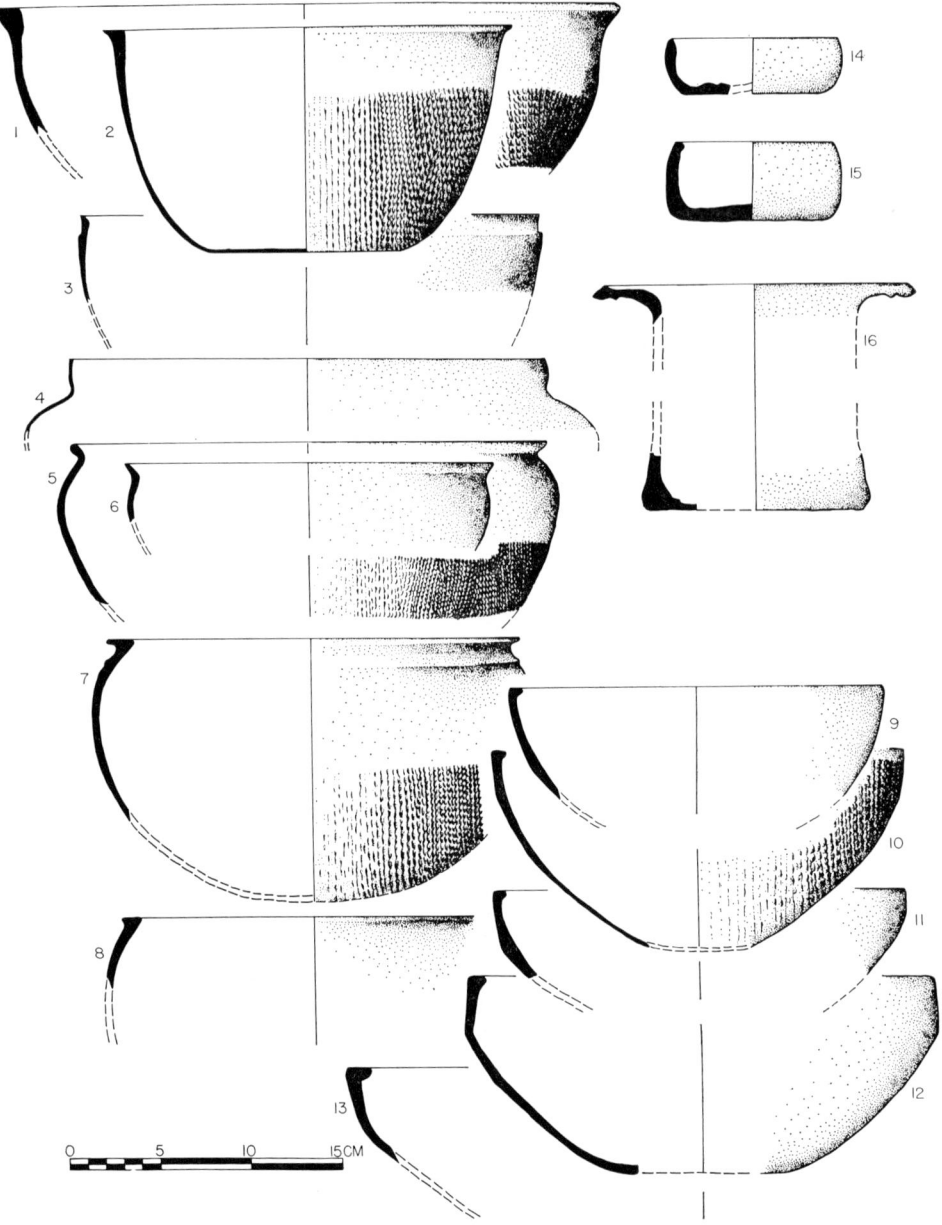

Fig. 48. Fine Red Ware, Fengpitou: Bowls.

bowls-basins with inverted lips (Fig. 48, *9–13*); and bowls-basins with flaring rims (Fig. 48, *1–8*). Some samples show a circumferential ridge just below the rim on the exterior surface (Fig. 48, *3,7*; Pl. 26, *C*). Some of these bowls and dishes were possibly used upside down, as covers or lids for vessels of slightly larger dimensions in the following categories. (b) *Basins, bowls, and dishes on ring feet* (Fig. 49; Pls. 28, 29). These vessels of the classical Chinese *tou* family, a characteristic form of the southeastern Lungshanoid cultures, consist of two basic components, a bowl, basin, or dish supported by a ring foot. They were separately made and then attached before firing. The upper part generally has two rim forms: one is straight (Fig. 49, *3–6*), and the other has a flaring and extended lip so that the outer edge of the lip has a diameter considerably larger than the diameter of the body of the vessel (Fig. 49, *7–11*; Pl. 29, *B,E*). The ring feet are of varying height and diameter, ranging from 2 to 14 cm high, and most have circular or rectangular window-like cutouts (Fig. 49, *12–19*; Pls. 28, 29, *A,C,D,F*). (c) *Jars* (Fig. 50; Pl. 27). Most of the jars—with clearly demarcated collars and bodies—are of considerable size. The collar is from 1.5 to 5 cm high and the mouth is 10 to 22 cm in diameter. The

FIG. 49. Fine Red Ware, Fengpitou: Long-neck Jars and *Tous*.

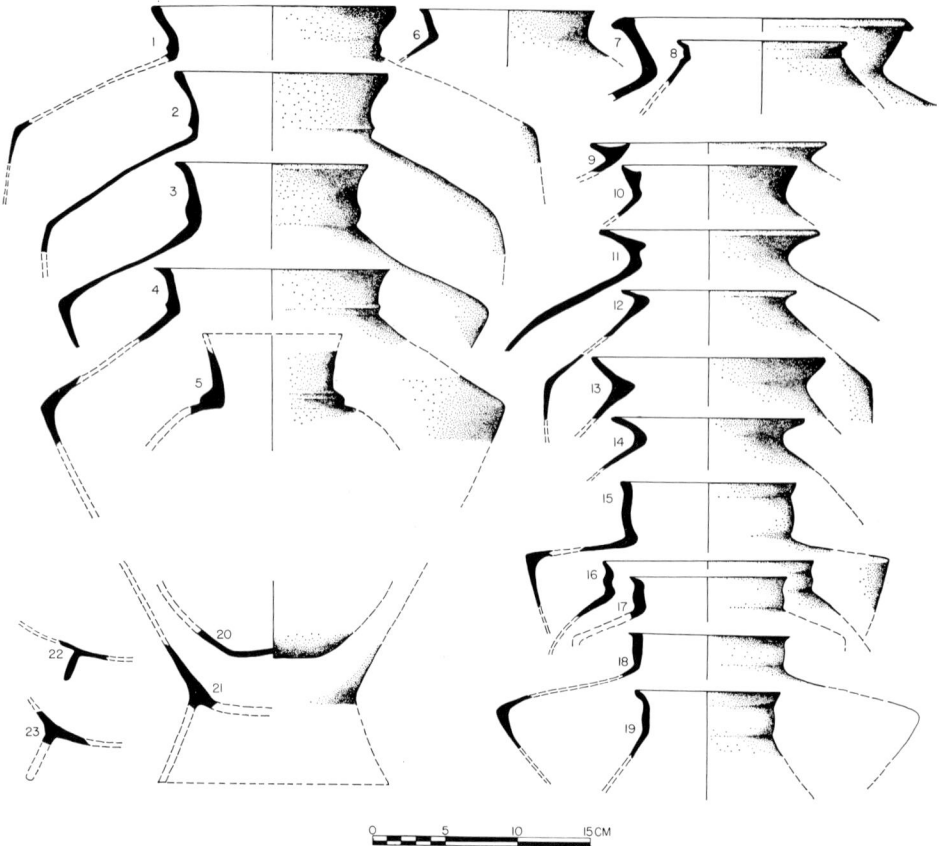

FIG. 50. Fine Red Ware, Fengpitou: Pots and Jars.

maximum diameter of the body may reach more than 35 cm. There is a large variety of rim shapes, but four are basic: straight (Fig. 50, *6–8*); with a circumferential ridge below the rim on the outside (Fig. 50, *1–5*); with a flat and wide lip (Fig. 50, *9–14*); and with a zigzag vertical section (Fig. 50, *15–19*). The base of the body is flat or slightly concave; many probably had a low ring foot. (d) *Long-neck bottles* (Fig. 49, *1,2*; Pl. 30, *B,C*). Only the necks of two such vessels have been found. One is 9.5 cm high and the other 13.5 cm. The diameter is 3.5 to 4.5 cm. The shape of the vessels below the neck is unknown. (e) *Tripods* (Fig. 51, *19–23*; Pl. 30, *E*). A large number of solid leg-like clay objects was found; they average 10 cm in length, and the base was evidently attached to a flat surface before it broke off. Some of these were probably knobs on lids (Fig. 51, *16–18*), but many have a base so placed that it was probably attached to the bottom of a basin to make a *ting* tripod. One of these leg-like objects was adherent to a piece of base sherd; it is unquestionably a tripod leg (Pl. 30, *E*).

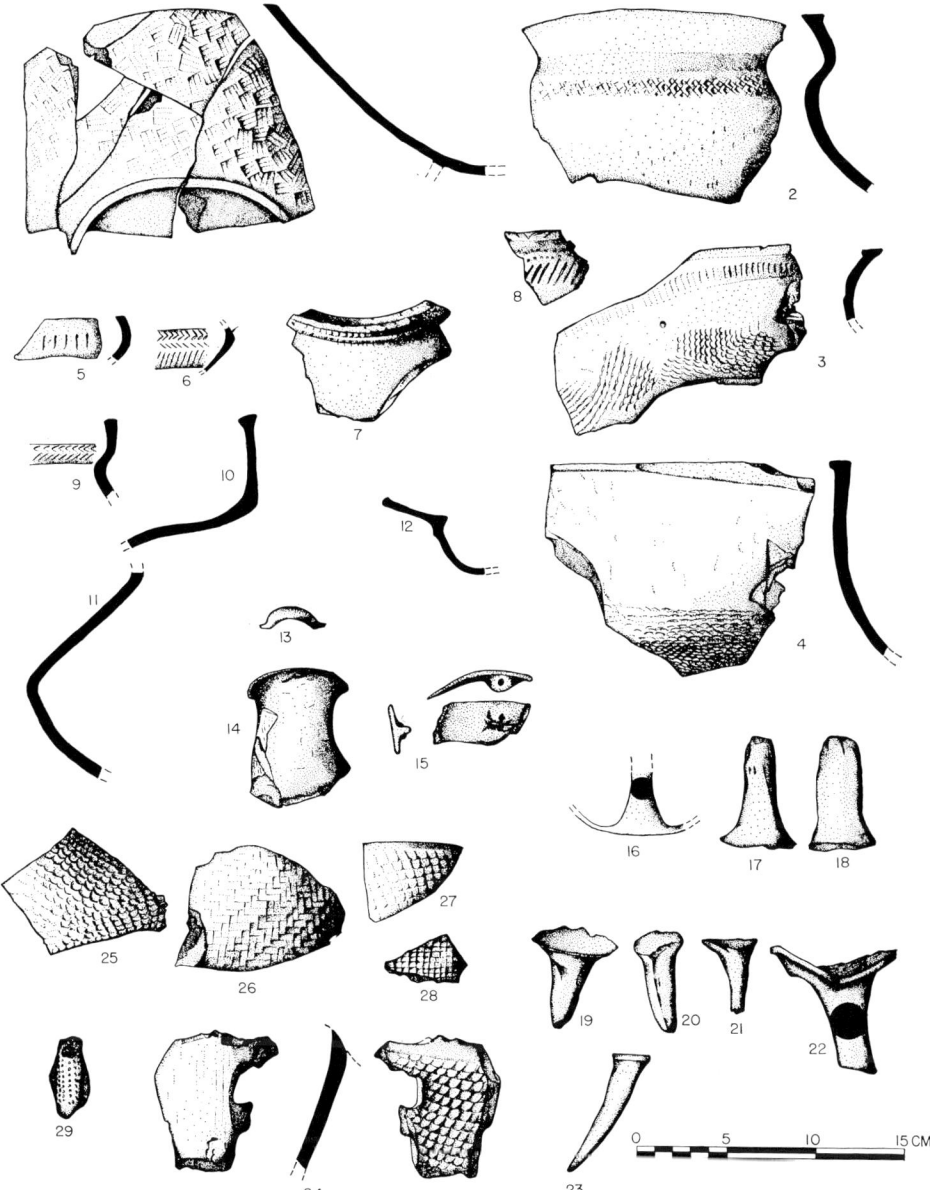

Fig. 51. Fine Red Ware, Fengpitou: Impressed Sherds, Lids, Lugs, and Tripods.

Besides shallow dishes that were possibly used inverted as lids, disk lids were also found (Fig. 51, *16*), which have cylindrical knobs on top. A piece of large handle (Fig. 51, *14*; Pl. 30, *D*), a small loop handle (Fig. 51, *13*; Pl. 30, *F*), and a rim sherd of a cup-like vessel with an interior ear (Fig. 51, *15*) were also recovered.

Decoration. Impressed decorations occur on the lower part of the body of many vessels below the shoulder. Most are cord impressions of very fine strands apparently made with a cord-wrapped paddle or stick (Pls. 25, *A,B*; 26, *B,E*). A few mat impressions (Pl. 25, *D*) and a very few check impressions also occur. All mat and check impressions occur on sherds of the harder and more burnished variety, but cord impression is universal.

The surface of the upper, unimpressed part of the vessels is mostly plain. A few jars and bowls have small and sparse units of incised parallel lines on the exterior or rows of dots on the lip (Fig. 51, *5–9*; Pl. 27, *C,D*). Vertical lines occur on a few rim sherds of bowls on the exterior below the rim and above the cord-impressed lower part, apparently made by impressing, in vertical series, the sharp edge of the paddle on the wet clay (Pl. 26, *C*). Circumferential ridges on the exterior of the collar and the body and the cut-out holes in the ring feet may also be described as decorative.

Sandy Red Ware

Paste. Inclusions of sands of observable size in the paste of this ware make the sherds feel rough to touch. A thin section of a sherd shows 15 per cent quartz and 5 per cent feldspar; the estimated temperature of firing is 600–650°C, and the average hardness is 4.5°. The color of the paste is uniformly dark grayish-red (9.8R/P3.0/1.0), both core and surface, and the walls are 5 to 6 mm thick. No evidence of a slip is observed, nor is there evidence of polishing. The manufacture is by hand; wheel marks are occasionally present on rim and ring-foot sherds.

Form. Vessels of this ware are classifiable into two major shapes: beakers and bowls, without a collar portion; and pots and jars, with a collar portion (Fig. 52). (a) *Beakers* (Fig. 56, *5–10*; Pl. 57, *A–D*) are cylindrical, 12–13 cm in diameter and in height, and have a flat base and two horizontal lugs below the rim. The lugs were made of a segment of clay coil applied to the body; they are of varying lengths, and some of the long ones are cut into several sections. The beakers are never decorated. (b) *Bowls* (Fig. 53; Pl. 53) are 12–18 cm in diameter and 5–8 cm high. (c) *Pots and jars* are of two kinds: those with wide mouth (Fig. 55; Pl. 55), about 15–25 cm in diameter and 10–15 cm in height in the body part, and those with constricted mouth, wide shoulders, and high bodies (Fig. 54; Pl. 52). Rim shapes of all forms of vessels are simple and straight or slightly flaring.

Ring feet (Fig. 56, *12–15*) and tripod legs (Pl. 57) are occasionally found. These were probably attached to bowls, and pots and jars, but the common forms of the latter are round-based and without additional support. Lids, however, are very common. They are dish-like, flat, plano-convex, or concave-convex (Fig. 56, *1–4*; Pl. 51). The edge of the flat disk is usually saw-toothed; plano-convex disks are straight-edged, and the concave-convex ones usually have wavy rims made by twisting the edge while the clay was wet and soft. At the center on top of the lids is a knob. It is usually stick-shaped; many of them have two branches at the upper end.

Fig. 52. Sandy Red Ware, Fengpitou: Principal Shapes of Vessels.

Decoration. Two major techniques of decoration were used in this ware: impression and incision-punctation. Impressed cord, mat, basket, and check marks occur in the lower parts of the vessels (bowls and pots). Incised-punctated designs occur on the lip and interior surface below the rim of bowls and on the lip, exterior surface of the collar, and the shoulder of pots and jars (Pls. 53, 55, 56). Vessels with incised designs tend to be plain in the other parts of the body, and the concurrence of impressed and incised designs on the same vessels is rarely observed. The incisions-punctations are of very simple designs, usually rows of dots and small strokes forming narrow bands.

Many rim sherds have on the interior surface of the rim isolated incised signs such as a single stroke, an X, a rectangle, or a circle (Fig. 57; Pl. 54). Their significance is not clear. They may be maker's or owner's marks or they may be marks to guide the positioning of the lid. No lids, however, have shown corresponding marks.

Sandy Gray Ware

Paste. In appearance and feel sherds of this ware are very similar to the sandy red, but the color, of course, is different and the paste is slightly coarser. Of a variety of shades of color, the most common sherds are brownish-gray (4.7YR5.4/113) and 4–4.5° in hardness. A thin section shows 25 per cent quartz, 10 per cent feldspar, and some mica, and its firing temperature is estimated at 600–650°C. The manufacture is entirely by hand; wheel marks are occasionally present on rim and ring-foot sherds. To judge from the prevalence of impressed marks, the shaping of the vessels was often done with the aid of paddles and anvils. Rims and appendages were attached to the body by hand, with folded-in edges (Pl. 61, *G*). Irregular depressions occur frequently on the interior of the vessels, apparently left by fingers.

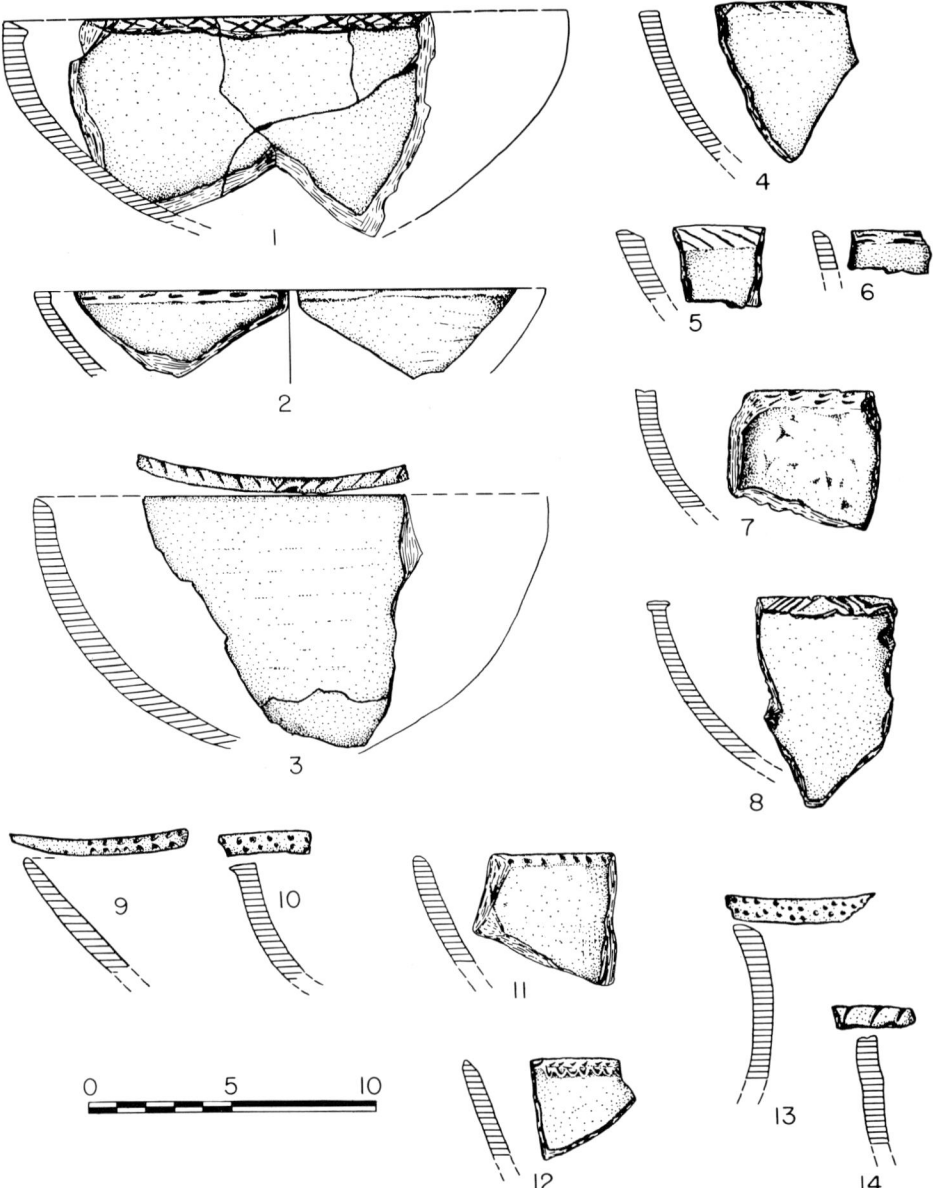

FIG. 53. Sandy Red Ware, Fengpitou: Bowls.

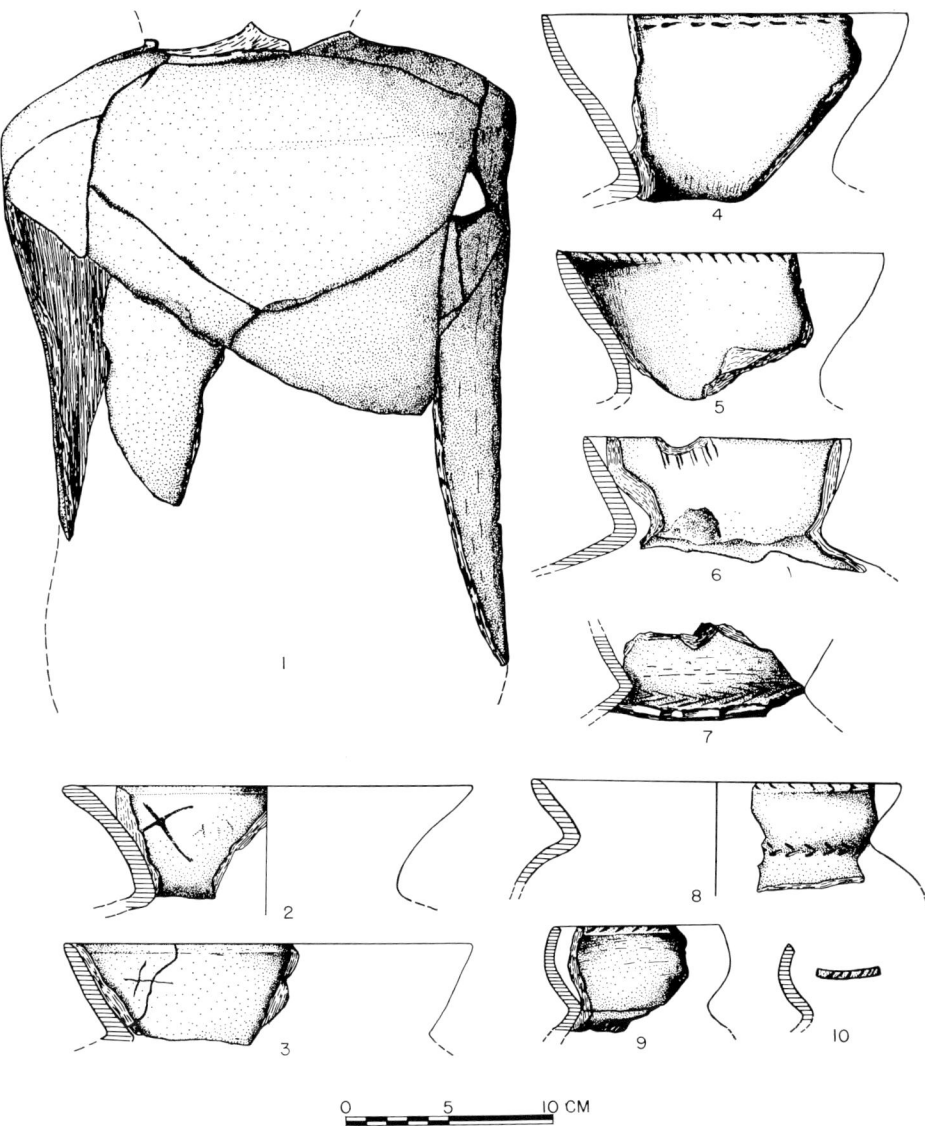

FIG. 54. Sandy Red Ware, Fengpitou: Pots and Jars.

Form. Rim, body, and foot sherds of this ware indicate three principal vessel forms (Fig. 58): *beakers* (Fig. 60, *1–5;* Pl. 59, *B*), about 10 cm high and 7–8 cm in diameter, cylindrical, and flat-based; *bowls and dishes* (Fig. 60, *6–8;* Pls. 60, *A*, 61, *A,C,E,F*), 20–22 cm in diameter and 5–8 cm high; and *pots and jars* (Fig. 59; Pl. 60, *B*), ranging in size from 15 to over 35 cm high and from 10 to over 25 cm in

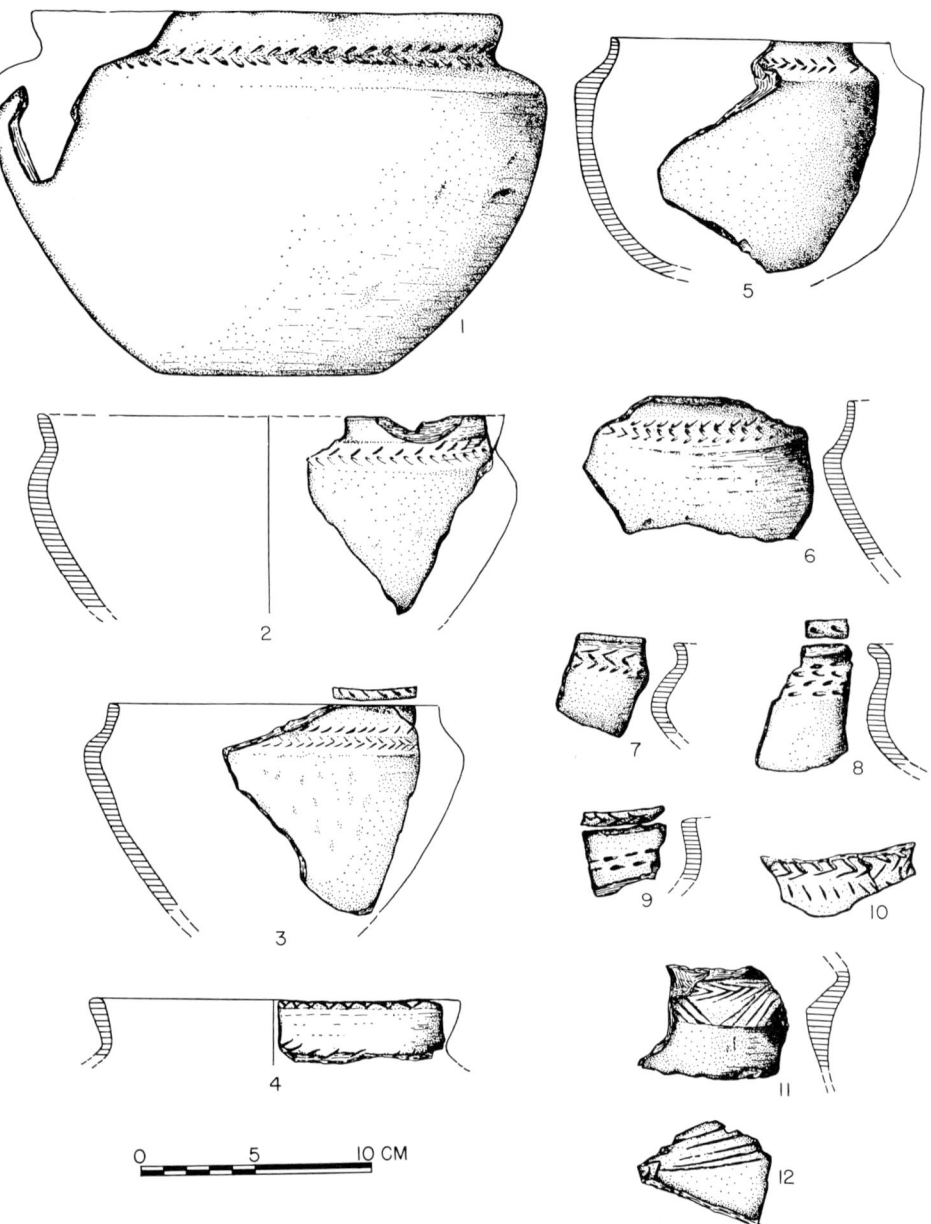

Fig. 55. Sandy Red Ware, Fengpitou: Jars and Basins.

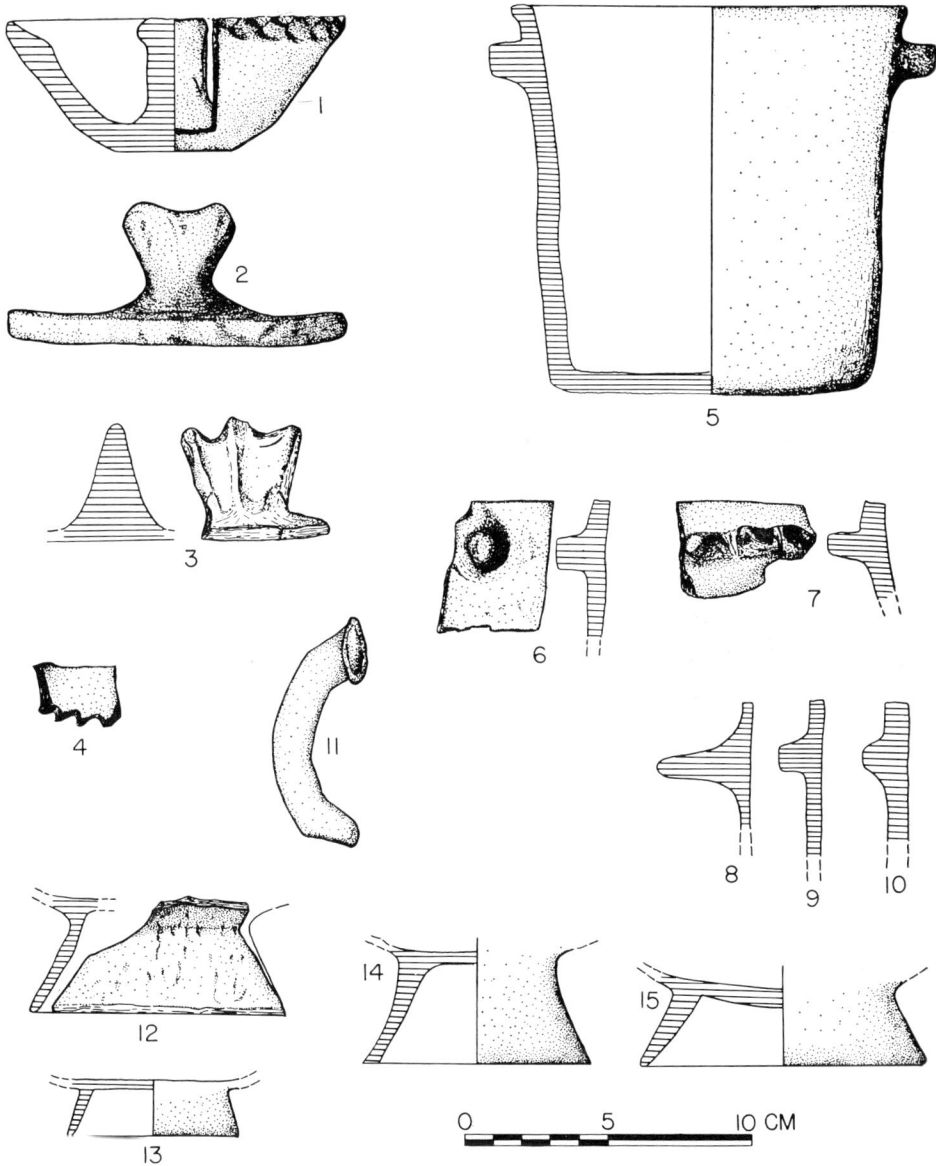

FIG. 56. Sandy Red Ware, Fengpitou: Lids, Lugs, Beakers, and Ring Feet.

diameter, consisting of collar with flaring rim, globular body and ring foot. Disk lids with knobs similar to the sandy red forms are common (Pl. 58).

Decoration. Again the decoration is made by impression and by incision. Among the impressed patterns cord and mat marks are few (Pl. 59, *D*), basket marks prevail

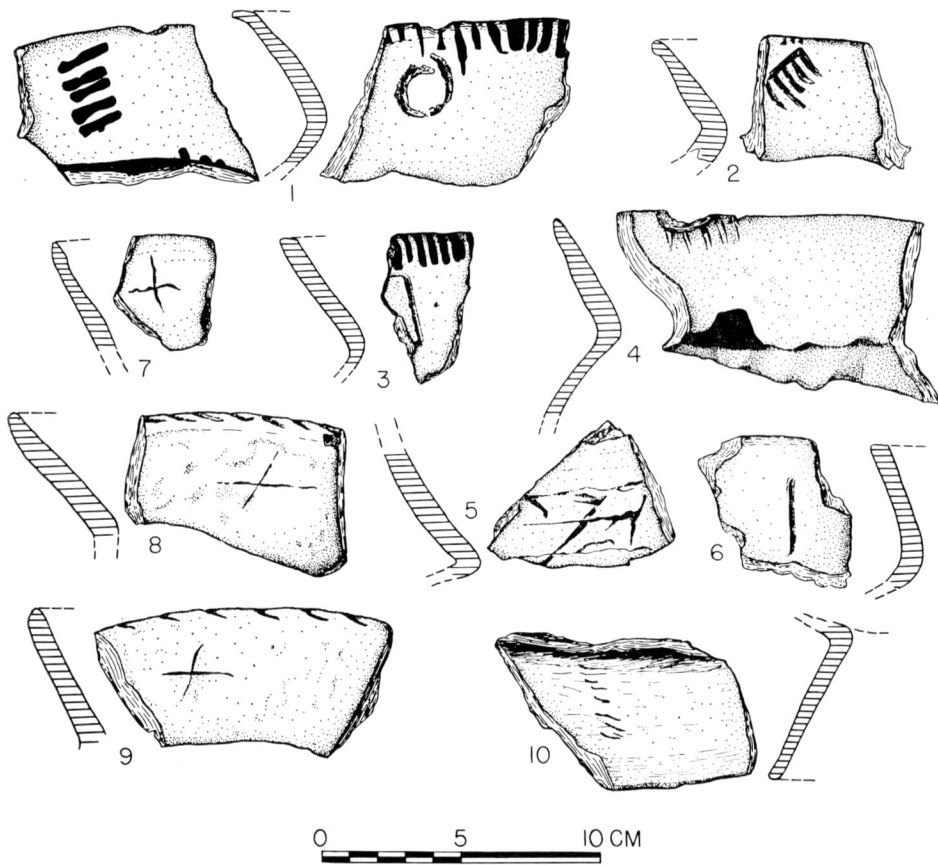

F<small>IG</small>. 57. Sandy Red Ware, Fengpitou: Incised Signs on Rims.

(Pl. 59, *A,B,E*), and check marks occur (Pl. 59, *C*). Other than rows of small dots incised or punctated on the lips of some pots (Pl. 61, *C,D*), the incised patterns of the sandy gray ware are exclusive to this category of pottery. They were incised by means of a group instrument (a "comb") at the root of the shoulders just below the collar. Three designs are most common: wavy lines (Pl. 62, *A–E*); units of parallel short lines arranged perpendicularly, forming radiating strokes from a series of nuclei (Pl. 62, *F,G*); and rows of cross-hatches (Pl. 62, *K,L*).

B<small>LACK</small> W<small>ARE</small>

Paste. The paste of this final category is characterized by the following features: thin (1–3 mm, about 2 mm in average, rarely exceeding 3 mm except the rim part), hard (on average 3.5°), and highly lustrous from polishing and burnishing. The color of the sherds of this ware ranges from ivory yellow (2.7Y7.5/2.6) to gray to jet black on the surface, but the core is always dark gray or black. (In preliminary

Fɪɢ. 58. Sandy Gray Ware, Fengpitou: Principal Shapes of Vessels.

analysis gray and black sherds were separated. Further analysis, however, has disclosed no meaningful differentiation between the two, and here they are combined.) Examination of two thin sections of the black sherds has shown 10 per cent quartz, 5 per cent feldspar, and some traces of mica, with the estimated temperature of firing placed at 550 to 600°C, and a thin section of a piece of yellowish sherd of this ware has yielded only 5 per cent quartz and only traces of feldspar and mica, with an estimated firing temperature of 550 to 580°C. A piece of black sherd contains a large amount of organic matter and reacts with H_2O_2, suggesting prolonged contact probably with cooking fire and a utilitarian use for some vessels of this ware.

The vessels were handmade, frequently from coils. The outer surface is carefully and elaborately polished, and the rims and ring feet were frequently smoothed on a wheel. Appendages were applied.

Form. The principal forms that can be reconstructed from sherds are bowls, beakers, and pots (Fig. 61). (a) *Bowls* (Fig. 62, *1–9;* Pls. 45, 46). About 20 cm in diameter and 5–10 cm high, the bowls have roundish bases and thickened rims. The rims often have flat lips on which decorative patterns occur. (b) *Beakers* (Fig. 62, *10–20;* Pls. 47–49). Beakers in this ware are of two kinds, both with a roundish base. The first has a slightly flaring rim (Pls. 47, 48), the other has a slightly inverted mouth (Pl. 49). Their decorative patterns are also different. Both are 10–16 cm high and 6–15 cm in diameter. (c) *Pots* (Pl. 44). The heights of the collar appear to cluster in two groups, resulting in two varieties of pots: those with high collar and smaller mouth, and those with low collar and wider mouth. The diameter of the body may reach 20 cm, and the height ranges from 10 to 20 cm; the collar part

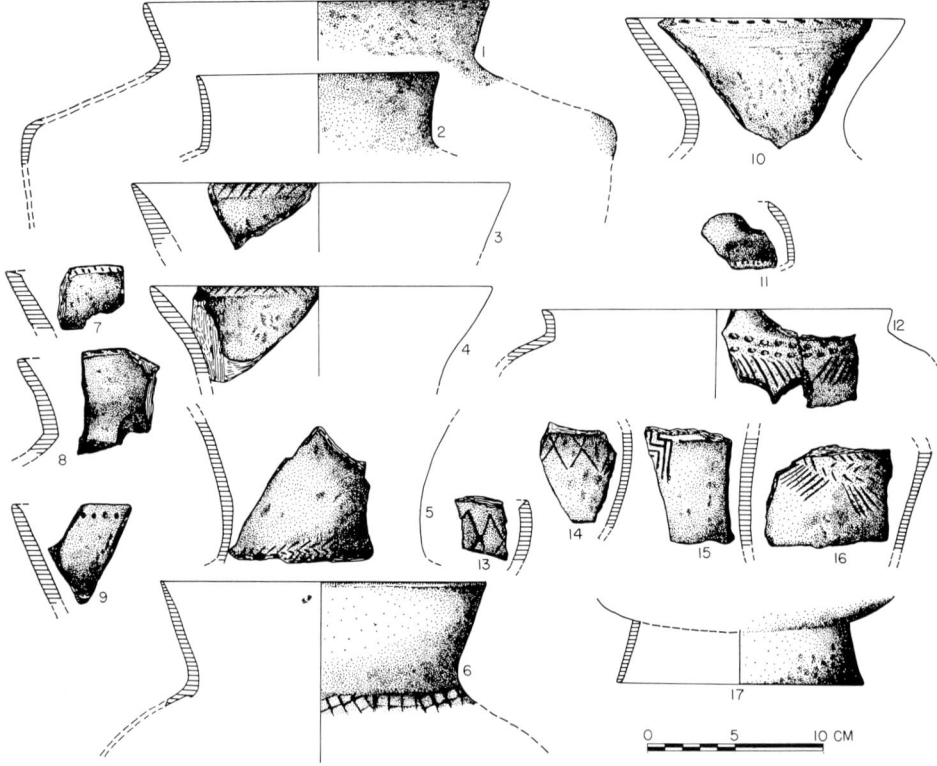

Fɪɢ. 59. Sandy Gray Ware, Fengpitou: Pots and Jars.

ranges in height from 1 to 4 cm. The base of the pots is roundish with a slightly concave center, and some pots were probably supported on ring feet.

Vessels of this ware have no appendages such as lugs or handles. Ring feet are few (Pl. 50, *A–E*) and are never cut out like the *tou* of the fine red ware. A piece is about 25 mm high but another is about 7 cm high and only 25 to 30 mm in diameter. These may have been attached to the base of the bowls, yielding the classical Lung-shan type of *tou*. A piece of sherd has a protrusion on one face and a corresponding depression on the other (Pl. 50, *F*), possibly a *li* tripod leg, but this is by no means certain.

Decoration. Decoration of this ware was done by incising and engraving—never by painting or impressing. The pots are mostly plain; rows of punctates occasionally occur below the collar, forming simple bands of triangles. Beakers are plain or heavily decorated over the entire exterior surface. Oblique parallel lines forming vertical bands of triangles and lozenges occur on beakers with inverted mouth (Pl. 49), and vertical rows of short, horizontal, parallel strokes engraved after the clay was dried occur on the surface of the beakers with flaring mouth (Pl. 48). The lips

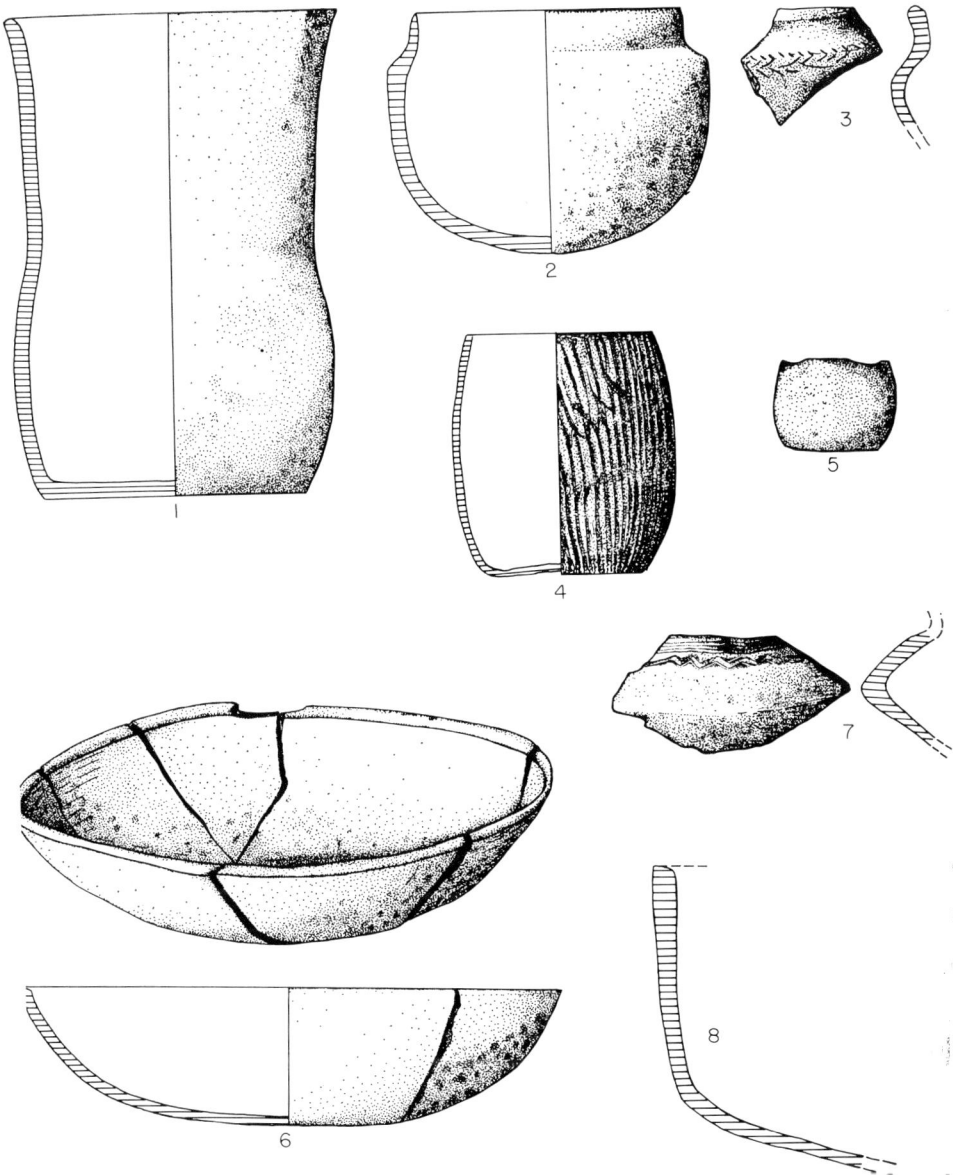

F<small>IG</small>. 60. Sandy Gray Ware, Fengpitou: Basins, Beakers, and Bowls.

and outside surfaces below the rims of bowls often have incised or combed patterns. These are usually wavy lines formed of dots or short strokes executed by means of a group instrument (comb) (Pls. 45, 46). The use of a shell comb, seen on some black potsherds found at the Ta-hu site near Tainan, is not observed at Fengpitou.

FIG. 61. Black Pottery, Fengpitou: Principal Shapes of Vessels.

Weapons

Offensive weapons kill both man and animals, and barehanded man is in fact more vulnerable than most animals. Inasmuch as arrows and spears are among the ordinary offensive weapons against man, there is little question that the projectile point category described above includes those that were used or made to be used in warfare. In addition, some large, polished stone implements with sharp edges and points were in all probability used exclusively in combat. These were all made of black slate, and are 15 to 20 cm in length. Two major classes are discernible: *swords* or *daggers* (Fig. 63; Pl. 78, *E–G*), in which the long edges are of the same length, and the point is at the center; and *ko* halberds (Fig. 64; Pl. 78, *A–D*), in which one of the edges is longer than the other, and the point is closer to one edge (shorter edge) than to the other. According to our knowledge of prehistoric and historic Chinese weaponry, these two classes of weapons were mounted differently. The haft or handle of a sword continues from the axis of the blade, whereas the *ko* halberd blade and shaft were attached at a right angle.

Ornaments, Artworks, and Signs

A few small adzes and chisels were found at the site, suggesting wood carving. Whatever ornamental, decorative, and/or socioreligious art that existed, however, has long since perished, and only in the following areas is there any evidence for prehistoric activities that were not directly utilitarian.

Rings (Fig. 65, *8–16;* Pls. 63, *F–Z;* 64, *A,B,D*). Many fragments of clay rings are encountered throughout the site. These are of various colors, pastes, and shapes, but two major groups can be distinguished by color—one is red and the other is gray-blackish. The red rings are mostly of a fine paste and are generally associated with the fine red pottery; they are either round in cross section or were made of two or three round rings attached together, and often bear incised patterns. The gray-black

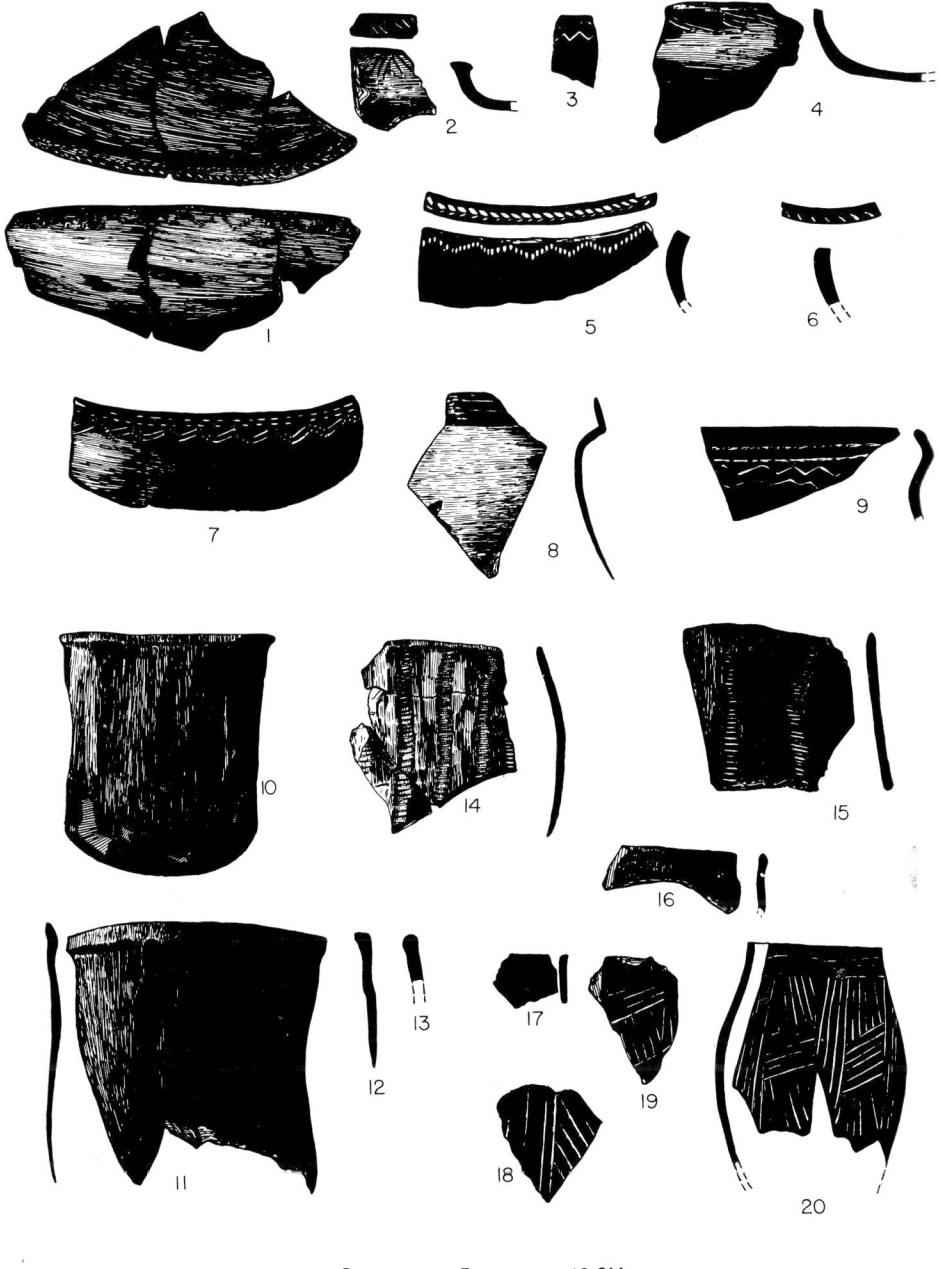

FIG. 62. Black Pottery, Fengpitou: Incised Patterns.

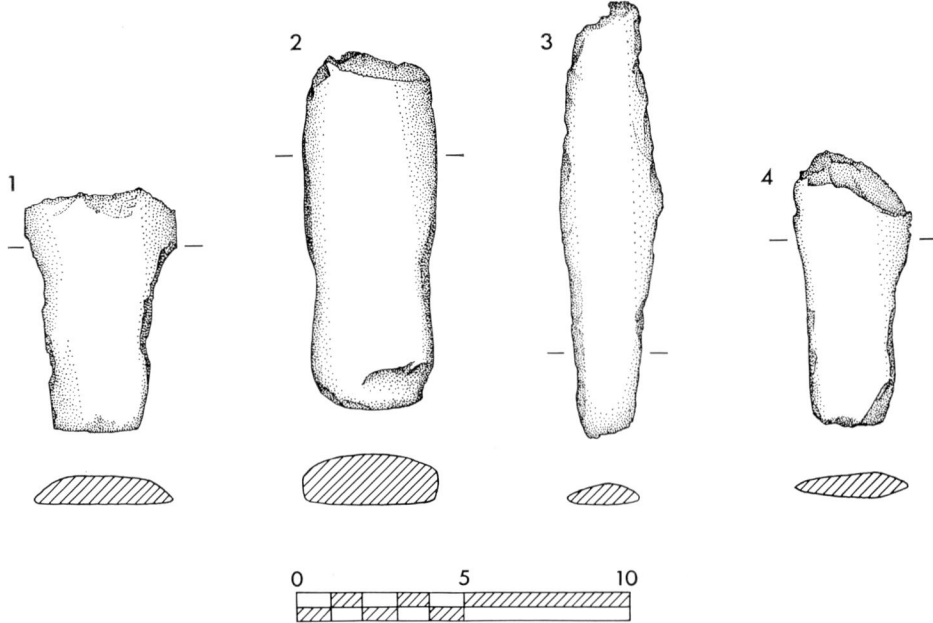

FIG. 63. Stone Swords and Daggers, Fengpitou.

rings, often associated with sandy red and sandy gray pottery, are of similar paste and shape, and are similarly decorated, but many are so broad that they can be called tubes rather than rings. Probably these clay rings were used as bracelets, armlets, or anklets.

Rings were also made of serpentine and jadeish materials (Fig. 66, *5;* Pl. 63, *K*) or of shell (Pl. 63, *F–H*), but these are much rarer. Serpentine-jade rings were largely confined to Locus P, and shell rings to Locus K.

Buttons (Fig. 66, *1–3;* Pl. 65, *G–J*). About a dozen thin disks of serpentine, some 4 cm across, have been recovered from the fine red pottery layers in loci P and V. Two small perforations occur near—but never at—the center of the disks. These were probably decorative buttons sewn on clothes and belts, such as those commonly found among the Paiwan aborigines of South Formosa at the present time. Buttons of shell (Pls. 64, *D;* 65, *E,F*) and of clay (Pl. 65, *C,D*) are also recovered.

Pendants and beads. Two perforated shells were found at Locus K, probably ornamental pendants (Pl. 65, *A,B*). A serpentine bead was found at Locus P (Pl. 65, *L*).

Figurines (?). A reddish clay object, seemingly the shape of an animal head, was found in a fine red ware layer in Locus P; it was covered with tiny punctated marks (Fig. 51, *29;* Pl. 30, *G*). A serpentine animal (?) figurine occurred in the same layer (Fig. 66, *6;* Pl. 65, *K*).

Ceramic decoration. Only the decoration of the Fengpitou pottery gives us any

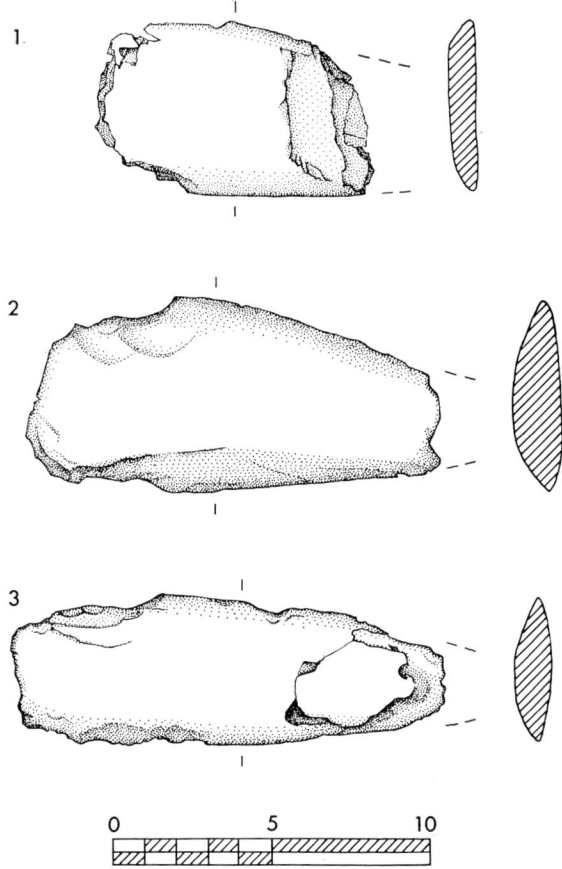

F<small>IG</small>. 64. Stone *Ko* Halberds, Fengpitou.

clue to the presumably wide use of decorative art among the people occupying the site. The techniques and designs of the Fengpitou ceramic decoration have been described in the section on pottery. It is interesting to note that, despite the great variety of techniques, the range of basic motifs is relatively limited. The wide use of the group instrument (for painting, incising, and engraving) and the prevalence of zoning, parallel lines, and diamond shapes made from solid–blank alternations and triangles of lines is apparent in patterns executed by whatever technique. The application of impressed patterns is a sure indication of the popularity of basketry.

Signs (?). About a dozen rim sherds found at loci K and N are distinguished by the occurrence of deeply incised signs on their interior surfaces. The patterns include short strokes, x-shapes, quadrangles, and whorls (Fig. 57; Pl. 54). The most obvious explanation of these signs is potter's marks, but there are too few of them for any sociological study of their significance (see p. 95, above).

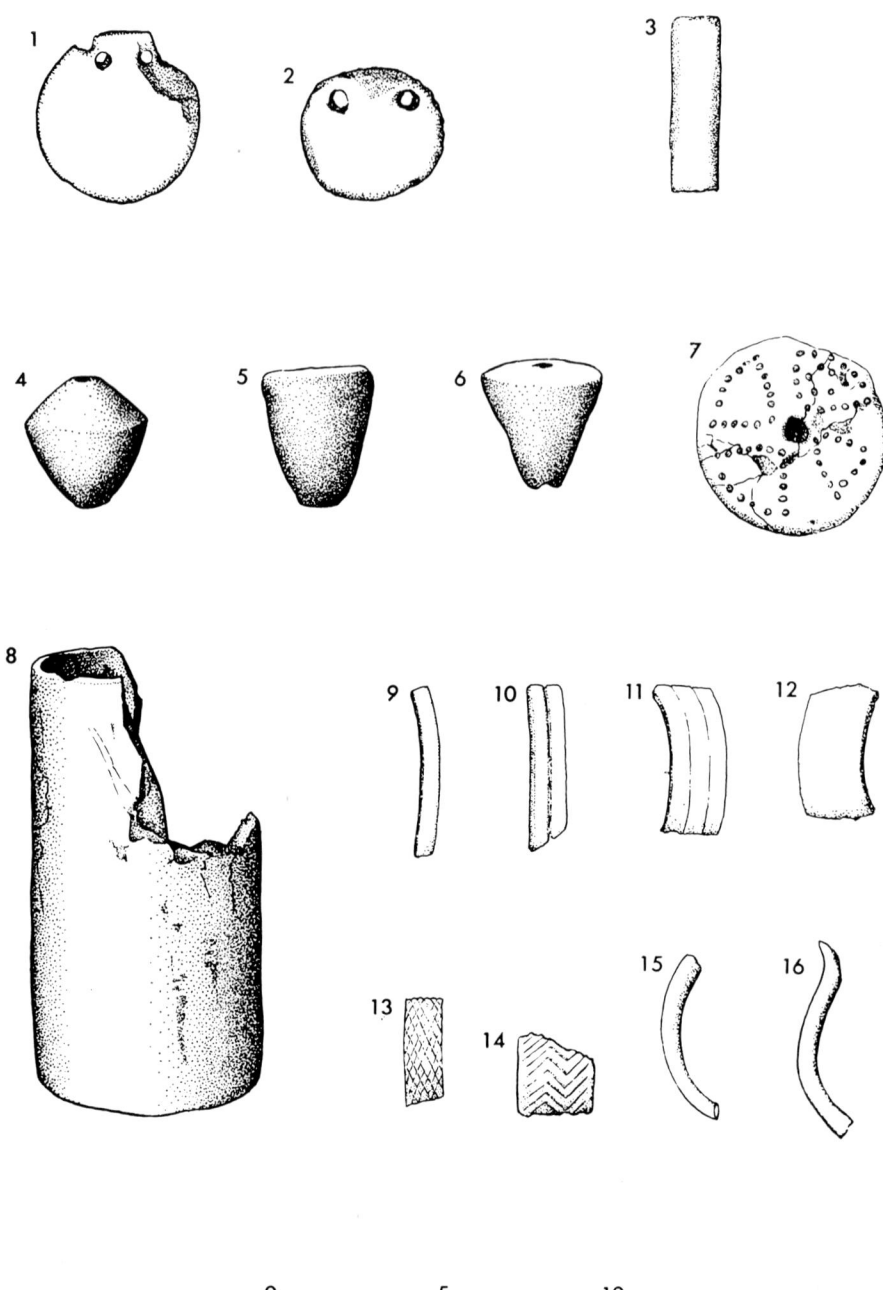

FIG. 65. Spindle Whorls, Rings, and Other Clay Objects at Fengpitou.

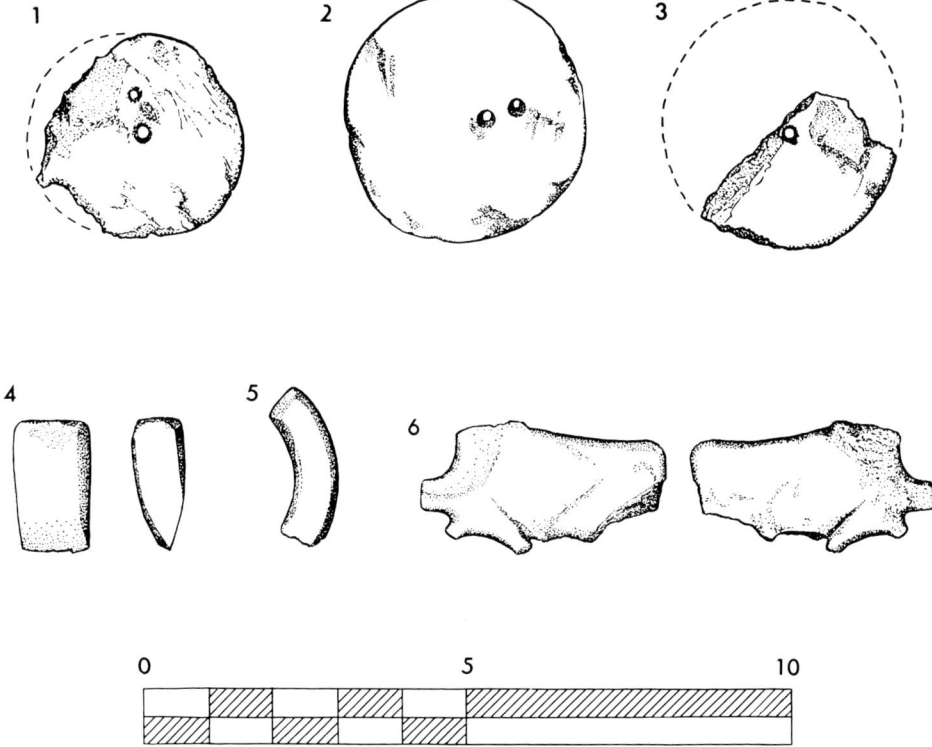

Fig. 66. Buttons and Other Serpentine Objects at Fengpitou.

Burials

No prehistoric settlement is complete without a burial area, and we were determined to find it. Midway in the excavation of the site it became clear that the habitations were distributed along the northern and the southern slopes of the hill, and their kitchen middens slightly downslope. For two reasons we decided to concentrate on the northern part of the site for tomb hunting: the northern slope is away from the sun and also away from the (presumably) major area of marine activities, and in many Neolithic sites in China the cemetery is known to be located in the northern part of the settlement. Sure enough, at the middle of the northern slope, in the area designated V, several fragments of human limb bones were collected from the surface and in the communication trenches. A flat area was cleared for excavation (Locus V) and a human burial was discovered in the first square (Pl. 5, B).

The V section (Chapter 1) exposes a thick layer of cultural deposits, but in the locus a large part of the upper level had been removed to make a flat plot for sweet-potato planting, and the human burial was only 45 cm from the present ground surface. It is in the undisturbed Layer 2 in squares V-E4, V-E5, and V-E9 (Fig. 67),

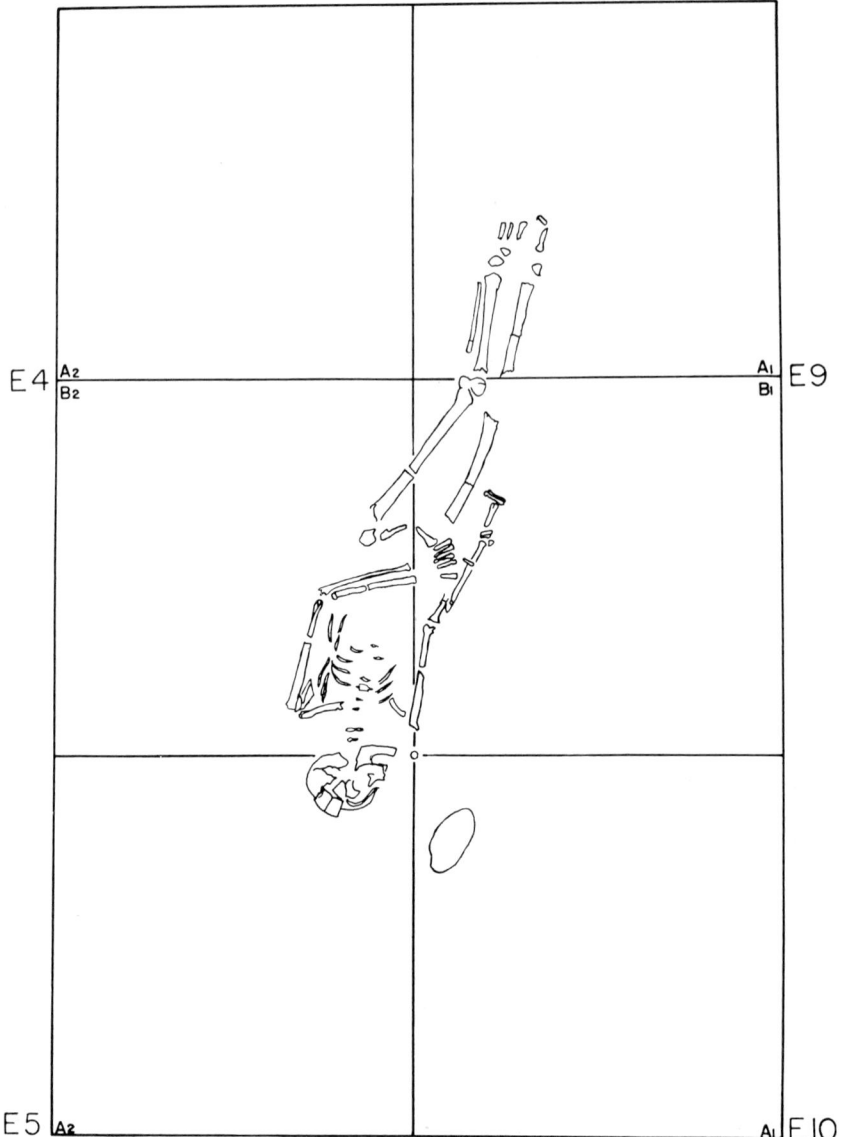

Fig. 67. V-M1: Lungshanoid Human Burial at Locus V, Fengpitou. (Upper side of figure is north; side of each square is 1 m.)

overlain by a clear and compact horizon of gray potsherds that shows no evidence of being intruded into by modern agricultural activities.

The skeleton (Fig. 67; Pl. 5, *A*) measures approximately 168 cm *in situ*. The head points toward the south and uphill, and rests on its right side, thus facing east. The skull (Pls. 103, 104) is almost complete but was crushed flat by pressure from above. The postcranial skeleton is nearly complete and was placed on the dorsal side in an extended posture in a south–north axis, slightly toward the east, and the ground on which the body rests has a slight gradient from the south to the north. The right arm is alongside the trunk, but the left arm is placed above the trunk with the left hand resting above the right wrist. The whole skeleton is surrounded by potsherds, animal bones, and other items of trash, and neither grave pit nor grave goods were recognized. The bones are dark ashy gray in color, and are so highly mineralized that practically the entire body would be needed for a carbon-14 determination. Since the *in situ* context is clear and there is no problem about the age, the first Lungshanoid skeleton that has so far been found in Southeast China south of Nanking has been left intact except for the two tibiae that were crushed (without providing a date) at the Radiocarbon Laboratory of Yale University.

The bones were placed in the custody of Mr. Hsü Tse-min of the Physical Anthropological Laboratory of the Institute of History and Philology, Academia Sinica, and his preliminary report appears in Appendix 2. The skeleton is apparently that of a male of advanced age, which in general exhibits Oceanic Mongoloid features.

Temporal Variations

Despite the fact that the material described above characterizes a single culture, the Lungshanoid occupation of the site at Fengpitou lasted for approximately 2,000 years. During this period marked or slight changes took place in both single items of material culture and their configurations. Each artifactual feature in archeology may be regarded as an empirical manifestation of a continuous and continuously moving behavioral tradition at a single fixed point of time, and at each point it assumes both a temporal (diachronic) and a contemporary (synchronic) dimension. The cultural and social change of a given unit of culture is the sum total of the archeological variations considered in the perspective of their temporal dimensions, both individually and in concert.

The complexity of the site of Fengpitou—the various parts of the site were occupied during different time intervals and have divergent contents—calls for a synchronized sequence of the site as a whole before consideration in either dimension of the artifactual variations can be reliably and meaningfully undertaken. This has been attempted in Chapter 2; the cultural sequence shown in Table 4 will provide the synchronic basis for the present study. Briefly, four temporal segments are distinguished, I–IV, designated respectively as Fine Red, Sandy Red, Lower Shellmound, and Upper Shellmound. Various types and modes of artifacts, as characterized above, did not occur in all segments, and the pattern of their occurrence and association differs from one segment to the next. Analysis will proceed from inidividual artifact types to their configurational occurrence.

THIN HOE-AXES

As shown in Table 6, two types of hoe-axes persisted throughout the Lungshanoid occupation, namely, the flat and the spatula-shaped types. Slate gained in popu-

TABLE 6. TEMPORAL DISTRIBUTION OF LUNGSHANOID STONE HOE-AX TYPES AT FENGPITOU

| | Flat | | | | | | Spatula-shaped | Perforated | Chipped | Large |
| | Basalt | | | Slate | | | | | | |
	Fragments	Symmetrical	Asymmetrical	Fragments	Symmetrical	Asymmetrical				
Surface	2	2	2		1		4		4	4
IV	3		1	1	3	1	12	2	2	2
III	2		1		1	1	1	1		
II	18	5	2			1	1	1	1	
I	13	2	2			2	7			

TABLE 7. TEMPORAL DISTRIBUTION OF LUNGSHANOID SLATE
KNIVES AT FENGPITOU

	Rectangular	Saddle-shaped	Semilunar	Leaf-shaped
Surface	1		3	3
IV	4	1	4	1
III				
II	1		4	
I	6		1	

larity as material for making the flat hoe-axes in later periods as opposed to basalt, but no significant change in shape can be discerned.

Perforated hoe-axes first appeared in segment II and then persisted to the end, but both the large and the chipped types are apparently segment IV innovations.

ADZES

Small adz-axes and chisels occur sporadically and throughout. Large adzes were made of four rocks: silicified greenrock, basalt, slate, and serpentine. Except for serpentine, which was used only in segment I for this purpose, neither preference of raw material nor shape underwent significant change during the occupation.

BOOT-SHAPED KNIFE

Unique occurrence of this type is in segment I.

HARVESTING KNIVES

Table 7 shows that both rectangular and semilunar (with straight cutting edge and curved back) types occurred side by side throughout the Lungshanoid occupation, but new shapes appeared in segment IV, including one saddle-shaped piece and several leaf-shaped specimens (both cutting edge and back are curved).

Stone Arrowheads

For the purpose of temporal analysis, five types of stone arrowheads are distinguished: perforated, triangular, broad-stemmed, narrow-stemmed, and leaf-shaped. Table 8 shows that triangular (with or without perforation) and broad-stemmed types are the earliest to occur, followed by leaf-shaped types, and segment IV witnesses the peak of leaf-shaped type and the appearance of the narrow-stemmed arrowheads.

Swords and Halberds

Of the four halberd pieces, one was collected on the surface, two were found *in situ* from segment I, and the remaining piece from segment IV. One sword piece came from segment III and two from segment IV. Apparently these weapons, broadly speaking, were characteristic of the later levels.

Miscellaneous Stones

Hammerstones and polishing stones are found throughout the Lungshanoid occupation. One net sinker came from segment II, and three waisted pebbles were found from segment I.

Stone and Shell Ornaments

Table 9 shows that the occurrence of the various kinds of ornaments is rather random, although greater use of shell for ornaments is seen in segment IV than previously.

Clay Rings

In pit 3 of Locus K, where the longest sequence of the site was uncovered, there are sufficient data on the typology and stratification of clay rings—bracelets and anklets—to indicate that segments I, II, and III are characterized by thin rings, but that segment IV is distinguished by the abrupt emergence of long clay tubes. Toward the end of the occupation, tubes all but replaced rings (Table 10). This sequence is confirmed by tabulations from Locus N (Table 11). At Locus P, where only remains of segments I and II were found, there is no evidence of clay tubes.

TABLE 8. TEMPORAL DISTRIBUTION OF LUNGSHANOID STONE
ARROWHEADS AT FENGPITOU

	Triangular Perforated	Triangular Unperforated	Broad Stemmed	Willow-Leaf	Narrow Steamed
Surface		2	4	4	5
IV		3	4	13	2
III					
II		1		4	
I	2	1	2		

TABLE 9. TEMPORAL DISTRIBUTION OF TYPES OF LUNGSHANOID ORNAMENTS AT FENGPITOU

	Jade and Serpentine					Shell		
	Button	Ring	Bead	Figurine	?	Button	Ring	Perforated
IV	3	2			1	2	3	2
III					1			
II	1	1	1			1		
I	1			1	1			

TABLE 10. DISTRIBUTION BY LAYER OF TYPES OF CLAY RINGS IN PIT 3, LOCUS K, AT FENGPITOU

	Gray-Black-Brown Ware												Red Ware				
	Long		Broad		Round		Double-round		Flat		Square		Broad		Round		Total (712)
	(no.)	(%)	(no.)	(%)	(no.)	(%)	(no.)	(%)	(no.)	(%)	(no.)	(%)	(no.)	(%)	(no.)	(%)	
IV																	
CL	96	75.59	4	3.15	24	18.90	3	2.36									127
L1a	77	91.67			5	5.95			1	1.19					1	1.19	84
1b	109	93.97	6	5.17	1	0.86											116
1c	60	92.31			5	7.69											65
1d	66	89.19			7	9.46									1	1.35	74
1e	67	84.81	2	2.53	3	3.80			3	3.80					4	5.06	79
L2	90	81.82	7	6.36	9	8.18			3	2.73					1	0.91	110
L3a	4	19.05	7	33.33	5	23.81	1	4.76	4	19.05							21
3b	2	7.69	8	30.77	10	38.46	3	11.54	1	3.85	1	3.85	1	3.85			26
III																	
3c					2				1								3
3d			1		1				1								3
3e					1		1		1								3
II																	
3f			1														1
3g																	
3h																	
I																	
3i																	

BONE, ANTLER, AND SHELL OBJECTS

Bone, antler, and shell implements were found from segments III and IV only, namely, from the shellmound layers, with a single exception. Table 12 shows that these objects are greater in number and more complex in typology in segment IV than in III.

TABLE 11. DISTRIBUTION BY LAYER OF TYPES OF CLAY RINGS IN PIT B, LOCUS N, AT FENGPITOU

	Gray-Black Ware						Red Ware	Total (205)
	Round		Broad		Long			
	(no.)	(%)	(no.)	(%)	(no.)	(%)		
IV								
L1b			8	*53.33*	7	*46.67*		15
1c			18	*42.86*	24	*57.14*		42
1d			30	*60.00*	20	*40.00*		50
III								
L2a			13	*72.22*	5	*27.78*		18
2b			14	*66.67*	7	*33.33*		21
2c	9	*27.27*	16	*48.48*	8	*24.24*		33
2d	7	*50.00*	4	*28.57*	3	*21.43*		14
2e			1		1			2
II								
I								
L3as							1	1
3a	3		3					6
3b	2		1					3

CLAY SPINDLE WHORLS AND OTHER OBJECTS

Top-like spindle whorls of clay were found throughout the occupation and in various areas, but segment IV has the largest variety of types (Table 13). Two clay tubes appeared in segment II, one perforated clay disk (weight?) was found in segment II and another in III, and a clay figurine came from segment IV.

POTTERY OTHER THAN PAINTED AND BLACK

The most profound and conspicuous change that took place at the site of Fengpitou within the Lungshanoid occupation concerns pottery: its paste, form, and decoration. I shall omit discussion of paste in this connection, because it has been described in Chapter 2, where it serves as one of the basic criteria for the chronological subdivision of segments I–IV.

Table 14 is a tabulation of the modes of rims and feet of the fine red sherds in Pit 3, Locus K. All basic shapes are common throughout the Lungshanoid occupation, but a significant shift occurs in the relative proportion of bowls and pots-jars: throughout segments I–III bowls number more than pots-jars, but this is reversed in segment IV. Some minor changes occur in the shape of the bowl. Curved walls were found only in the last two segments, and ridged pieces were found in II and III only. The same change in bowl–jar proportion is also noted in Pit E8 of Locus P.

TABLE 12. TEMPORAL DISTRIBUTION OF TYPES OF LUNGSHANOID BONE, ANTLER, AND SHELL IMPLEMENTS AT FENGPITON

| | Chisel | Polished antler | Awl | Graver | Projectile Points | | | | | Shell implements | Fish vertebrates |
					Deep-notched harpoon	Notched harpoon	Narrow-stemmed point	Triangular point	Broad-stemmed point		
Surface		S(1)	S(3) U(1) V(1)					K(1)			
IV	K(5) N(1) S(4) V(2)	V(1)	K(7) N(2) S(4) V(7)	N(1)		N(2) S(1) V(2)	K(2) S(2) V(1)	K(3) V(1)	V(1)	K(3)	K(1)
III			K(1) N(3) V(2)	N(1)	V(1)						V(1)
II	K(1)										
I											

TABLE 13. TEMPORAL DISTRIBUTION OF TYPES OF LUNGSHANOID CLAY SPINDLE WHORLS AT FENGPITOU

	Type 1	Type 2	Type 3
Surface	P(1), U(1), V(3)		U(1), V(1)
IV	B(1), K(1), S(1), V(4)	K(1)	
III	N(1), V(3)		
II	K(3), P(2)		
I	P(1), V(1)		

In P-E8, from Layers 3a, 3b, 2c–f of segment 1, among the 437 fine red sherds, 147 (33.64%) are jar sherds and 232 (53.09%) are bowl sherds. Among the 59 fine red sherds from Layers 2a and 2b of segment III, only 14 are bowl sherds (23.73%), and jar sherds increase to 24 (40.68%). It will be shown below that in the two sandy wares—red and gray—there are invariably more pots and jars than bowls. The increase in fine red ware must be accounted for by the greater need for storage containers than serving vessels.

TABLE 14. DISTRIBUTION BY LAYER OF POTTERY MODES IN THE FINE RED WARE IN PIT 3, LOCUS K, FENGPITOU

	Lid	Cup	Bowl A	B	C	D	E	F	G	H	Dish	Pot-Jar A	B	C	D	E	F	G	H	I	Leg	Ring Foot
IV																							
CL			1	3				6						7					1	1			
1a						1	1					1								1			
b		1					1							2				8		1			
c				1												1							
d		1				1	5													2			
e			1			1								1									
2			1	1							2	2		3					3				
3a				1		3		1	1		1			2	1								
b		1		5					2		6							1				1	
III																							
3c			1											2			1						
d				4				1			1											1	
e			5	14	1		1	1		1		1		9			1			1			
II																							
3f		1	4	5			4			1				11			1	2					2
g				17			1	1			3			1		10							
h	1					10								4			6		1				
I																							
3i			3	1								1							2				2

Bowl — A B C D E F G H

Pot-Jar — A B C D E F G H I

In the tabulations for sandy red (Table 15) and sandy gray (Table 16) shapes, it is noted that no drastic change took place.

In decoration, some significant changes are discernible. Table 17 indicates the relative occurrence frequencies of various decorative techniques throughout pit 3 of Locus K. In both the red and gray series there is a consistent decrease of impressed sherds as opposed to plain sherds. Incised sherds are few compared with the total, but within itself there is a marked increase of incised pieces in segment IV. Among the impressed sherds, cord and check patterns decrease from early to late levels, but basket-impressed pieces increase. At Locus B (Table 18), placed within segment IV on grounds of ceramic paste, there is a predominance of basket-impressed patterns, a fact confirming its contemporaneity with the segment IV levels in K. The decrease of impressed pieces in the total sherd count is also confirmed by the tabu-

TABLE 15. DISTRIBUTION BY LAYER OF POTTERY MODES IN THE SANDY RED WARE IN PIT 3, LOCUS K, FENGPITOU

	Lid		Bowl			Pot-Jar				Ring Foot
	A	B	A	B	C	A	B	C	D	
IV										
CL	3						51			
1a	4		1			1	80			1
b		2	12			13	96		1	
c		7	7	5			39			1
d			7		1		72			
e	1		7				63			2
2	1		10	1			118			1
3a		3	5				46			2
b	2	1	24			4	135			
III										
3c			10			1	37			5
d			7				59			1
e			8				38			
II										
3f	1						32		1	7
g	1		8				33			2
h			1					2		
I										
3i										1

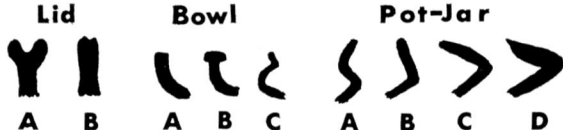

lation of sherds from Locus N (Table 19), but here basket impressions are consistently abundant for the sandy gray ware, although in the sandy red ware, check pattern prevailed in the beginning and basket pattern increased toward the end. The relative proportion of basket and check impressions in P (Table 20) again places this locus with segments I and II of K. In Locus V (Table 21), exactly the same changes are noted with reference to pottery decoration: (1) from segments I to IV there is a consistent decrease of impressed sherds; (2) the major categories of impressed patterns are the same throughout the site's occupation; (3) cord impressions were conspicuous in segment I but declined afterward; (4) basket impressions are the leading pattern for the sandy gray ware and increase in frequency of occurrence in sandy red; (5) check impressions constitute an appreciable percentage in segment I in sandy red, but are gradually squeezed out by the ever-increasing basket impressions; (6) incised sherds are a minority of the decorated pieces but their oc-

TABLE 16. DISTRIBUTION BY LAYER OF POTTERY MODES IN THE SANDY GRAY WARE IN PIT 3, LOCUS K, FENGPITOU

| | Lid | Beaker | Bowl | | Pot-Jar | | Ring Foot |
			Regular Rim	Thickened Rim	Inverted Rim	Regular Rim	
IV							
CL					1	13	
1a						7	
b		1	1		1	15	
c						8	
d						15	
e				2		15	
2	1	2	3			3	1
3a		1	2			14	1
b	4	2	3			52	1
III							
3c	1	2	27			62	
d		1	8	2		28	2
e		1	11			73	
II							
3f		1				35	3
g	1		1			18	
h			1				
I							
3i						1	

currence significantly increases during segment IV (Table 22); and (7) finally, in segment IV are several rim sherds on which apparent signs were incised, a feature nonexistent heretofore.

BLACK POTTERY

As shown in Table 23, the beautifully polished, thin black pottery is characteristic of the shellmound layers (segments III and IV), whereas only three sherds of this ware were recovered from segment II in pit 3, Locus K. Of the four major forms of vessels (beaker, bowl-dish, high-collared pot, and low-collared pot), the beaker and the low-collared pot were the first to emerge, the proportion of serving vessels as against storage vessels is consistently high, and segment III saw the climax of the beaker and segment IV the peak of the bowl-dish.

In decoration, Table 24 shows that the number of decorated black sherds increased, as against plain sherds, during the final segment. Of the four major categories of decorative designs (A, rows of engraved short horizontal parallel lines; B, pairs and wavy rows of short incisions; C, zoned long parallel lines; D, short oblique incisions in clusters below the rim), A was the earliest to occur, in segment II, and

TABLE 17. DISTRIBUTION OF MAJOR CATEGORIES OF DECORATIVE PATTERNS IN THE SANDY RED AND GRAY WARES IN PIT 3, LOCUS K, FENGPITOU*

	I	II	III	IV
Sandy Red				
Plain	61	989	918	11,329
	(57.55%)	(60.67%)	(62.32%)	(71.52%)
Wheel marks	10	169	158	685
	(9.43%)	(10.37%)	(10.73%)	(4.32%)
Incised		5	2	125
		(0.31%)	(0.14%)	(0.79%)
Impressed				
Cord	35	238	46	569
	100.00%	*50.96%*	*11.65%*	*15.37%*
Basket		103	223	2,918
		22.06%	*56.46%*	*78.84%*
Mat		33	25	27
		7.07%	*6.33%*	*0.73%*
Checker		93	101	187
		19.91%	*25.57%*	*5.05%*
Total	35	467	395	3,701
	(33.01%)	(28.65%)	(26.82%)	(23.36%)
Total	106	1,630	1,473	15,840
Sandy Gray				
Plain	14	465	1,997	5,532
	(100.00%)	(61.18%)	(66.83%)	(74.25%)
Wheel marks		42	91	98
		(5.53%)	(3.05%)	(1.32%)
Incised				26
				(0.35%)
Impressed				
Cord		3	1	40
		1.19%	*0.11%*	*2.23%*
Basket		101	637	1,388
		39.92%	*70.78%*	*77.33%*
Mat		4	5	3
		1.58%	*0.56%*	*0.17%*
Checker		145	257	364
		57.31%	*28.56%*	*20.28%*
Total		253	900	1,795
		(33.29%)	(30.12%)	(24.09%)
Total	14	760	2,988	7,451

* By number of potsherds.

TABLE 18. NUMBER AND PERCENTAGES OF VARIOUS DECORATIVE PATTERNS IN THE SANDY RED AND GRAY WARES IN PIT 1, LOCUS B, FENGPITOU

Sandy Red						Sandy Gray						
Plain	Incised	Impressed			Total	Plain	Incised	Impressed				Total
		Basket	Checker	Total				Cord	Basket	Checker	Total	
6,758	25	256	25	281	7,064	4,299	17	5	174	26	205	4,521
(95.67%)	(0.35%)	*91.10%*	*8.90%*	(3.98%)		(95.09%)	(0.38%)	*2.44%*	*84.88%*	*12.68%*	(4.58%)	

TABLE 19. DISTRIBUTION OF VARIOUS DECORATIVE PATTERNS IN THE FINE RED, SANDY RED, AND SANDY GRAY WARES IN PIT B, LOCUS N, FENGPITOU*

	Layer 1	Layer 2	Layer 3
Fine Red Ware			
Plain	176 (82.63%)	456 (59.69%)	279 (50.36%)
Wheel marks	1 (0.47%)	29 (3.80%)	23 (4.15%)
Incised	2 (0.94%)		3 (0.54%)
Impressed			
Cord	34 *100.00%*	270 *96.77%*	249 *100.00%*
Mat		9 *3.23%*	
Total	34 (15.96%)	279 (36.52%)	249 (44.95%)
Total	213	764	554
Sandy Red Ware			
Plain	2,874 (82.73%)	2,236 (74.06%)	518 (78.72%)
Wheel marks	9 (0.26%)	35 (1.16%)	1 (0.15%)
Incised	9 (0.26%)	4 (0.13%)	7 (1.06%)
Impressed			
Cord	41 *7.03%*	85 *11.42%*	30 *22.73%*
Mat	22 *3.77%*	38 *5.11%*	8 *6.06%*
Basket	396 *67.92%*	425 *57.12%*	32 *24.24%*
Checker	124 *21.27%*	196 *26.34%*	62 *46.97%*
Total	583 (16.78%)	744 (24.64%)	132 (20.06%)
Total	3,475	3,019	658
Sandy Gray Ware			
Plain	1,511 (74.76%)	3,890 (68.97%)	503 (67.97%)
Wheel marks	5 (0.25%)	21 (0.37%)	6 (0.81%)
Incised	6 (0.30%)	1 (0.02%)	
Impressed			
Cord	1 *0.20%*	7 *0.41%*	3 *1.30%*
Mat	3 *0.60%*	13 *0.75%*	2 *0.87%*
Basket	328 *65.73%*	1,354 *78.36%*	168 *72.72%*
Checker	167 *33.47%*	354 *20.49%*	58 *25.11%*
Total	499 (24.69%)	1,728 (30.64%)	231 (31.22%)
Total	2,021	5,640	740

* By number of potsherds.

TABLE 20. CONTRAST IN AMOUNT OF IMPRESSED DECORATIVE PATTERNS BETWEEN THE LOWER AND UPPER STRATA IN PIT E-3, LOCUS P, FENGPITOU*

	Fine Red Ware		Sandy Gray Ware				
	Plain	Impressed Cord	Plain	Impressed			
				Cord	Basket	Checker	Total
Upper stratum	11,409	2,305 16.81%	11,403	62 4.55%	545 39.96%	757 55.50%	1,364
Lower stratum	9,750	2,500 20.41%	1,043				

* By weight of potsherds in grams.

TABLE 21. DISTRIBUTION OF VARIOUS DECORATIVE PATTERNS IN THE FINE RED, SANDY RED, AND SANDY GRAY WARES IN PIT W-3, LOCUS V, FENGPITOU*

	Layer 1	Layer 2	Layer 3
Fine Red Ware			
Plain	125 (81.17%)	858 (79.52%)	1,724 (61.46%)
Wheel marks	1 (0.65%)		
Impressed			
Cord	27 96.43%	168 76.02%	1,025 94.82%
Mat	1 3.57%	53 23.98%	56 5.18%
Total	28 (18.18%)	221 (20.48%)	1,081 (38.54%)
Total	154	1,079	2,805
Sandy Red Ware			
Plain	199 (63.58%)	527 (68.26%)	1,984 (89.21%)
Incised	2 (0.64%)		
Impressed			
Cord	2 1.79%	5 2.04%	22 9.17%
Mat	2 1.79%	4 1.63%	9 3.75%
Basket	84 75.00%	91 37.14%	71 29.58%
Checker	24 21.43%	145 59.18%	138 57.50%
Total	112 (35.78%)	245 (31.74%)	240 (10.79%)
Total	313	772	2,224
Sandy Gray Ware			
Plain	498 (71.55%)	5,049 (66.74%)	1,400 (54.26%)
Incised		1 (0.01%)	
Impressed			
Cord	3 1.52%	8 0.32%	5 0.42%
Mat	1 0.51%	6 0.24%	2 0.17%
Basket	133 67.17%	2,095 83.30%	1,006 85.25%
Checker	61 30.81%	406 16.14%	167 14.15%
Total	198 (28.45%)	2,515 (33.25%)	1,180 (45.74%)
Total	696	7,565	2,580

* By number of potsherds.

TABLE 22. OCCURRENCE OF INCISED DECORATIONS ON POTTERY OF
THE SANDY RED WARE IN PIT 3, LOCUS K, FENGPITOU*

	Bowl: Incised Lip	Low-Rim Jar-Pot: rows of short incised strokes on lip and at root of collar	High Rim Jar-Pot: rows of short incised strokes on lip and at root of collar	High Rim Jar-Pot: incised lip only	Incised Body Sherds
IV	38	21	57	2	8
III		1			
II	1				
I					

* By number of potsherds.

TABLE 23. OCCURRENCE OF VARIOUS VESSEL FORMS IN THE BLACK
WARE IN PIT 3, LOCUS K, FENGPITOU

	Beaker	Low Rim Jar-Pot	High Rim Jar-Pot	Bowl
IV	9	2	8	26
	20.00%	*4.44%*	*17.78%*	*57.78%*
III	13		1	3
	76.47%		*5.88%*	*17.65%*
II	2	1		
I				

B followed in segment III. The other two were all segment IV innovations, and, within segment IV, D was the latest to appear.

PAINTED POTTERY

Table 25 and Figure 68 indicate that the painted pottery occurred in all four temporal segments of the Lungshanoid culture, although its presence did not become conspicuous until segment III. Only two painted sherds (of beakers) appear in segment I and only one (of jar) in segment II throughout the site. Then painted pottery blossomed fully and dramatically in the Lower and Upper Shellmound segments, even more elaborate and complex in the upper than in the lower. In individual elements of design, whorls and parallel lines appeared first. In overall composition, beakers were always completely decorated on the exterior, but whorls were more popular on beakers during segments I III and on jars during segment IV. Other contrasts between III and IV are notable in Figure 68.

CONFIGURATIONAL CHANGES

According to the analyses of temporal variations of individual artifacts as well as changes in settlement data, the following conclusions appear to be justified: (1) the Lungshanoid occupation is characterized by a single and continuous culture tradition, and (2) during the occupation at the site of Fengpitou a series of interrelated changes

TABLE 24. DISTRIBUTION BY LAYER OF PRINCIPAL INCISED AND ENGRAVED DECORATIVE
PATTERNS ON BLACK POTTERY IN PIT 3, LOCUS K, FENGPITOU*

	A. Vertical rows of short horizontal engraved lines on beaker (Pl. 48)	B. Rows of punctates on lip and below rim of bowls (Pl. 46, *A,D,H*)	C. Zonal rectangles and lozenges of incised lines on beakers (Pl. 49)	D. Clusters of short incised lines on outside of rim of bowls (Pl. 46, *C,E*)
IV				
1a				
1b			1	2
1c	1	3		1
1d	1		1	
1e			4	
2	2	4	2	
3a		8	2	
3b		5		
III				
3c	1			
3d		3		
3e	2			
II				
3f				
3g	1			
3h				
I				
3i				

* By number of potsherds.

took place which subdivides the total occupation into four settlements. The configurational characterization of each of the settlements can be stated as follows.

The Fine Red Ware Settlement (ca. 2400–1900 B.C.). When the Lungshanoid people arrived at the site of Fengpitou in the middle of the third millennium B.C., they found a bare hill which had been uninhabited for a long time. They quickly occupied the entire hill, except for the western third. The major area of occupation was apparently the top of the terrace and the northern slopes; the southern, seaward slopes have yielded relatively thin and scattered remains. Apparently the people's living was based mainly on farming and hunting, for the marine resources were not yet tapped. No shellmounds are located.

Agriculture was apparently the principal mode of subsistence. Flat hoe-axes are abundant, most made of basalt which is not produced locally but appears to have originated in the Pescadores. Another probable cultivating implement is the spatula-shaped hoe-axe of slate. Adzes of greenrock, slate, basalt, and serpentine were rectangular and of excellent workmanship. Implements with a lateral (as opposed to terminal) cutting edge include a single boot-shaped knife (*hache pédiforme*) and a number of slate knives. The latter were probably harvesting knives and include both rectangular and semilunar varieties.

TABLE 25. DISTRIBUTION OF MAJOR DESIGN ELEMENTS OF THE PAINTED POTTERY DECORATION IN PIT 3, LOCUS K, FENGPITOU*

	Hooks and Spirals	Hooks Below Horizontal Lines	Groups of Straight Lines	Short Strokes on Interior Rim	Chevrons Probably on Ring Foot	Cross-Hatching	Groups of Dots	Cross-Hatching, Groups of Lines	Total Sherds with Identifiable Decor Elements by Layer
IV									
C1		1		1			1		3
1a									—
b			1			1	4	2	8
c			3			2		1	6
d			6		1		4	1	12
e	1	2	20	1	2	2	10		38
2	1	2	23	2			11		39
3a		5	4	1			1		11
b			1				1		2
III									
3c			8		1				9
d			4		1	1			6
e	1		2	1					4
II									
3f			2						2
g			2						2
h		1							1
I									
3i	1								1

* By number of potsherds.

A house was located at the eastern end of the terrace top. It is about 4.5 m wide and of undetermined length, with raised floors and entrance at one end. Probably it was a timber structure constructed on wooden piles.

No remains of bone, antler, or shell implements were found. Top-shaped spindle whorls of clay are abundant. Personal ornaments consist of jade-serpentine buttons, rings, and beads and clay rings. There is a single piece of a figurine carved of serpentine, and a small jade adz.

In pottery, the predominant ware is the fine red. Its shapes include bowls (the most abundant), pots, jars, and beakers. Ring feet are important, producing *tou* stands with cut-out holes characteristic of the Lungshanoid. *Ting* tripods also occurred. The primary decorative treatment of this ware is cord impression. Sandy red and gray wares occurred also, and the leading shape is the pot or jar, but there are also bowls in significant numbers. Lids and pedestals both occur. Cord impressions are abundant in these wares, and there are also impressed check and basket designs. Two painted sherds are found: one a small beaker with painted hooks or

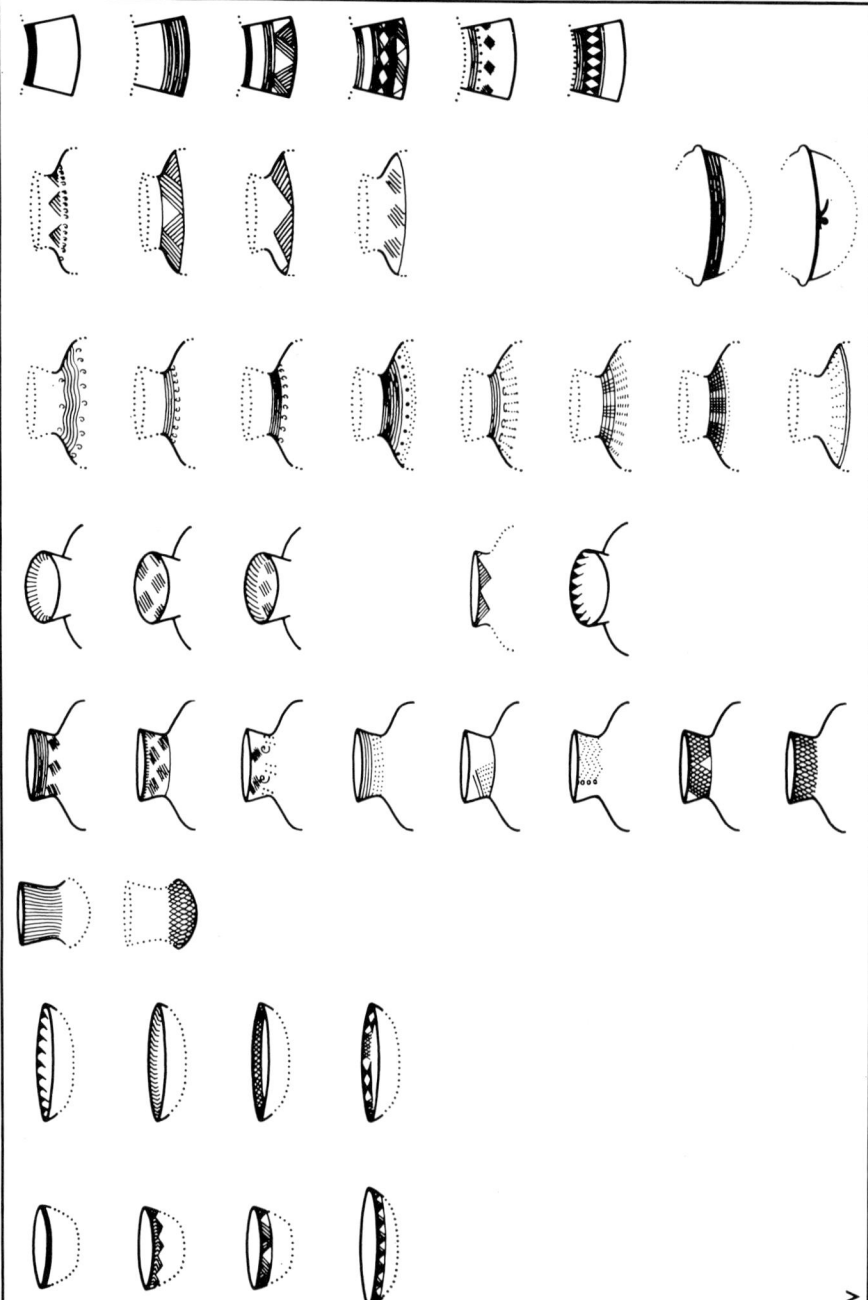

FIG. 68. Painted Decorative Designs on Pottery at the Four Lungshanoid Settlements at Fengpitou.

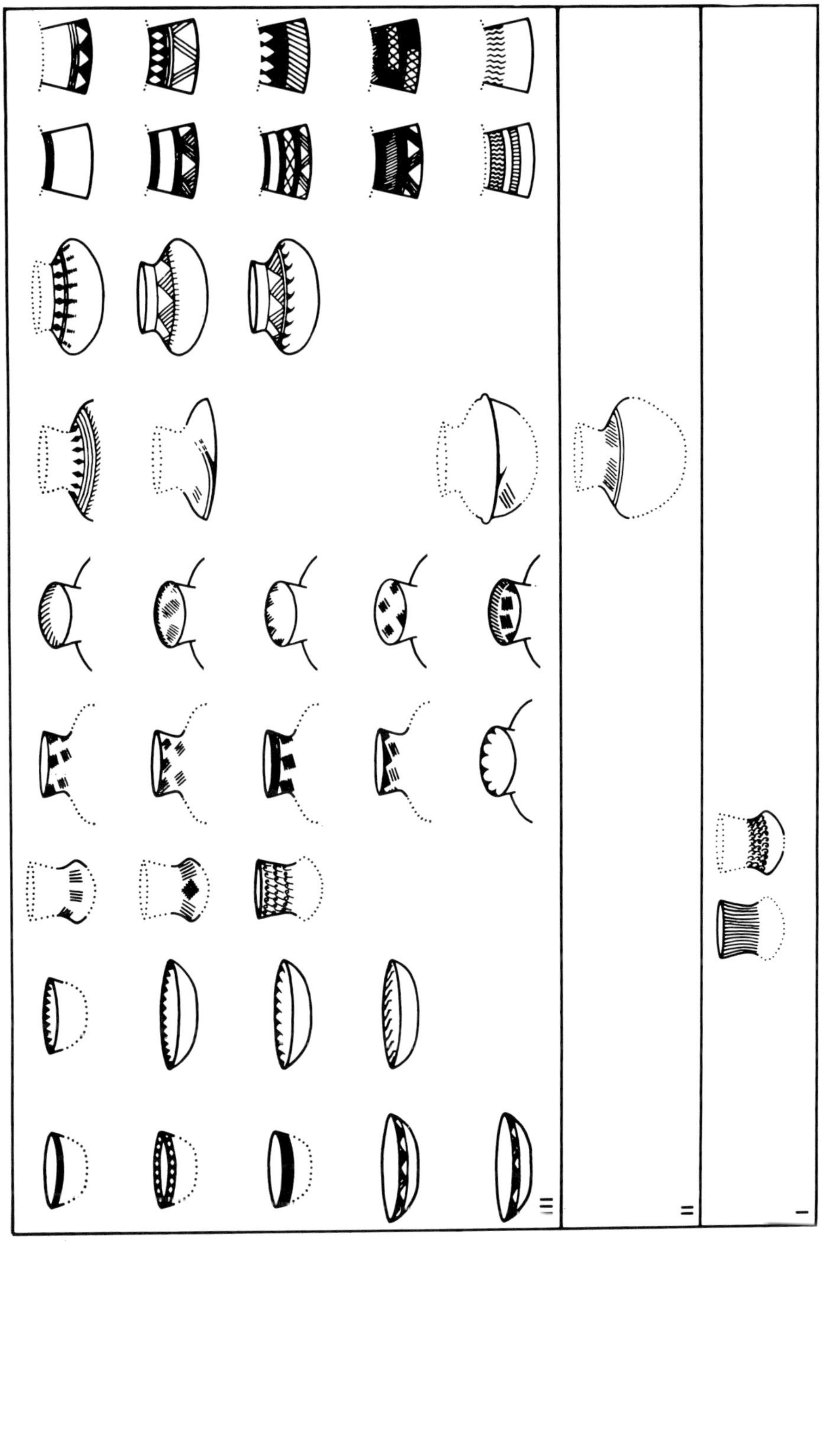

FIG. 68—*Continued.*

whorls on the exterior, and the other a small beaker with painted parallel lines vertical from rim to bottom. No burnished black pottery is in evidence. If we distinguish between storage and serving wares—the former being jars and the latter bowls and beakers—then it is clear that the sandy red and gray pottery was made mainly for storage purposes, and the serving bowls and beakers were made in the fine red ware and only occasionally of painted pottery.

The Sandy Red Ware Settlement (ca. 1900–1400 B.C.). This component is best defined at loci K and P, namely, the center of the southern slope and the eastern end of the top, whereas at other parts of the site only traces of it have been located. At both N and V there is a distinct break between the red ware layers below and the shellmound layers above, but at K and P an intermediate layer occurs before the shellmound began to accumulate but in which sandy red ware (rather than fine red) already predominated. Apparently, activities were somewhat restricted during this period, although the same culture continued.

Flat and spatula-shaped hoe-axes continued, but new types of hoe-axes occurred, including both chipped and perforated types. Rectangular adzes of various kinds continued. The same types of arrowheads continued, but leaf-shaped forms appear. Semilunar slate knives increased. The technological, industrial, and ornamental remains continued, but bone implements and shell ornaments appear in small numbers.

All major wares continued, but sandy red ware was leading, impressed sherds decreased, and among the impressed pieces basket patterns increased. Another significant change is the increase of elaborate serving pottery. Painted pottery continued, and the painting with group instruments occurred for the first time. Burnished black pottery occurred for the first time, in the shapes of beakers and bowls. Some of the black beakers have vertical rows of incised and engraved short strokes.

The Lower Shellmound Settlement (1400–900 B.C.). The site during this period exhibits profound changes from the previous stage. Habitation was apparently concentrated along both the north and the south slopes, whereas the top of the terrace has relatively little cultural remains. This could be the result of truncation of the hilltop, but it must at least be partially accounted for by the growing emphasis upon the marine and riverine resources surrounding the hill. A burial area is located on the northern slope of the hill.

Stone implements probably involving agriculture continued—flat, spatula-shaped, and perforated hoe-axes—as well as rectangular adzes. Neither slate knives nor arrowheads have been found, but this is surely accidental. For the first time, large quantities of shells appeared in the trash area. The species of mollusks are few—with oysters and clams predominant—and the individual mollusks are large in size. Presumably this resource was only beginning to be exploited.

A growing number of bone and antler implements was recovered from the site. Bone artifacts include harpoons. The other aspects of the technological, industrial, and ornamental features remained the same.

In pottery, the same wares persisted, but sandy gray ware replaced sandy red as the leading component. Basket impressions surpassed all other kinds of impressions in quantity. Black pottery continued and increased, and jars and pots appeared in addition to bowls and beakers. Aside from the incised line rows, comb incisions were applied to the lips and rims of the bowls. The most noticeable feature in ceramic change is the great increase of painted pottery, which indicates a growing elaboration of serving wares as well as a growing importance of the storage jars.

The Upper Shellmound Settlement (900–400 B.C.). This is the Lungshanoid climax, with the most elaborate cultural inventory and widest area of occupation. Within a period of about 500 years, cultural debris of over 2 meters accumulated, as opposed to the less than 2 meters for the previous three components (with a total of 1,500 years) combined.

Flat, spatula-shaped, and perforated hoe-axes persisted, but more chipped hoe-axes and a new type, the large hoe-ax, were added to the inventory. In addition to the rectangular and semilunar slate knives, saddle-shaped and leaf-shaped varieties obtained. In most pottery wares, jars are in greater abundance than serving pieces, indicating storage needs for grains and intensified agricultural activities.

Hunting continued, and the narrow-stemmed stone points and stemmed bone points appeared. A far greater variety of shell is recognized, and the individuals are smaller in size, suggesting either population pressure or a growing dependence upon the marine resources, or both.

Bone, antler, and shell implements increased in variety and in number. There are new types of spindle whorls. Ornaments of both jade and serpentine occur in larger quantities. Clay rings continued, but clay tubes—probably armlets and wristlets—appeared.

Sandy red pottery was most common, and incised decorations increased at the expense of impressed patterns. Among the impressed pieces the basket impressions increased at the expense of check designs. In form, the same varieties continued, but with growing variations. In both black and painted pottery the decorative designs became more elaborate, and this settlement has the greatest complexity of incisions on black pottery. In other words, the grain storage pots increased, but at the same time there was a greater elaboration in the serving ware, some of which may have specialized uses. A denser population and a growing sophistication of culture would seem to call for a growing complexity of social organization, and the increased abundance of weapons—first seen in the previous stage—and the appearance of incised signs on pottery rims are indications of the same nature.

Contemporary Variations

The archeological assemblage of a prehistoric community at a given point of time includes some essential elements of a system of culture-society and/or a series of subsystems within the total system. By studying the "contemporary variations" of artifacts and their assemblages one reconstructs the place or places each variation occupies in a larger cultural-social context and speculates on the roles it had performed in the system or subsystem. Such studies can be undertaken at this site in at least two ways. The first is the analysis of the relative quantitative or qualitative weight of each variation in the category and/or each category in the system, as well as the ways in which these categories can be constructed into a hierarchy. The second is the associational and spatial distribution of these variational attributes.

A precondition to any such study is the determination of the synchronism of the relevant variations. Obviously such studies can achieve the most significant degree of reliability at single-component sites or sites where the demarcation between components is clearly defined stratigraphically. With a thickly stratified (and continuously inhabited) site such as Fengpitou, where changes in artifacts are relatively slight both horizontally and chronologically, these studies are necessarily conceived broadly and must center on variations that are persistent through a wide range of both time and space. Each of our settlements covers a time span of approximately 500 years, which can be translated into roughly twenty generations in terms of individuals. Considering the amount of change that can be discerned in the archeological record, as far as this particular site is concerned, I think that a 500-year time bracket is sufficiently synchronic for my purpose which is to detect broad trends of social and cultural patterns but omit minor fluctuations.

The Fine Red Ware Settlement

The only available evidence of the cultural volume of each of the components is potsherds. Actual sherd account for Locus K is 366 for the Fine Red Ware Settlement; that for N is 6,027; for P, 54,950; and for V, 38,395. According to the formula proposed in the beginning of this chapter (B is to be multiplied by 2,500, K by 1,000, N by 2,000, P by 250, S by 600, and V by 500) the total sherds estimated for the entire occupation will number approximately 46 million. On the basis of restorations it can be assumed that approximately 100 sherds represent a complete vessel, and accordingly there are about 460,000 pottery vessels for this component over a period of 500 years. In other words, about 1,000 pottery vessles were broken—and presumably replaced—each year during this period. This would give some indication of the volume of people who inhabited the site, although no analogy is available for the number of pottery vessels each individual might have used (broken) during an average year.

The relative weight of each *kind* of implement can be estimated only in very general terms, since the precise use of each type of artifact is not sufficiently clear for this purpose. Among the implements for subsistence activities, 70 per cent are apparently for cultivating, 10 per cent are adzes, and 5 per cent arrowheads, percentages that undoubtedly give some indication of the relative intensity of agriculture and hunting. No fishing implements are recovered, and no mollusk shells are found at the site. Among the ornaments, those made of stone are about 5.5 per cent of the total stone artifacts, and 1.7 per cent of the clay objects (including pottery) are rings. Among the sherds with known shapes, 56 per cent are serving vessels (cups, bowls, etc.), while 44 per cent are for storage and cooking (jars and pots). All these are indicators that together point to a culture primarily based on agriculture, with a relatively low yield per capita and relatively low degree of elaboration. The workmanship of the artisans was applied generally to artifacts that were directly involved in subsistence and domestic activities.

Spatially, the culture was apparently rather homogeneous throughout the habitation area. The activities seem to have been more intensive in volume in some regions of the site (top of the terrace) than in others (slopes), but no significant variations can be discerned between different parts of the site.

The Sandy Red Ware Settlement

The volume of occupation, using the sherd count as the indication, is shown by the approximately 44 million pieces of potsherds. This is a slight decrease from the previous segment (46 million), but since the area of occupation is restricted to the top of the terrace and the center of the southern slope, the population must have had a greater density.

Among the subsistence-related implements, 72.34 per cent are cultivating implements, 14.89 per cent adzes, 10.64 per cent arrowheads, and 2.13 per cent fishing gear. This indicates that the place of hunting and fishing apparently increased relative to farming, an inference supported by the appearance of bone implements, but the accumulation of shellmounds was yet to begin. Among the pottery vessels, the storage and cooking vessels jumped to 74 per cent as opposed to serving bowls and dishes. It must be concluded that, although the cultivating implements declined in percentage among the total artifacts, the agricultural yields drastically increased. Obviously in this stage there was a marked advance in the entire cultural elaboration. Six and a half per cent of the total stone artifacts can be described as ornaments, although clay rings decreased to less than 1 per cent of the total pottery objects. Again no horizontal subdivision of the site can be made according to the spatial distribution of the cultural variables.

The Lower Shellmound Settlement

That there was a great expansion of culture during this segment is shown by the dramatic increase of sherds to approximately 111 million, just less than three times the previous volume. This means that more than 2,000 pottery vessels were possibly broken during the course of a single year at this village. The area of occupation did not expand to any significant extent; the density of population must then account for the increase in volume.

Agricultural implements are now 53.85 per cent; adzes, 30.77 per cent, and hunting implements, 15.38 per cent. Shellmounds began to accumulate. These indicate that, in addition to cultivation of plants, hunting, fishing, and shell-gathering activities became much more extensive, probably contributing to the population increase. One third of the total implements were made of bone and antler as against stone, but this could be due to the ideal preservation conditions afforded by the shellmounds. Over 7 per cent of the stone artifacts are ornaments, although clay rings are still less than 1 per cent of the total pottery. Both black and painted pottery increase in quantity. Thirty-two per cent of the pottery vessels are known to be serving ware; the other 68 per cent are for storage and cooking.

This settlement also witnessed the first indication of a well-defined community patterning. Habitation remains were scattered around the hill along both the north and the south slopes, and the only area where burial remains have been located is the central part of the northern slope. The distribution of stone, bone, and pottery artifacts does not show well-defined subdivisions within the site with regard to groups, but in painted decorations of pottery there is a very clear-cut distinction of two parallel styles, each prevailing in one half of the village. Although the painted pottery found at the site exhibits similar characteristics relating to paste, shape, and technique and general style of painted decorations, the northern half of the site— as exemplified by Locus V—is characterized by jars with lower rims, the rarity of painted designs on rims, and the bands of triangles consisting of parallel lines around the upper part of the shoulder just below the neck. The southern slopes of the site are characterized by higher rims of jars, scattered units of parallel strokes over the rims and the upper part of the body, and concentric rings and hooks and dots around the upper part of the shoulder. This southern slope style is typified by painted sherds from loci K and N; these two areas evidently are closer to each other stylistically than either is to V. There are, however, minor but consistent differences within themselves. All the hooks and whorls in the painted patterns in Locus K were painted clockwise, whereas many of the hooks in Locus N were counterclockwise. This last distinction could have been due to individual differences, although the persistence of this distinction at these areas throughout the deposits would seem to indicate group rather than individual distinction. The contrast in painted designs between V, on the one hand, and K and N, on the other, can only lead to the conclusion that the group or groups inhabiting the northern part of the village favored one substyle in pottery painting, whereas those along the southern part of the site favored another substyle.

THE UPPER SHELLMOUND SETTLEMENT

This settlement marks the peak at the site of Fengpitou in the volume of culture. No fewer than 196 million pieces of potsherds were accumulated during a period of some 500 years, and this means that as many as 3,800 pottery vessels were broken and thrown into the trash mound every year, approximately a 60 per cent increase. The area of occupation now covered the entire site, and the increase in cultural volume indicates more intensified activities as well as an absolute volume increase. As stated previously, the variety of shellfish collected increased, but the individuals were smaller in size. Shellfish were thus apparently collected on a greater scale and more indiscriminately, again indicating a larger population.

Among the subsistence-related implements, 46.91 per cent are cultivating implements, 13.58 per cent adzes, and 39.50 per cent arrowheads (of both bone and stone). A greater variety of agricultural implements was made. Apparently a growth in complexity in agricultural activities came about alongside the growing dependence upon hunting, fishing, and shellfish collecting. The bone–stone implement ratio is now more than 50 per cent. Serving wares account for 25 per cent of the total pottery vessels, and storage jars the other 75 per cent. All of these point to a highly elaborate and developed Neolithic type of culture and society. The absolute increase of both painted and black pottery, and the greater percentage of ornaments in the total artifact assemblage (13.68 per cent of stone artifacts are ornaments, and almost 3 per cent of the potsherds are clay rings) point to a greater degree of cultural elaboration than before.

The north–south subdivision within the village shown in the painted decorative patterns on pottery, first distinguished in the previous segment, continued into this stage.

Part II. Tapenkeng

Chapter 5. The Site

AT THE center of Taipei basin in the northern end of Formosa lies Taipei, the most populous city of the island, and capital of Nationalist China. The three major rivers in the basin—Keelung in the east, Hsintien in the south, and Takokan in the southwest—merge in the vicinity of Taipei to form the Tamsui River, which flows northwestward to the Formosa Strait (Fig. 91). Flanking the Tamsui Valley on both banks are two conspicuous but inactive volcanoes: Tatun on the northeast and Kuanyin on the southwest.

Tapenkeng,[1] perhaps the most important prehistoric site in the Taipei basin, is on the northern slope of the Kuanyin volcano, near the Tamsui estuary (lat. 25°09′14″N, long. 121°24′28″E, geographical coordinates 2322-11-NE, L892-UT-51R-39508293). It is in the administrative district (*hsiang*) of Pa-li, of T'ai-pei County (*Hsien*); the modern settlement closest to the site is Pei-t'ou-ts'un. About 10 km south of Pei-t'ou is the district town of Pa-li, formerly a resort featuring a stretch of sandy beach that has long been closed. Buses (of the Provincial Bus Authority) run frequently between Taipei and Pa-li, a ride of about fifty minutes, circling the Kuanyin volcano along the river on a road about half of which is paved. The village of Pei-t'ou has a flag stop. One of several trails leading to the summit begins at the flag stop. Proceeding south, there are about 800 meters of paddy fields before the trail begins to ascend (Pl. 8, *A*); 40 or 50 meters above, scattered prehistoric remains on the surface begin to be seen to the east. This has proved to be the main part of the site. West of the trail there are also prehistoric deposits, but the ground is more eroded and the remains are not extensive.

Before describing the site a brief account of the topography of this area is necessary. Kuanyin is a volcanic body at the southwestern end of the Tat'un volcanic group. It is basically conical, but its summit consists of several small peaks, the highest of which is 611.5 m above sea level. The volcanic body has a radius of 800 to 1,500 m, and its piedmont zone is extended by the Tananwan Formation of the Pleistocene period (consisting of sands and gravels, with thin layers of limonite), making a total radius of 2,000 m. Viewed from above, Kuanyin is dissected by a radial system of valleys—among which Chih-k'eng, Nei-yen-k'eng, T'ien-tzu-p'u-k'eng, Ting-liao-k'eng, Wu-shan-ting-k'eng, Mi-kou-k'eng, Kamalan-k'eng, Ta-p'en-k'eng (=Feng-kui-tou-hu-k'eng), Lao-ch'ien-k'eng (upper course), and Wu-ku-k'eng (upper course) are the most important. It is also encircled by stepped circular terraces (Fig. 69); in most places five or six terraces are distinguishable along the

---

[1] The correct romanized spelling is Ta-p'en-k'eng. *K'eng* in Chinese refers to a deep ravine-like valley in a radiating valley system surrounding a mountain. Ta-p'en-k'eng is one of these *k'eng* in the Kuanyin volcano and has been used to designate the site located on a terrace next to it.

137

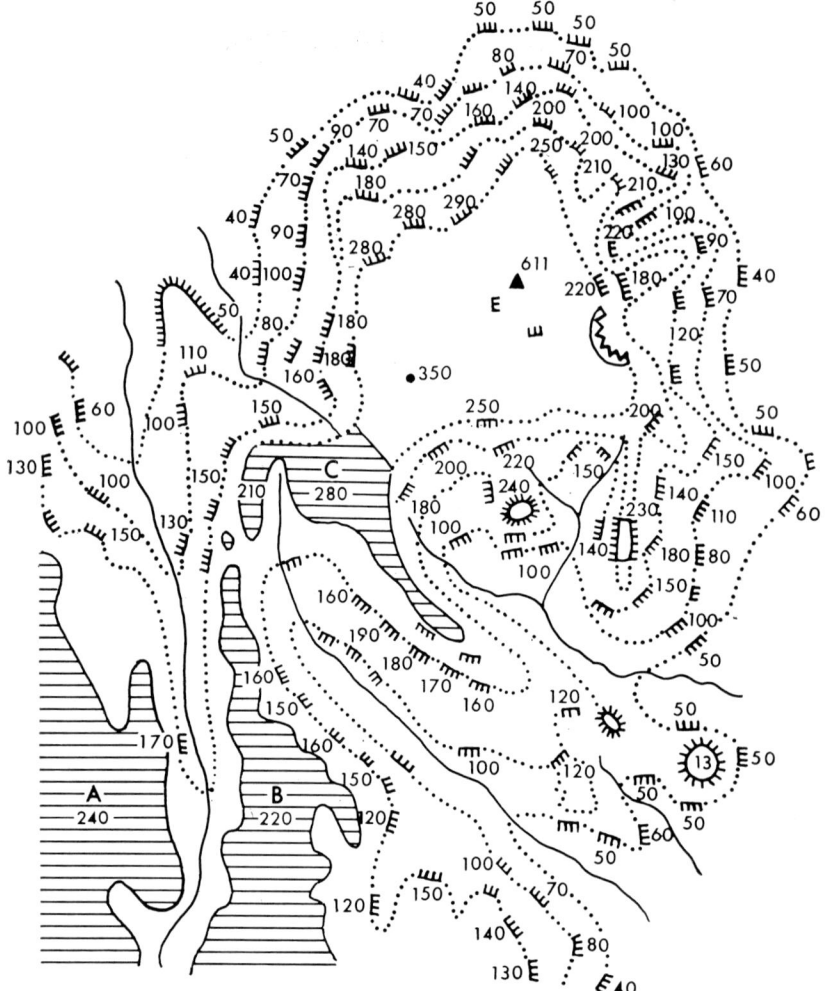

Fig. 69. Kuanyin Volcano Terraces. (Scale = 1:65,000; redrawn from C. C. Lin 1957.)

radius. The terraces observed on the northern and northwestern slopes of the Kuan-yin volcano are shown in Table 26.

The prehistoric site of Tapenkeng covers an area of approximately 500 m east–west and 350 m north–south which is divided into two terraces, Ting-p'u (or the Upper Slope) below (40–50 m in altitude) and Hsia-yüan (or the Lower Garden) above (70–80 m in altitude). Between them is a terrace scarp with a gradient of 35 to 40°, but the terraces themselves are only slightly inclined slopes. The Upper Slope belongs to Kao & Co., of Pei-t'ou village. Much of it is barren, and the rest is rented to tenant farmers who plant sweet potatoes and peanuts in small plots. The

TABLE 26. TERRACES ON WESTERN AND NORTHWESTERN SLOPES OF KUANYIN VOLCANO*

Terrace	1	2	3	4	5	6
Height						
Range (m)	10–20	40–60	40–100	130–160	190–210	260–290
Average	15	50	80	150	200	280
Foundation rocks	Tananwan Formation	Andesite and Tananwan Formation	Andesite	Andesite	Andesite	Andesite
Gravels	none	yes	yes	yes	yes	yes
Width						
Maximum (m)	400	400	350	300	150	400
Average	150	150	150	150	100	250

* Based on data supplied by C. C. Lin.

Lower Garden is owned by a Dr. Chang of Chin-shan (near Keelung on the north coast) and is looked after by his foreman Chang, a farmer, also from Pei-t'ou village in the plain. Most of the Lower Garden is covered by bamboo groves, cultivated for the shoots, and the rest is a *hsiang-ssu* tree (*Acacia confusa* Merr.) plantation. On the northern edge of the Lower Garden there is a small shrine, referred to locally as Ta-mu-kung. This small brick-and-tile structure contains a large number of animal and human bones, placed here by the farmers who encountered them in cultivating the fields and gathered them together to be sacrificed to out of deference and fear. This shrine is the only permanent structure in the general area, and we used it as the only fixed point for surveying (Fig. 70).

The Upper Slope corresponds to the second terrace of the Kuanyin terrace system, and the Lower Garden to the third terrace. Cultural remains occur on these terraces and in the regolith bed of the terrace scarp. In view of their uniform and systematic nature, these second and third terraces are considered to be coastal terraces—rather than river terraces or lava plateaus—formed by exposure as the result of periodic upheaval of the land or lowering of sea levels.

North and west of the terraces on which prehistoric remains are found is the Pa-li coastal plain (Pl. 8, *B*), which shows a zonal distribution stretching from the left bank of the Tamsui estuary in the northeast to Hung-shui-hsien-k'eng in the southwest, with a total length of 3,700 m. It is about 1,500 m wide at the northeastern and about 1,000 m wide at the southwestern end. The town of Pa-li and Pei-t'ou village are on the plain. Alluvial deposits, mainly sand and mud beds, are found on the left bank of the Tamsui River, in riverbeds in the radial valley system of the Kuanyin volcano, and in the courses of the extended rivers on the coastal plain.

The archeological investigation of Pa-li district is a recent affair. In the museum of the Department of Archaeology and Anthropology, National Taiwan University, are a few artifacts supposedly collected from this district during the Japanese occupation, but the details of their provenance are not available. Kokubu Naoichi (1944: 30–44) located a prehistoric site toward the end of World War II at Miao-hou, near the village of Tu-ch'uan-t'ou, on the left bank of Tamsui farther up from Pei-t'ou. In the winter of 1957, Professor Lin Ch'ao-ch'i of the Department of Geology, National Taiwan University, discovered the shellmound of Shih-san-hang, near the village of Ting-ku, north of Pei-t'ou and directly on the seashore. In June 1958, Mr. Sheng Ch'ing-ch'i, of the Commission for Historic Research of Taipei Prefecture, discovered the site of Tapenkeng when he revisited the Shih-san-hang site. His account of this first discovery (Sheng 1960) follows:

> On March 15th, 1956, I visited the district of Pa-li. I noticed that the northwestern slopes of Kuanyin Shan were mostly gently and slightly inclined—ideal topographical features for prehistoric occupation—and speculated on the possibility of finding some sites there. On June 28th, 1958, I went to investigate the Shih-san-hang site [discovered by Professor Lin], and went up the Kuanyin Shan to take a look. I took the trail starting from the bus flag stop and headed southeast. After a little over one half kilometer I began to climb. The slopes were wide and flat, and prehistoric remains were found along the trail. . . .
>
> Remains began to appear at an altitude of about 30 meters. At an altitude of about 40 meters many stone and ceramic remains and some ashy debris were visible on the eroded surfaces and profiles. I used my small trowel to excavate to a depth of half a meter, but the bottom of the cultural deposits was not reached. Following the trail to an altitude of from 70–100 meters, the slope became steep, and the remains fewer and eventually disappeared. The remains scattered in an area about 3–400 meters from north to south and about 250 meters from east to west, but the major concentration occurred in an area about 100 meters square in an altitude of 40 to 50 meters. Stone fragments and potsherds were encountered everywhere in the area. This was the largest site I have seen in the western part of Taipei and was the best preserved site of all.
>
> We visited the site again on June 28 and July 1, 1958, and March 5, 1959, and made extensive surface collections. The finds can be described as follows:
>
> (1) Stone implements. We collected 48 stone implements and 1 engraved piece. These include 1 stepped chisel, 1 fragment of arrow, 1 hammer, 1 ball, 2 reworked hammer-stones, 1 fragment of chipped and pecked knife, and the rest are chipped, pecked, or polished spades, hoes, and axes. The most important type seems to be the great variety of rectangular stone hoes. . . .
>
> (2) Pottery. Fifty-four pieces of potsherds have been collected, including check-impressed and basket-impressed sherds and plain sherds of white, red, and gray colors.

On March 21, 1959, the staff of the Department of Archaeology and Anthropology, Taita, undertook another surface-collection trip at the Tapenkeng site, and stone implements, potsherds, and some mollusk shells were collected, leading to the belief that this was again a shellmound site (Yang 1961). Thus the extensive nature of the site was recognized, but its details were still unknown.

The Commission for Historic Research of Taipei Prefecture undertook two seasons of excavation at Tapenkeng, and its significance became immediately apparent. The first lasted from April 17 to May 2, 1962, and the second from February 18 to March 11, 1963. In addition to Sheng and Mr. Wu Chi-jui of the Commission, Mr. Liu Pin-hsiung of the Institute of Ethnology, Academia Sinica, was invited to direct the excavations. Mr. Liu's account of the excavations follows (Liu 1964):

The first excavations on the Tapenkeng site were undertaken in April, 1962. The bamboo grove east of the Tamukung temple is designated as Excavation Area A, and the pine grove west of the temple as Excavation Area B. . . .

A shell midden area behind the temple in Excavation Area A, approximately 10 metres in diameter, was first selected for trial excavation, and eleven pits were dug . . . and the following general stratigraphy was uncovered. The topmost layer is the surface soil, with a maximum depth of 15 cm.; below this is a layer from 10 to 15 cm. deep of grayish soil containing mollusc shells. Underneath this is a layer of dark, grayish loose soil, about 40 to 50 cm. deep. This layer gradually changes into a dark, brownish soil below, around 20 cm. thick. All these strata contain a large number of potsherds and, except for the surface soil and the topmost portions of the grayish, shell-containing layer, are undisturbed. Under the dark, brownish layer is yellow-brownish sterile soil containing boulders. . . .

From the twelve trial pits opened during the first season of work at the Tapenkeng site, many cultural remains have been brought to light. . . . Among the stone implements are stepped adzes, flat chisels, polished hoes, chipped hoes, polished arrowheads, tubular beads (of soft, jadeish material), hammer-stone, stones with depressions, pillow-shaped artifacts with sockets, and grinding stones. In addition, there are iron objects (arrowheads and nails), coins, glass beads, glass rings, porcelain sherds of various ages, and many univalval and bivalval mollusc shells and animal bones. Potsherds constitute the majority of finds uncovered from the site. About half of these have plain surfaces; the other half are decorated. Those with plain surfaces or with pitted patterns were low-fired, reddish-brown or gray-brownish in colour, and with pastes and shapes similar to the ceramics of the upper stratum of the Yüanshan shell-mound. Sherds with net or checker patterns are much harder and reddish-brown, analogous to the so-called Ketagalan ware. . . .

The second season of excavation at Tapenkeng was carried out in 1963 with three aims.

i. To examine the stratified relationships of the various cultural phases at the site and the cultural contexts of mainland Chinese types, on the basis of detailed excavations, and to establish a cultural sequence in northern Taiwan and an absolute chronology;

ii. To excavate the natural and cultural remains of the shell middens in order to procure relevant data on the dating and cultural relationships of the shell-mound;

iii. To obtain a variety of cultural remains from the site to amplify our knowledge of its cultural contents.

Work began in Excavation Area C, a spot with scattered shell middens at the southern end of Tingyüan fields behind the Tamukung temple. Two trial pits, 1 m. square, were opened, but very few remains were found.

Attention was then focused on Excavation Area D, the spot locally known as Hsiayüan . . . where sweet potato was planted; there prehistoric remains were found scattered on the surface. . . .

The cultural stratum in Excavation Area D has a depth of 90 to 100 cm. and contains two different cultural phases. The upper phase is 80–90 cm. in thickness, containing gray-brownish or reddish-brown ceramics of coarse paste with plain surface, and characterized by ringfeet, handles, and clustered incisions on the handles. The most common stone implements were stepped adzes and arrowheads. This phase of the Tapenkeng culture is apparently related to similar cultural assemblages from the upper stratum of the Yüanshan shell-mound. . . .

The lower phase has a depth of approximately 10 cm. and is predominantly characterized by cord-marked potsherds. These are reddish-brown or dark brown, hand made of coarse paste, sand-tempered, and with thick and heavy walls; a few are plain, but most sherds are impressed with cord marks, and a very few exhibit basket patterns. Similar corded-ware phases have been found heretofore from the lower stratum of Yüanshan. . . .

Besides its stratification of cultural phases, the Tapenkeng site is important because of the discovery of a bronze arrowhead, the first bronze weapon from the prehistoric period to be found on the island of Taiwan. It was sifted from the earth from layer 5 (40–50 cm. deep) in D-3a [of the Upper phase]. . . .

 After the excavation of Area D was completed, Area A at Tingyüan was re-excavated. . . . The cultural phases brought to light . . . are as follows. The lowest phase is characterized by gray-brownish and reddish-brown potsherds and can be synchronized to the upper phase at Hsiayüan, described above. Both of these phases are apparently related to Yüanshan culture. Above this at Tingyüan is a phase characterized by thick, reddish-brown potsherds with checker impressions, similar to the ceramic phase identified at the Botanical Garden of Taipei city, . . . Lying above this phase is another characterized by reddish-brown, hard potsherds with net patterns, similar to those found in the upper layer of Chiang-t'ou A, . . . and the Shihsanhang shell-mound. . . . The uppermost phase of the Tingyüan site is characterized by modern potsherds and porcelain sherds of Chinese origin and is apparently of modern Chinese culture.

 Excavation Area A at Tingyüan and Area D at Hsia-yüan, at Tapenkeng, combine to make the following archeological sequence by phases:

 Fifth, modern Chinese phase (Tingyüan IV)
 Fourth, hard pottery with net patterns (Tingyüan III)
 Third, thick pottery with checker patterns (Tingyüan II)
 Second, reddish-brown pottery with plain surfaces (Tingyüan I and Hsia-yüan II)
 First, corded-ware phase (Hsia-yüan I)

From this account—as well as from personal communication—it is clear that Liu's excavation areas A, B, and C are located in the Lower Garden, and his excavation area D in the Upper Slope.[2] D has two cultural phases, corded ware and Yüanshan, and A has four, Yüan-shan, Botanical Garden, Ketangalan, and modern Chinese. These five phases of culture include all the major known cultural horizons in the Taipei area, and here they occur, according to Liu, in stratified relationship. The significance of this sequence is clearly recognized by Liu, who makes the following speculations (Liu 1964: 220):

> The two seasons of excavation at Tap'enk'eng and vicinity have produced several important discoveries. Two of them are of far-reaching significance: the stratification of no fewer than five phases of prehistoric and historic cultures, and the finding of the bronze arrowhead, coins, and other artifacts of mainland Chinese affinities.
>
> It has been known that the prehistoric cultures in northern Taiwan can be grouped into the following phases: the corded-ware phase; the phase of red-brown, coarse pottery (or the Yüanshan culture, also known as the culture of Stepped Adzes); the phase of checker-impressed pottery; and the phase of hard pottery with net patterns. The sequential order in which these different ceramic phases were introduced into northern Taiwan has long been in dispute among specialists, but in the absence of stratified sites no agreement can yet be reached. The new findings at the sites at Tap'enk'eng not only contribute a stratigraphical sequence of five different cultural phases to the prehistory of northern Taiwan, but also provide artifacts of mainland Chinese affinities that help to date some of these cultural phases in absolute years.

---

[2] Here we have a first-rate confusion. As described before, the terraces in the area are referred to by the local farmers as (from bottom up) Hsia-p'u (Lower Slope), Ting-p'u (Upper Slope), Hsia-yüan (Lower Garden), and Ting-yüan (Upper Garden). The remains occur in Ting-p'u and Hsia-yüan only. Liu erred in calling Ting-p'u Hsia-yüan, and Hsia-yüan Tingyüan. All these names in Liu's preliminary report should be so corrected. In this report, we will simply use the names Upper Slope and Lower Garden to facilitate reading.

The two important features of Tapenkeng—the stratification of several cultural phases and the occurrence of a bronze arrowhead of the Shang type—mentioned by Liu were also behind our decision to explore the site again in 1964. In selecting a site to excavate in the northern part of Formosa, we believed that Tapenkeng offered the best potential to throw light on the prehistory of the area as a whole. Our purpose was to work out a minute stratigraphy at the site in the hope that many facets of cultural change in the area might find a reliable temporal location, and also that a series of carbon-14 dates would help erect an absolute chronological framework for the prehistoric sequence. Scientific analyses would also effect a better understanding of the cultural and environmental milieu of the successive prehistoric phases in the area. Finally, it was hoped that a more complete assemblage could be obtained here from the earliest cultural stratum characterized by cord-marked pottery, a stratum whose existence had long been known on the island but had never been excavated.

The Yale–Taita excavation was carried out from July 8 to October 27, 1964. The permanent staff consisted of Chang, Pearson, and Kress of Yale; Lin, Sung, Huang Shih-ch'iang, and Miss Ch'en Ching-yüan of Taita; and Wu Chi-jui of the Commission for Historic Research. Miss P'an Hsiu-ying and Miss Chang Ch'eng-mei of Taita and Miss Canta Pian of Cambridge, Massachusetts, joined the dig during July and August; Stephen McKinnon of Yale during July, August, and part of September; Mrs. Hu Hsiu-kui of Taita in September and October; and Mrs. Chang Jui-li of Academia Sinica in the latter part of October. The permanent male staff had quarters in the upper floor of the Farmers' Association building in the town of Pa-li, where a temporary laboratory was also set up, and the women resided in the Sacred Heart Middle School for Girls during July and August and in a rented house at Pa-li during September and October. The weather was extremely dry and hot, and the working day (Monday–Friday) was from 9 to 4:30, with a one-hour lunch break. An army truck, through the courtesy of the Chinese Youth Corps, transported the crew daily from their residences to the flag stop at Pei-t'ou village, from which point on they took the fifteen-minute walk to the site. Two workmen were employed throughout at the site, and another was hired at the laboratory to wash the artifacts. Additional workmen were used from time to time at the site as the need arose.

Several factors had to be considered for the determination of excavation tactics. Since the site was huge and the ground rock-hard, total or even extensive excavation was out of the question within our time limits. The Lower Garden, with its dense bamboo groves, posed a difficult problem. Here the area was wide and open and cultural deposits were thick. Farmer Chang, the foreman, made extravagant compensation demands; meeting them was possible within our resources but would set an unfortunate and unheard-of precedent which would inevitably make subsequent archeological work in this area extremely difficult. On the other hand, the area had been excavated by the Commission for Historic Research, and we knew something about its stratigraphy. It was abundant in Yüan-shan and post-Yüan-shan remains, but no corded-ware component was reported. At the Upper Slope, the vital stratification between the corded ware stratum and the Yüan-shan layers was revealed, and we wanted to know more about this. Mr. Kao, landlord of this stretch of land, was gracious and his conditions were reasonable. We finally decided to concentrate in this area, but also to make a specific effort to tackle the terrace scarp where we expected the Upper Slope and the Lower Garden stratigraphies to join. Therefore, the area we eventually excavated was the northeastern part of the site.

Seven pits 1 × 1 m (designated TP 1–7) and twenty pits 2 × 2 m were excavated (Fig. 70). Bulkheads 1 m wide were left between neighboring pits (Pl. 9, *A*), but some of these were dug because of necessity. It was discovered that the ancient land surfaces have slight inclines, but the degrees and gradients varied extensively (Fig. 71). For microstratigraphical analysis a 2 × 2 m pit was considered too large; thus, each pit was further subdivided into four or sixteen smaller squares (Pl. 9, *B*). Natural stratification was followed whenever possible, but the dryness of the earth made this extremely difficult, expecially in upper levels. Within each natural stratum and wherever it was not possible to recognize natural stratification with certainty, artificial strata of 10 cm each were divided. The resultant unit (50 cm square in horizontal dimensions and 10 cm deep) was thus the basic unit of find control; all sherds and stone fragments within such a unit were bagged together except for remarkable finds which were specially numbered and whose coordinates were taken.

Five of the seven test pits lined the northern edge of the second or Upper Slope terrace; the other two were on the eastern edge of the third or Lower Garden terrace, 50 m to the south. The twenty excavation pits were clustered in five loci designated respectively L, M, N, P, and Q from north to south. L had six pits; M had one; N, four; P, five; and Q, four (Fig. 70). These pits revealed a north–south profile of the site 76 m long (Fig. 71), and represented an appreciable part of the Upper Slope portion of the site. The Lower Garden part of the site was known through two test pits only, but the Commission's excavations provided general knowledge.

The workmen first assisted in clearing the surface; occasional burning was necessary to clear away the undergrowth. Then each member of the staff was put in charge of a pit and instructed to dig down very carefully with a hand trowel and, if necessary, a convertible spade-and-pick. All artifacts (stone fragments, potsherds, and anything else that did not belong to the earth) were collected and bagged according to the control unit, but rocks and structural features were left in the ground. For numbered pieces, three-dimensional coordinates were taken. Excavation proceeded at 10-cm intervals, as stated, and as a rule a new pit was not opened until the old one was dug to the bottom. Bags of artifacts were carried back to the laboratory to be washed the next day. Preliminary classification and description were performed in the laboratory, and photographs taken, before the finds were transported back to the Department of Archaeology and Anthropology at Taipei. During November and December, and again intermittently during March, April, and May, 1965, the author carried out most of the necessary processing work in the laboratory at Taita,

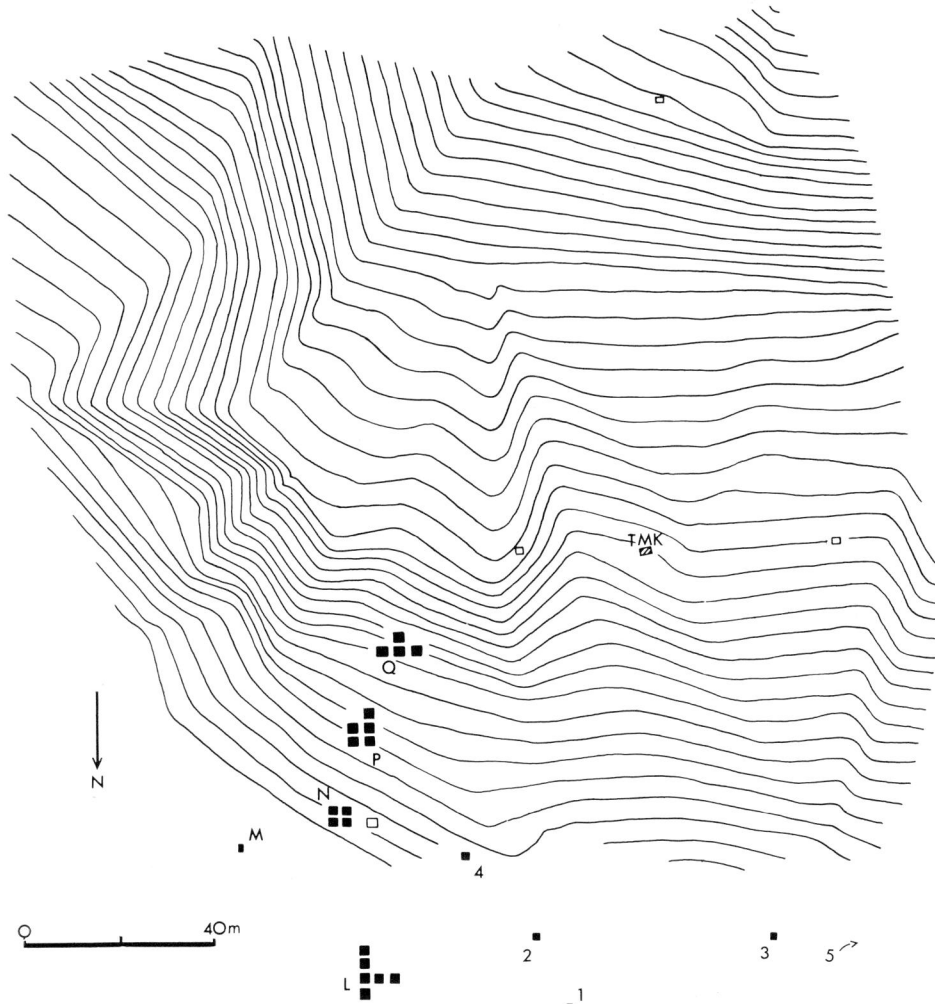

FIG. 70. Plan of the Area of Excavation at Tapenkeng. (TMK = Ta-mu-kung.)

with the assistance of students Ch'en, P'an, and Chang, and a complete photographic record was made in March and April, 1965, by Pearson and the author.

Locus L

This is at the northernmost (and lowest) region of the Upper Slope (Figs. 72, 73; Pls. 9, *A*; 11, *A*). The surface was mostly barren, and the earth rock-hard. The bottom was reached in most pits at about 75 cm from the surface. The top 15 cm or

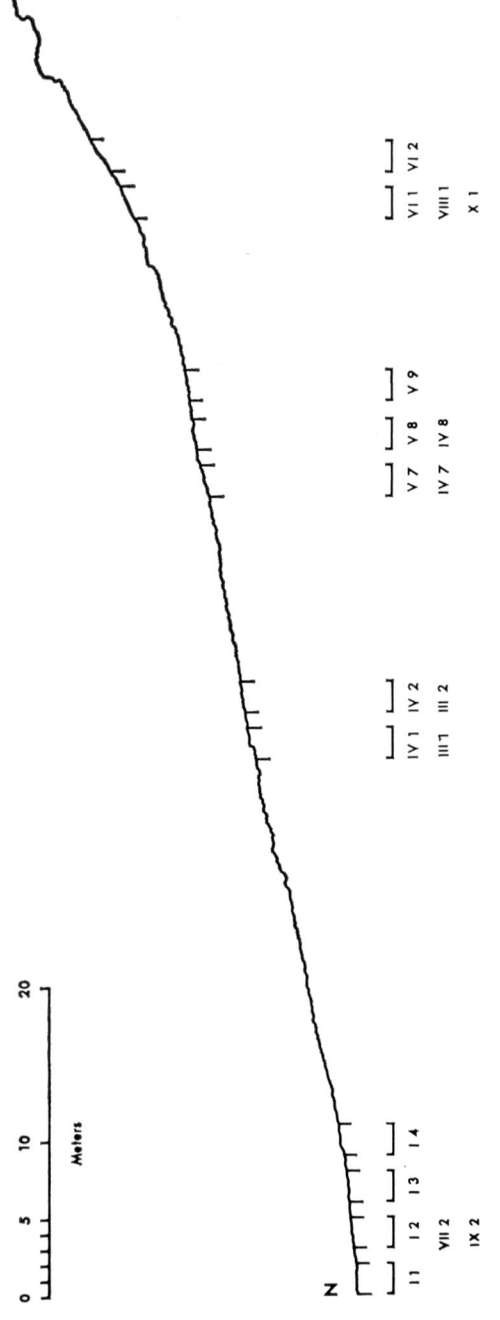

FIG. 71. North–South Section of the Site of Tapenkeng in the Excavated Area.

so was blackish surface soil; below this, to a depth of about 40 or 45 cm, was a layer consisting of gray-brownish earth with Yüanshan-type potsherds (Figs. 72, *b;* 73, *b*). Below this layer were scattered andesite rock fragments and slabs, forming a rough surface at some places (Pl. 11, *A*). Under these rocks was softer, yellowish, porous clay containing scattered cord-marked pottery (Figs. 72, *a;* 73, *a*). Potsherds disappeared at a depth of about 75 cm, but the yellow clay continued in varying degrees until another huge and impenetrable layer of andesite rocks was reached.

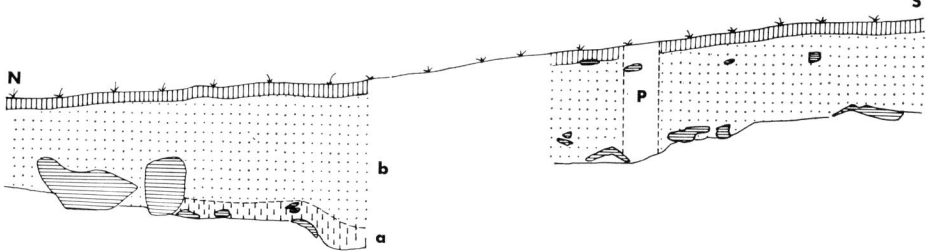

FIG. 72. Locus L, Pits I-1 and I-2, Tapenkeng: East Walls. (I-1 at left, I-2 at right; total length: 5 m; *a* = Corded Ware stratum; *b* = Yüan-shan culture stratum; *p* = section destroyed by taking soil samples for pollen analysis. Total north–south length: 5 m.)

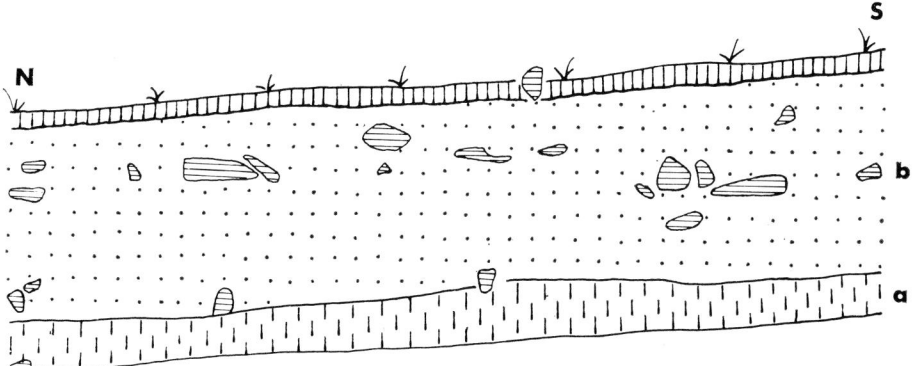

FIG. 73. Locus L, Pit I-3, Tapenkeng: East Wall (North–south length: 2 m).

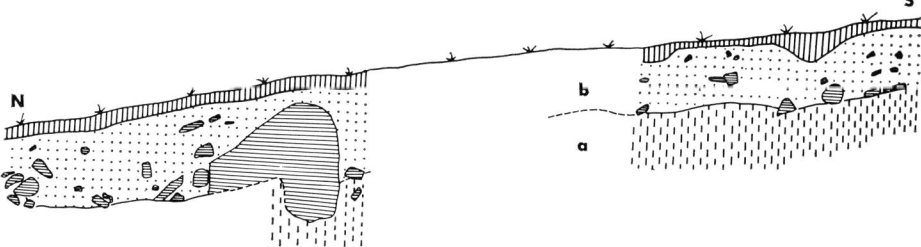

FIG. 74. Locus N, Pits IV-1 and IV-2, Tapenkeng: West Walls. (*a* = Culturally sterile; *b* = Yüan-shan culture. Total north–south length: 5 m.)

Locus M

Only a single pit was dug here. A dark, brownish layer again overlay a yellowish layer; both were noticeably sandy. A single potsherd was found in the upper layer. This area, at the extreme northeastern border of the site, can be considered sterile.

Locus N

The stratification of Locus L was repeated here, but there was an extraordinarily abundant amount of andesite rocks and slabs (Fig. 74). Only the Yüan-shan stratum was brought to light (Fig. 74, *b*), although Area D in the Commission's designation, from which a cord-marked pottery layer was reported beneath the Yüan-shan stratum, was only 4.7 m to the west.

Locus P

Five pits were opened, but only one was dug to the bottom (Fig. 75; Pl. 11, *B*). The stratification was identical with Locus L, but the cultural deposits here were thicker—to a depth of about 1.5 m. Again a layer of scattered andesite rocks and

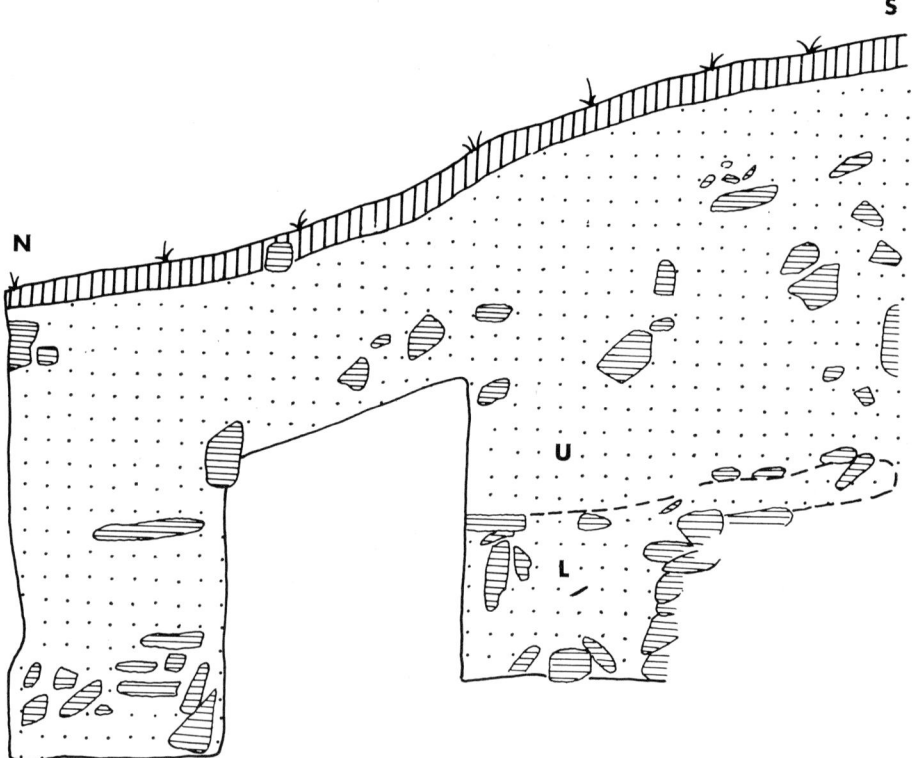

FIG. 75. Locus P, Pit V-7, Tapenkeng: East Wall. (*L* = Corded Ware culture stratum *U* = Yüan-shan culture stratum. North–south length: 2 m.)

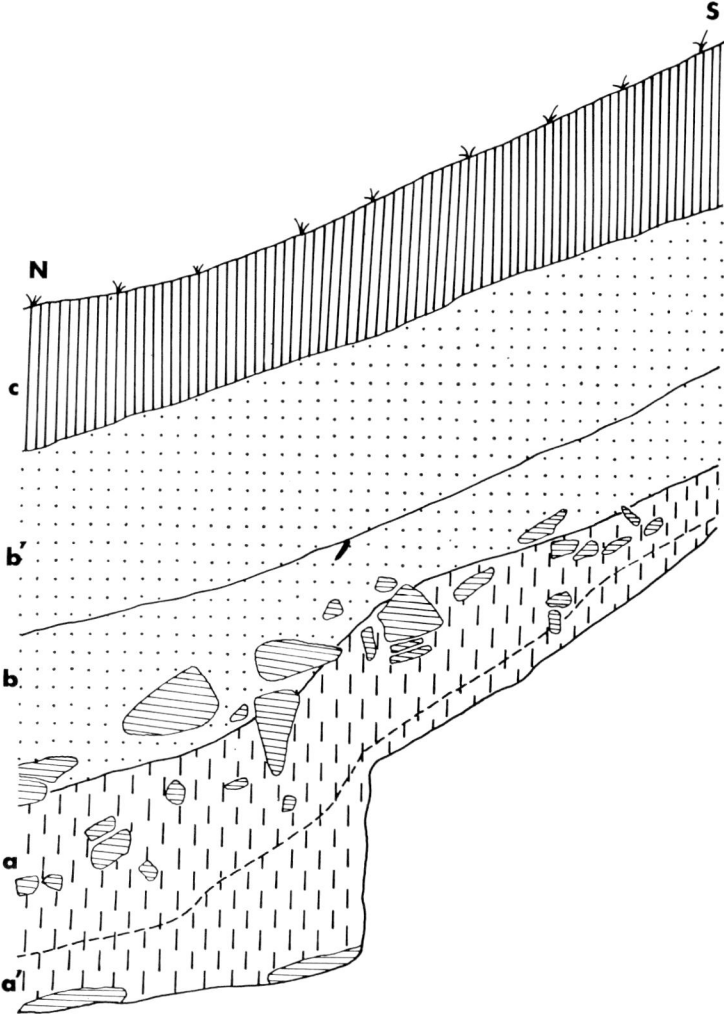

FIG. 76. Locus Q, Pit VI-1, Tapenkeng: East Wall. (*a* and *a'* = Yellow loam, *a* being Corded Ware culture stratum and a' culturally sterile; *b* = Yüan-shan culture stratum, pre-kiln layer; *b'* = Yüan-shan culture stratum, post-kiln layer. North–south length: 2 m.)

slabs separated the corded-ware stratum from the Yüan-shan (Fig. 75). At the upper levels of the Yüan-shan stratum were found a greater number of post-Yüan-shan remains that were known to be abundant in the Lower Garden area, about 20 m south of Locus P.

Locus Q

The southernmost locus of excavation in this season, Locus Q (Figs. 76, 77; Pl. 10), was perhaps the most revealing. The top 25 cm of dark, loose, surface soil (Figs. 76,

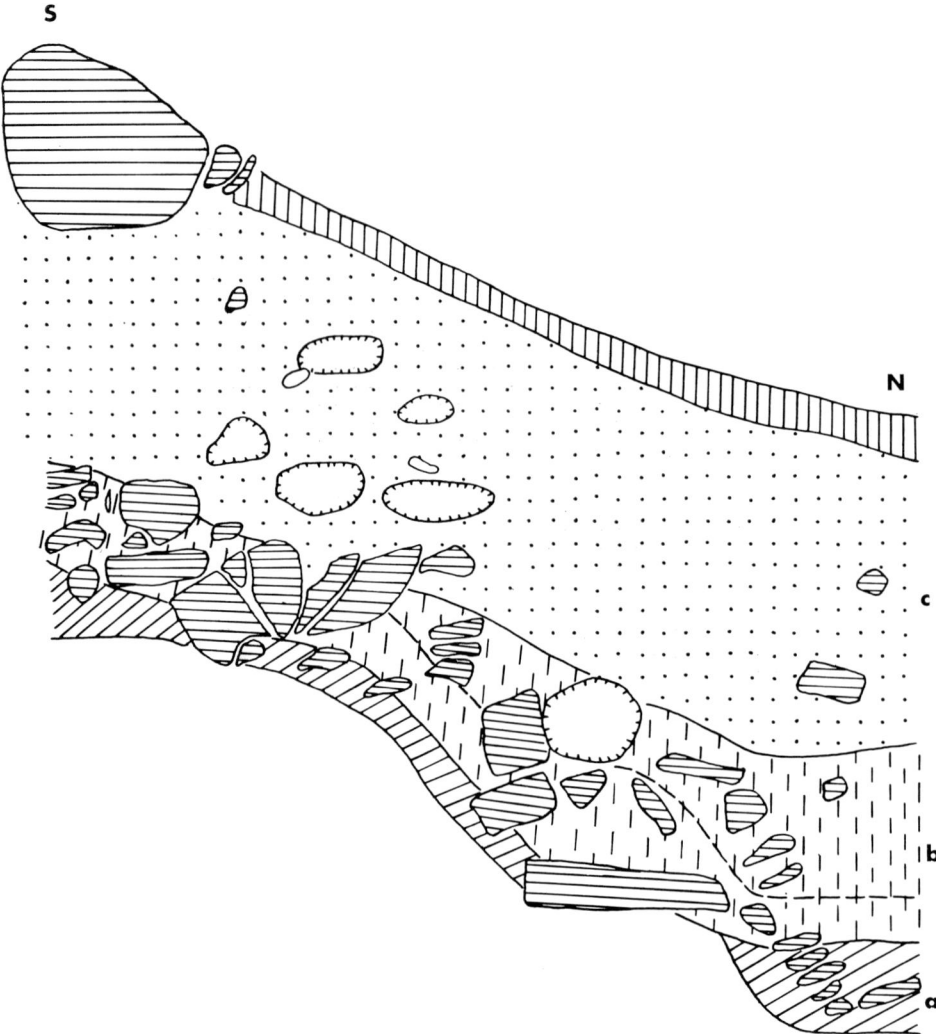

FIG. 77. Locus Q, Pit X-1, Tapenkeng: West Wall. (*a* = Yellow loam, sterile; *b* = Corded Ware culture stratum; *c* = Yüan-shan culture stratum. South–north length: 2 m.)

c; 77, top layer) contained a large number of modern artifacts such as iron objects, Ketangalan sherds, and Chinese porcelain. The brownish layer underneath this was again Yüan-shan in age, but its upper levels contained a large number of post-Yüanshan artifacts (Figs. 76, *b,b′*; 77, *c*). Within the Yüan-shan layer a pottery kiln was brought to light (Pl. 12). A very clearly marked layer of andesite rocks and slabs separated the Yüan-shan from the cord-marked pottery layer of yellow clay below (Pl. 10, *b*). The yellow clay continued below the occurrence of potsherds to a depth of 2.2 m before the dark, hard surface of lava basalt base was reached

(Figs. 76, *a,a′*; 77, *a,b*). This area is situated right at the terrace scarp between the Lower Garden and the Upper Slope, and its stratification thus combines the Commission's Lower Garden and Upper Slope. In a single vertical cut, therefore, there was a complete sequence of the prehistoric and early historic cultures in the northern part of Taiwan, from the earliest known cultural phase down to the modern Chinese (Pl. 10, *a,c*). This section was the deepest cultural profile ever reached in Formosa before the Fengpitou excavations, and it remains the most stratified profile at any one site.

Test Pits 1–5

These five pits were roughly on the same east–west line as Locus P, but they yielded a much wider cross section of this part of the site. The P stratification was repeated in all these pits, but in none of them were cultural remains prolific or deep.

Test Pits 6–7

These, at the eastern part of the Lower Garden, repeated the Commission's Lower Garden stratigraphy; namely, a thicker deposit of post-Yüanshan remains, traces of Yüanshan-type artifacts, and an absence of cord-marked pottery in the lowest stratum.

Chapter 6. History of Neolithic Settlement

THE problems of synchronization at the site of Tapenkeng are vastly different from those at Fengpitou. The area of excavation here is smaller, but the sequence is greater in cultural complexity. Similar sequences are encountered at all excavated loci, and their cross-dating is less difficult. The problem is therefore less one of cross-dating different parts of the site with an emphasis on the horizontal analysis of the settlement than one of detailed examination of the long chronological sequence itself with the entire site as a single unit. Since the site's chronological sequence to a considerable extent mirrors the prehistory of Taipei basin, the focal point in the method of analysis is necessarily determined by the advantages the site has to offer. For this purpose, again, a variety of approaches was tried, leading to the following results.

Stratigraphy

The geological structure of the area surrounding the site of Tapenkeng can be divided into the following formations, from base to top: the Toukoshan group, of early Pleistocene age and base rock of the Kuanyin volcano, which began eruptions during the later formation of the group; important eruptives of the Kuanyin volcano; the Tananwan Formation; the Link'ou Formation (= the higher terrace deposits); middle and lower terrace deposits; and alluvial and coastal plain deposits.

A series of Kuanyin eruptives has been recognized by T. Ichimura (1950), and two of them occurred at the site: (1) Wushanting lava, consisting of augite olivine basalt, black in color, extremely porous in texture, containing abundant, large augite phenocrysts. Large and small fragments of this lava are scattered on the surface throughout the site, probably derived from disturbances, for this lava is the second oldest in the series according to Ichimura. (2) Niuliaop'u lava, consisting of hornblende-bearing 2-pyroxene andesite, very compact and nonporous, almost free of olivine, and containing large augite phenocrysts. This lava is found at the bottom of pits in Locus Q.

The Tananwan Formation encircles the Kuanyin volcanic body, and consists of layers of white or yellow-grayish coarse-grained quartz sands, yellow-brownish sands of medium to fine grain, and light yellowish-gray and white clay. Thin layers of limonite occur within this formation, and the sandy and clay layers often contain small concretions shaped like sandpipes or irregular thin cakes, in which limonite occurs. This formation makes up the base rock of the site at loci L, M, N, and P.

The Link'ou Formation constitutes the higher terrace on the Kuanyin volcanic body, ranging in altitude from 220 to 290 m. The lower part of the terrace is a gravel bed, 40 or 50 m thick; the gravels are mostly hard silicate sandstones, but quartz, slate, andesite, and basalt gravels are also found. The upper part of the terrace is a lateritic soil bed, dark reddish-brown in color and 1 to 6 m thick, consisting of clay minerals and residual mineral grains of weathering, including quartz, zircon, magnetite, augite, and hornblende. The high terrace must have provided much of the rock used by the Tapenkeng stonemakers, and a small number of prehistoric implements has been collected on this terrace, above the Tapenkeng site.

There are five middle and lower terraces, some of which are erosional, the others depositional. The latter are divisible into a lower gravel bed and an upper loam bed, but the lower beds have rare gravels and thin regoliths. The first, second, and third terraces are lower terraces, with gray regoliths, and the fourth and fifth are middle terraces with lateritic soil regoliths. The cultural remains occur in the second and the third terraces.

The alluvial valleys of the Tamsui River and the radial valley system and their extended courses on the coastal plain have gravel, sand, and mud deposits, but the coastal plain itself consists of dune sands and marine sands. Magnetite grains are rich in these deposits and were used in the late prehistoric period for smelting. The topsoil on the coastal plain is cultivated.

This geological stratified sequence, observed in the area as a whole, is not revealed at the site in any single cut, but it provides a basic stratigraphical yardstick against which the stratification phenomena in the various loci can be matched. According to field observations in the excavated parts of the Lower Garden (third terrace) and the Upper Slope (second terrace and the terrace scarp between the second and the third), the underground stratigraphy is as follows.

iv. Topsoil, blackish and loose, containing organic materials; apparently cultivated; 10 to 20 cm thick. On the surface are scattered large porous augite, olivine, basalt fragments, probably rolled fragments of the Wushanting lava. Very heterogeneous cultural content, but modern Chinese porcelain sherds, iron objects, and hard, gray potsherds with impressed check designs (so-called Ketangalan ware) are particularly notable. The Lower Garden has an undisturbed layer of this late prehistoric occupation, but the remains of this period in the Upper Slope were probably derived from the higher terrace.

iii. Dark brown loamy earth, from 30 to 100 cm thick. A particle-size analysis, in a Coulter counter, shows that the earth of this layer is loamy in character, and an X-ray refractometer and microscopic analysis indicate that the loam consists primarily of ihleite and kaolinite ingredients. In addition, it contains many fragments of quartz, magnetite, andesite, and basalt, as well as a small number of mineral grains of hornblende, augite, limonite, and zircon. It is evident that the original rocks of the soil in this layer are sedimentary, such as sandstone, and volcanic, such as andesite and basalt. The predominant pottery in this layer is the Yüan-shan ware, but in upper levels pottery of several other wares occurs in increasing amounts.

ii. Breccia of andesite slabs, of varying thickness and intensity. These slabs, sometimes as large as 60 cm to a side and 10 cm thick, consist of hornblende-bearing 2 pyroxene andesite and frequently exhibit a raised ridge along the axis. The breccia possibly came from the Niuliaop'u lava, and was probably derived from talus activities. This layer indicates that there was a considerable time interval between the overlying Yüan-shan stratum and the cord-marked pottery stratum underneath. Sherds of both strata are found in this layer.

i. Yellow loam, 40 to 50 cm thick in some areas, absent in others. It contains cord-marked pottery, but Yüan-shan sherds are virtually lacking.

o. Base rock. Lava in Locus Q, and Tananwan Formation in the other parts of the site.

This stratigraphy can be considered the basic chronological yardstick at the site of Tapenkeng. The first culture on the site was established upon the surface of the Tananwan Formation and its corresponding yellow loam; it is characterized by cord-marked pottery. The remains of this culture were then overlain by a layer of andesite slabs, probably parts of a conical talus structure. Whether the corded ware occupation was terminated here as a result, or whether these lava-derived andesite slabs descended upon an abandoned settlement, it is not possible to state by the stratigraphical evidence alone. The Yüan-shan culture came subsequently and occupied the site for a considerable length of time. There was again an interval between the termination of the Yüan-shan occupation and the arrival of the Ketangalans who inhabited the Lower Garden part of the site until the modern historical period.

The following problems at Tapenkeng awaited solution: the absolute dating of the cord-marked pottery occupation; the nature and the length of the interval between the corded ware occupation and the subsequent Yüan-shan occupation; the absolute dating of the Yüan-shan occupation; the nature and length of the interval between the Yüan-shan and the Ketangalan occupations; and the absolute dating of the Ketangalan occupation. Finally, changes within each of the three occupations are important, but these concern problems of cultural change rather than of chronology.

Soil Change

The nature and length of the interval between the corded ware and the Yüan-shan occupations are of the utmost importance in the culture history of not only the Taipei basin but also the island as a whole. The corded ware has long been postulated to be *the* earliest ceramic manifestation on the island, but the site of Tapenkeng demonstrates the first occurrence of this cultural phase at the bottom of a stratified sequence that has been excavated to an appreciable extent. A series of carbon-14 dates has placed the Yüan-shan culture firmly on an absolute chronological basis, and the stratigraphical interval between the corded ware and the Yüan-shan gives a significant indication of the antiquity of the former culture in this part of the island. From the following stratigraphical and soil-change evidence it is possible to state for a fact that between these two cultural occupations there is a chronological discontinuity.

1. An andesite slab layer separates two loam layers, and it is probably a part of a talus structure.

2. Peaks of ihleite and kaolinite minerals appear throughout the strata in Locus Q in an X-ray refractometer (reported by C. C. Lin 1966: 30), but such peaks become

TABLE 27. CHEMICAL ANALYSIS OF SOIL SAMPLES FROM PIT VI-1, LOCUS Q, TAPENKENG*

Sample Depth (cm)	Loss of Ignition	SiO_2	Al_2O_3	Fe_2O_3	TiO_2	CaO	MgO	pH (%)
0	8.21	63.49	16.72	5.45	0.78	0.98	1.32	6.40
20	9.94	64.12	15.71	5.20	0.59	0.72	1.03	6.40
40	6.89	66.32	17.84	4.70	0.90	0.49	0.85	6.50
60	8.30	63.89	19.63	3.97	0.50	0.73	1.27	6.60
80	10.32	60.36	22.34	4.50	0.75	0.68	0.84	6.50
100	9.64	59.11	23.87	3.79	0.63	1.16	0.59	6.70
120	10.22	56.39	27.12	3.91	0.65	0.78	0.60	6.50
140	8.13	61.61	11.76	3.74	0.80	0.89	1.00	6.50
160	9.14	58.30	23.71	5.78	0.85	1.12	0.67	6.40
200	10.86	56.79	24.98	4.50	0.96	0.97	0.66	6.70

* Reported by Hsinchu Window Glass Works, Inc., Hsinchu, Taiwan. Figures for soil samples are percentages.

obscure in the layers between these two occupations. This suggests that the surface of the corded ware occupation underwent a long period of exposure and was subject to extensive weathering before the Yüan-shan deposits began to accumulate over it; the ihleite and kaolinite crystals were therefore weathered and decomposed to become noncrystalline soil.

3. A chemical analysis of soil samples taken from Q-VI-1 (courtesy of Hsinchu Window Glass Works, Inc.) shows unmistakable changes between the two occupations in question. The major components of soil by layers are shown in Table 27.

Three of these components, Al_2O_3, Fe_2O_3, and TiO_2, are particularly indicative (Fig. 78). In the topsoil (0–60 cm), Al_2O_3 is low, having a percentage of 15.71 to 16.72. This component increases, however, toward the lower levels; at 120 cm it increases to as much as 27.12 per cent. After this there is a sharp drop, to 11.76 per cent at 140 cm, apparently because of the fact that during a long period of exposure the fine grains of Al_2O_3 were washed away by water. After 160 cm, when the corded ware layer is reached, there is again an increase of this component.

The presence of iron tells a similar story. The two peaks of iron are in topsoil (0–20 cm) and the surface of the corded ware occupation (140–160 cm), whereas within the occupational layers iron content is relatively lower. It is apparent that on a long-exposed surface where the fine Al_2O_3 clay ingredients were being washed away and where chemical weathering takes place, the iron content—augmented by the relatively heavy magnetite grains—is larger than below the surface. The two peaks of iron thus indicate two comparable surfaces that were subject to weathering during long periods.

The change of TiO_2 follows a different pattern. Within the Yüan-shan occupational layers, the TiO_2 content fluctuates. From the corded ware occupational surface down, however, there is a constant increase of this mineral. The soil of these two layers is apparently characterized by different chemical components.

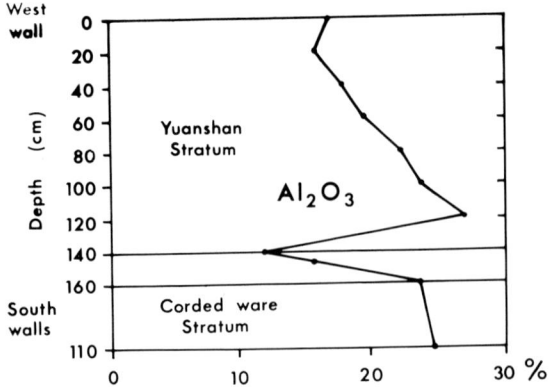

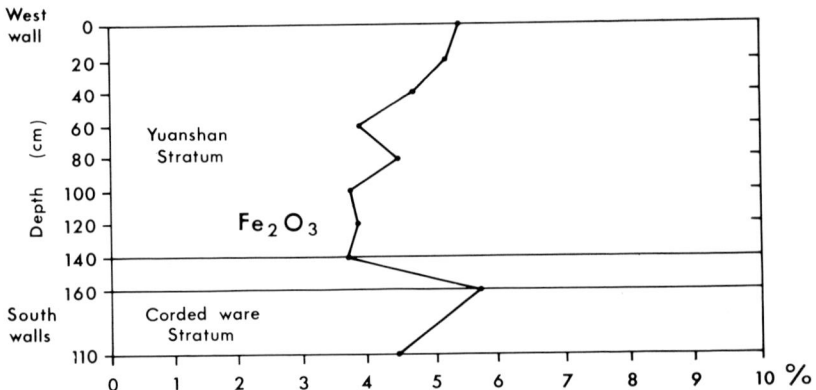

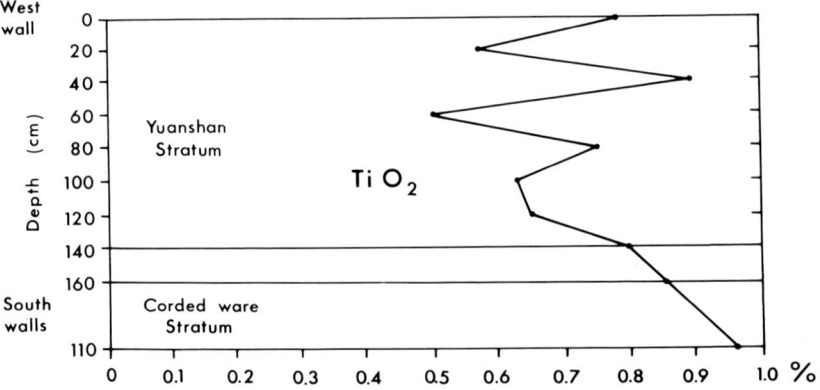

FIG. 78. Percentage Changes of Three Chemical Components in the Soil Samples from Locus Q, Pit VI-1, Tapenkeng. (Data supplied by C. C. Lin.)

Ceramic Seriation

The overwhelming majority of artifacts found from all cultural strata at the site of Tapenkeng are potsherds. The ceramic wares at this site are quite complex but are clearly demarcated into the following groups.

Corded wares. Cord marks appear on a variety of ceramic wares of the island, but the term *TPK Corded* can be used to designate those of a specific category with characteristic features of paste, form, and decoration, first stratigraphically recognized from a cultural context at this site. Sherds of this category are easily identifiable by their size and then by their paste. The vessels indicated by the sherds are quite large, ranging from 20 to 35 cm in diameter, and the individual sherds are thick, somewhere around 5 to 12 mm for body sherds and 20 to 25 for rim sherds at their thickest part. The paste is very coarse, with large amounts of coarse-grained inclusions of quartz and other minerals. Firing was not thorough; a hard pinch or squeeze with two fingers usually reduces a sherd to a powder. The leading shapes are bowls and jars. Rims are always thin toward the lip, and in many cases a raised ridge occurs between the lip and the neck, dividing the rim into two well-defined zones. Lug handles occasionally occur on the shoulder, and a low ring foot (sometimes with small circular cutouts) is sometimes attached to the bottom. The surface is sometimes coated and then impressed with cord marks. Incised patterns as a rule appear on the lip, on the exterior surface of the rim, and occasionally on the shoulder. Two patterns predominate—short parallel strokes and wavy lines. Two closely parallel lines always form the fundamental unit of composition. After the impression or incision was made, a red pigment was often applied to the surface.

Since the colors of the sherds—cores and surfaces—are notably heterogeneous, in the initial classification the corded wares are grouped into the following classes: (1) red; (2) gray-cored red; (3) buff; (4) gray-cored buff; (5) buff, with finer paste and yellow or white slip; (6) buff, with finer paste and yellow or white slip, and gray core; (7) brown; and (8) black. Some of these varieties were subsequently eliminated as irrelevant.

Brown fine ware. Very rarely found, this ware differs from the buff fine corded in that it never has cord marks and that it has a thinner body and finer paste.

Yüan-shan ware. This is the ceramic ware first recognized and best represented by the shellmound pottery at the site of Yüan-shan in Taipei city. The core is gray or buff, but the surfaces are always brown-gray coatings. Sand and grit inclusions are many; in fact the paste is uniformly coarse-grained. The surface is mostly plain; simple incisions and ring impressions are seen on the rim, the handle, and the ring foot. Red pigment is sometimes applied in broad strokes but irregular patterns. The predominant shape is a jar, with medium-sized mouth, broader shoulder, and vertical strap handles with one end at the shoulder and the other at the rim; the upper surface of the handle merges with the lip. The bottom is usually rounded, and a ring foot—occasionally with cut-out holes—is attached to some. Most vessels have lids. All vessels were molded by hand. Four varieties are distinguished for preliminary analysis: gray-cored, buff-cored, sandy hard, gritty gray.

Sandy red. Brightly red or orange in color, this ware is relatively coarse of paste but lacks conspicuous inclusions. In shape it is similar to the Yüan-shan plain, but bowls are developed. No decorative pattern of any kind has been recognized.

Sandy brown. This ware is mainly chocolate in color, but some sherds are reddish or blackish. Paste is finer than Yüan-shan plain, and the body is harder.

Geometric impressed wares. The color, paste, and shape of this class are heterogeneous, but in contrast to all other types it includes all sherds with impressed decorative designs. The following classes are further divisible: red-checked, buff-checked, buff-chevroned, gray-lozenged, and herringboned.

Glazed and stone wares. These are evidently modern, but are not necessarily all introduced from the Chinese. They include porcelain, glazed ware, and stoneware.

These wares and their varieties provide the categories for preliminary seriation for the purpose of chronology. More detailed descriptions and analyses will be presented in another section on pottery. For the present purpose, two pits of the greatest depth are selected: VI-I in Locus Q, and V-7 in Locus P. The ground surface of the various occupations varies within the shortest distance; that is, the greatest depth of a certain occupation may be reached at 120 cm below the ground in one of the four or sixteen smaller units within a pit, but it may not be reached in an adjoining unit until 130 cm. In the unit farther down, 140 cm may be the boundary. For this reason, a column of 50×50 cm is used for this analysis in Locus P, and 1×1 m in Locus Q (see block graphs in Figs. 79, 80).

These seriation graphs give rise to the following observations:

The first occupation at the site is characterized by a variety of corded wares. The small amount of Yüanshan-type ware sherds in these layers may reasonably be regarded as intrusive.

Between the corded and the Yüan-shan ware strata is a layer representing a considerable time hiatus; this is indicated by the mixed occurrence of both sherds in Locus Q and by the sterile layers in Locus P, and it corresponds to the stratigraphical layer of andesite slabs.

The Yüan-shan ware has the longest life span at the site. In lower levels it is the only ware that occurs. In upper levels it sometimes gives way to other wares. The kiln in Locus Q serves as a clear indicator of this change. It is possible to subdivide the Yüan-shan occupation into the two subperiods: pre-kiln and post-kiln.

In the post-kiln subperiod of the Yüan-shan occupation, the geometric impressed wares begin to occur and increase in quantity, together with sandy red and sandy brown. On the strength of this evidence, the Historic Research Commission's conclusions must be modified. In other words, the Botanical Garden ceramics do not constitute a separate and independent cultural phase but were a minority component of the Yüan-shan occupation.

Modern historical pottery occurs in the topsoil, together with iron objects.

Carbon-14 Dates

The following carbon-14 determinations are reported by the Radiocarbon Laboratory, Yale University (B.P. = before 1950):

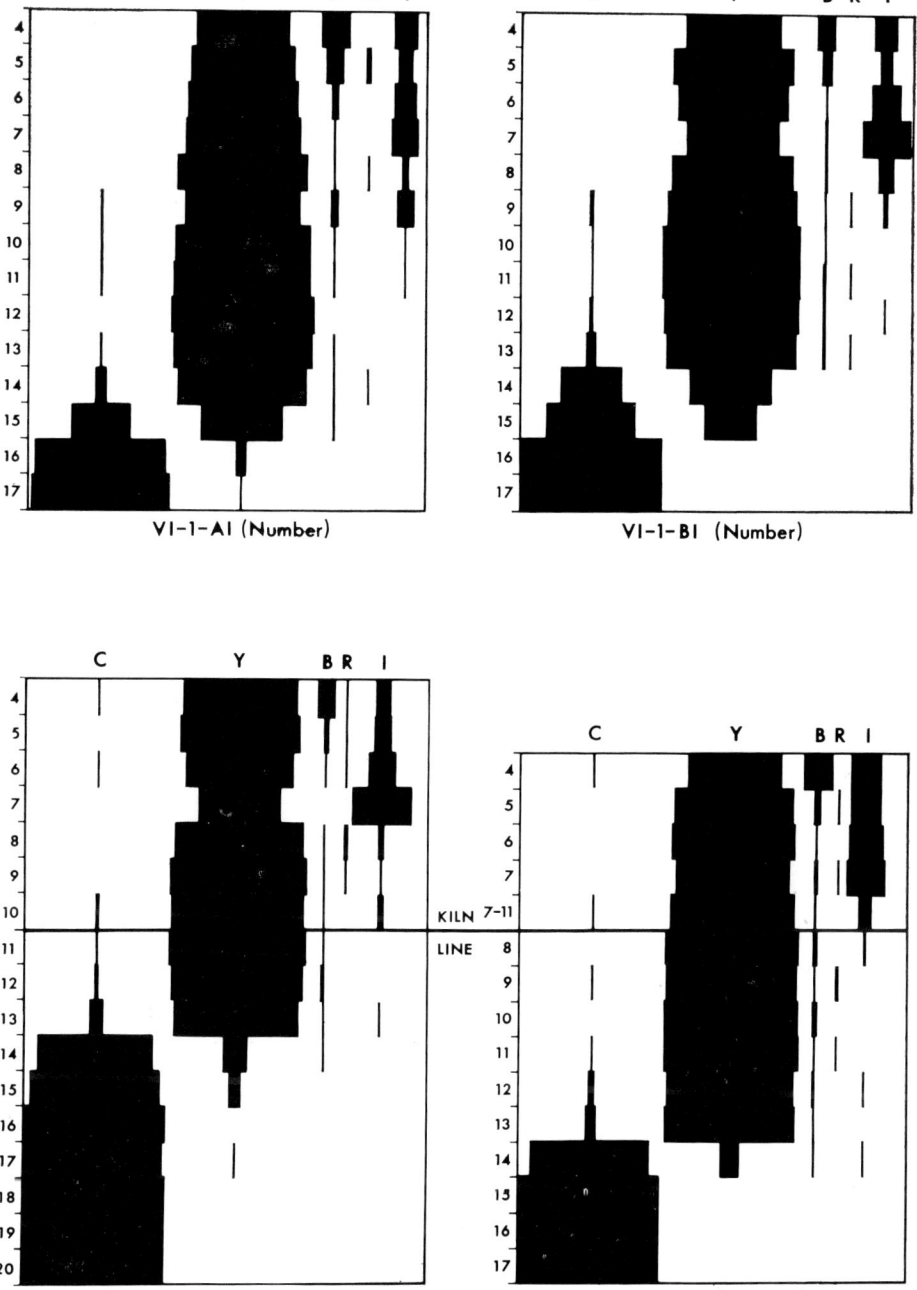

FIG. 79. Graphic Representation of the Percentage Changes of Major Wares at Locus Q, Pit VI-1, Tapenkeng. (C = Corded ware; Y = Yüan-shan ware; B = TPK brown ware; R = TPK red ware; I = Botanical Garden impressed ware.)

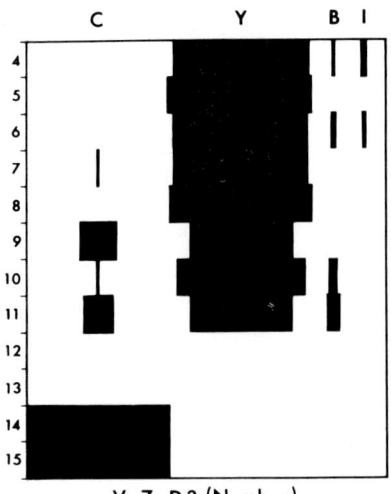

V-7-D3 (Number)

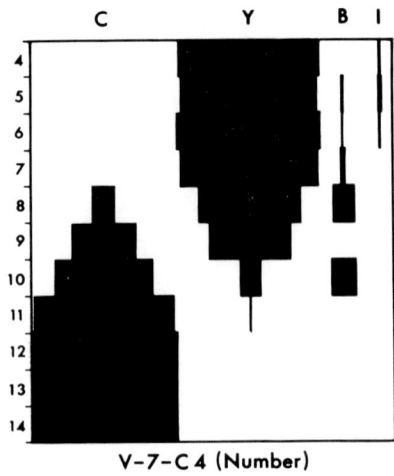

V-7-C4 (Number)

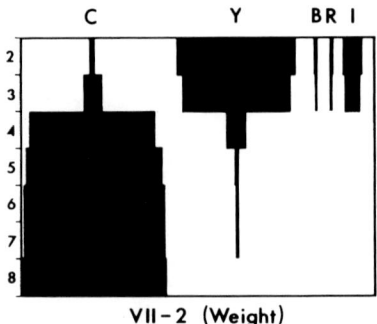

VII-2 (Weight)

FIG. 80. Graphic Representation of the Percentage Changes of Major Wares at Locus P, Pits V-7 and VII-2, Tapenkeng. (For key to abbreviations, see Fig. 79.)

Y-1552	charcoal, from Locus Q, pits VI-1-165	
	cm and X-1-135 and 165 cm	19,670 ± 450 B.P.
Y-1551	charcoal, from Q-VI-1-142 cm	2,850 ± 200 B.P.
Y-1498	charcoal, from Q-VI-1-70–90 cm	2,030 ± 80 B.P.

The samples were all taken from Locus Q, which has the longest stratigraphy. Chunky organic materials such as shells and bones are absent throughout the excavated part of the site, but small fragments of charcoal were collected from many layers with great care. Most were too small to enable dating, except for samples Y-1551 and Y-1498. Y-1551 was derived from the bottom of the Yüan-shan occupation, and it dates from about 1000 B.C. Y-1498 was collected around the kiln, and its date of about 100 B.C. marks the beginning of the post-kiln period of the Yüan-shan occupation. This means that the Yüan-shan occupation of the site at Locus Q dates from around 1000 B.C. to the early centuries of the Christian era, a conclusion of great significance when it is compared with the dates of the Yüan-shan culture at the Yüan-shan Shellmound, as will be discussed in Part III.

From all indications it was clear that a considerable time interval was involved after the corded ware occupation came to an end and before the Yüan-shan occupation began around 1000 B.C. But no one expected that the interval could have been so great as to warrant a date of 19,670 B.P. for the corded ware occupation. (Another piece of charcoal, collected from the corded ware horizon in Q-X-1-138 cm gives a date of 3,080 ± 350 B.P. The size of this sample is very small, and the date is much too recent to be accepted as the more correct of the two from this occupation. See Part III for the latest possible date of this culture in Taipei basin.) A communication from Dr. Minze Stuiver concerning sample Y-1552 reads, in part:

> Upon receipt of your last two letters of March 5th I talked extensively with our technician about the samples . . . Y-1552 is considered to be quite normal . . . Contamination of samples will practically always make them younger, so this cannot explain the problem . . . In order to make a sample older, material containing no C14 should be added. However, the amount needed to reduce an age of 5000 to for instance 20,000 years is very large; seven times the amount of the original sample. This large additional amount of foreign material should certainly be noticed in the laboratory . . . in my opinion the date of Y-1552 could be normal. [Letter dated March 11th, 1965, addressed to Chang at Taipei.]

If the carbon-14 reading is reliable, that leaves the question of its archeological context. These samples were collected from the corded ware occupational layer without the slightest doubt. The only question is the time when the wood was converted to charcoal, and the underground context gives no indication about this. For the moment we shall let the date go without comment, and be satisfied with the probability that the corded ware occupation was "considerably earlier" than the Yüan-shan occupation. This chronological problem is of great importance in East Asia archeology, and will be discussed in Part III.

No carbon samples were collected from the post-Yüanshan stratum at the site of Tapenkeng. The Carbon-14 Laboratory of the National Taiwan University, however, has reported two dates from the site of Shih-san-hang, a Ketangalan settlement on the coast northwest of the Pei-t'ou village:

NTU-7   shell, from Shih-san-hang   1,044 ± 209 B.P.
NTU-8   charcoal, from Shih-san-hang   1,145 ± 206 B.P.

According to pottery and stone implements, the Shih-san-hang site and the latest occupation at the site of Tapenkeng are on the whole contemporary, and it is probable that the date of 800 or 900 of this era for the former site falls within the time range of the Ketangalan occupation at Tapenkeng as well.

Historical Accounts and Historically Datable Finds

In 1963 a bronze arrowhead was discovered in the Upper Slope at the site of Tapenkeng, in Area D near our Locus N, from a context of Yüan-shan pottery.

[It] is typologically analogous to the Shang dynasty arrowhead of the two-winged, long-shafted, and stemmed type known from the site of Hsiao-t'un. The only other possible Bronze Age source of the Tapenkeng arrowhead in Eastern Asia would be the area of the Dongson Culture in Southwest China and Indochina, but the typology of Dongson arrowheads appears to differ from our specimen. Most of the bronze arrowheads unearthed at Shihchaishan near Chinning in Yunnan are of the socketed variety; a few are stemmed, but their shafts are prismatic instead of flat. The site at Dongson in North Vietnam . . . has yielded bronze arrowheads with spearhead-like elongate shafts with hollow sockets at the end: . . . [they] are obviously different from the Yin types at Hsiao-t'un. Thus there is little doubt that the Tapenkeng arrowhead is of the Hsiaot'un type and that its historic connections must be sought for in that direction. Bronze arrowheads of the Hsiao-t'un type have been found elsewhere in South China . . . and Father Finn is of the opinion that this type of bronze weapon was introduced into Hong Kong during the Western Han dynasty at the latest. . . .

  Unless on the basis of evidence not now available it can be shown that the people of the upper phase of Hsiayuan brought a bronze culture with them when they immigrated into northern Taiwan, the best assumption is that the Hsiayuan II bronze arrowhead was imported from South China, possibly by way of Hong Kong. The three-winged bronze arrowhead replaced the Hsiao-t'un two-winged type in North China from the period of the Warring States (c. 450–221 B.C.). If the two-winged bronze arrowhead of Hsiayuan was imported directly from North China, it cannot have been at a later date than the Warring States period. If, on the other hand, it can be by way of South China, its date still cannot be later than the Han dynasty. With this evidence we may now date the upper stratum of the Hsiayuan site (i.e. the Yuan-shan culture) to the interval between the Shang dynasty and the end of the Han, or about from 1600 B.C. to A.D. 200 [Liu 1964: 220–1].

This chronological range can be considerably narrowed. South China archeology, which is now much better known than in Father Finn's day, makes it clear that there was intensive development of the Eastern Chou culture by the Warring States period. That is to say that the two-winged arrowhead of the Hsiao-t'un type was no longer the prevailing type of arrowhead in Fukien and Kwangtung before 400 or 500 years B.C. The presence of this type at Tapenkeng indicates contact with the mainland before that date, even though the artifact itself could have survived much longer. This is in agreement with the carbon-14 dates.

The excavations in 1964 did not discover more bronze arrowheads, but a piece of bronze bracelet was found in Locus L from the Yüan-shan layer, lending even stronger credence to what is suggested by the bronze arrowhead with reference to chronology and culture contact. There is absolutely no evidence that Tapenkeng's Yüan-shan culture was a bronze-casting culture.

There is no indication of any kind about the termination date for the Yüan-shan culture at Tapenkeng, although it would be unlikely to assume that it lasted much longer into the Christian era. The beginning date for the next culture, the Ketangalan, is again uncertain, but this culture lasted into the period with historical documents. The Chinese arrived in the neighborhood of Pa-li in the latter years of K'ang-hsi (1662–1722; Ch'ing Dynasty), and made a settlement there in the first years of Yüng-cheng (1723–35). In the early part of Ch'ien-lung (1736–95), the settlement grew into a town that is referred to as Pa-li-p'en in *Taiwan Fu-chih*. The subsequent lowering of Tamsui River water levels in this region gradually caused Pa-li-p'en to decline, and the town of Hu-wei (Tamsui) across the river eventually became the leading port in northern Taiwan. Under T'ung-chih (1862–74), Pa-li-p'en sank into insignificance.

When the Chinese came into the northern part of Taiwan they encountered aborigines known as the Ketangalan. The Ketangalan pottery, typified by the site of Ao-ti, is found in great quantity from the top layer at Tapenkeng, primarily on the Lower Garden terrace. The Commission for Historic Research discovered in this layer a coin:

> It bears an incomplete inscription with two characters, *t'ung* (circulation) and *li* (part of the reign name of the Ming dynasty, either Wan-li, 1573–1619, or Yung-li, 1647–62). This coin appears to date the Ketangalan culture in northern Taiwan to the middle or later part of Ming [Liu 1964: 222].

In view of the fact that in the Ming and Ch'ing dynasties coins circulated long after their first minting, these coins do not necessarily indicate Ketangalan contact with the Chinese earlier than the early years of the Ch'ing Dynasty when there were documented records of Chinese entry into the place. From various parts of the Lower Garden we collected several early Ch'ing Dynasty coins (the earliest from K'ang-hsi). These, plus iron metallurgy and porcelain (Pl. 101), suggest very close contacts with the Chinese during the seventeenth century.

Chapter 7. The Corded Ware Culture

THE Corded Ware culture at the site of Tapenkeng occupied a relatively restricted area compared with the subsequent occupations. No cord-marked pottery stratum was reported by Liu from the Lower Garden, and our test pits TP-6 and TP-7 in this same region reached the bottom after the Yüan-shan layers. Test pits 1–5, spanning the northern edge of the Upper Slope, revealed no Corded Ware occupation either. On the basis of the excavated material, one can state with considerable certainty that the Corded Ware culture occupation was confined to the eastern part of the Upper Slope in an area approximately 80 m north–south. Within this area, corded ware layers occur throughout, showing no tendency of clustering. (Although we did not find a Corded Ware layer in Locus N, corded sherds were reported from the Commission's Area D, immediately west of Locus N.)

Stone Implements

Among the small number of stone implements unearthed from the Corded Ware layers at Tapenkeng, three groups of artifacts are conspicuous.

1. *Pitted pebbles* (Fig. 81, *10,11;* Pl. 24, *B*). There are six of these quartz-sandstone river pebbles, in average 10 cm in diameter, the heaviest almost 1 kg in weight. One end, both ends, four sides, the whole circumference or a part of it, or the center of one of the broad faces or both centers of these pebbles are pitted—apparently signs of wear after long use for striking, hammering, or knocking. These were probably general-purpose hammerstones, used to flake stones, press leathers, knock open shells, and so forth. As previously stated, Sung Wen-hsün suggests that those with pitted centers were used for knocking open mollusk shells. No shells were found at the site.

2. *Axes.* Six implements can be described as axes, each of a different type. (1) A chipped long ax (Fig. 81, *1;* Pl. 23, *A*), of dark gray arenaceous slate and planoconvex in cross section, a little over 7 cm long. The cutting edge, shorter than the butt end, shows wear, so that it was probably not a blank. (2) A polished small (5.5 cm long) adz of brownish gray slate (Fig. 81, *2;* Pl. 23, *C*). On one broad face there are two chipped notches in the middle of each long edge, suggesting a rudimentary form of the "step" of the stepped adzes, apparently a hafting device. (3) A small (3.6 cm long) ax of serpentine, beautifully polished and completely intact (Fig. 81, *3;* Pl. 23, *D*). The cutting edge is made up of two ground faces, one narrow and the other very broad. (4–6) Fragments of polished rectangular adzes. Two are the butts of gray siliceous slate adzes (Pl. 23, *F,G*), and another (Fig. 81, *4;* Pl. 23, *B*) the butt part of an apparently stepped adz.

3. *Points.* Five, all of slate and all of the same form (Fig. 81, *5–8;* Pl. 23, *H,J–M*). They are polished, thin, and flat, have a straight base 2–2.5 cm wide, with a small perforation at the center. All five are broken at or above the perforation and the

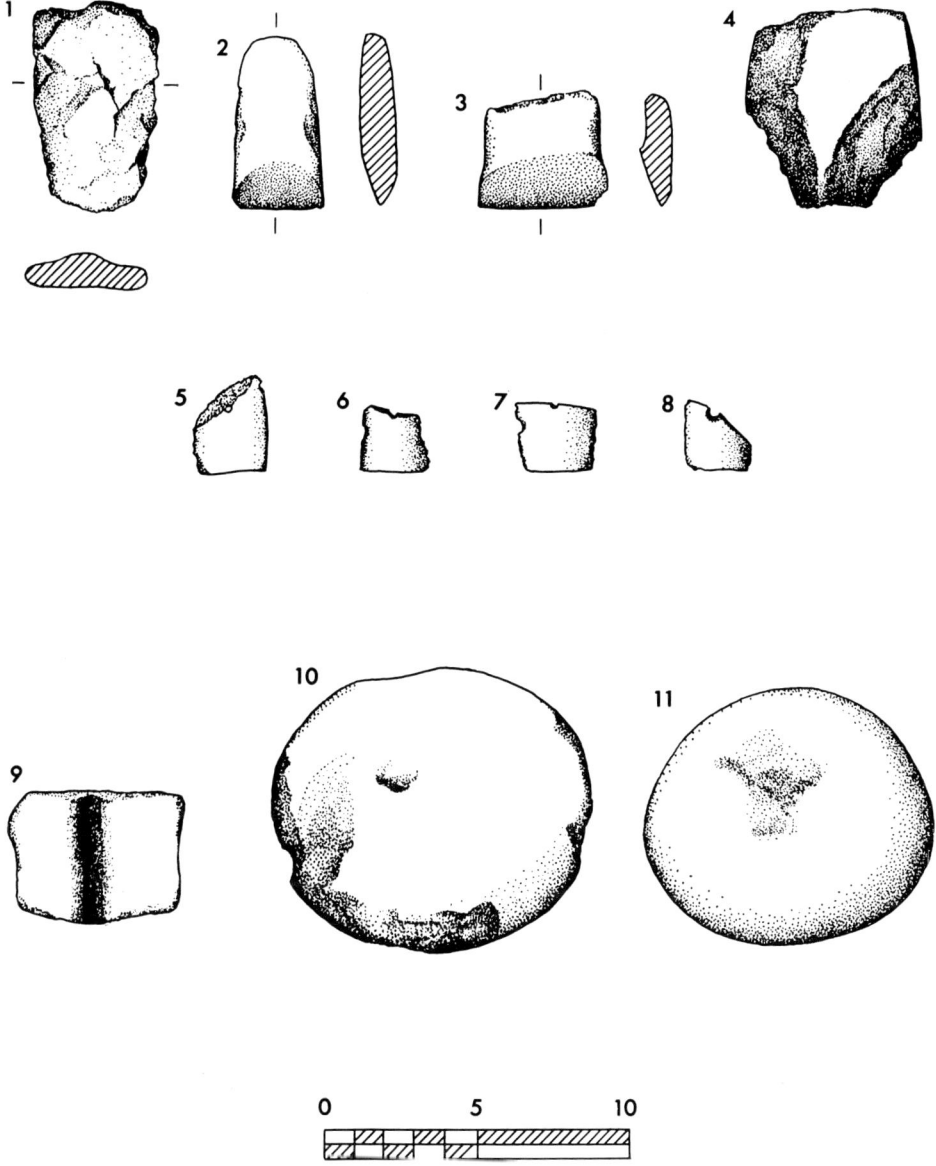

FIG. 81. Stone and Clay Artifacts from the Corded Ware Stratum at Tapenkeng.

point parts are missing. One has a small notch on a side above the perforation (Fig. 81, *5;* Pl. 23, *H*). To judge by size, these were probably arrowheads.

In addition, there is a fragment of a polished and perforated disk of siliceous slate (Pl. 23, *I*), and half of a tubular disk of clay with a hole at the center (Fig. 81, *9;* Pl. 24, *A*). Their uses cannot be ascertained.

By and large, the stone industry of the Tapenkeng Corded Ware culture is characterized by polished implements of remarkable workmanship, and the basic rock, except for hammerstones of sandstone, is slate.

Pottery

This ware is, of course, corded by definition, and in fact practically all the jars and bowls are covered with cord marks. It does not necessarily mean, however, that every sherd of this ware exhibits cord marking or that there is no pot or bowl that does not bear a cordage mark. This has to be stated because some collectors have faced the problem of having to refer to a plain piece of sherd as "cord marked," and have questioned our identification.

Cord marking was widespread on Formosa in its prehistoric period and occurs on many wares. The kind of corded ware that is involved here has certain specific properties and characteristic features. As Tapenkeng is the first site where the ware was found in demonstrably stratigraphical conditions and in scientifically controlled cultural context, we suggest that henceforth this ware be referred to as the TPK Corded. Some quick identification markers of this ware, primarily formulated according to the Tapenkeng data but known to be applicable also to the pottery of other sites, are as follows. Coarse paste containing a noticeably large amount of sand or grit inclusions (analyses of four thin sections reveal 30 to 35% quartz, 5 to 15% feldspar, and traces of mica or iron minerals). Walls are on the thick side; buff, brown, or red exteriors have cores of the same color or show insufficient oxidation. Firing temperatures are estimated within the 400–500°C range, achieved in open kilns with wood or straw fuels. Sherds are relatively soft and loose as a rule; body sherds are usually covered with cord marks (Pl. 17) that have large strands and were deeply impressed. Long lines of incisions occur in pairs or in groups in place of the cord marks on some sherds. There are two typical rim forms: (1) very low rim with thick neck and thin lip that flares (Fig. 82); (2) a raised ridge separating the lip from the neck on the exterior. Incised patterns often occur above the ridge and cord marks below it (Fig. 83). The rim itself is *never* cord marked.

Paste. Although rather uniform in shape and decoration, this ware is very heterogeneous in paste and color. For the purpose of a more realistic description as well as distributional analysis, eight varieties are distinguished.

1. *Red.* Red or "dark carmine" (Munsell scale 4.5R3.7/7.1) throughout, this variety contains an observable amount of quartz inclusions and is relatively soft (2° in a scale of 10). The body sherds range from 2 to 14 mm in thickness, and the rims are considerably thicker at the neck. There is no evidence of the use of a wheel, fast or slow. The rim was made as an integral part of the body, in contrast to the Yüan-shan ware which had rims applied to the body.

2. *Red with gray core.* This is the red corded with gray or black core, but the red color is a little darker (dark red, 3.5R3.6/5.3), and the paste a little harder (2.5°).

3. *Buff.* This ware is separated from the red primarily according to color, and the constrast is very distinct. It can be described as "brilliant yellow" (9.6YR7.8/9.6),

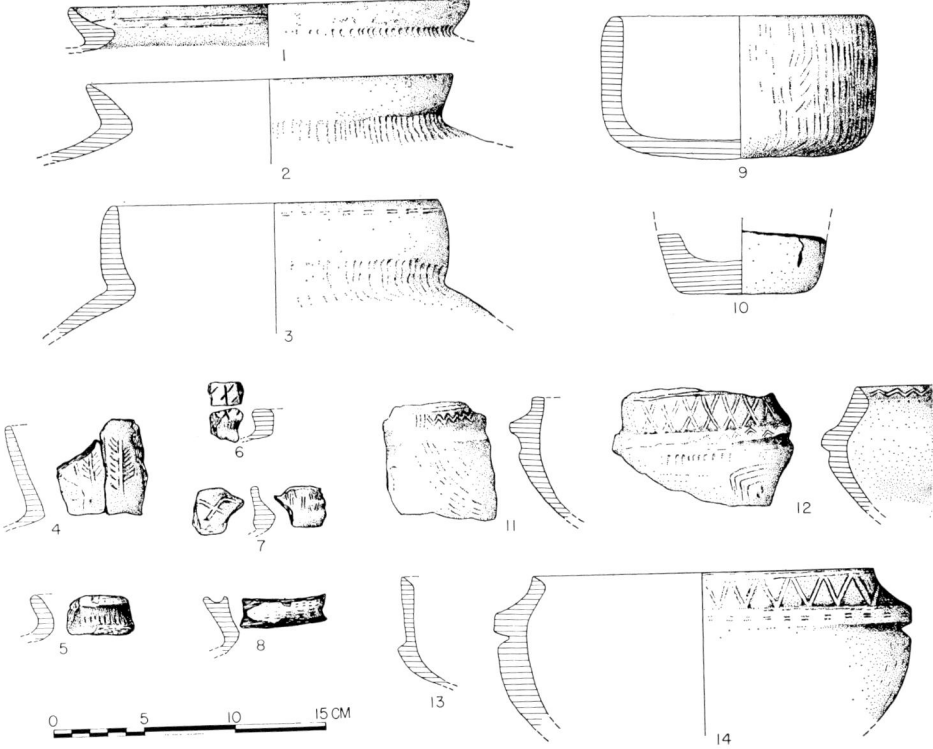

Fig. 82. Corded Ware, Non-ridged Rims, Tapenkeng.

and its hardness is 2°. The inclusions, thickness, and manufacture are identical with the red.

4. *Buff with gray core*. This ware is "cinnamon" (7.6YR6.3/4.2) in color and 2° in hardness; it is distinguished from the buff primarily by its dark core. In paste, thickness, and manufacture this is no different from the previous wares.

5. *Fine buff*. Very few sherds of this variety are found. "Light brownish-gray" (5.0YR7.0/1.3) in color and only 1.5° in hardness, these sherds are thinner (2–8 mm) and are made up of finer grains with fewer and smaller inclusions. A yellowish or whitish coat covers the exterior and interior surfaces.

6. *Fine buff with gray core*. Closely similar to the above, but even thinner (2–6 mm) and finer.

7. *Brown*. "Dark reddish-brown" (10.0R3.5/2.2) in color and 2° in hardness, this ware is separated from the red mainly by its darker and grayer color; but this could have been due to different preservation conditions.

8 *Black*. The black exterior of this variety is probably due to secondary coloration, e.g. cooking and long wear. It is made into a separate category because sherds of this kind cannot be otherwise classified.

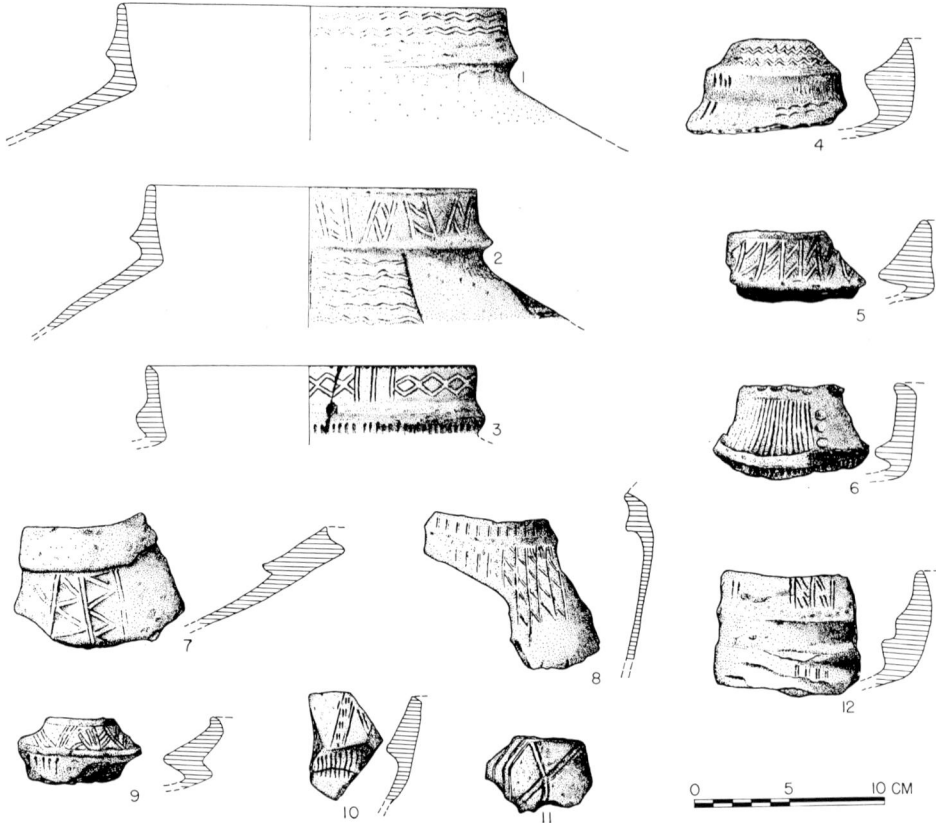

FIG. 83. Corded Ware, Ridged Rims, Tapenkeng.

Form. Only two basic shapes of vessels are present in this ware: bowls (Fig. 82, *9–14*) and jars or pots (Figs. 82, *1–8*; 83). Each includes several major varieties, and different shapes often exhibit different pastes.

1. The jar or pot is universal, i.e. exhibits all paste varieties. Its model form is: low rim, medium mouth, wide shoulder, globular body, rounded bottom, and (not always necessarily) an applied ring foot. The diameter of the mouth averages (from observation) around 15–25 cm, and that of the body, probably around 20–30. The height is estimated at approximately 20–50 cm. The shoulder is curved rather than rounded into the lower part of the body. The ring foot is invariably low, at most no more than 25 or 30 mm. Three or four perforations (circular, small) sometimes occur near the bottom on the upper portions of the ring foot (Pl. 18, *F–J*). Two lug handle sherds of the buff varieties have been found; presumably a pair was attached to the shoulder at the maximum diameter of the body (Pl. 22, *J*).

The rim sherds fall into two major groups, flat and ridged. The flat rim (Pl. 18, *A,C–E;* Fig. 82, *1–8*) flares a little; the lip is in most cases much thinner than the neck, but some rims are of uniform thickness, giving rise to a flat lip on which decorative patterns often occur. Other rims have an interior bevel in the lower part, seemingly for the support of a lid, although no lid sherds can be identified. The ridged rim has a raised circumferential ridge below the lip and above the neck (Pls. 19, 20; Fig. 83); the lip is again either thin and sharp or flat. The ridge can be very low or very high; the thickness of some of the high-ridged rims at the ridge part often exceeds the height of the rim. Incised patterns as a rule occur on the exterior of the rim above the ridge. It is a reasonable inference that the exterior surface of the rim of this type was raised in order to execute and display the incised pattern, for the rims are low and decoration was difficult. Among sherds of the buff-with-gray-core variety, some have two ridges instead of one (Pl. 19, *B;* Fig. 83, *12*).

2. The bowl is made of all varieties of paste except for the red and brown varieties. Red bowls with gray cores are about 20 cm high, and the walls are quite straight. The whole exterior is covered with cord impressions, and the lip exhibits short incised strokes (Pl. 18, *B;* Fig. 82, *9*). Bowls made of the buff varieties are more complex, some possessing a raised ridge along the circumference below the rim, a form absent in red bowls (Pl. 21; Fig. 82, *11–14*).

Decoration. Except for the rims and the lower edges of the ring feet, the entire body of the vessel is normally covered with cord-like impressions. From the closeness of the adjoining strands, the depth of the negative impressions, and the overall pattern, it is probable that the patterns were impressed over the wet surface by rouletting, lengthwise, a cord-wrapped stick and by using a cord-wrapped paddle (Pl. 17).

In addition to the cord marks, the corded ware jars and bowls are clearly *decorated* in two ways—by painting and incising.

The surface of the sherds is generally in a badly eroded condition, primarily because of the loose texture, and only traces of a red pigment are detected on a few sherds. It is extremely difficult to state in a general way whether the red pigment is the remnant of a slip or part of a painted design. On one sherd (Pl. 21, *D;* Fig. 83, *3*), however, where both red pigmentation and incision are present on the rim, it is clear under a binocular microscope that the red pigment extends into the bottom of the incised groove, showing that the red pigment was applied after the incision was made. This makes it likely that the red color, if not a red design, was applied for a decorative purpose. Another large piece of body sherd was found in Locus Q on which are vertical rows of red stripes, approximately 10 mm wide (Pl. 17, *E*). These were applied over the corded surface, and were clearly intended for decoration.

Incised patterns occur on the rim, the shoulder, and occasionally on the ring foot. They are particularly developed on the raised rims with ridges, which are apparently designed for this decorative purpose (Fig. 83; Pls. 19, 20). The overwhelming majority of the incised patterns were executed with a pair of incising instruments (Pls. 21, 22). There were apparently pairs of different sizes for patterns of different sizes. The incision was done while the clay was still wet, for some of the rounded wavy lines could not have been incised otherwise. But the margins of the incisions are not

TABLE 28. NUMBER OF SHERDS OF DIFFERENT VARIETIES OF CORDED WARE IN LAYERS 13-20, IN PIT VI-1 (QUADRANT A2), LOCUS Q, TAPENKENG

	Fine Buff	Buff	Gray Core Buff	Gray Core Red	Red	Brown	Total
13		9	15	7	8	8	47
		19.15%	*31.91%*	*14.89%*	*17.02%*	*17.02%*	
14	1	10	35	7	19	12	84
	1.19%	*11.90%*	*41.67%*	*8.33%*	*22.62%*	*14.29%*	
15	3	40	52	35	44	13	187
	1.60%	*21.39%*	*27.81%*	*18.72%*	*23.53%*	*6.95%*	
16		9	29	16	17	13	84
		10.71%	*34.52%*	*19.05%*	*20.24%*	*15.48%*	
17	2	107	287	67	93	43	599
	0.33%	*17.86%*	*47.91%*	*11.19%*	*15.53%*	*7.18%*	
18		23	50	22	21	40	156
		14.74%	*32.05%*	*14.10%*	*13.46%*	*25.64%*	
19		21	35	23	9	32	120
		17.50%	*29.17%*	*19.17%*	*7.50%*	*26.67%*	
20	2	5	18	2	7	2	36
	5.56%	*13.89%*	*50.00%*	*5.56%*	*19.44%*	*5.56%*	
Total*	8	229	538	181	224	163	1,343
	5.36%	*17.05%*	*40.06%*	*13.48%*	*16.68%*	*12.14%*	

* Total number of each variety includes sherds in upper layers.

noticeably raised, suggesting that either the incision was applied while the clay was already beginning to harden or the incised surface was scraped after the incision was completed. There is no evidence that the incised patterns cover previously applied cord marks; it is possible that blank areas were left on the shoulder in applying the cord impression, or that the incision was executed before the cord impression.

There is a variety of incised designs. Indentations and dotted lines frequently occur along the lip, and bands of square or rectangular units decorate the exterior surface of the rim and the shoulder. These units are filled with obliquely placed parallel strokes or wavy lines. These and other rare variations (such as rim interior incisions) are seen in Figures 82, 83 and Plates 18–22.

Temporal and Spatial Variations

Several varieties of the corded ware have been described on the basis of paste, and rim forms and incised patterns also show great diversity. These variations are very difficult to interpret, owing to the small depth and the small area. Whatever changes there were occurred within a depth of no more than 40 cm of deposits in all areas, and whatever horizontal dimension that can be observed must be discerned within an area that is only 80 m long. After repeated analyses of the several variables described above, no clear-cut patterns of change—either horizontal or chronological —can be distinguished. Table 28 shows only that the division into the various paste varieties of the cord-marked pottery occurs throughout the corded ware occupation, and that the buff varieties are quantitatively greater than the red. Other aspects of the pattern of distribution are not clear.

In decorative designs, Locus Q has the greatest variety; loci L and P have simple designs of much smaller numbers. It should also be pointed out that Locus Q has yielded the largest number of stone implements as well, and it is likely that living activities were more intensified on the southern—upslope—part of the site than on the northern.

Chapter 8. The Yüan-shan Culture

THE main occupation of the site of Tapenkeng, spanning from approximately 1000 B.C. to the early centuries of the Christian era, is that of the Yüan-shan culture. This culture was first identified at the Yüan-shan Shellmound at the northern end of Taipei city in the early years of the twentieth century and has since been found to be widespread in the Taipei basin. The general characteristics of this culture at the Tapenkeng site can be described as follows.

1. The settlement was extensive and the subsistence was based on agriculture but supplemented by hunting and fishing. Mollusk-shell collecting is not in evidence at the site.

2. The technology is basically one of an advanced Stone Age level. A variety of rocks was employed for the making of specialized implements by polishing, chipping, and pecking. Pottery was a principal container, and other clay objects were widely used. Objects of bone, shell, and antler have not been found at the site, but their use can be presumed.

3. No clearly discernible remains of houses are found, but isolated post holes indicate the use of timber, and rocks were probably cemented with clay to build foundations of walls.

4. A pottery kiln foundation was found, constructed of wattle-and-daub. This suggests that dwelling houses also had mud-and-reed walls.

5. The pottery is characteristically of the Yüan-shan type. The basic form is the jar or pot with a flaring mouth, a lid, two vertical strap or loop handles, and a ring foot attached to the roundish bottom. The paste is visibly sandy, and the wall is relatively thin. A red slip or coat was frequently applied onto the exterior surface, and single-unit incised designs occur often on the handles and infrequently on the rims and the ring feet. There is positively no impressed decoration in the Yüan-shan ware, and the impressed ware that appears in the upper levels was apparently intrusive from another culture.

6. Stone-making implements and blanks are found scattered at the site. The diagnostic forms of stone artifacts are chipped hoes, shouldered axes, stepped adzes, triangular projectile points with central perforations, and grooved pebbles. An important negative trait is the absence of polished stone knives.

There is little doubt that the Corded Ware culture at the site of Tapenkeng can be identified with the Corded Ware culture at Fengpitou. There is likewise little question that the Yüan-shan culture at Tapenkeng stems from an entirely different tradition from the Lungshanoid culture of Fengpitou. The contrasts between the two are distinctive and wide-ranging.

House Remains

Short rows of post holes, each about 3 cm across and 3 to 6 cm deep, were located at Locus N from different levels of the Yüan-shan occupation. No overall patterns can be discerned, however, and whether these were made during or after the Yüan-shan occupation cannot be established. Large numbers of andesite rock fragments and slabs are found throughout the Yüan-shan occupation, mixed with Yüan-shan sherds and stone implements. These are found in particular abundance at loci N and P. In Locus N a hole—12 cm across and approximately 14 cm deep—was formed by several andesite slabs (Pl. 13, *A*), and at Locus P several andesite fragments were found attached with hard, plaster-like clay layers (Pl. 13, *C*). These seem to suggest the use of andesite rocks and slabs for constructing the foundations of house walls, a custom that prevails among the present farmers down in the coastal valley (Pl. 13, *B*). It is possible that the Yüan-shan inhabitants utilized natural stones for house wall foundations, cemented them with clay, and supported the walls with timber posts. But if such was indeed the case, all the houses have been completely destroyed by repeated disturbances during the last two thousand years, and no residential patterns can be clearly recognized.

At Locus L, two isolated post holes were located. Each is about 10 cm in diameter and 25 cm deep. The top appears near the bottom of the Yüan-shan stratum, and the lower, pointed end was inserted into the layers with corded ware sherds. Unquestionably, these indicate timber posts of Yüanshan-period houses; unfortunately, they are too isolated and ill-preserved to yield any significant information about the house.

Chunks of burned clay were scattered throughout the site. Inferring from the reed impressions in the burned clay fragments of the kiln in Locus Q (Pl. 12, *D,E*), we may further speculate that some of the upper portions of the Yüan-shan house walls were constructed of wattle-and-daub.

The Pottery Kiln

A horseshoe-like structure of burned clay was located at Locus Q, pit VI-I (Fig. 84; Pl. 12). Although the ground here forms a slope, the plane of the structure is fairly level. The opening of the horseshoe faces north and down. The southern part is about 80 cm below the present ground surface, but the northern ends are only 45 cm below the ground (Fig. 85). The distance between the two arms is 130 cm, and the radius north–south is about 60 cm. The structure itself was made of clay, probably reinforced with reeds, and repeated burning converted the clay into hundreds of small lumps of bright red color. The structure is about 30 cm high but only 3 to 10 cm thick. It is apparent that a level ground surface was built on the terrace scarp, and a half-ring of clay was built on the surface. No other use for this structure can be conceived than as the base of an open, bonfire-type of pottery kiln. The clay wall was presumably built so that any water flowing from uphill would be diverted from the fire.

The kiln, as stated above, serves as a significant marker of time. Impressed and other kinds of pottery are abundant in levels above and in front of the kiln—probably in a caved-in depression—but behind and below the kiln potsherds other than the characteristic Yüan-shan ware are extremely rare. In the clay of the structure are mixed Yüanshan-type sherds. Probably the kiln was built at a time when the

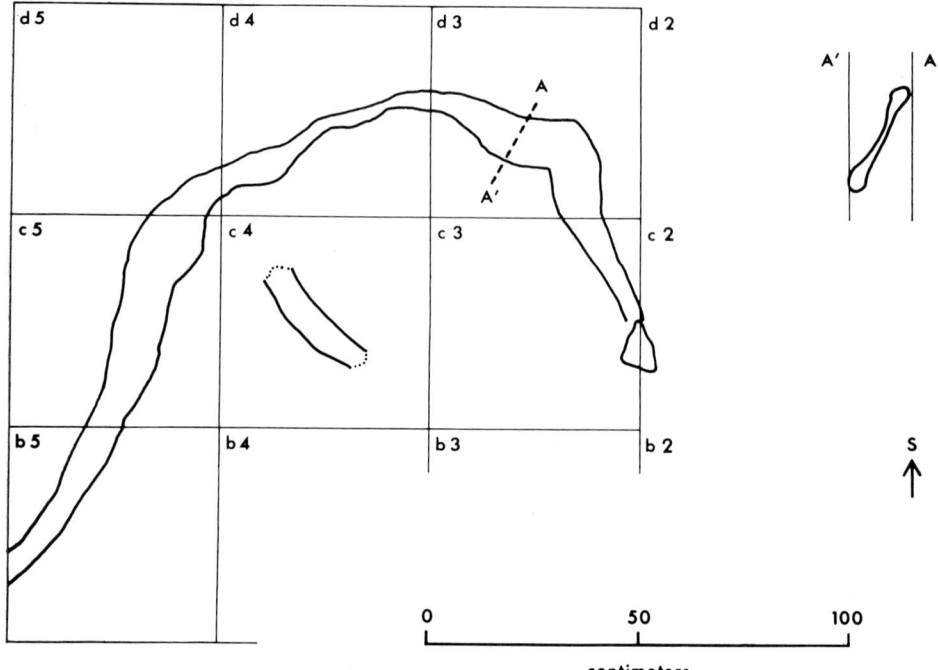

FIG. 84. Ground Plan of Kiln at Locus Q, Tapenkeng.

Yüan-shan was the only prevailing type of pottery. It subsequently fell into disuse, and this region served as a trash heap for an occupation in which new ceramic elements occurred in increasing quantities.

The Subsistence Implements

The stone implements at the site of Tapenkeng are remarkably abundant; our total collection has more than four hundred pieces. Three basic categories can be distinguished: hoe, adz, and arrowhead. There is no evidence of either the crops planted or the animals hunted. The Yüan-shan Shellmound of Taipei city has yielded a large number of animal bones (mostly deer) and bone implements. Small deer prospered as late as the ethnographic present in the forests at the base of the Kuanyin volcano.

There are no shellmounds of the Yüan-shan stratum at the Tapenkeng site. They are abundant in the Lower Garden, but their pottery content is post-Yüanshan. The most important shellfish at the Yüan-shan Shellmound, *Corbicula maxima* Prime, is very abundant at the estuary of the River Tamsui, and oysters are consumed by the modern villagers. In view of the fact that the coastline was much closer to the site during the occupation than it is at present, there is no doubt that shellfish collecting was easy for the Tapenkeng inhabitants. Other marine and riverine

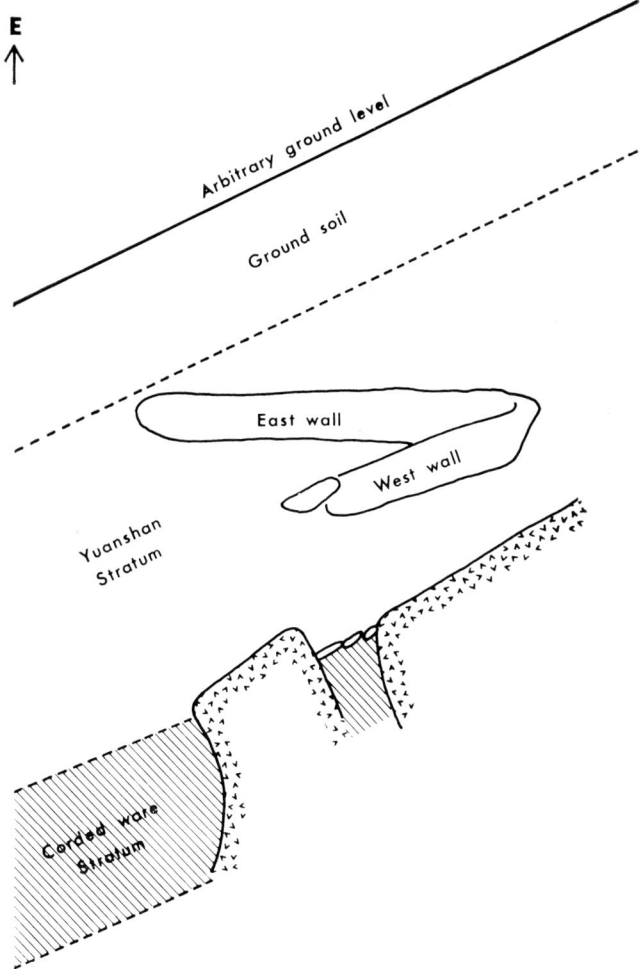

FIG. 85. Stratigraphical Position of Kiln in Relation to Depositional Units at Locus Q, Pit VI-1, Tapenkeng. (Horizontal width of section represented: 2 m.)

resources, such as fish, were also within easy reach, and their exploitation to some extent can be assumed. However, the conspicuous absence of shellmounds at the site, plus the fact that Tapenkeng's occupation followed the Yüan-shan Shellmound, may suggest that the inhabitants here were more advanced gardeners.

CHIPPED AND GROUND HOES

Hoes are the single most abundant artifact at the site (Fig. 86, *1*; Pl. 91); 34 were excavated and at least 50 others were collected on the surface of the Upper Slope alone. With very rare exceptions made of basalt, the overwhelming majority of these hoes are made of one rock: gray augite-hornblende andesite. The size is quite

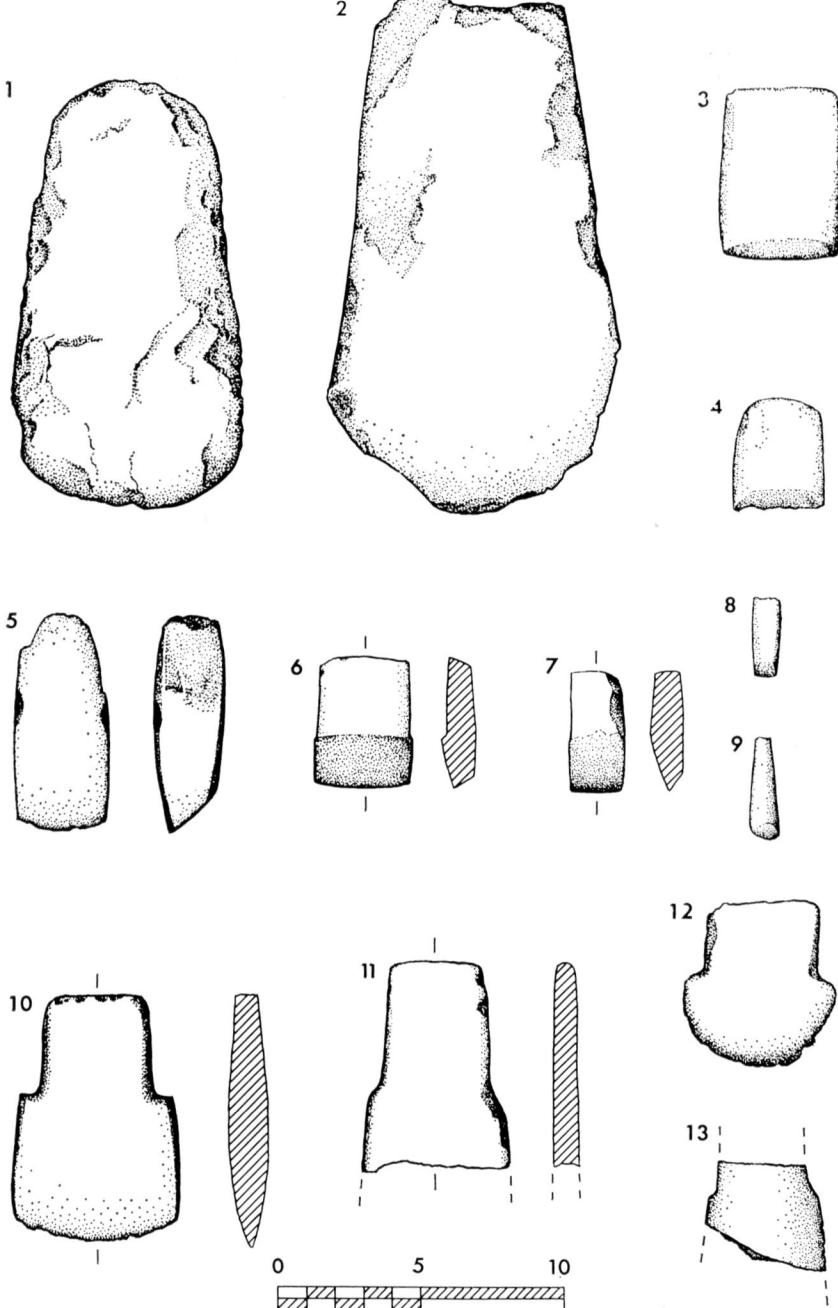

Fig. 86. Stone Hoes and Axes of the Yüan-shan Culture at Tapenkeng.

uniform: approximately 11–17 cm long, 8–12 cm wide, and 1.5–3 cm thick. All are made with the same technique: chipping around the edges, polishing the two broad faces a little, and sometimes grinding the butt. These hoes were presumably so commonplace and were intended for such everyday earth-digging work that the makers needed no more than a rough outline and paid little attention to the details. The hoes were probably hafted perpendicularly to wooden handles (Pl. 90, *D*), and all wear-marks occur on one broad side.

POLISHED FLAT HOES AND THICK HOES

Completely polished hoes at the Tapenkeng site fall into two groups (Fig. 86, *2;* Pl. 90, *B,C,E–H*). The first consists of those made of gray augite-hornblende andesite; the butt is ground flat, and the cutting edge is ground from both sides and is rounded in side view. The size and thickness of this group are very close to the chipped-and-ground hoes, and the cross section is relatively flat (Pl. 90, *E–H*).

The second group consists of two samples, both made of dark gray, hard, compact, silicified medium- or coarse-grained sandstone. They are much larger than the flat hoes: about 17 or 18 cm long, 9 or 10 cm wide, and the body is thicker—about 3.5 cm. The cross section is lentoid, and all edges are ground and rounded (Pl. 90, *B,C*).

AXES AND ADZES—EXCLUSIVE OF SHOULDERED AND STEPPED TYPES

One huge ax (20.8 cm long, 10.5 wide, 4.4 deep, and 1,255 g in weight) was excavated from the topsoil at Locus L. It was made of dark gray, hard, compact, muscovite-bearing medium-grained sandstone flake; the flaking surface was left intact, and the cortex surface has a few large flaking scars (Pl. 90, *A*). The margins were slightly retouched. No sign of wear is observed, and it could be a blank.

A mid-section of a possibly plano-convex polished ax, of brownish-gray, hard, muscovite-bearing medium-grained sandstone, with a width of 5 cm and a depth of 1.9 cm, was excavated from Locus P.

Two fragments of thick rectangular adzes are recovered from Locus Q, one of andesite and the other of dark gray and brown siliceous slate. Both are highly polished.

The remaining adzes excavated from the site are all of small size (two about 2 cm long, and five about 4 cm long), polished, with a cutting edge that is straight in side view and asymmetrical in profile. Four are made from hornblende andesite, two from green serpentine, and one from greenish-black, siliceous slate. All show signs of wear along the back side of the cutting edge (Fig. 86, *3,4;* Pl. 96, *C–J*).

SHOULDERED AXES

Nine shouldered axes (complete or fragmentary; Fig. 86, *10–13;* Pl. 93) were found, three of them from the surface. They are all of gray, augite-hornblende andesite, and are of one shape: 6 or 8 cm long, 5 or 6 cm wide, and a little over 1 cm thick, with straight butt base, rounded or angled shoulders, and rounded edge on the broad side. All the excavated ones came from near the surface.

STEPPED ADZES

Thirty-one stepped adzes, almost all complete, were excavated at the site (Fig. 86, *5–7;* Pls. 94, 95). One of them is made of yellow-brown, medium-grained sandstone, and two others are of serpentine. All the rest are made of gray, brown, or black siliceous slate or augite-hornblende andesite. The sizes vary considerably; the shortest is 2.3 cm long and the longest 10.5 cm, but the majority (23) fall within 3 to 8 cm in length. The width is mostly from one half to two thirds of the length, and there is a single piece with a greater width than length. The thickness varies greatly in proportion to the length and the width. The distribution of the thickness–breadth index of 28 stepped adzes is as follows:

30–35	1	60–65	0
35–40	7	65–70	2
40–45	2	70–75	2
45–50	7	75–80	0
50–55	3	80–85	1
55–60	2	85–90	1

It is apparent that the mode is 35–50.

An andesite stepped adz, no. 53, found in III-2-c2-2 at Locus N, is of especial interest. It is apparently a reject, the face broken, but the edge not yet ground sharp (Pl. 94, *I*). The step is clearly shown on a broad face, indicating that in making the stepped adzes the step was completed before the cutting edge was ground. The step itself offers another criterion for subdividing the stepped adzes: those with steps running all the way across the back (Fig. 86, *6,7*), and those with only two steps along the edges of the back but without interconnecting in the middle (Fig. 86, *5*). There are 18 of the former, but 10 of the latter. Among the remaining pieces, one has a thin, shallow groove instead of a step. The continuously stepped adzes were excavated throughout the different layers, but the partially stepped adzes were excavated from the upper, post-kiln, levels.

CUTTING IMPLEMENTS

The well-defined polished stone knives, so characteristic of the Lungshanoid horizon in southeastern China in general and at Fengpitou in particular, are not present at Tapenkeng, nor in the Yüan-shan culture as a whole. In their place are roughly shaped, elongated flakes with a long cutting edge that probably served the same or similar uses. Eight of these pieces were recovered at Tapenkeng, five of medium- or fine-grained sandstone, two of andesite, and one of black schistose slate (Pl. 92, *M–P*).

ARROWHEADS AND SPEARHEADS

Next to the chipped-ground hoe, arrow- and spearheads are the most abundant artifact category at Tapenkeng, 53 pieces having been excavated (Fig. 87, *1–11;* Pl. 98). All are made of gray or black (schistose or phyllitic) slate, and are polished.

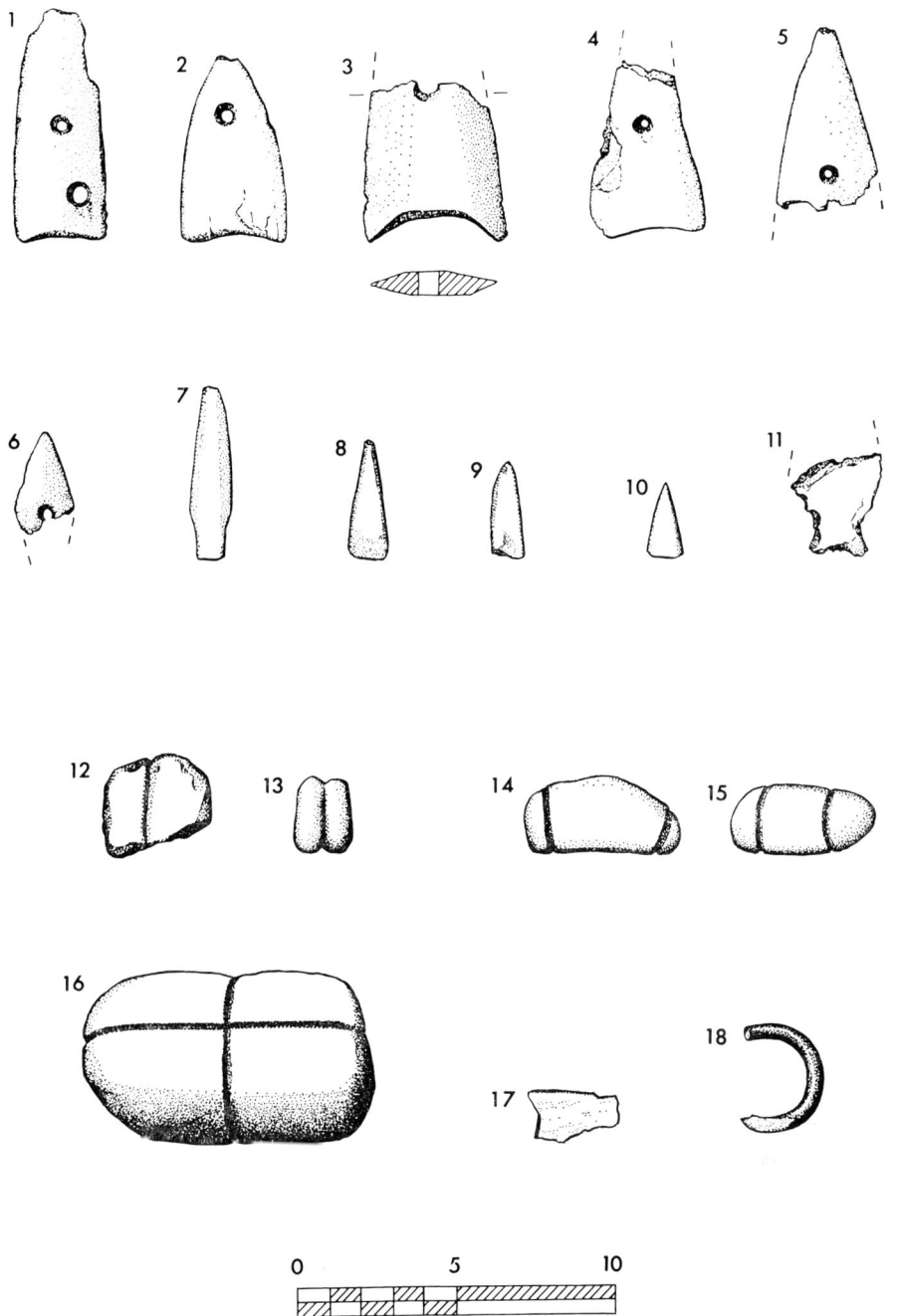

FIG. 87. Stone Points, Grooved Stones, and Stone Ornaments from the Yuan-shan Culture Stratum at Tapenkeng.

The majority are of an elongated triangular shape, with a straight or concave base and one or two perforations at the center or near the point (Fig. 87, *1–6*). Many are broken near the hole, and the complete ones are sometimes as long as 8 cm, but 5 or 6 cm seem to be the rule. Another type, which includes seven pieces, is thin and triangular, without holes. A third type, including only three specimens, is willow leaf-shaped (Fig. 87, *7–9*). All the willow leaves were excavated from the upper levels, probably intrusive from the Lungshanoid culture to the south of the area.

Grooved Stone Objects

There are three classes of grooved stone objects (Fig. 87, *12–16;* Pl. 92, *A–F, H,I,L*). The first consists of two surface findings, both river pebbles with circumferential grooves at both ends, a characteristic form of net sinker on Formosa (Pl. 92, *H,I*). The second is a single piece of pebble with two side notches, of unknown use (Pl. 92, *L*). The third includes six yellow sandstone fragments, apparently ground and grooved for use as weights (Pl. 92, *A–F*). Bigger ones are heavy enough for net sinkers, but the light ones were more likely loom weights.

Technology

Stone Working

Implements indicating stone manufacture are found throughout the site, not only in the excavated strata but also extensively on the surface. In all likelihood stone manufacture was a household affair, and no portion of the site can be described as being a stone workshop exclusive for that purpose. Two groups of finds can be described under the present heading—tools for stone making, and raw material, blanks, and wastes.

Stone-making tools include hammerstones, grinding stones, and whetstones (Pl. 89). All hammerstones, about twenty in number, are pebbles of hard, compact, fine- or medium-grained sandstone, some elongated and others roundish. The long ones have wear-marks at the ends, the round ones have them along the edges and/or at the centers. These hammerstones could have been used for food preparation as well as for making implements. One piece of stone mortar-like container was found, indicating that some of the elongated pebbles were probably pestles.

More than a dozen small grinding stones—held in the hand and used for polishing—are found (Pl. 89, *D,E*). A few of them are of sandstone but most are made from reddish-brown mudstones that were originally nodules in shale beds. It is possible that for coarser work the sandstone gives better results, but the mudstone is good for fine polish. Grinding lines, and in one case a groove, are clearly visible. All sides are used.

Several fragments of larger whetstones are found, invariably of dark gray, muscovite-bearing, fine-grained sandstone. The top has a depression ground smooth by repeated use (Pl. 89, *A,B*).

About a dozen sandstone pebble flakes and cores with flaking scars were found

(Pl. 89, *C*). No wear-marks are visible, either to the naked eye or under a micro-scope, and they were probably blanks. Since so few of the implements were made of sandstone, it is difficult to say what these objects were intended for. Scores of slate pieces and fragments are found, many bearing saw-marks (Pl. 89, *F,G*). These were mostly intended for arrowpoints. Apparently a rough shape was first sawed from the rock, and a perforation was made before the edges were sharpened. Many half-holes on the edges of the slate fragments indicate that rows of holes were drilled before sawing or breaking in order to prevent the rock from splitting and flaking. Only one reject can be related to other definite types of stone artifacts, i.e. the broken stepped adz (Pl. 94, *I*).

SPINNING AND WEAVING

Twenty spindle whorls were recovered at the site, in average 4 cm in diameter and 3 cm high (Pl. 100, *A–C,E,G–I*). With a single exception (conical on one side and flat on the other; Pl. 100, *E*), all of them are biconical in shape and have a hole at the center. One of the spindle whorls shows clearly in cross section that the hole was made from both directions while the clay was still soft. Rows of punctates sometimes decorate the surface.

Some of the grooved sandstone pebbles, as previously stated, may have served as loom weights.

POTTERY MAKING

Pottery of the Yüan-shan culture at Tapenkeng is above all (in contrast to the Lungshanoid pottery) characterized by the coarse texture of its paste. Percentages of sand inclusions (quartz, feldspar, and mica) in the various wares will be described below, but it can be generally stated that in Lungshanoid pottery the quartz content as a rule never exceeds 25 per cent, whereas in the Yüan-shan wares it is never below 35 per cent. The only exception to this rule is the buff impressed pottery of the upper levels of the Tapenkeng site, which has only 5 per cent quartz and was prob-ably fired at a temperature as high as 750°C. This indicates a considerable improve-ment in pottery-making technique during the Yüan-shan occupation at Tapenkeng and all other wares were fired at temperatures ranging from 450 to 600°. This range of temperature suggests the use of an open kiln and wood or straw fuel. The clay foundation of the kiln recovered at Locus Q bears this out. Whether the appearance of improved pottery above the kiln level is an event related to the abandonment of the kiln itself, is an interesting question.

All pottery vessels were made by hand. There is no evidence of either the use of wheel or the coiling technique in the construction of the vessel, and neither pottery-making implements nor an area of pottery making (other than the kiln itself) has been recovered. Several rim sherds found near the kiln are deformed (e.g. twisted contours), and may have come from rejects.

The construction of a vessel appears to follow these steps: a clay disk was placed on a board as the base and the body was built on top of it, with fingers and fist pressing inside; the collar and the ring foot were built separately and then applied to the body; and the handles were finally applied to the exterior surface. When it was dry the surface was further burnished slightly. Incision was done when the clay was still wet, but painting was most likely applied after the burnishing. Impression by means of a carved paddle was used only on the Botanical Garden impressed ware, and this appears only in post-kiln levels. The use of the anvil-and-paddle technique was probably also introduced at the same time, but again it was apparently confined to the Botanical Garden impressed ware.

Pottery

Yüan-shan Type

Paste. Sherds of the well-definable Yüan-shan ware (Pls. 80, *A–E,G;* 81; 82, *A–D,G–K;* 83, *A–D,G–N;* 84; 85; 86, *E*)—first typified by pottery at the Yüan-shan Shellmound—are of rather coarse texture, containing a large amount of sand inclusions of observable grain sizes. A thin section has shown 35 per cent quartz, 10 per cent feldspar, and some mica, and its firing temperature is estimated at 550–600°C. (A sherd of the same type from the Yüan-shan Shellmound has yielded 55 per cent quartz and 5 per cent feldspar, with an estimated firing temperature of 500–560°C. Compare the high percentage of quartz and feldspar, principal ingredients of the "sand inclusions," in the Yüan-shan ware with those in the Lungshanoid wares.) The average hardness of the sherds is only about 2°. The core of the sherds is in most cases light brown or gray (3.2YR5.5/3.8), but some are a much lighter "ivory" (10.0YR8.4/2.3).

The pottery was handmade and does not exhibit evidence of coiling. The wall is in average 3 to 5 mm thick. The exterior surface is always coated in a light brown or grayish wash. The body was made first, and then the collars, lugs, handles, and ring feet were applied. Some sherds exhibit evidence of dark red patches or stripes on the exterior surface in irregular and unpatterned shapes.

A small number of sherds of this ware is darker gray in color (5.5/ and 6.3/) and harder (3.5–4°). Apparently these came from vessels of larger size (Pl. 86, *E*).

Form. The pottery remains are very fragmentary and badly preserved, and the vessel forms can only be reconstructed from sherds. The principal form of the pottery vessels in the Yüan-shan ware is the jar with a lid, a collar, two strap or loop handles, a globular body with roundish base, and a ring foot. A few rim sherds appear to come from bowls (Pl. 82, *A–C*), but the whole shapes of the bowls cannot be reconstructed.

Twenty-five sherds of lids were recovered. All are disk-shaped with a convex upper face, a concave lower face, and a knob. The diameter of the disk is 10 to 14 cm, and the diameter of the knob is 2 to 3 cm. The knobs are low and nipple-like (1) (Pl. 80, *G*); short (15 mm) cylindrical (1); long (20–25 mm) cylindrical (10) (Pl. 80, *C,D*); long cylindrical, with a hole cutting horizontally across the middle (2); with a constricted base and vertically incised lines encircling the base (4); with a polygonal top (2) (Pl. 80, *E*); or phallus-like (1) (Pl. 80, *B*). A lid is made of stone (Pl. 80, *A*).

Rim sherds of jars fall into two classes: those with mouths of small diameter and those with mouths of large diameter. In both cases the height of the collar is mostly 3 or 4 cm, but the small mouths are below 5 cm across (Pl. 81, *C–E*) and the large mouths are usually above 10 cm (Pls. 81, *F*; 82, *D,G–K*). Small mouths occur on double- or triple-mouth jars (Pl. 81, *A*, Yüan-shan Shellmound) and occasionally those of long-neck bottles (Pl. 81, *G*); a few of them exhibit a small spout.

Most of the rim sherds belong to the regular large-mouth jar type (*kui*). The overwhelming majority of them have a rounded, thinned lip, or slightly thickened lip, but many sherds show lips which are more than twice as thick as the wall. The wall of the collar is straight or curves slightly inward or outward. A few have twisted wavy lips, and two sherds have a spout.

Handles and lugs are all applied to the exterior surface of the body. The majority of the handles are paired and placed vertically at the collar part; one end is attached to the upper edge of the rim, its upper surface extending to the upper surface of the lip (Pl. 83, *J*), and the other end is attached either to the base of the collar or to the middle of the shoulder. These vertical handles are straps (with flat cross section) (Pl. 83, *J–N*) or loops (with round cross section) (Pl. 83, *G–I*). Handles of a second category are horizontally placed, in pairs, at the maximum diameter of the body. These are long and flat (Pl. 83, *C,D*), long and round with one or two holes (Pl. 83, *A,B*), or simple lugs. Smaller lugs on the body surface shaped like nipples are probably decorative (Pl. 84, *H*).

Body sherds are extremely fragmentary but of rather uniform thickness. The exterior surface is always coated or slipped unless heavily eroded, and the interior surface often exhibits depressions caused by fingers in the process of body construction. Many sherds show an angular curve and are probably the part where the shoulder curves down toward the belly. Base sherds are distinguished by stripes of a rough surface to which the ring foot was attached. These rough surfaces indicate that the coating of the pot was done after the ring foot was applied.

Ring-foot sherds are many; aside from bowls, which are few, all jars seem to be ring-footed. The diameter seems to range from 10 to 20 cm (which, plus the diameter of the rim sherds, helps to suggest the size of the body), and their heights cluster around two medians, 6 cm and 12 cm. Largely speaking, these ring feet are low (Pl. 85).

Decoration. In sharp contrast to the Lungshanoid wares at Fengpitou, paddle impression as a decorating technique is completely absent in the Yüan-shan ware; check-stamped pottery and a few other impressed designs occur in the impressed ware here at Tapenkeng in association with the Yüan-shan ware during a late phase of the occupation of the site, but cord- and basket-marked pottery, the mainstay of the Lungshanoid, is not seen at all. On the other hand, heavy coating is a Yüan-shan characteristic. Most of the area of the vessel is left undecorated except for an occasional red or brown slip, and the decorations are executed by one of three techniques—incision, ring impression, or painting.

Incision was most often used; the techniques were sophisticated and a variety of tools presumably used. Most of the patterns are made up of short strokes by very fine tools with pointed ends, apparently executed with heavy and fast scratching-like movements. On the exterior (upper) surface and the knob of the lid, a stroke sometimes occurs on the top of the knob and a series of them at the base, but very often at the center of the concave interior (lower) surface of the disk there are patterns consisting of a single stroke, two punctates, four strokes forming a cross, rows of lines (Pl. 80, *E*), or rows of dotted lines. They may be signs of some sort, for the hidden location of these patterns does not suggest a decorative purpose. Incised lines and dots often occur on the upper surface of the thickened lip or on the exterior or interior of the collar, making up rows of sparse lines and dots, cross-hatches, lozenges, and checkerboard patterns (Pl. 82). Similar designs also occur on the exterior of the ring foot (Pl. 85). A pair of short, incised strokes, slanting toward each other at the top, or two to four such pairs, often occur on the upper surface of the handles (Pl. 83, *J,L–N*). At the Yüan-shan Shellmound, where potsherds are better preserved, some body sherds exhibit incised net patterns, i.e. checkerboard patterns with punctates at the intersections like the knobs of nets (Pl. 84, *G*). This pattern has not been found here.

Impressions of rings, about 4 mm in diameter, occur on the interior of some rim sherds, and ring impressions of larger diameters forming rows occur on a large ring foot of huge dimensions (Pl. 86, *E*). Painted designs are rarely seen at the site; only traces of them are discernible on some sherds. The Commission for Historical Research of Taipei Prefecture has in its collection a large sherd, found at Tapenkeng southeast of our excavated area, that exhibits unpatterned red painting applied with a large brush. A few sherds painted in red, with dots and parallel-line designs, have been found at the Yüan-shan Shellmound. Such painted decorations have not been found on our excavated sherds here, but evidently painting was one of the decorating techniques at Tapenkeng also. In addition, lugs and clay crosses pasted on the walls (Pl. 84, *C,F,H*), circumferential ridges on ring feet, cutouts in the ring foot, and pressed wavy rims (Pl. 82, *I,J*) are rare decorative devices in the Yüan-shan ware.

TPK RED

Paste. Bright or dull orange or brownish-buff (6.9YR5.5/5.8) in color throughout, sherds of this ware are hard (4°), coarse of texture, and rough to touch. A thin section shows 65 per cent quartz, 10 per cent feldspar, and some mica, with an estimated firing temperature of 450–500°C, but the inclusions are not so conspicuous or large as in the Yüan-shan ware, and the texture is uniformly coarse. The manufacture is similar to that of Yüan-shan ware, but the walls are more even in thickness and the finger-made depressions on the interior surface are not so conspicuous.

Form. Lid sherds are rare, and only one knob form occurs, i.e. short (2.5 cm), cylindrical, with a diameter of 3 cm. Rim sherds are again of jars and bowls, and body sherds and ring-foot sherds abound. There is, however, no evidence of the angular shoulder curve, and the ring feet are better applied to the base. Handles are all vertical and cylindrical. The upper end is attached to the lip, and the lower end to the middle of the shoulder. Two handles have small rivets at the lower end, presumably inserted into the body for firmer attachment (Pl. 83, *E,F*).

Decoration. A rim sherd of a bowl has a strip of clay applied to the wall just below the rim (Pl. 86, *B*), and small round holes occur in the ring foot (Pl. 86, *C*). Otherwise the sherds of this ware are undecorated.

TPK Brown

Paste. Sherds of this ware show a wide range of colors, from reddish to blackish, but most are coffee or grayish and brown (0.1YR3.6/1.5) throughout. Rather hard (3.5°) and coarse, they contain a large amount of sand inclusions but feel less rough than TPK Red. A thin section shows 60 per cent quartz, 20 per cent feldspar, some mica, and some organic matter that reacts with H_2O_2. The firing temperature is estimated at 450–500°C. Manufacture is by hand. Coating is heavy, similar to the Yüan-shan ware, and red slip occurs on some sherds.

Form. Again two vessel forms can be reconstructed from sherds: jars-pots and bowls. The jar or pot differs from both Yüan-shan and TPK Red wares in that it lacks lid, handles, and ring foot and consists of a high collar and a globular body. The base shape is unclear but is probably roundish.

Decoration. Two rim sherds of pots exhibit incised designs on the interior, consisting of short strokes arranged in meandering rows (Pl. 82, *E,F*).

Botanical Garden Impressed

Paste. In appearance, sherds of this ware (deriving its name from the Botanical Garden site, in Taipei city, where the ware was first recognized) are far from homogeneous, in color, texture, or hardness. But they can be clearly contrasted to the sherds of the other wares by their impressed decorative patterns and by their generally finer texture. Three major subcategories are easily distinguishable. (1) Red or "maroon" (7.8R2.7/2.1), with check impressions (Pl. 87, *A*). These are generally coarse and hard (2.5°). A thin section exhibits 50 per cent quartz, 10 per cent feldspar, and some mica, and its firing temperature is estimated at 650–700°C. (2) Buff or "cream" (3.3Y8.6/4.5), with check impressions (Pl. 87,*B*); generally softer (1.5°) and of fine texture. A thin section shows only 6 per cent quartz, 3 per cent feldspar, and some mica and organic matter, with an estimated firing temperature of 700–750°C. This is the highest firing temperature known in the prehistoric pottery of Taiwan. (3) Buff or "sunset" or "pale orange" (7.7YR8.0/6.0), with chevron impressions (Pl. 87, *E,F*); somewhat harder (3°) and of finer texture.

Walls of the sherds are generally thicker than the other wares; an average of 5 mm or more is the rule. These are all handmade, presumably with the aid of carved paddles. Heavy coating occurs. Because of the fine texture the surface is often heavily eroded away by water, giving a "washed" appearance.

Form. Pot (with a collar and a globular body) is the only vessel form that can be reconstructed from the sherds. Rim sherds are straight, slightly flaring, or curving inward. A lid with a short cylindrical knob was found (Pl. 80, *F*). Vertical and horizontal handles similar to the Yüan-shan ware forms are found but are very rare. Base is roundish or flat. A neck sherd of a long-neck jar was found.

Decoration. Check impression is the most common decoration of this ware. These check patterns vary in size of units but are apparently impressed on the surface of the vessels (below the base of the collar) in units, e.g. by means of a carved paddle or a stamp (Pl. 87, *A–D*). Chevron impressions are found on some two dozen sherds (Pl. 87, *E,F*); and mat (Pl. 87, *G*) and herring-bone (Pl. 87, *H*) impression each occurs once.

KETANGALAN WARES

These are hard (3°), gray (7.1/) or "cinnamon" (7.6YR6.3/4.2), and thin (2–3 mm), giving a metallic sound when knocked. Check impressed and with a concave base and a thickened base rim, sherds of this ware are known to represent the pottery of the historic Ketangalan tribes (Pl. 101, *G–J*). They occur at the site only in the topsoil and will not be described here.

PORCELAIN AND STONE WARE

Contemporaneous with the Ketangalan ware, sherds of porcelain and stone wares of Chinese origin again occur at the site only in the topsoil (Pl. 101, *K–M*). These will be omitted from discussion.

Utensils Related to Pottery

A considerable number of small disks made of potsherds was found throughout the site in different layers (Pl. 100, *L,M*). Their pastes vary but correspond to the pottery of the horizons in which they occur. Each of these disks is 4.5 to 5 cm in diameter and is largely circular in shape, although the cutting along the edges is not very neat. Two of the disks have a small perforation at the center (Pl. 100, *J,K*). Three possible uses can be suggested for them: pottery scraper, spindle whorl, or pot lid. The second can probably be ruled out on the ground that these are too light and that spindle whorls abound but are of other shapes. The third, use as a lid or stopper, is perhaps the most reasonable, because one type of pottery found at the site has a small mouth into which the disk could fit, and the perforation at the center gives seat for a string in place of a knob.

Scattered throughout the site are fragments of rather large pyramidal andesite, pumiceous, and sandstone rocks, 15 to 20 cm high and 14 to 16 cm in diameter at the base (Pl. 99, *B*). A few have two depressions on a side, giving rise to a handle-like projection in between. The shapes vary in actual details, and the archeologists working at the site earlier believed they were seeing stone sculptures of a very primitive kind. At the Yüan-shan Shellmound a few fragments of clay pot supporters were collected, which are rather comparable in shape (Pl. 99, *A*) (Sung 1957). These stone ones at Tapenkeng probably served similar purposes.

Ornaments

About two dozen fragments of jade and serpentine ornaments have been recovered. These include a serpentine pendant (Fig. 87, *17;* Pl. 100, *W*) and two perforated tubular beads (Pl. 100, *P,Q*); the rest are bracelets and/or anklets (Fig. 87, *18;* Pl. 100, *R–Z, a–e*). Most if not all of the bracelets consist of two halves, at both ends of which are small perforations for the attachment of strings.

One piece of bronze was found at Locus L, pit IX-2-d1, level −26 cm. It was broken in the process of excavation into seven pieces. Restored, they make up a fragment of probably a bracelet. The length of the arc is 20 mm, the height 16 mm, and the thickness 2 mm. One of the edges was the original margin of the bracelet (Pl. 100, *O*). This is the only bronze artifact discovered in 1964 at the site, but it lends greater credence to the authenticity of the bronze arrowhead discovered here in 1963 (on the Upper Slope, in Area D, near our Locus N).

Temporal and Spatial Variations

Since the area of excavation at Tapenkeng is very small and is confined to the northeastern part of the prehistoric village, we do not recognize significant patterns of variation within the Yüan-shan culture in terms of spatial distribution. Remains of structures have been recovered at loci L, N, and P, remains of stone manufacture are scattered throughout the site, a pottery kiln occurs at Locus Q, and potsherds are more abundant at the central portions of the site than on the northern edge. These are some aspects of spatial variation that are immediately apparent.

On temporal variation there is a larger amount of data. As described in Chapter 6, the Yüan-shan culture at the site is represented in the ceramic sequence by the entire segment after the corded ware layers and before the Ketangalan layers, in layers 4 through 13 at Locus Q, pit VI-1. Artifacts have been recorded in layers of 10 cm throughout the 1-meter depth of Yüan-shan deposits, and analyses have been performed on every aspect of the artifact distribution, but major change within the Yüan-shan culture can be observed only at one point, namely at the level of the pottery kiln. This change is manifest in the following aspects:

1. The kiln fell into disuse.

2. In the earlier levels sherds are basically classifiable as a single ware, i.e. the Yüan-shan type. From the later strata sherds of the Yüan-shan ware continue, but the other wares either emerge for the first time at the site or have gained immensely in popularity. These other wares of a later date include TPK Brown, TPK Red, and Botanical Garden Impressed.

3. Sherds of the buff Botanical Garden Impressed ware represent a significant improvement in pottery-making technology. The texture is extremely fine and the temperature of firing is at least 200°C higher than for the other wares, suggesting

major improvements in kiln construction and firing techniques. This may very well be related to the abandonment of the kiln. The introduction of the paddle-and-anvil technique also coincides with these other changes.

4. In stone inventory the same Yüan-shan artifact types continue from the earlier to the later levels, but in the later levels new varieties of arrowheads (willow-leaf-shaped) and stepped adzes (discontinuous steps, as opposed to the continuous steps) appear.

These indications together would seem to justify a division of the Yüan-shan culture at Tapenkeng into two temporal segments, pre-kiln and post-kiln. The two segments represent a single culture tradition, but during the post-kiln period intrusive elements representing a superior ceramic technology and the Lungshanoid culture tradition (primarily the willow-leaf arrowhead and the impressed pottery) appear to have made a strong impact upon the Tapenkeng Yüan-shan culture. This interpretation will have a strong bearing upon the prehistoric problems of Taipei basin, and will be discussed again in that connection.

Part III. Comparative Studies

Chapter 9. Fengpitou and Tapenkeng in the Postglacial Stratigraphy and Prehistoric Archeology of Formosa

TO ESTABLISH the placement in time and in culture history of the Neolithic settlements at the sites of Fengpitou and Tapenkeng and to explore the ecological conditions under which cultural similarities and differences can be understood, it is necessary to piece together the available bits of information on the postglacial stratigraphy and prehistoric archeology of the island of Formosa. This undertaking had not been attempted in any interdisciplinary manner until very recently, and the information that is now available is necessarily incomplete.

Climate and the Changes of Shoreline

Until evidence of man appears on Formosa from Pleistocene deposits no useful purpose will be served by reviewing the data of climatic and geological change on the island before the last glaciation (C. C. Lin 1963). Whatever geological evidence for glaciation is available, however, seems to be attributable to the latest Würm phases:

> Cirque groups, arêtes, terminal moraines, central moraines, Rundhöcker, rocks and gravels with glacial scourings, roches moutonnées, Trogschluss, Zungenbecken, Talgletscher, and other glacial formations in the Nanhutashan region (el. 3,740.3 m) of the Backbone Range of Taiwan; cirque groups at Chungyangchienshan (el. 3,703.4 m), Lumoulamolushan (3,270.9 m), Pilushan (3,370 m), Tunghohuanshan (3,416 m), and Ch'ilaichushan (3,558.9 m); cirque groups, Kartreppen, morainic mounds, terminal moraines, glacial valleys, arêtes, cirque lakes, and roches moutonnées near Hsüehshan (3,884 m) in the Hsüehshan range; the small cirque groups between Tapachienshan and Hsiaopachienshan, and the cirque groups north of Tapachienshan and Hsiaopachienshan, and the cirque groups north of Tapachienshan on the eastern slope of Tahsüehshan, and in the Yüshan range. The mechanical weathering is rapid and severe in the mountainous regions of Taiwan, and formations from older glaciations have not survived to this date [C.C.Lin 1964: 205].

Some elements of the modern biota on the island, such as the Formosan salmon (*Oncorhynchus formosanus*) in the upper Tachia River and the high-latitude flora and insects of the island, are considered to be glacial remnants surviving from the Ice Age (Lin 1964: 206), but weighty evidence of past climatic change is provided by pollen fossils collected by Matsuo Tsukada from Sun-Moon Lake in central Formosa (Tsukada 1966, 1967). A core of sediments was collected from the bottom of the lake to a depth of 12.79 m, which dates back to over 60,000 years B.P. Four pollen zones, T1, T2, T3, and R, are established in relation to a series of decreases or increases of the boreal and subtropical elements that are clearly affected by major climatic changes (Fig. 88).

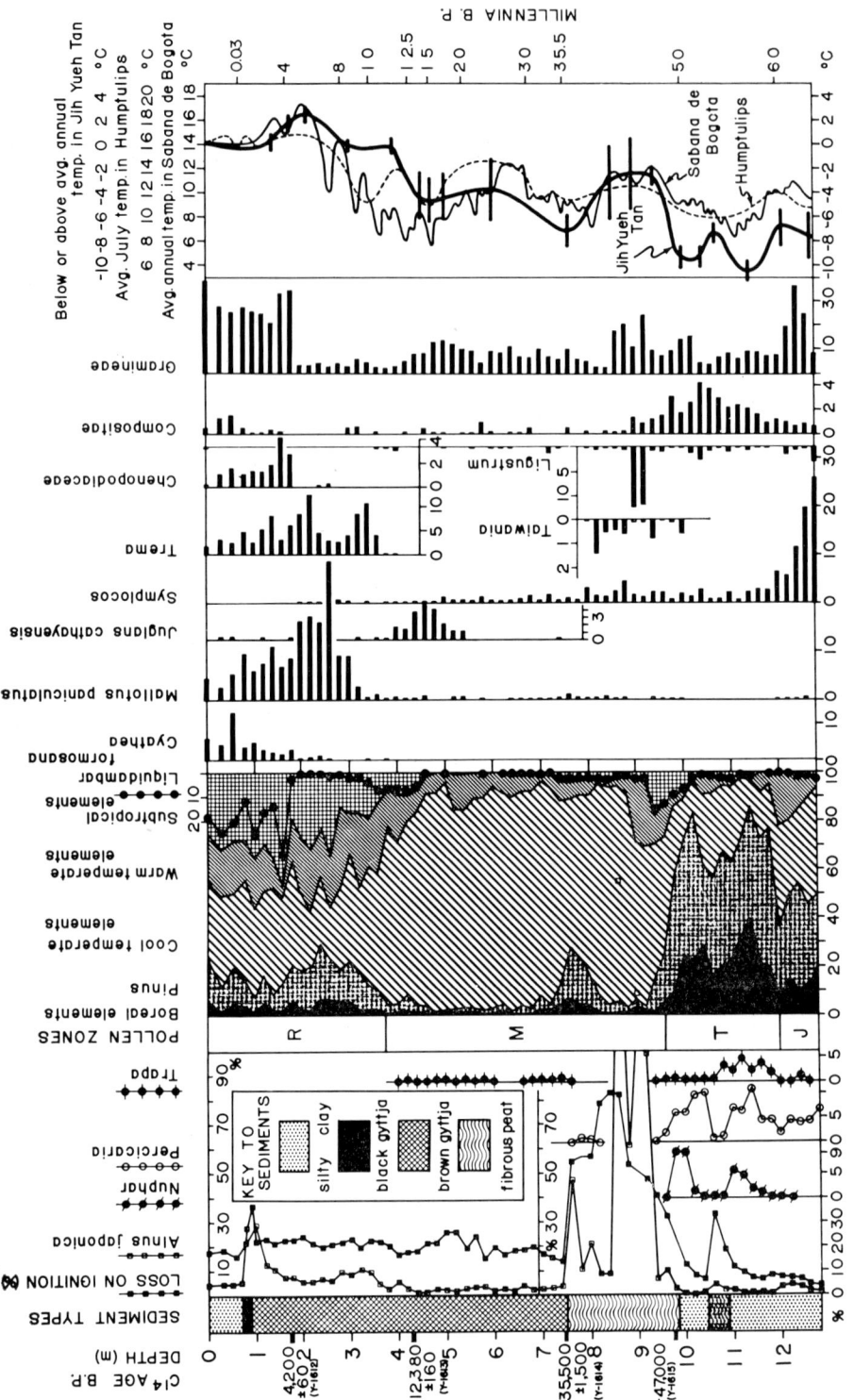

FIG. 88. Pollen Diagram for a 12.79-m Core from Jih-t'an, Central Taiwan (*after* Tsukada 1966).

192

Zone T1. A moderate climate is indicated by pollen species, although the temperature was 5.0 to 9.0°C lower than it is at present in the area, and radiocarbon dates place the T1/2 boundary at approximately 60,000 years B.P. This time interval can be tentatively correlated with the third interglacial of the Himalayas.

Zone T2. This stage opens with a fast expansion of the boreal elements and pine and ends with the displacement of the boreal by cool-temperate elements. The peak of the boreal forests suggests a remarkably cold climate with a reduction of annual temperature of from 8.0 to 11.0°C, and this zone appears to correspond to the early fourth glacial of the Himalayas or the early Würm of the Alps.

Zone T3. The dominance of the cool-temperate elements distinguishes this zone, but several species that show minor changes indicate a relatively warm interval at the beginning of this stage, about 40,000 to 48,000 years B.P., followed by a slightly colder climate with a temperature approximately 4.0 to 6.0°C lower than at the present. This may correspond to the main Würm or the main phases of the fourth glacial, preceded by a period of interstadial; but more pollen diagrams are needed before a conclusive subdivision of the T3 zone can be accomplished.

Zone R (Recent). This zone begins with the destruction of primeval forests and with the rise of the subtropical and warm-temperate species, indicating a rapid amelioration of climate from about 14,000 to 12,000 B.P. A hypsithermal (climatic optimum) is recognized from 8,000 to 4,000 years B.P., and it may have a temperature 2.0 to 3.0°C higher than at present. At the middle of Zone R, dated to 4,200 ± 60 B.P., the steep increase of grass pollen (about one third of the total grass pollen is considered by Tsukada to be cereal species), together with *Liquidambar* and Chenopodiaceae, suggests intensified agricultural activities.

Before Tsukada's work we knew next to nothing about late Pleistocene climatic and vegetational sequences, and therefore the Jih-yüeh-t'an pollen diagram marks the beginning of a new era in the island's Pleistocene studies, even though many more such profiles must be obtained before generalizations can be made. The Jih-yüeh-t'an sequence indicates that the following significant changes in past climate took place that are pertinent to prehistoric research.

1. From approximately 60,000 to 12,000 B.P. the island of Formosa had a cold–cool-temperate climate, with a temperature perhaps 4.0 to 10.0°C below that of the present and a boreal forest, suggesting correspondence with the fourth glacial of the Himalayas. Subdivisions can certainly be made within this prolonged interval, and a major interstadial is already indicated.

2. From about 14,000 to 12,000 B.P. a rapid amelioration of climate began, as is indicated by the rise and expansion of subtropical and warm-temperate forests. At the same time there is the beginning of evidence of the removal of primeval forests by burning and the continuous growth of secondary forests and shrubs. The implications of this evidence for human history will be discussed at length a little later.

3. From about 8,000 to 4,000 B.P. there is a period of climatic optimum or hypsithermal, which gradually loses force after 4,000 years B.P.

4. During the latter half of the hypsithermal or late fifth millennium B.P. the

Jih-yüeh-t'an core exhibits conclusive evidence of intensified agricultural activities and probable evidence of cereal agriculture.

Evidence of human occupation is available on the island only since the beginning of the postglacial period,[1] but for the study of culture history the relevance of the information concerning climatic changes, vegetational shifts, and agriculture-related activities is already apparent. Closely related to these, particularly the climatic changes, are changes in topography of the western coastal areas—where prehistoric sites are concentrated—caused largely by shifts in shorelines.

Lin (1964: 205) is convinced that "the eustatic movement of the Taiwan Quaternary is probably a glacial eustacy associated with climatic changes, as elsewhere in the world. Major regressions indicate cold glacial periods, whereas major transgressions, warm interglacial periods." The postglacial peak of transgression apparently is related to the climatic hypsithermal, although transgression–regression fluctuations not only can be assumed but are also evident. The major evidence for shoreline changes consists of the distribution of prehistoric sites chronologically arranged and the distribution of shellmounds containing various proportions of marine mollusks. These phenomena will be looked into presently. Additional evidence of coastal eustacy is provided by written records, the distribution of peats, and geological sediments along the coastal areas.

These lines of research combine to provide a chronological framework for the placement of prehistoric sites and also a suggestive context for the study of cultural ecology in prehistoric times.

The Southwest Coast

The southwest coast refers to the strip about 60 km long between the Tsengwen and the Hsia Tamsui rivers (Fig. 89), which is treated as a unit for discussion because it is the second best-known region on the island archeologically. (The best known region is the Taipei basin.) Prehistoric cultures in this area also tend to exhibit common characteristics that contrast with regions to the north and south, although the cultural boundaries are not at all clear-cut.

A list of prehistoric sites in this region published by Kokubu in 1941 contains the names of fifty-six localities. Among the thirty-one prehistoric shellmounds discussed by C. C. Lin in 1960, nine are new to Kokubu's list. In early 1965 when we were excavating the sites at Fengpitou, we discovered six new sites in the vicinity. These make a total of seventy-one prehistoric sites whose exact locations and characteristic contents are known. At very few sites, however, had there been test excavations on any considerable scale, and at only a single site—Fengpitou—was there extensive excavation.

A result of the meager excavation is the fact that very few stratigraphical data are available to enable correlations with geological and geomorphological information. According to Lin's recent studies (1966), the scattered postglacial deposits in this region, referred to as the Tainan Formation, consist of two substages: Akungtien

---

[1] See footnote on p. 216.

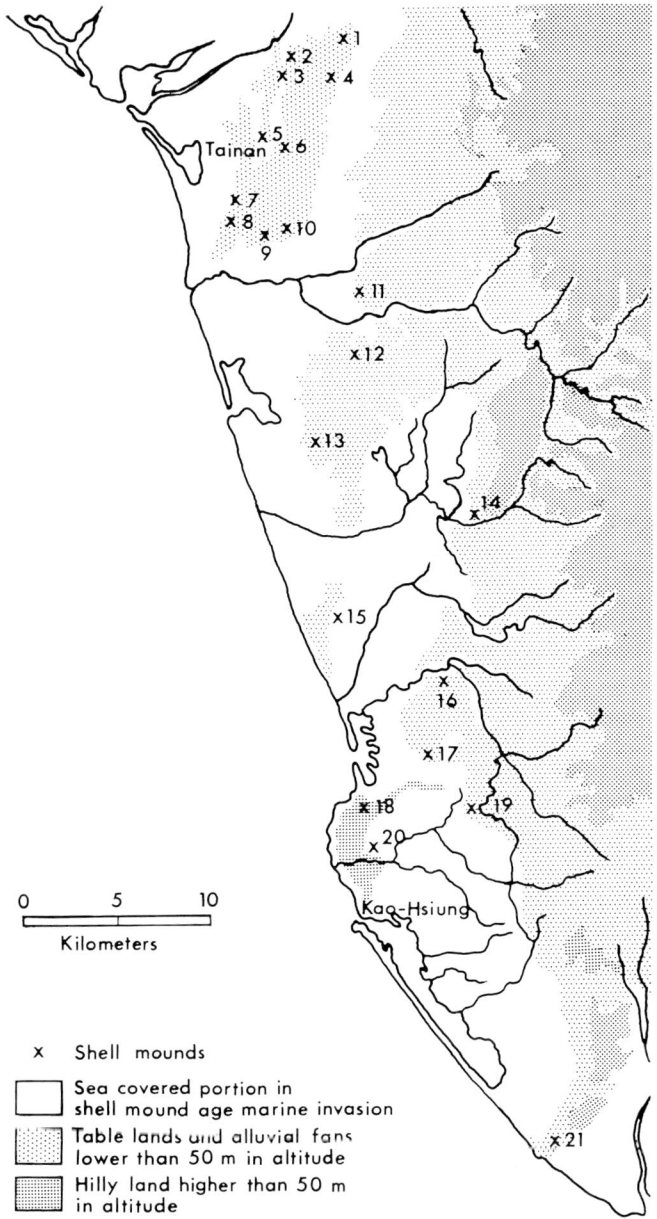

Fig. 89. Prehistoric Sites on the Southwest Coast. (*1*, Niao-sung; *2*, Liu-chia-ting; *3*, San-pen-mu; *4*, Wang-liao; *5*, Tainan Post Office; *6*, Tainan Tung-men-wai; *7*, Pa-chiao-chiao; *8*, An-tzu; *9*, Shih san-chia; *10*, Niu-ch'ou-tzu; *11*, Chung-chou; *12*, Ta-hu; *13*, Wu-shu-lin; *14*, Hsiao-kang-shan; *15*, Lo-ti; *16*, Hou-chin; *17*, Tso-ying; *18*, T'ao-tzu-yüan; *19*, Fu ting-chin; *20*, Shou-shan: *21*, Feng-pi-t'ou.)

coral reefs (ca. 8,000–7,000 B.P.) and Hutoupei shell formations (ca. 7,000–5,000 B.P.), both being dated by carbon-14 determinations. Archeological remains, however, have not been located from formations typical of this period; it is not certain, therefore, whether the prehistoric sites as a whole fall above—and after—the entire Tainan Formation, or whether some of them coincide with it in time. The principal device for a chronological study of the sites in the southwest coastal region, therefore, must be a careful use of the horizon concept, taking into account the distribution of some of the diagnostic features that characterize the successive cultural strata at the Fengpitou site. Fengpitou is thus exceedingly important for the study of the prehistoric southwest as a whole.

SITES AND THE LANDSCAPE: ANCIENT AND MODERN

Topographically the southwest coastal region is composed of three longitudinal components: the coastal alluvial plains, about 5 km wide east–west; the hills above 50-m altitude in the east; and the alluvial fans and tablelands between the plains and the hills. All the prehistoric sites under discussion are distributed on the tablelands or on their perimeters. Three of these—Tahu, Houchin, and Fengshan—are western protrusions of the hills to the east, and, detached from these, Tainan Tableland, Loti Hill, and Shoushan Hill, are isolated plateaus. During the postglacial transgression, when the shoreline was farther inland, most of the prehistoric sites were at or near the water's edge; the three interior tablelands were directly on the coast, and the three isolated tablelands were partially submerged and appeared as offshore islets.

That the transgression took place during the period of prehistoric occupation is conclusively shown by the shellmounds, where marine mollusks prevailed (C. C. Lin, 1960, enumerated seventy-one species of mollusks, of which one is a land snail, six are freshwater species, and the rest marine). The molluscan species contained in the prehistoric shellmounds differ from the modern population in significant ways: *Telescopium telescopium*, widespread in prehistoric periods, and *Batissa* sp., which has been found from two sites, no longer occur in this region. The prehistoric *Corbicula subsulcata* is now completely replaced by *C. fluminea*. On the other hand, *Turritela terebra cerea* and *Sanguinolaria* spp., which are very abundant and widespread in modern waters, have very rarely been recovered from prehistoric localities. The change in the mollusk populations may have resulted, according to Lin, from "the rapid accumulation of sands and muds, the frequent fluctuations of sea levels, the rapid shifts of coastal topography, and possibly climatic changes" (1960: 75).

If the climatic sequence indicated by the Jih-yüeh-t'an core is not a strictly local phenomenon, then it is quite likely that the transgression and climatic change in the southwest was a part of a hypsithermal period in postglacial Taiwan. From the shellmound at Niao-sung, northernmost Tainan tableland, charred fragments of a certain plant that occurs today only in the southernmost region of Formosa are reported, supporting the inference of a climatic optimum for at least that part of the prehistoric period.

In short, at the maximum of transgression the southwest coastal region of Taiwan consisted of a strip of low coastal terraces and three major offshore islets, surrounded by very shallow seawater with a molluscan population characterized by at least thirty-one species, the most common being *Telescopium telescopium, Terebralia semistriata, Anadara scapha, A, (Tegillarca) granosa; A, (T.) nodifere, Ostrea (Crassostrea) gigas, Gafrarium tumidum, G. (Circe) scriptum tumefactum, Meretrix petechialis, Chione (Anomalodiscus) squamosa, Anomalocardia (Cryptonemella) producta,* and *Katelysia (Hemitapes) virginea.* The shallow lagoons provided marine resources such as shellfish, crabs, turtles, and fish. Over the hills to the east primeval forests and mangroves presumably abounded, consisting of tropical and/or subtropical plants and inhabited by a large variety of mammals. Deer and wild boar were among the commonly found mammals from prehistoric sites.

CERAMIC HORIZON STYLES

In ordering archeological sites in this area, pottery is often the sole criterion when absolute chronological information is lacking. On the basis of pottery styles and characteristics, Kokubu (1941: 196) classified the prehistoric sites in this region into four groups having: (1) plain reddish-brown or gray pottery as the principal ceramic component; (2) a variety of combed pottery; (3) cord-marked pottery; and (4) a combination of combed, cord-marked, check-impressed, and plain pottery. A recent study of Kokubu (1962a: 65) attempts to arrange the groups of sites in chronological order according to altitude of the sites: (1) cord-marked pottery sites, on the 20-m contour line, are considered to be the oldest; (2) sites with combed black pottery and fine-paste black pottery, on the 13–15-m contour lines, follow; (3) sites with plain, coarse-textured, and reddish-brown pottery, on the 10-m contour line, are considered the latest prehistoric; and (4) sites with Chinese porcelain sherds, on the 7-m contour lines, are the latest. Kokubu's classifications of sites and their chronological assessment were undertaken without the benefit of any stratified sites, but the notion of an earliest cord-marked pottery stratum showed interesting foresight.

The excavations at Fengpitou show conclusively that the coarse-textured cord-marked pottery does characterize a prehistoric segment of culture and that this indeed is the earliest ceramic complex in the region. Kokubu's "plain, coarse-textured, and reddish-brown or gray pottery" no doubt corresponds to the lower and the upper shellmound settlements at Fengpitou, for at the latter site the principal ceramic components were what we have described as the sandy red and the sandy gray. The Fengpitou excavations, on the other hand, raise the following two questions regarding Kokubu's classifications. Fine red pottery of Fengpitou, that characterizes a whole settlement at the site, does not have a place in Kokubu's cultural grouping for the region. Is it possible that Kokubu has grouped these sites under his "cord-marked pottery" categories? At Fengpitou the combed and plain black pottery constitute only a part of the settlements that are above all characterized by the sandy red and the sandy gray wares. In this region as a whole, are there sites characterized by black pottery alone?

Let us examine the fine red pottery first. "Fine, burnished, red pottery" is said to have been found at the site of Niu-ch'ou-tzu on the southern tip of Tainan Island and at the site at T'ao-tzu-yüan on the northern end of Shoushan Island, but at neither site is it said to be quantitatively predominant. Neither of the sites, on the other hand, has been excavated; it is entirely possible that the fine, burnished red pottery indicates an earlier cultural horizon than the sandy red pottery. But we found fine red pottery in 1965 to be the leading ceramic component at the sites of Tung-ting-shan and Chung-ts'u, on the southeastern slopes of the Fengshan table-land not far from the site of Fengpitou. At the site of Chung-ts'u, especially, cultural debris was solidly packed with sherds of this kind, with a depth of over 1 m, reminiscent of the deposition of this ware at the lower Lungshanoid strata of Fengpitou. Farther south, at the site of K'en-ting on the southern tip of Formosa, fine, burnished red pottery again prevails in association with shell ornaments and cist graves. It is possible, according to the available evidence, that a cultural horizon characterized by this fine red pottery occurred in the southern part of this region.

The red burnished pottery at Fengpitou was followed by the ceramic horizon characterized by sandy red and sandy gray wares in association with painted and black pottery. It is indicated that such a mixture of wares also occurred in the rest of the region, and that black pottery alone does not characterize a separate cultural group. For his black pottery category Kokubu (1941: 196) listed the sites of Ta-hu and Liu-chia-ting. No excavations of these sites were undertaken, but the brief descriptions given according to surface collection and test diggings enumerate "combed, burnished black pottery, thick gray coarse pottery, reddish-brown plain pottery, and check-impressed pottery" for Ta-hu (Kokubu 1962a: 65–6) and "reddish-brown coarse plain pottery and burnished black pottery" for Liu-chia-ting (*ibid.*, pp. 61–2). The different wares at the sites are not quantified, but it is plain that these sites stand out among the sandy red and sandy gray group because of the occurrence also of burnished black pottery.

It is thus apparent that the third group of sites in the southwest coastal region is characterized by the common occurrence of sandy red and sandy gray sherds. Some of these sites are distinguished for a great number of burnished black pottery sherds, and others for painted sherds. Neither the painted nor the black pottery constitutes a separate group. Tsuboi's observation (1956) that there was a painted pottery stratum and a black pottery stratum at Fengpitou has proved to be erroneous by our excavations.

According to the occurrence of diagnostic pottery wares on the various sites in the southwest coastal region, the categorization and classification shown in Table 29 are probably warranted (Kokubu 1941, 1962a, 1964a; C. C. Lin 1960; K. C. Chang 1954a).

SHELLMOUNDS

Another criterion that may be helpful in placing the prehistoric sites in the southwest coastal region concerns the shellmounds: their presence and absence, and the

TABLE 29. PREHISTORIC CERAMIC HORIZONS AND MAJOR SITES IN SOUTHWEST TAIWAN

Ceramic Horizon	Sites	Painted Pottery	Black Pottery
Sandy red–sandy gray wares group	Niao-sung		x
	Liu-chia-ting		x
	San-pen-mu		
	Liu-chia-ting—Yen-hsing		
	Pa-chiao-chiao		
	An-tzu		
	Shih-san-chia		
	Niu-ch'ou-tzu (upper horizon)		x
	Tung-men-wai (Tainan city)		
	Wang-liao		
	Chung-chou		
	Ta-hu		x
	Hu-nei		
	Wu-shu-lin		
	Hsiao-kang-shan		
	T'ao-tzu-yüan	x	x
	Tso-ying		
	Fu-ting-chin		
	Feng-pi-t'ou	x	x
Fine, burnished red ware	Niu-ch'ou-tzu (middle horizon)		
	T'ao-tzu-yüan		
	Feng-pi-t'ou		
	Tung-ting-shan		
	Chung-ts'u		
Coarse cord-marked ware	Niu-ch'ou-tzu (lower horizon)		
	Tung-men-wai (?)		
	Wang-liao (?)		
	Feng-pi-t'ou		

species of shellfish they contain. Shellmounds did not begin to accumulate at Fengpitou until the red and gray sandy pottery components occurred; and then the proportions of the various species changed as the shellmounds grew. No other sites in this region are known to contain a pure cord-marked pottery assemblage, but this culture was apparently not one associated with extensive shellfish collecting. The only stratigraphically verified fine, burnished red pottery sites, Tung-ting-shan and Chung-ts'u, are without any trace of shellmounds, a situation identical with the Fengpitou condition. All the sites where the sandy red and gray potsherds predominated have also yielded shellmounds, and we can safely say that shellfish gathering was probably associated with these particular ceramic wares.

No internal evidence enables us to place the sites of this third group in a finer chronological order, but some indication of relative antiquity might be inferred by the progression of a shellfish population in which *Ostrea gigas, Meretrix petechialis,* and *Anomalocardia producta* were diagnostic species, to one in which *Chione squamosa* and *Ostrea vitrefacta* were becoming predominant. The subdivision of the

TABLE 30. GROUPING OF PREHISTORIC SITES IN SOUTHWESTERN TAIWAN ACCORDING TO THEIR MOLLUSK REMAINS

Molluscan Level	Sites
Chione squamosa, Ostrea vitrefacta	An-tzu D
Chione squamosa, Ostrea gigas, Meretrix petechialis	Niao-sung
	Liu-chia-ting
	Pa-chiao-chiao
	An-tzu A-C, E-H
	Shih-san-chia
	Niu-ch'ou-tzu (upper horizon)
	New Cemetery (Tainan city)
	Chung-chou
	Ta-hu
	Hu-nei
	Hsiao-kang-shan
	Lo-ti A, C
	K'o-k'o-tzu
	Hou-chin
	Lung-ch'üan-ssu
	T'ao-tzu-yüan
	Tso-ying
	Fu-ting-chin
Ostrea gigas, Meretrix petechialis, Anomalocardia producta	San-pen-mu
	Tainan Post Office
	Tung-men-wai (Tainan city)
	Wu-shu-lin
	Lo-ti B, D-F

sandy red–gray sites (with shellmounds) shown in Table 30 is suggested (Kokubu 1962a; C. C. Lin 1960).

Since these sites have not been excavated, and stratigraphical and quantitative information given in current descriptions of them is not entirely reliable for this purpose, this table can be said only to give some indication of the occurrence of earlier and later cultural components at the respective sites within the third group of sandy red and sandy gray, which presumably lasted a considerable length of time and underwent changes of appreciable magnitude.

SUMMARY AND CONCLUSIONS

On the basis of the current available information about the sites characterized above, the prehistory of the southwest coastal region of Formosa can be summarized as follows.

Cord-marked pottery culture. The only cord-marked pottery level that is well defined by excavated materials is the lower stratum at Fengpitou, and the extent of its distribution in the southwest is unclear. The corded sherds of this stratum are coarse-textured, thick, and have characteristic rim shapes and decorations as described in Part I. "Cord-marked pottery" is said to have been recovered from many sites in the southwest (Pl. 24, *I*), but the precise nature of these sherds and their stratigraphical positions are not clear. Since cord impressions occur on both the fine red and the sandy red–gray sherds, we have no way of knowing whether the cord-marked pottery of the other sites is of the early or later variety. At the site of Niu-ch'ou-tzu, however, cord- and mat-impressed red and gray sherds are found and are said by Kokubu (1962a: 64) to resemble those of Liang-wen-kang. If this kind of corded ware formed a distinct cultural horizon at Niu-ch'ou-tzu, the fact remains to be verified by excavations, for this ware was described there together with later varieties of pottery and stone implements.

Fine red pottery horizon. Only at two or three sites on the southern part of the Fengshan tableland has the archeologist uncovered cultural strata containing fine red ware as the predominant ceramic component, and the characterization of the fine red ware settlement at Fengpitou is the only cultural characterization available for this ware.

This horizon is defined by burnished red pottery in the shapes of bowls, jars, and pedestaled basins and by slate knives, triangular and stemmed arrowheads, flat hoes, boot-shaped knives, and rectangular adzes. Serpentine and jadeish disks with a pair of holes are also characteristic. Its cultural affiliations will be discussed later, but in general it bears striking resemblance to the Lungshanoid horizon of the southeastern Chinese coast. Many of the stone implements were made of a kind of olivine basalt that is produced only on the Pescadores (Hayasaka and Rin 1934). Liang-wen-kang (Kokubu 1960), on the Pescadores, has yielded cord-marked pottery of the fine red ware, and is suggestive of contact between the Pescadores and southwest Taiwan during this period.

Sandy red–gray pottery horizon. The bulk of the prehistoric sites in the southwest belong to a horizon characterized above all by the coarse-textured red and gray pottery that is typical of the shellmound settlements at Fengpitou. Shellfish gathering must have formed an essential part of the subsistence pattern of the inhabitants of the southwest coastal region from about 1500 B.C. onward, as indicated by the carbon-14 dates from Fengpitou.

The common denominators of the cultural remains of this horizon, in addition to the sandy red and gray sherds and shellfish collection, can be described as follows. Stone implements are mostly hoes, but there are also arrowheads, knives, spatula-shaped hoes, rectangular adzes, chisels, and spearheads or halberd heads. Two basic materials were used: olivine basalt and slate. In range of types the shellmound settlements of Fengipitou are representative.

Many of the potsherds are plain, but check-, cord-, and basket-impressed and incised pieces are also common. Painted pottery (in dark red pigment) occurs only at Fengpitou and T'ao-tzu-yüan. Burnished, fine black pottery is found at a number of sites, and incised decorations are common. Of particular interest are the wavy and spiral patterns incised on the black pottery with comb-like instruments or with

Anadara shell edges. Other characteristic clay objects include spindle whorls, rings, and bracelets.

The most commonly encountered animal bones from the shellmounds are those of deer (*Cervus unicolor*) and wild boar (*Sus taivanus*), and dog (*Canis familiaris*) bones are found at least at one site (Kokubu 1962a). Teeth and vertebrae of sharks and other fish are also common. Shell rings are found, either for ornamentation or as instruments. Bone and antler implements are found widely but, except at Fengpitou, in small numbers.

Human burials are found at Fengpitou and T'ao-tzu-yüan. The burial at the former site has been described in Part I. At the latter site a burial urn was unearthed, containing a few fragments of the bones of a child, not much more than six years old. A human skull was also found at T'ao-tzu-yüan in a nonburial context, suggesting to some scholars the possibility of head-hunting (Kokubu 1964a). In this connection a human mandible found at the Niao-sung shellmound by Sueo Kaneko in 1939 is of great interest:

> This mandible has a hole, 6.5 mm to 4.5 mm in diameter—apparently a postmortem mutilation—bored through it in the median part of its corpus. It is glossy all over, and particularly at the posterior opening of the hole, indicating that it was continually handled and carried about by a string passed through the hole. It appears to the author [Professor Kenaseki] that it has been used for some time as a "human jaw handle" of a gong, a practice still to be met with among the Ifugao and Bontok Igorot folk in the northern mountainous region of Luzon Island. It is attached as a sort of "Netsuke" to one end of a string by which a bronze gong is held or carried about and prevents the string, with a heavy gong held at its other end, [from] slipping downward through the hand that holds it [Kanaseki 1957: 351].

Human mandibles for such use in the Philippines were usually taken from an enemy's head, and this instance suggests not only the practice of head-hunting but also the occurrence of ceremonial musical instruments and the close cultural ties between prehistoric southwest Formosa and the aboriginal cultures of the northern Philippines.

Central Taiwan

Central Taiwan is defined to include the coastal plains and terraces from Hsinchu in the north to the Choshui River in the south, and the upper courses of the major river valleys flowing into Formosa Strait, including the Taan, Tachia, Tatu, and Choshui rivers (Fig. 90). Prehistoric sites happen to cluster in this region, and the remains show common characteristics that separate them from the cultures described above for southwest Taiwan and the cultures farther north.

The topography of this region is not unlike that of the southwest: hills in the eastern part, a narrow strip of coastal plain in the west, and several major rivers flowing from the hills down to the coast. Prehistoric sites are situated along the edges of the hilly region, above the coastal plain, and in the upper valleys. Topographically, these sites can be grouped into three clusters: along the western edge of the hills in the north, along the banks of the Tatu River on the hilly flanks of the

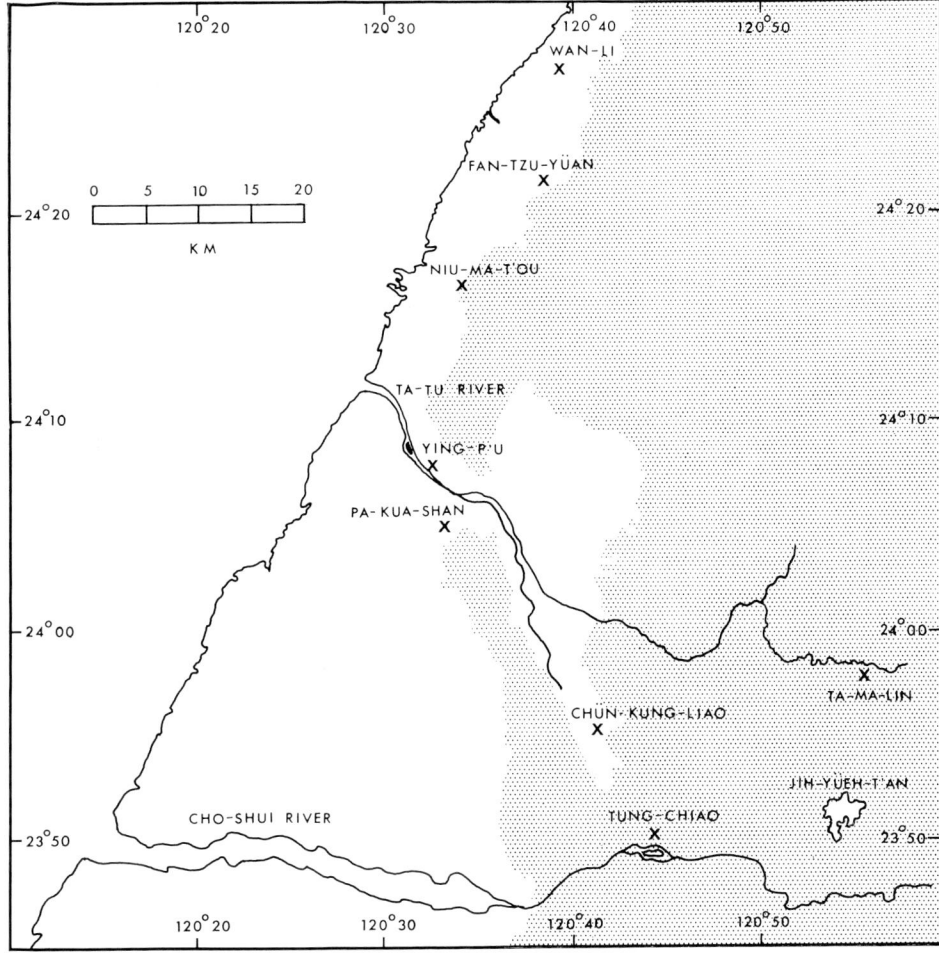

FIG. 90. Prehistoric Sites in Central Taiwan.

Taichung basin, and in the middle course of the Choshui River. The vast plains south of the region, in Yünlin and Chiayi prefectures, have yielded very few prehistoric sites, making the transition from central Taiwan to the southwest coast unclear at the moment.

With pottery characteristics as horizon markers, a chronological arrangement has been made of the prehistoric sites located in the region except for the Choshui Valley (Table 31). A brief description of the various sites and their cultural strata follows.

NIU-MA-T'OU HORIZON

The first stratigraphical evidence that the cord-marked red pottery was the earliest culture in central Formosa came in January 1954 when a stratified site was

TABLE 31. Prehistoric Ceramic Horizons and Major Sites in Central Taiwan

Horizon	Region								
	Miao-li	Yüan-li	T'ieh-chan-shan	Shui-yüan-ti	Ma-t'ou-lu	Ch'ing-shui	Ta-tu	Wang-t'ien	Chang-hua
Modern Chinese	Surface collections	Surface collections	Surface collections		Surface collections				Surface collections
Protohistoric				Surface collections	Upper horizon				Pa-kua-shan (upper horizon)
Fan-tzu-yüan	Hou-lung-ti shell-mound	Yüan-li shell-mound	Fan-tzu-yüan shell-mound and cemetery						Pa-kua-shan shell-mound
Ying-p'u				Upper horizon	Lower horizon	Niu-ma-t'ou (upper stratum)	Ying-p'u		Pa-kua-shan (lower horizon)
Niu-ma-t'ou			P'ing-ting	Lower horizon		Niu-ma-t'ou (lower stratum)	Ting-chieh	Hsia-ma-ts'u	

investigated at Shui-yüan-ti, southeast of the town of Tachia, on the bank of the Shuiwei River, a tributary of the Tachia. Very eroded and fragmentary sherds of a coarse texture, occasionally impressed with cord marks, were found in a band lying below a well-delineated layer of black-grayish sherds (Sung and Chang 1954). Similar sherds have been collected at several sites scattered in the region, but the only extensive information about this cultural horizon came from Niu-ma-t'ou, near the town of Ch'ing-shui, on the coast between the Tachia and Tatu rivers.

The site of Niu-ma-t'ou was first discovered by Kokubu in 1943. Three seasons of survey and test digging were undertaken in 1950, 1954, and 1955 by Liu Pin-hsiung. Liu's description of the stratigraphical situation is as follows (Liu 1955: 71–2):

> The great majority of sherds are red and cord-impressed, scattered over the entire hill. Black sherds are next in quantity and are distributed only in the northwestern part of the hilltop and on the western slope....
>
> Beneath a layer of secondary deposits are two undisturbed cultural strata: Black pottery stratum in the upper and the red, cord-marked pottery stratum in the lower layer.... According to my observations of the exposed sections, within the red pottery stratum plain sherds are situated in the upper portion and the corded sherds tend to occur in the lower part.

The red pottery of the lower stratum is red, orange, and/or buff in color and is said to be handmade. The paste is very fine or coarse and sand-tempered. One sherd shows evidence of burnishing. The principal surface treatment resulted from impression of very fine cord patterns, and a few sherds are incised. The shapes are bowls, jars, beakers, and ring feet; the last include one piece with cutouts.

Current knowledge about the Niu-ma-t'ou horizon in central Taiwan is definitely insufficient for conclusions concerning its cultural characteristics and chronological position. It is doubtful, nevertheless, that this horizon is identical with the Corded Ware horizon of the southwest or of the Taipei basin, for the characteristic rim forms and decorations of the latter sherds are lacking in central Taiwan from this layer. This horizon can more likely be compared with the fine red ware of Fengpitou.

YING-P'U HORIZON

Aside from the Niu-ma-t'ou horizon in which red ware predominates, all prehistoric sites in central Taiwan are characterized by the overwhelming occurrence of gray and black pottery. Within these sites themselves a further subdivision can be made between an earlier stratum, known by incised gray pottery of coarse, soft paste, and a later stratum characterized by impressed black pottery of fine, hard paste. The former stratum can be designated as the Ying-p'u horizon, and the latter the Fan-tzu-yüan horizon.

The Ying-p'u horizon is typified by the sites at Ying-p'u (Kanaseki and Kokubu 1949a, 1953), Ta-ma-lin (Shih 1953; C. Liu 1956a), and Chün-kung-liao (C. Liu 1960a), and the Fan-tzu-yüan horizon by the sites at Fan-tzu-yüan (Shih and Sung 1956; Sung 1962), Ma-t'ou-lu (Sung and Chang 1954), Pa-kua-shan (Kanaseki and Kokubu 1953), and Tung-chiao (P. Liu 1954). These two horizons are said to occur in stratigraphic relationship at the site of Pa-kua-shan. Carbon-14 dates at Ying-p'u place this horizon at approximately 1100–200 B.C., and the site at Fan-tzu-yüan has produced a single C-14 date of A.D. 850 ± 80.

Ying-p'u. The prehistoric site near the village of Ying-p'u, on the northern bank of the Tatu River, was first investigated by Kokubu in 1943, and subsequent work was done at the site in the 1940s by various scholars. Highly polished black sherds painted in black pigment, combed black sherds, and tripod feet in the shape of animal legs were among the finds at the site, recalling the Lung-shan culture of southeast China, which stimulated discussions about the prehistoric relationship between Taiwan and coastal (or even north) China (Kaneseki and Kokubu 1949a).

Excavations at the site were undertaken by the staff of the Department of Archaeology and Anthropology, National Taiwan University, from November 18 through December 24, 1964, in collaboration with the staff of the Yale expedition. By agreement, the results of these excavations will be reported by Professor Sung of Taita. The following descriptions concern only those aspects of the Ying-p'u culture that are relevant to the present study.

Archeological remains are scattered near Ying-p'u in an area several hundred meters wide directly on the level alluvial plain on the north bank of the Tatu River. Our excavations disclosed a single-component occupation characterized by two principal ceramic wares: sandy and fine gray pottery. The shapes of the pottery include such features as lids similar to the sandy red lids at Fengpitou, bowls, high jars, pedestaled basins, and tripods. The major decorative designs are incised and punctated; dark red and black paintings occur in a few cases, and check impressions are rarely found. There are applied lugs of small size on a few rim sherds. The overall characters of the gray pottery of this horizon are very closely similar to the shellmound settlements' sandy red and sandy gray wares, but red pottery is rare here, and the painted pottery is much simpler. Very few stone types can be categorized. These include rectangular adzes, chipped and polished knives, and a few other types of implements. Large numbers of carbonized seeds of plants have been found, and two sherds bear impressions of grains, possibly paddy husks.

Three carbon samples collected at the site were processed by the Yale Radiocarbon Laboratory and gave the following determinations: Y-1630, 2,970 ± 80 B.P.; Y-1631, 2,810 ± 100 B.P.; and Y-1632, 2,250 ± 60 B.P. These three samples came from the same general area, at different depths from near the bottom to near the top. They indicate a range from 1100 to 200 B.C. for the occupation of the site.

Ta-ma-lin. About 40 km up the River Tatu from Ying-p'u and 450 m above sea level is the site of Ta-ma-lin, near the town of P'u-li. Archeological investigations at the site took place in 1938, 1947, and 1949. The pottery is very similar to that of Ying-p'u, but here greater numbers of check-, basket-, and cord-impressed sherds were found. Differing from the site of Ying-p'u, however, the site at Ta-ma-lin has yielded a large number of chipped and polished stone implements, including such types as triangular arrowpoints, rectangular and perforated knives, rectangular adzes, net sinkers with two circular grooves at each end, and *ko* halberds. Most of the stone implements were made of either slate or schist.

In addition to habitation remains, five stone cists were uncovered during the 1949 excavations by the Academia Sinica and the Department of History, National Taiwan University, but no skeletal remains were found in the cists. Cist burials are very rarely seen on the western coastal areas of Taiwan; in addition to Ta-ma-lin, they occur only on the southern end of the island (Shih 1953).

Niu-ma-t'ou (upper horizon). The pottery from the upper layer at Niu-ma-t'ou is essentially like that of Ying-p'u. Commonly found decorations, however, are rows of small circles impressed with a reed. According to P. Liu (1955), who has reported remains at the site, the diameter and the thickness of the rings indicate that the stems of millet were used for making the impressions.

Shui-yüan-ti, Ta-chia. From the black pottery layer overlying cord-marked red pottery layer at the site, fragments of black pottery and stone implements were collected. The most characteristic stone implements at this horizon are the polished stone knives with two protrusions at the ends, the so-called "saddle-shaped stone knives" (Sung and Chang 1954).

Chün-kung-liao. This site is midway between Ying-p'u and Ta-ma-lin on the Tatu River, and its ceramic and stone inventory is similar to both sites. The descriptions of the pottery at the site are fuller than those of other sites (C. Liu 1960a):

> A great amount of pottery was obtained from the site, but all was in fragmentary state,

including rim-body-base- and shoulder sherds, amounting to 1,122 pieces. On 62 of these decoration could be ascertained, which amounts to 5.53% of the total sherds. Incised parallel and feather-like patterns occur most frequently, while incised wavy lines and impressed circles are also found. The surface color of the sherds is of great variety, but according to their paste, temper, color and method of manufacture, they could be sorted tentatively into ten types.

1. Manufactured by paddle and anvil. Tempered with fine sand. Black to deep gray colored. Surface hardness from 2.0 to 3.0.

2. Hand moulded. Fine clay paste, tempered with fine sand. Black to deep gray colored. Surface hardness from 2.0 to 3.0.

3. This type is similar in most ways to group 1, from which it differs only by the light grayish color of the surface. Surface hardness 3.0.

4. Gray colored. The manufacture and paste are similar to those of 1. Surface hardness from 1.0 to 2.0.

5. The surface color varies from black, grayish-black, to brown. Other items are identical to group 1.

6. The surface color varies from light brown to brownish orange. The core is usually grayish-black. In other details the sherds are similar to group 2.

7. The surface is covered with a thin slip, dark-red or brown in color. The core is usually grayish-black. Other details are similar to group 1. Surface hardness 2.0.

8. Hand moulded. Brown colored. The paste is tempered with coarse sand. Plain, without decoration. Surface hardness from 2.0 to 3.0.

9. Hand moulded. Tempered with coarse sand. Light red to brownish-orange colored. Plain, not decorated. Surface hardness 2.0.

10. Hand moulded. Tempered with coarse sand. Grayish-black colored. Surface hardness from 1.0 to 2.0.

The last four types account for 144 sherds, but the frequencies of occurrence of the first six types are not given.

Fan-tzu-yüan Horizon

Black and gray pottery continued in central Taiwan after the previous horizon, but profound changes in the cultural characteristics occurred at the various sites. Pottery became harder, was better made, and was commonly impressed with checks, chevrons, and herringbone patterns. Stone implements were not so well made as in the previous horizon, and the coastal sites featured knives chipped from pebble flakes. Human burials were found from two sites near Ta-chia; prone posture was the rule, and in some cases the heads of the dead bodies were covered with an overturned basin.

Another major change is that all coastal sites are now characterized by shellmounds. Two leading mollusk species, *Melanoides crenulatus* and *Corbicula maxima*, no longer occur in the area today, indicating similar ecological changes suggested by the shellmound contents in the southwest (Kokubu 1962a). The animal bones from the Yüan-li shellmound include deer (*Cervus unicolor, C. taivanus, Muntiacus reevesi micrusus*), wild boar (Suidae), rodents (Sciuridae), carnivores (Viverridae, *Canis familiaris*), and monkey (Cercopithecidae), indicating the range of some of the animals hunted at the time (C. Su 1959).

One carbon-14 date is obtained from the Fan-tzu-yüan site: Y-1499, 1,100 ± 80 B.P. (A.D. 850 ± 80).

SUMMARY

Because of the large number of sites in the area, central Taiwan's prehistory is well known in its broad outline, but the small number of well-excavated sites prohibits detailed characterizations of the prehistoric cultures.

If Tsukada's conclusions about the vegetational history of the Jih-yüeh-t'an area are valid, central Taiwan's occupation by men with agricultural capabilities can be dated to more than ten thousand years before the present. Very early cultures occurred on the island of Formosa, as attested by the corded ware strata in the north and in the south, but this cultural layer has yet to be located in stratigraphical contexts in the central regions.

The earliest known prehistoric culture in this region is the one characterized by the cord-marked red pottery comparable to the fine red ware horizon in the southwest which began around 2500 B.C. If its occurrence in the central region began at a similar date, it is very likely that this horizon was responsible for the evidence of intensive agriculture in the Jih-yüeh-t'an area around 2300 B.C.

Sandy gray ware was the leading ceramic component at the site of Fengpitou around 1400 B.C., as described in Part I. Probably around that date the same cultural horizon emerged in central Taiwan in the form of the Ying-p'u horizon. The stone inventory and the ceramic shapes and decorations of this horizon are very similar to the shellmound settlements at Fengpitou, and the Ying-p'u dates (1100–200 B.C.) also correspond very closely with the shellmound settlements in the southwest. The area between central Taiwan and the southwest, unfortunately, has not been explored archeologically, and at this moment it is quite uncertain whether direct connections can be ascertained between these two cultures. Some evidence exists, however, suggesting that millet and rice were being planted at this time both in the central region and in the southwest.

The Ying-p'u horizon gave way to the Fan-tzu-yüan horizon in central Taiwan some time after the beginning of the Christian era. Shellmounds did not occur in central Taiwan until this time, suggesting that the black pottery tradition did not come into this area, and the local resources were not tapped until a later date than in the southwest.

Prehistoric sites of the same tradition—characterized by chipped stone implements and check-impressed black and gray pottery—have been found widely in central Taiwan and particularly in the upper courses of the Tatu and Choshui rivers (C. W. Liu 1956a,b, 1960a,b), close to the habitats of the central groups of the modern aborigines. Check-impressed pottery remained to be manufactured and used by such ethnographically known groups as the Bununs. It is entirely possible—in fact, it has been repeatedly suggested—that some of the central aboriginal groups are direct descendants of the prehistoric inhabitants described above.

Northern Taiwan

Northern Taiwan in terms of prehistoric archeology consists of the Taipei basin and the coastal regions. The basin is encircled in the north by the Tat'un Mountains, in the west by the T'aoyüan Tableland, and in the east and south by the Hsüehshan Mountains. The whole basin is drained by the Tamsui system: the Takokan River from the southwest, the Hsintien River from the southeast, and the Keelung River from the east merge at the center of the basin, where the metropolis of Taipei lies, and form the lower course of the Tamsui River which flows north-northwest into Formosa Strait (Fig. 91).

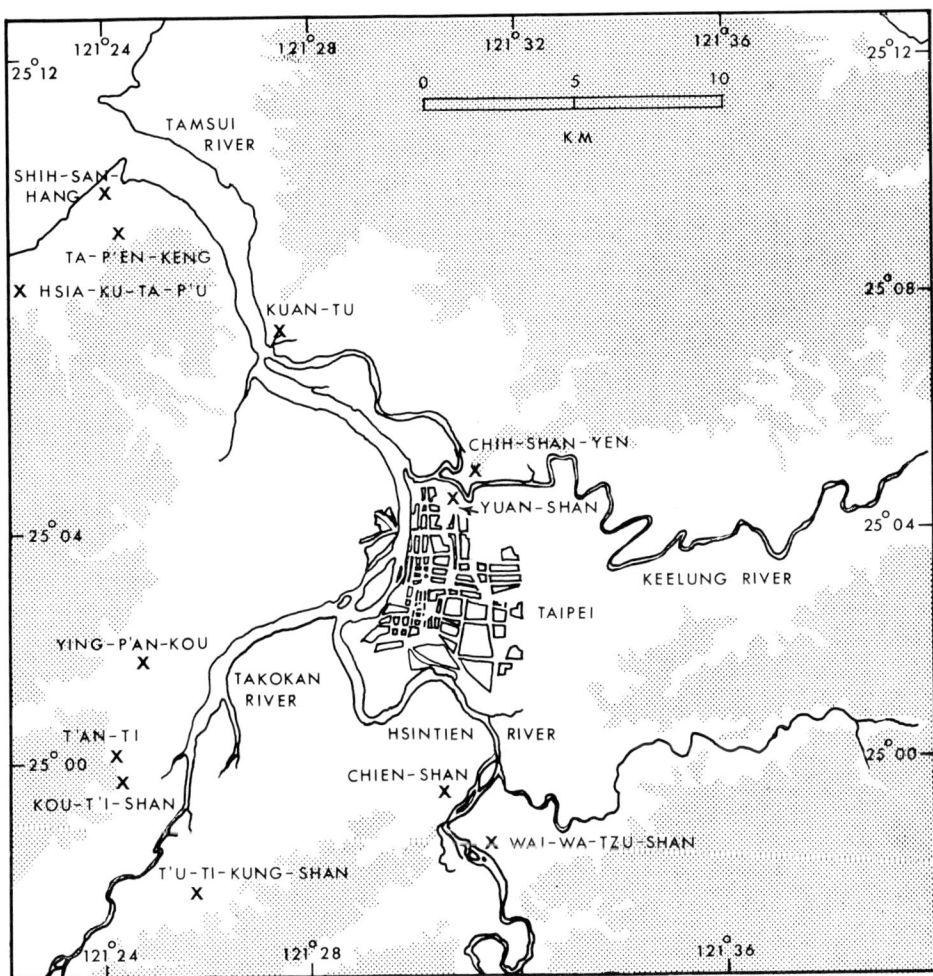

FIG. 91. Prehistoric Sites in North Taiwan.

Prehistoric sites have been found widely on the coast and throughout the basin, and they fit within a fairly tight chronological framework according to the geological history of the basin, carbon-14 dates, and the typological classification of the prehistoric assemblages and the stratigraphical information concerning the various cultural groups at Tapenkeng and elsewhere.

The geological history of the basin has been summarized by C. C. Lin (1964: 207–10) as follows:

> The Taipei basin is a tectonic basin, formed during the Tientzuhuian Age [Middle Pleistocene] when laterization of the land surface took place. Shortly after its formation the Taipei basin was submerged under sea water and became the ancient Taipei lake, which lasted from the Sungshan formation … through the end of the Milunian Age [final Pleistocene]. After the Milunian the lake water drained away because of the collapse of the banks, and the whole region became a large swamp. A variety of lacustrine plants was abundant in the swamp which, in combination with plants washed into the basin as well as other native plants of the basin, subsequently formed the Taipei peats. In the peats have been found fossils of wild cattle and other mammals. Radiocarbon has dated the formation of the peats at about 4880 ± 300 years ago (Report no. WR-1016, Geochemistry and Petrology Branch, U.S. Geological Survey). Shortly afterward the basin surface tipped from the southeast toward the northwest, and the northwestern portions of the Taipei basin became a marshy and lacustrine region. Prehistoric men inhabited the neighbourhood of Yüanshan, on the eastern periphery of the lacustrine region, and their remains are known as the Kunghsia shell-mound. Another transgression took place, bringing the sea water again into the Taipei basin through the Kuantu pass. The Kunghsia shell-mound was submerged, and its inhabitants apparently moved onto higher land; the archaeological site at Yüanshan shell-mound was apparently formed at this time. Another minor regression brought men down into the river valleys. A subsequent transgression, however, once more transformed the basin into a lacustrine region, larger in area than the previous Yüanshan shell-mound period. Fresh-water molluscs all but disappeared at this time, and salt-water and semi-fresh water species thrived. Another regression again extended the shoreline toward the sea, and such early sites as the Hsihsinchuangtzu shell-mound were formed in the low valleys along river banks. Early documents record that the last transgression took place in 1694 when an earthquake brought about the depression of a part of the basin and the entry of sea water. As far as can be judged, the surface of the basin at that time dropped not less than 3 metres. Since the 17th century the Taipei basin has been devoid of sea water.

The history of Taipei basin will provide an enormously useful yardstick for archeological purposes when enough sites have been excavated and their geological positions studied. Unfortunately, such sites are still rare, and a broad correlation is possible only when cultural classifications are first made according to archeological remains and when some of the key sites are correlated according to carbon-14 dates.

It has long been established that four major cultures can be classified for northern Taiwan during its prehistoric period: Corded Ware, Yüan-shan, Botanical Garden, and Shih-san-hang (K. C. Chang 1954b). The importance of our excavations at Tapenkeng lies primarily in the new information according to which the interrelationship of these four cultures is rendered understandable. A quick survey of the prehistoric picture that emerges as a result of our excavations at Tapenkeng follows.

Corded Ware Culture

Sites at which the early variety of cord-marked potsherds have been recovered include Hsia-ku-ta-p'u (P. H. Liu 1964) (Pl. 24, *C,D*) and Tapenkeng on the coastal region south of the Tamsui estuary; Lao-peng-shan and eight other sites on the coast between Tamsui and Keelung (C. Sheng 1962a); Ch'ing-yün-yen, Chih-shan-yen (Pl. 24, *E,F*), and Yüan-shan on the banks of the main course of the Tamsui; and possibly along the upper courses of the Takokan River (Sheng 1962b). These sites indicate a distribution sphere in the western part of the area, mainly the valley of the lower Tamsui, near its estuary, and along the coastal regions in the north and south. The eastern part of the Taipei basin and the eastern coasts south of Keelung have not yet yielded remains of this kind, but potsherds of the same variety are found in abundance along the eastern coast of Taiwan, from Suao in the north to Ch'ang-pin (Pl. 24, *G,H*) in the south. Whether or not the corded-ware remains on the eastern coast belonged to the same culture of the lower Tamsui and the north-western coast will be discussed presently. The description that follows will be confined to the area of the lower Tamsui and its vicinity.

Of all the sites, Tapenkeng has yielded the greatest number of finds from this layer and the greatest variety of ceramic types and stone implements. The potsherds from all the sites, however, form a distinctive group. They are handmade, sand-tempered, rather thick and heavy, and light or dark brown in surface color. The characteristic forms are bowls and globular jars; the latter often have a low flaring rim and a low ring foot, occasionally perforated. The cross section of the rim is characteristically triangular; that is, the lip is very thin but the thickness of the rim increases before the neck is reached. Sometimes there is a ridge along the lower part of the rim so that the exterior surface of the rim tends to be horizontal or sloping rather than vertical. The exterior of the body is generously impressed with cord marks of thin or thick strands, apparently done with a cord-wrapped stick or paddle. Incised decorative patterns occur frequently on the lip, the external surface of the rim, and occasionally on the shoulder of the jar. Red pigment was sometimes applied over the cord marks in brushy but distinctive patterns. Relatively few stone implements have been found; they include pebbles retouched along the circumference or at the centers of both sides, chipped stone hoe-like implements, polished rectangular adzes, and perforated triangular slate points.

Stratigraphically, the Corded Ware culture lies at the bottom of Tapenkeng and Yüan-shan (Chang 1954a), lower than the remains of the Yüan-shan culture. The discussions in Part II on Tapenkeng would leave little doubt that the Corded Ware culture was the earliest known prehistoric culture in northern Taiwan and that its date could be as early as several millennia before Christ. This culture is also closely related to the Corded Ware culture at the site of Fengpitou, where it has been shown to predate by a considerable interval the Fine Red Ware culture of the third millennium B.C.

Yüan-shan Culture

Yüan-shan, the first prehistoric culture found on Taiwan, came to light through the discovery of Yüan-shan Shellmound in 1897. Intensive excavations were undertaken at the shellmound in 1951 and 1952, but the results remain to be published. The estimates of the age of this culture ranged from "several thousand years ago" to the Ming Dynasty (Sung and Chang 1964); before its dating became established the status of this culture could not be known in the larger context of Formosan and eastern Asian prehistory. Our excavations at Tapenkeng and the work of the Yale Radiocarbon Laboratory in determining the dates of the carbon samples from Tapenkeng and Yüan-shan are an initial step toward a fuller understanding of this culture in these respects.

At least twenty prehistoric sites found in northern Taiwan can be assigned to the Yüan-shan group (C. Sheng 1960), and at least three of them have been excavated: Tapenkeng, Yüan-shan Shellmound (Chang 1954a), and T'u-ti-kung-shan (Sheng *et al.* 1961). Their major concentration is along the Hsintien River and in the lower Tamsui Valley, i.e. the northern and eastern portions of the Taipei basin; few of them have been found on the coast, and only rarely have Yüan-shan remains been brought to light in the Takokan River valley.

The characteristic features of the Yüan-shan stratum at Tapenkeng are also characteristic of the Yüan-shan culture as a whole. The pottery is characterized chiefly by a buff sandy ware, with the jar (restricted mouth, occasional spout, vertical strap handles, and low ring foot) as the principal form. The exterior of the vessels has a thin coat or slip, in most cases left plain but sometimes brushed with discernible designs in red and dark brown pigment, incised with short, oblique parallel strokes and net patterns, and impressed with small rings (Pl. 84, *A,B,D,E, G,J*). In addition to vessels, clay objects include spindle whorls and pot supporters.

The stone inventory of Yüan-shan Shellmound, very similar to that of Tapenkeng, includes such distinctive Yüan-shan types as shouldered axes, stepped adzes, long spatula-like hoes (*patu*), and perforated triangular points. Many rings and beads made of jade and serpentine were found in the assemblage, and from the shellmounds were recovered bone and antler points, chisels, and awls.

Shellmounds occur at some of the sites on the lower Tamsui River, and the predominant shellfish is *Corbicula maxima* Prime, a semimarine species currently found only near the estuary, attesting to the geological changes taking place at that time (Tan 1934). It has been suggested that the Yüan-shan inhibitants followed the retreat of marine mollusks along the lower Tamsui River, and the carbon-14 dates of the shellmound and of the site at Tapenkeng tend to bear this out, but no shellmounds were found at Tapenkeng from the Yüan-shan stratum.

In fact, the carbon-14 dates of Yüan-shan Shellmound and the Yüan-shan stratum at Tapenkeng pose new problems as they solve old ones. As the excavations at Tapenkeng were taking place in summer and fall of 1964, a series of carbon samples was collected at Yüan-shan Shellmound, three of which have been given the following results at the Yale Radiocarbon Laboratory:

Y-1547   Shell, 200 cm below surface   3,860 ± 80 B.P.

Y-1548   Shell, 120 cm below surface   3,540 ± 80 B.P.

Y-1549   Shell, 40 cm below surface   3,190 ± 80 B.P.

This means that the occupation at the shellmound lasted approximately from 2000 to 1000 B.C. The first date is probably close to the beginning date for the Yüan-shan culture as a whole, for two carbon dates available (4,880 ± 300 and 4,249 ± 281 B.P.) seem to indicate that the extensive Taipei peat antedated the beginning of the significant Yüan-shan occupation at about 2200 B.C. in Taipei basin. In Part II it has been reported that the Tapenkeng occupation by the Yüan-shan people took place from about 1000 B.C. through the early centuries of the Christian era. In other words, it may have taken the Yüan-shan culture more than a millennium to expand from the heart of Taipei basin to the estuary of the Tamsui River. The geological changes affecting the eastern part of the Taipei basin could have made this possible. But this would suggest that the Yüan-shan culture as a whole lasted in northern Taiwan for more than two thousand years. Cultural changes that occurred during these two thousand years are rather negligible; significant changes that occurred at the last phase of the Tapenkeng sequence are more likely related to external influences (see below) than to internal changes within the Yüan-shan culture.

The fact that the earliest Yüan-shan culture remains are in the heart of the Taipei basin but that more recent sites occur near the coast poses problems concerning the origin of this culture. These will be discussed toward the end of this chapter.

BOTANICAL GARDEN CULTURE

First recognized at the Botanical Garden in the southern part of Taipei city, this culture is characterized by a fine-paste, thick-walled brown and buff pottery with check impressions (Pl. 88). The stone implements are similar to those in the Yüan-shan inventory, but chipped hoes and axes are as abundant as polished ones, shouldered axes are fewer, and the stepped adzes are characteristically thick rather than flat, as are the Yüan-shan type. *Patu*-type long hoes occur (Pl. 97), but a bend is conspicuous in the long section, whereas the Yüan-shan type is usually straight. In distribution, these types occur mostly in the Takokan Valley and in the lower Tamsui River, and few if any have been located in the eastern half of the Taipei basin (Sheng 1960).

The contrast between the Botanical Garden and the Yüan-shan cultures has long been recognized, but before their respective ages were known, their interrelationship was difficult to ascertain. The 1943 excavations of the Kuan-tu shellmound by Kanaseki and Kokubu (1953) showed that "check-impressed potsherds" occurred stratigraphically above Yüan-shan remains, but these potsherds are said to be of the northern coastal type or of the Ketangalan culture. Our excavations at Tapenkeng demonstrate beyond reasonable doubt that at least at the lower Tamsui area the Botanical Garden elements *intruded into* the Yüan-shan occupation around 700 to 500 B.C. Since Botanical Garden remains do not occur at Yüan-shan Shellmound, which antedates the entire Tapenkeng sequence, it seems probable that the Botanical Garden culture did not occur side by side with the Yüan-shan culture at the heart of the Taipei basin, and also that in the basin as a whole this culture emerged some time during the latter half of the Yüan-shan occupation, that is, after 1000 B.C.

This leads to two hypotheses: the Botanical Garden culture could have developed out of the Yüan-shan culture, or it could have arisen independently in the southwestern part of the Taipei basin in the Takokan Valley. The second alternative is strengthened by the fact that in this area and in the coastal region of Hsinchu the northern cultural remains and pottery of central Taiwan affinities are said to occur in mixed contexts (Kokubu *et al.* 1949; C. Sheng 1963a, 1965). Geometric stamped and impressed pottery is characteristic of the central Taiwan prehistoric cultures as far back as the second millennium B.C., and it is entirely possible that the Botanical Garden culture represents a northern offshoot of the impressed pottery traditions and horizons. The question cannot be considered solved, however, until the relative chronology of this culture is known throughout its area of distribution so that its greater antiquity in the southwest is demonstrated.

SHIH-SAN-HANG CULTURE

If the Botanical Garden culture as a whole can be dated to follow the Yüan-shan culture in time, despite its initial overlaps, then it is likely that this culture, beginning just before the Christian era, lasted in the western part of the Taipei basin through most of the first millennium. The culture following this, characterized by gray, hard, check-impressed pottery, is distributed mainly along the northern coast of Taiwan and is identified with the Ketangalan people known from early historic accounts and from ethnographical studies. The best-excavated site of this culture is Shih-san-hang (Yang 1961; Sheng 1960) on the coast west of Tapenkeng where remains of the same culture are found on top of the Yüan-shan culture strata (see also C. C. Lin 1965).

Prehistoric Taiwan: A Summary

Archeological data from Taiwan have been accumulating since the end of the last century, and excellent work has been undertaken by a number of archeologists, despite the small size of the island. Our work from 1964 to 1966 has contributed to the general pool of prehistoric archeology in only a small way. On the other hand, the many and varied problems Formosan archeology still has to face obviously cannot be solved overnight, and quick and complete solutions were not a part of our aim for this project. What we have achieved that can be said to be of more than minor importance in the history of Formosan archeology may include: carbon-14 dates, application of intensive excavation techniques and an interdisciplinary approach, and the excavation of two stratigraphically significant sites and the quantification of the typological variations throughout the occupation layers, resulting in pictures of cultural change that have wide implication. New information thus derived has without question helped to place a great variety of existing information into a somewhat newer perspective, and to clarify and identify a number of urgent problems that await further research.

THE CHRONOLOGICAL SCALES

Both macro- and microenvironmental analyses provide essential information for cultural ecological studies of prehistoric cultures and are useful for their chronological significance. The macroenvironmental changes of overriding importance concern climatic fluctuations, which are indicated by the palynological research undertaken by Tsukada and by geological evidence. The hypsithermal interval shown in Tsukada's pollen diagram from Jih-yüeh-t'an goes a long way toward providing interpretive factors for the transgressive and regressive changes of the shorelines and the changes of marine fauna that are revealed in prehistoric shellmounds. Microenvironmental studies, such as the seriation of shellfish species at Fengpitou and the soil analyses undertaken at both Fengpitou and Tapenkeng, help to cross-date different parts of the same site as well as different sites in adjoining regions.

Typological classifications of cultural remains and the stratigraphical studies of the various cultures have long been standard procedure in chronological research of Formosa, and the excavations of the stratified sites at Fengpitou and Tapenkeng with prolonged occupations further underline the wide-ranging significance of such work. What has not been hitherto apparent is, however, the importance of quantification in dealing with cultural remains in the process of change and in making comparisons between neighboring cultural assemblages, both within and between sites. The seriation data obtained at Fengpitou and Tapenkeng are the first ever made available in the archeology of the island, and their significance in tightening the chronological controls at the respective sites and regions is readily apparent.

The application of the carbon-14 method to the prehistoric archeology of Taiwan is long overdue; the enormous usefulness of the method is amply demonstrated by the twenty or so carbon-14 dates obtained during the past two years by the radiocarbon laboratories of Yale University and of National Taiwan University.

The application of this and other conventional dating techniques has resulted in a somewhat tighter chronological placement of prehistoric sites in Formosa, as is shown in Figure 92 (cf. K.C. Chang 1954a, 1956; Sung 1965).

HUMAN OCCUPATION DURING THE PLEISTOCENE

Despite the speculative role of Formosa in Pleistocene Sino-Malayan faunal migrations when a land bridge connected the island with China and the Philippines, no conclusive evidence of Paleolithic man has been brought to light. Ino claimed the recovery of two stone implements from the Pleistocene deposits in the Pescadores, but the circumstances of the discovery are unclear. While we were excavating at the site of Fengpitou, C. C. Lin investigated the Pleistocene deposits in the neighborhood of the Fengshan tableland and discovered a limestone fissure deposit near Chung-ts'u, northwest of Lin-yüan, from which mammalian fossils of ap-

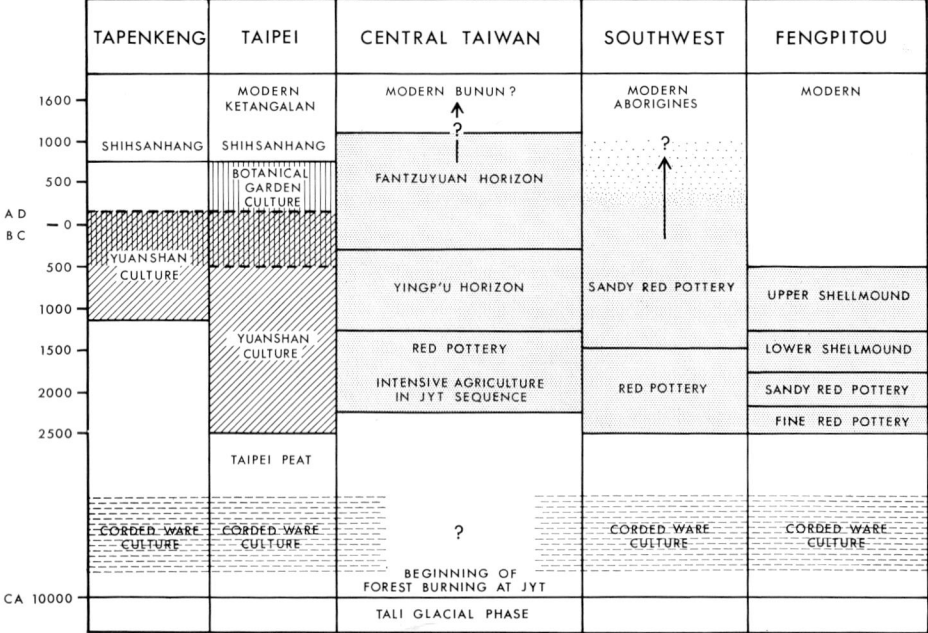

Fig. 92. Prehistoric Cultures in Taiwan and Their Chronological Placement.

parently Upper Pleistocene age were collected. On a piece of long bone some incisions were observed, possibly made by an artificial agency. Additional findings will be necessary before any human occupation during the Pleistocene can be verified.[2]

The Corded Ware Occupation and the Problem of the Early Form of Agriculture

The establishment of the cord-marked pottery as a cultural horizon and the clarification of its characteristics are probably the most significant contributions of our current work. It has been suggested by Kano, among others, that the oldest cultural stratum on the island is characterized by cord-marked pottery, and the excavations at Yüan-shan Shellmound and Tapenkeng tended to bear this out stratigraphically. But no corded ware stratum was known from the south, and

[2] While proofs of this monograph were being read, a preliminary report came from Taiwan concerning new finds of chipped flake implements, not in association with pottery, from beneath cord-marked pottery layers in several cave sites (Pa-hsien-tung) near the village of Chang-yüan, at the northern end of Taitung Prefecture on the southeast coast. These finds were made in January and February 1969 by the staff of the Department of Archaeology and Anthropology, National Taiwan University, under the direction of Professors W. H. Sung and C. C. Lin. Further reports concerning these finds are eagerly awaited.

incomplete knowledge of this cultural layer led to the erroneous conclusion that the cord-marked pottery stratum in central Taiwan also belonged to the same cultural horizon. New data from the north and south are sufficient for a characterization of this cultural layer, which has led to a re-examination of the evidence of central Taiwan and a reclassification of the cord-marked pottery layer in that area. It is now evident that there are two cord-marked pottery horizons on the west coast: an earlier one characterized by thick, coarse brown-buff sherds, and a later one characterized by fine, soft, red-orange sherds. The latter horizon probably belongs to the Lungshanoid and will be discussed below. The oldest ceramic culture on the island is represented by the cord-marked pottery of the coarser kind.

Current available archeological data indicate two clusters of corded ware sites, one in the southernmost areas of the western coast and the other in the lower Tamsui Valley and the northwestern coast. These two clusters, almost 200 km apart, share a number of essential characteristics such as the paste, general shape, surface features, and decorative techniques and patterns of the pottery; polished rectangular adzes; retouched river pebbles; and perforated triangular slate points. In contrast to all other prehistoric cultures in Formosa, the two clusters of corded ware remains belong, without any question, to a single culture derived from a single source. On the other hand, each of the two clusters exhibits some distinctive features, such as the ridged rims in the northern group and the delicate curvilinear incised patterns in the southern.

The age of this culture is uncertain, but apparently it antedates, by a considerable interval, the subsequent prehistoric cultures that began around 2500 B.C. Apparently of considerable antiquity, the Corded Ware culture is rather elaborate, nevertheless, as indicated by the occurrence of well-polished stone implements (adzes and points) and by the complex incised decorative patterns on pottery. The small number of stone implements that are apparently for cultivating purposes (chipped hoes) and for woodworking (adzes), as well as the common occurrence of retouched pebbles and points, seems to suggest that hunting and collecting were of great importance, and the absence of the characteristic stone knives that came with the subsequent grain-growing cultures indicates that the Corded Ware culture did not possess the techniques of intensive agriculture if, indeed, it had any agriculture at all.

At this juncture, however, the palynological sequence at Jih-yüeh-t'an is of great significance. It may be recalled that at about 9000 B.C. the vegetational history at the Jih-yüeh-t'an area underwent a clear and persistent change accounted for by the continuous burning of the primeval forests and the continuous replacement of secondary growths. Accidental burnings of the forest (such as forest fires) cannot account for the persistence of the new pattern of growth, and forest clearance by human hands is not likly to have been undertaken except for plant cultivation. Since the sequence at 4,200 B.P. shows evidence of intensive farming and of grain cultivation, the contrast seems to suggest that the earlier form of agriculture was characterized by the cultivation of root and fruit crops. During this period—from

11,000 to 4,200 B.P.—the only known prehistoric culture on the island of Taiwan was the Corded Ware culture described above, and the conclusion naturally follows that this culture was associated with an early form of root and fruit cultivation.

Such a conclusion, although it is credible on the grounds of comparative significance, would not be warranted by the available material. In the first place, one could not generalize about the history of farming of the entire island on the basis of a single palynological profile, however reliable it might be. Second, no well-established Corded Ware culture sites or components have been found in the central part of Taiwan (Liu and Liu 1957). The possibility, however, should be kept in mind so that continued investigations along the same paths may eventually lead to better-established results (see K. C. Chang, 1967b, for further speculations).

The corded ware sites on the east coast remain to be mentioned. At Hsin-ch'eng, near Suao, in the northern part of the east coast, a burial site was found from which cists and cord-marked pottery of essentially the same form and decoration were recovered (Utsurikawa and Miyamoto 1937; Sheng 1963b). At the southern end of the eastern coast, the site at Ta-p'ing, near Ch'ang-pin, has yielded similar pottery, although the paste contains a much larger amount of sand and grit of greater size. At both these sites, however, pottery of the Yüan-shan type has been discovered from apparently the same horizon and cultural context. These suggest that the eastern coast was a backwater, so to speak, in which survivals of earlier forms of culture persisted in mixed forms (Pearson 1966). Excavations throughout the eastern coastal area would be needed for a better understanding of its prehistoric cultures.

The Yüan-shan and the Botanical Garden Cultures

Beginning about 2500 B.C., the Yüan-shan culture emerged at the heart of the Taipei basin, a culture characterized by a distinctive pottery ware (sandy buff, plain, incised, ring-impressed, and paint-brushed) and a distinctive stone inventory (chiefly stepped adzes, shouldered axes, and perforated triangular arrowheads). Agriculture of an intensive nature is indicated by the abundance of stone hoes of several varieties, the large number of pottery jars presumably for storage, and the general elaboration of the cultural makeup. Bones of domestic dog were known from the sites. But shellmounds, bones of deer, wild boar, and monkey, implements of bone and antler, stone arrowheads and sinkers, all testify to the continued importance of hunting, fishing, and shellfish collecting. Human burials are known to have taken place in the shellmounds, and tooth extraction was practiced.

Compared with the Lungshanoid cultures in central and southern Taiwan at about the same time, several interesting points may have a bearing on the origin of the Yüan-shan culture. The characteristically Lungshanoid slate knives and stemmed arrowheads are absent, which may reflect the relative unimportance of grain agriculture. The decorative art of the ceramics is very dissimilar to anything that is known from the Lungshanoid sites either in Taiwan or southeast China, even though some of the basic pottery forms (such as the pedestal jars) may have Lungshanoid affinities. Aside from the stepped adz, which is a Lungshanoid characteristic, the stone inventory recalls nothing known in the Lungshanoid, but the shouldered axes point to the prehistoric cultures along the Gulf of Tonkin. From none of the burials at Yüan-shan Shellmound have shovel-shaped incisors been observed (a perforated shovel-shaped incisor suggests the occurrence of head-hunting and also the fact that a different morphological feature from the Yüan-shan inhabitants was found among the human group from which heads were obtained). All of these points combine to suggest the interesting possibility that the Yüan-shan inhabitants, despite Chinese influences, were essentially a non-Chinese strain both physically and culturally.

Two alternative interpretations concerning the origin of this culture thus present themselves. The Yüan-shan culture could have been a native outgrowth at Taipei basin of the Corded Ware culture, or it was an intrusion from a non-Lungshanoid origin somewhere in eastern Asia. We shall come back to this problem after taking a wider perspective than the island of Formosa.

During the latter half of the Yüan-shan occupation, from about 1000 B.C. to the Christian era, contacts between Taipei basin and mainland bronze cultures are indicated by the discovery of bronze objects at Yüan-shan Shellmound and at Tapenkeng. But no basic change occurred that is consonant with a bronze culture, and the bronze objects must be regarded as trade items.

Basic changes in the prehistoric scene in the northern part of Taiwan did occur, however, after about 500 B.C., with the emergence of the Botanical Garden type of archeological sites. The problems concerning the origin of this new type of site in the western part of Taipei basin have already been discussed. It is likely that the new phase of culture emerged in the southwestern portion of the area, in the valley of the Takokan River, as a direct result of cultural contacts with the Lungshanoid culture in central Taiwan in the form of impressed pottery. A comparison of the Yüan-shan and Botanical Garden sites, however, discloses that basic subsistence patterns differed from one type to the other. Shellmounds cease to be an important feature of the Botanical Garden sites, which are found on more level and lower ground than the Yüan-shan sites. Massive chipped and polished hoes and large stone adzes (including the stepped variety) occur in large numbers. It is possible that, even though the check-impressed pottery marks a decisive division from the Yüan-shan pottery in terms of style, the Botanical Garden type of sites represents a culture of higher levels of plant cultivation. The higher firing temperature for the Botanical Garden-type sherds than the Yüan-shan sherds also indicates advances in technology.

The Lungshanoid Cultures

Also beginning around 2500 B.C., a tradition decisively different from the Yüan-shan culture but essentially of the same strain as the Lungshanoid cultures of southeast China, occurred in central and southwest Formosa. One encounters, at different areas and different time periods, three major types of pottery of this culture: fine-paste, cord-marked red; sandy, incised brown-buff; and incised and impressed black wares.

The fine-paste, cord-marked red pottery occurred first, both in the southwest and in central Taiwan. The forms include bowls, *tou*-pedestaled basins and bowls, large, wide-mouthed jars, and thin, long-necked jars. The associated stone implements include flat polished hoes, stemmed arrowheads, rectangular and saddle-shaped slate knives, and rectangular adzes. Neither the shouldered ax nor the stepped adz, so typical of the Yüan-shan culture, was found here. The intensive nature of the agricultural activities at the red pottery sites is merely indicated by the character and amount of their stone and pottery artifacts and by the temporal coincidence with the intensive farming shown by the Jih-yüeh-t'an sequence. Shellmounds are not found at this level.

The sandy brown-buff and the black pottery occurred in Taiwan at about the same time, that is, about the middle of the second millennium B.C. Cord, basket, and mat impressions and incisions (including the shell-combed) are distinctive decorative patterns, and jars, bowls, basins, pedestaled jars and bowls, and *ting* tripods are the characteristic pottery forms. Shellmounds occur in great abundance, in which bones of deer, wild boar, monkey, fish, crab, and turtle are found. Both the Jih-yüeh-t'an sequence and the grain impressions on pottery suggest intensive grain agriculture (probably of millet and rice) as does the occurrence of hoes, slate knives, and other agriculture-related artifacts. Several distinctive burial patterns are recognized, and head-hunting is again indicated.

The variety and change of pottery throughout the Lungshanoid sites are very interesting and suggestive. While internal development from one type of pottery to another is far from impossible, it seems more likely, from the variety of pottery and stone inventories at the Lungshanoid sites, that the Lungshanoid inhabitants arrived at the island in different waves at different localities at different times. This will be further discussed in Chapter 11.

Chapter 10. External Affinities of the Corded Ware Culture of Taiwan

THE Corded Ware culture of Taiwan forms a discrete unit for comparison because of its temporal isolation from the subsequent cultures and its lack of entanglement with later cultural remains in a stratigraphic sense, at least along the western coast. From other areas than Taiwan, however, there is a paucity of comparative data. Published descriptions of the cord-marked pottery of the Far East (with the exception of Japan) are scarce and scattered. The Formosa data, therefore, are unique in many ways, and the origin and relationship problems of this culture must remain inconclusive for the time being.

The comparative data in the immediate neighborhood of Formosa of cord-marked pottery can be described under three geographical divisions: Japan and the northern Ryukyus, southeast China and northern Indochina, and the Philippines.

Japan and the Northern Ryukyus

Japan seems to be the most logical place in which to seek affinities with the Taiwan material, for Japan has not only extensive and enormous remains of a long and wide ceramic tradition of cord-impressed pottery (the Jomon) but also the earliest dated pottery of the kind. If our Corded Ware culture can be given a date anywhere near ten thousand years ago, then the early Jomon pottery of Honsho, dated more than 10,000 years B.P. (Oba and Chard 1963), deserves immediate attention.

However, aside from the fact that both the Japanese and the Formosan pottery are cord marked and that occasional incised patterns are common to both, there is little indication that there was any direct and close cultural relationship between the two areas. The shapes of the Formosan cord-marked pottery and the decorative motifs of the incisions are found but rarely—if at all—in Japan, and the characteristic Jomon shapes and decorations (e.g. Kidder 1957) are completely absent from the Taiwan data. Moreover, the associated stone and bone artifacts in Formosa derive evidently from a cultural strain different from their Japanese counterparts.

The geographical locations of the Corded Ware culture sites in Formosa—clustering on the lower Tamsui and on the northwest and southwest coasts—would point to a westerly direction of direct and close contact with Formosa.

Southeast China and Northern Indochina

It has long been postulated that the earliest pottery of north China was characterized by cord marking (Ward 1954: 133; Chang 1963: 56–7), and the hypothetical *Sheng-wen* horizon, a horizon of cord-marked pottery antedating the earliest known Neolithic culture of the painted pottery stage, is beginning to be substantiated (P. C. Su 1965). Recent findings in Kiangsi, in central China, moreover, have disclosed an early ceramic assemblage characterized by cord-marked pottery in an area intermediate between North China and the southeastern coast.

This is the archeological site found in a limestone cave—Hsien-jen-tung (*Cave of the Spirits*) in early 1962, northeast of the town of Wan-nien, in northeastern Kiangsi (Kuo and Li 1963). Three cultural strata are distinguished: Hsien-jen-tung I, characterized by cord-marked potsherds; Hsien-jen-tung II, yielding potsherds similar to the lower stratum of the Ying-p'an-li site, or a local facies of the Lungshanoid horizon; and a recent, disturbed layer at the top.

Of great interest in the present connection are the findings from the earliest stratum. These include:

1. Twelve hearths or clusters of burned clay fragments.

2. Two fragmentary human skulls, a human mandible, and a piece of femur, which represent four individuals, including two adults (one male, one female), a child of eight, and an infant. The skull of the child has shovel-shaped incisors, a usual Mongoloid feature.

3. Bones, teeth, and shells of wild animals, including *Pseudaxis hortulorum* (largest number), *Hydropotes inermis* (many), *Sus scrofa* (many), *Ovis* sp. (many), *Arctonyx collaris, Mustela* sp., *Viverricula* cf. *malaccensis pallida, Paguma larvata, Felis bengalensis, Felis* sp., *Lepus* sp. *Aquila* sp., *Gallus*, turtles, crabs, and mollusk shells (many). Many of the long bones are broken, and two deer antlers show artifactual incisions. The fauna as a whole indicates humid and warm environment.

4. Stone implements, 40; 24 of these are chipped from sandstone pebbles and can be referred to as choppers and chopping tools; 16 stone artifacts are polished, including pointed tools, a chisel, a perforated disk, and 6 grinding stones.

5. Bone implements, 36, most polished, including eyed needles, awls, a knife, and a harpoon.

6. Antler and teeth artifacts, 4, including chisels, a knife, and worked pieces.

7. Shell artifacts, 52, including perforated shells, ornaments, and other fragments.

8. Potsherds, over 90 pieces. The description of these potsherds is of importance and is quoted in full as follows:

> *Paste:* Sandy Red ware. Coarse texture; tempered with quartz grains of various sizes, the largest 1 millimeter in diameter and 0.5 millimeter in thickness; tempering materials exhibited very unevenly in the paste. Other tempering materials were used, but are oxidized and occur in grayish-whitish powder form. Firing was low, and the paste is loose and easily breakable; the sherds are difficult to remove from the soil during excavations. The thickness of the sherds varies from 0.7 to 1.4 centimeter; the thickness of a single sherd varies from one portion to another. The color of the core is reddish-brown; one piece exhibits red, gray, and black. The interior surface of the sherds is uneven, indicating that the pottery was handmade.
>
> *Shape:* Too fragmentary for shape determination. The rims are mostly straight; there are a few that are flaring or inverted. No neck or shoulder sherds. Body sherds show large arc angles. No appendages. No flat base sherds. One restorable pot: lip slightly flaring; upper part of the body vertical; lower part slopes inward to form a possible round base. Thick but uneven. Both exterior and interior impressed with cord-marks. Remaining height 18 cm, the diameter of the mouth 20 cm.

Decoration: All of the sherds are cord-marked. Strands vary in thickness; thick strands 2.5 mm wide, but fine ones only 1 mm. Techniques of decoration include (1) cross-impressed: most common, fine, resembling check patterns; (2) segment-impressed: impressed in units; (3) parallel: fine and regular, thick and fine strands; (4) irregular: often smeared; (5) interior-exterior: impressed on both sides; patterns on the two sides are often not identical.

In addition to cord-marking, there are sherds that were smoothed and exhibit parallel lines. A few rim sherds exhibit one or two rows of circular impressions; a few of these penetrated through the sherds or cracked the walls. On the lips are also found irregular indentations [Kuo and Li 1963: 7].

This site is highly important for several reasons. Stratigraphically, the Hsien-jen-tung cave site repeats the Fengpitou stratigraphy of cord-marked pottery underlying the Lungshanoid, indicating that at the heart of China the cord-marked pottery horizon definitely predates the Lungshanoid. This phenomenon is recurrent in the southern part of South China, but the geographic location of this site underlines its significance. The shovel-shaped incisor gives definite evidence of the characteristics of the people, something completely lacking for this culture in the rest of China. The faunal evidence gives clear indication of the ecological conditions of the site, and the natural remains and the multiple stratifications within this cultural layer (Kuo and Li 1963: 3–4) suggest strongly that the subsistence basis of the culture was hunting, fishing, and collecting. Unfortunately, besides the stratigraphy and the paste and decoration of the pottery, which are of very broad nature and do not give specific comparative information for the study of the Corded Ware culture of Formosa, the remains of the site are so restricted in range of typology that little comparison can be drawn directly between them and our Formosan materials.

Elsewhere in the mainland, large numbers of cord-marked pottery sites—in many cases stratigraphically underlying Lungshanoid or Geometric remains—have been located in Kwangtung Province, southwest China, and northern Indochina. The easternmost sites are found in the lower Hankiang Valley of easternmost Kwangtung, about 370 km directly west of Fengpitou across the Formosa Strait and South China Sea. For the purpose of this study only the coastal sites will be considered; these can be grouped as follows according to their geographical locations.

1. Lower Hankiang Valley, near the city of Ch'ao-an, eastern Kwangtung (Mo 1961a). Here is a series of shellmound sites, where prehistoric assemblages definitely distinct from the well-known Geometric Neolithic remains of the area were located in the late 1950s by the provincial Commission for the Preservation of Ancient Monuments. These sites have yielded, in addition to mollusk shells, animal bones and other habitation remains, a large number of stone and bone implements, and potsherds. The stone implements are mostly chipped pebble choppers, scrapers, and a kind of pointed instrument that the investigators describe as an oyster pick. Roughly or partially polished stone adzes were also found. Potsherds are described as very coarse grit or shell-tempered. Some of them are painted in brown pigment, some incised, and others impressed with cord marks. The descriptions of the pottery

are too brief and cryptic, and the illustrations too poor, for a clear impression of its characteristics, but the apparently early age, the predominance of a hunting–fishing–collecting way of life, and the geographic propinquity to the Formosan sites all command close attention and suggest important comparative data for the future.

2. Northeast Kwangtung, in the county of Wung-yüan (P'eng 1961). A series of limestone caves yielding early habitation remains was located in 1959 in this area. The remains include chipped and roughly polished stone implements, mollusk shells, animal bones, and "coarse, sandy gray and red potsherds with cord-marks." A stalagmite crust occurs in one of the caves over the cultural remains, suggesting a considerable antiquity, and these cord-marked sites are the closest to the Hsien-jen-tung site of Kiangsi in geographic proximity.

3. Lower Pearl Valley. In the Pearl Delta, in addition to the late Neolithic Geometric pottery, coarse and primitive-looking cord-marked pottery has long been found, and its great antiquity long suspected (Schofield 1940: 279; Mo and Li 1960). Where chipped stone implements occur, the associated pottery is usually described as coarse and cord marked (Mo 1959). The postulated antiquity of the corded pottery is given stratigraphical credence by archeological excavations of two shellmound sites on the east bank of the delta in 1961 (Mo 1961b). Some of the potsherds, moreover, are painted in brown and red pigment.

In the summer of 1966 the author visited City Hall and the Feng P'ing Shan Museums in Hong Kong and also a number of prehistoric sites, where many data seem to be relevant. Sherds with wavy lines incised by group instruments over corded surfaces are found in the Hoifung collection of Father Maglioni, and are said to have come from the SOW site. Cord-marked sherds of very coarse paste are seen in well-defined horizons at the site of Lao-fo-san I (New Territories) and the site of Man-kok-tsui (Lantau Island) (Pl. 102), although the excavators of the latter site did not discover any clear-cut stratigraphic relationship of this kind of pottery with the geometric-impressed wares (Davis and Tregear 1961). Excavations in the future at these Hong Kong sites may yet disclose more abundant information about this layer of culture.

4. Western coastal Kwangtung. Coarse, cord-marked potsherds were found in association with chipped and roughly polished pebble implements, shellmounds, and bone artifacts in Tung-hsing Hsien, directly east of North Vietnam (Mo and Ch'en 1961). From a limestone cave in Ling-shan, nearby, cord-marked sherds and distinctively Mongoloid skeletal remains were found indisputably in an early Neolithic context (Ku 1962: 196, 199).

5. North Vietnam. Archeological assemblages similar to those in Kwangtung, where cord-marked pottery occurs in association with crude chipped and partially polished stone implements, have been located in the Bacson district of North Vietnam (Mansuy 1924, 1925). Many of the chipped pebble axes resemble the chipped ax of Tapenkeng, but the form is perhaps too general to be of specific comparative significance. Interesting parallels, however, can be seen in the clay cylindrical tubes

(Mansuy 1925, his Pl. XII: *8a,b*) and in the group instrument-incised rectilinear patterns found from a number of Bacsonian sites (Saurin 1940).

The Philippines

Some of the incised patterns from Tapengkeng have very close affinities in the pottery of the so-called Kalanay complex of the central Philippines (Solheim 1964a), where, however, they are found in a cultural context apparently different from the Corded Ware culture of Taiwan.

Summary

The Corded Ware culture is without doubt a local manifestation of the widespread cord-marked pottery horizon in the eastern part of Asia, which is of considerable antiquity. Intensive excavations of the prehistoric sites with predominantly cord-marked pottery in the Far East have been scarce, with the exception of the Jomon sites of Japan, and the sites of Tapenkeng and Fengpitou thus occupy a unique position in the literature on Southeast Asia in terms of the amount of material.

Comparative studies suffer, however, from the paucity of relevant data, and it is yet impossible to determine the origin of the Corded Ware culture of Taiwan. Japan has the largest amount of information on this kind of pottery, but it is unlikely that direct connection can be made between Taiwan and Japan at this time. In terms of geographical propinquity, associated cultural remains, and stratigraphy, close affinities are indicated with the cord-marked pottery assemblages along the southern coast of China and in northern Indochina, where they are referred to as late Hoabinhian and Bacsonian, but the data from these areas are far from adequate for specific conclusions. The Corded Ware culture of Formosa was also probably among the cultures that gave rise to the Kalanay ceramic complex of the Philippines, but the nature of the connection is not clear.

Chapter 11. The Lungshanoid and Yüan-shan Cultural Affinities in China and Southeast Asia

IT WAS stated in Chapter 9 that after approximately 2500 B.C. two major cultures arose on the western coastal areas of Taiwan: the Yüan-shan culture in the north and the Lungshanoid cultures in the center and southwest. The external affinities of the successive phases of these two cultures are clearly indicated by the available comparative materials, which can be described and discussed under three regional headings: southeast coastal China (Fig. 93), the South China Sea coasts and the Gulf of Tonkin, and the Philippines. Interrelationships with the Ryukyus and Kyushu are negligible for our present purposes (Kokubu 1964b; Pearson 1966).

Southeast Coast of China

Before the advent of historical civilizations in the southeast coastal areas of China—Shang and Western Chou in the northern regions and Eastern Chou in the south, but Ch'in and Han (ca. 200 B.C.) throughout and intensively—the prehistoric cultures were broadly grouped into two major cultural horizons, Lungshanoid and Geometric (Chang 1964b,d). Except for Yüan-shan, the cultures on the western coast of Taiwan fall within the Lungshanoid category without any serious questions. The Lungshanoid horizon of southeast China, however, is a very broad integrative concept, and it includes a number of more restricted local and temporal manifestations. In order to trace the origins of the various Lungshanoid cultures in Taiwan it is necessary to trace each of them back to its specific regional and temporal phase on the mainland. It must be pointed out, however, that, although the various Lungshanoid phases are well understood in their temporal and spatial relationship on the western coast of Taiwan as the result of our research, they have been formulated in only a preliminary manner on the Chinese mainland. Much light can be shed on the mainland cultural chronology by the Taiwan data but, needless to say, conclusive correlations are out of the question.

The temporal and spatial interrelationship of the various Lungshanoid phases on the mainland is best documented in the provinces of Kiangsu and Chekiang, in the southern part of the Huaiho drainage system, the lower Yangtze, and the lower Chientangkiang River. The most recent studies of the Neolithic cultures of the area recognize three different "cultures": Ch'ing-lien-kang, Liu-lin, and Liang-chu, all three of which fall within the broadly conceived Lungshanoid cultural horizon. Moreover, some archeologists believe that these cultures, of somewhat different geographical distribution, are also chronologically successive (Chiang 1959; KKYCS 1962; Tseng et al. 1963; H. Chang 1964). A brief characterization of each of them follows.

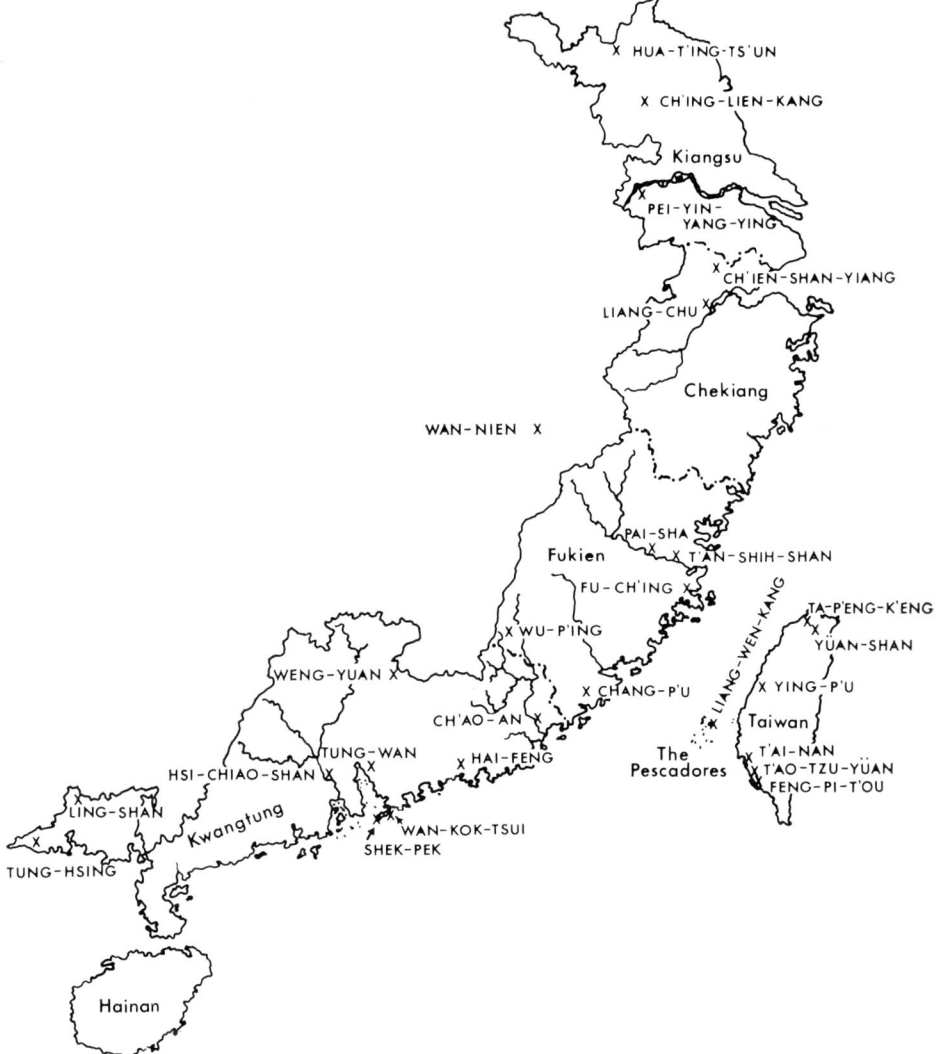

Fig. 93. Prehistoric Sites on the Southeast Coast of China.

Ch'ing-lien-kang Culture

First recognized at the site of Ch'ing-lien-kang in Huai-an Hsien, northern Kiangsu, in 1951, this culture is now known to be concentrated throughout the province of Kiangsu and the adjacent areas in Anhwei and Chekiang. It is characterized by:

> Large numbers of polished stone implements, typical of which are flat, rectangular adz; square and flat chisel; and rectangular knife with multiple perforations. A small number

of perforated stone hoes. Stepped adzes and shouldered axes are occasionally found. Most of the pottery is red in color, sandy or very fine of paste. Gray and black wares occur but rarely. Most of them are handmade and highly polished; and tripods and ring-footed vessels are the most common shapes. The principal tripod is *ting* . . . and the principal ring-footed vessel is *tou;* some of the ring-feet have cut-outs. Handled mugs, jars, pots, and bowls are also found. At some sites a small number of painted sherds occur . . . A variety of ornaments, including rings, beads, and pendants of jade and agate . . . The inhabitants lived on hills and terraces near the rivers, engaged principally in farming. Remains of rice husks occur at a few sites . . . Bows and arrows, fish spears, and net sinkers were implements for fishing and hunting [KKYCS 1962: 30–1].

Liu-lin Culture

So far three sites of this type of Lungshanoid culture have been located, all in the northernmost part of Kiangsu. Its distinctive feature is an instrument made of a pair of deer teeth hafted to a bone handle, said to be for harvesting purposes. Large numbers of bone and antler implements are found at all sites. Sandy red *ting* tripods, fine-paste red bowls, and black mugs and high-pedestal *tou* vessels with cutouts are characteristic of the pottery vessels. Painted potsherds are many, the painting invariably executed on red pottery. Jadeish ornaments are also found (C. Tseng *et al.* 1963: 4).

Liang-chu Culture

First discovered at the site of Liang-chu, near Hangchow, in 1936, this culture has now proved to be widespread in southern Kiangsu and northern Chekiang. The stone implements include a great number of large, polished, and flat axes, knives, and hoes, many having an oblique handle and some of which have perforations. Stone spearheads and arrowheads, chisels and knives, and stepped adzes occur. Bone and antler implements are found. The pottery is characterized by fine-paste, well-made black pottery with incised and, occasionally, painted decorative patterns. The leading shapes are jars with lugs, pots and bowls, and pedestaled *tou* with cut-outs (C. Tseng *et al.* 1963: 5; KKYCS 1962: 31–2).

The chronological interrelationship among these three cultures, according to recent study (C. Tseng *et al.* 1963: 10; H. Chang 1964: 470), is that the Ch'ing-lien-kang culture is the earliest, and the Liang-chu culture the latest. Since the first has a more northerly distribution, it is implied that the chronological sequence was a southward expansion of the Lungshanoid cultures from their homeland in the north.

The archeological evidence from Formosa, however, seems to indicate that the earliest Lungshanoid phase reached Formosa. It is suggested here that the fine red cord-marked pottery phase of southwest Formosa is related to the Ch'ing-lien-kang culture; that the sandy red pottery (including painted and black pottery) is a cultural phase comparable in time to the Liu-lin culture; and that the gray and black pottery of central Taiwan is related to the Liang-chu culture. To trace the connections of these cultures in Formosa to their counterparts in Kiangsu and Chekiang it is necessary to review the problem of the southern limits of the Lungshanoid cultural distributions on the mainland, and in this review the prehistoric sites of the province of Fukien must play a significant role.

The Fine Red Ware Phase of Southwest-Central Taiwan

The first Lungshanoid phase in Taiwan is the one characterized by the fine-paste, cord-marked red pottery, recovered from the lower strata in the southwestern sites and in central Taiwan. The shapes of the pottery (especially the high-pedestal basins and dishes with cutouts, and *ting* tripods), the use of a wheel in the manufacture of pottery, and the stone inventory (especially flat hoes, rectangular adzes, and rectangular slate knives) that characterize this phase of Taiwan Lungshanoid would identify it with the broad Lungshanoid concept. The fact that it is an early phase of the Lungshanoid in Formosa is very significant in extending the southern limits of the Ch'ing-lien-kang culture, for the closest affinities of this phase on the mainland must be found in that culture.

Ting tripods and *tou* with cut-out ring feet of fine red paste are the most distinctive features of the fine red ware Lungshanoid phase of Taiwan, and the Ch'ing-lien-kang culture is the closest thing to it anywhere in the region. Differences between the two groups are many and profound, to be sure, but together they contrast sharply with all the other Lungshanoid phases. A major problem is the lack of well-defined assemblages of this type of culture (primarily characterized by red pottery) in the intermediate areas.

Tracing this phase of culture back to the mainland, the first site one encounters is at Liang-wen-kang of the Pescadores (Kokubu 1960). Two loci of remains were found at the site, both yielding deposits of shell middens. Fragments of chipped hoes of basalt and hard sandstone occur, together with potsherds with cord marks and narrow rims. The sherds are reddish-brown, thin at the middle but relatively thick at the rim, which sometimes flares. The cord marks are very fine and thin, probably applied by means of a cord-wrapped paddle. Dark brown, brown, or light reddish painting was occasionally applied on the lips, presumably after the pottery was fired. The shape is apparently characterized by flat-based vessels, but a piece of ring-foot fragment was collected. The cord-marked red pottery and the stone artifacts made of olivine basalt strongly indicate the close ties between the Liang-wen-kang remains and the Fine Red Ware Settlement of Fengpitou, but the paucity of the remains at the former site makes further comparisons difficult.

Similar ceramic assemblages have not been located in Fukien and southern Chekiang. The connection with the Ch'ing-lien-kang culture is inconclusive in view of this geographic gap.

The Sandy Red or Gray, Painted, and Black Pottery Phases of Southwestern Taiwan

Sandy red pottery became predominant in Lungshanoid II of Fengpitou; and similar assemblages, including painted pottery, black pottery, and a characteristic Lungshanoid stone and bone complex, have been shown to be widespread in the southwestern coastal areas of the island. There is no question that this Lungshanoid phase of Taiwan is closely related to similar prehistoric assemblages on the mainland. Prehistoric remains very closely similar to Settlements III and IV of Fengpitou have been recovered from the site of T'an-shih-shan, near Foochow, in central Fukien (C. Lin 1955, 1961; Lü *et al.* 1964; C. H. Chang and Lü 1965).

First discovered in 1954, the site of T'an-shih-shan has undergone five seasons of excavation. It is on a small hill of that name, about 300 m long, 10 to 40 m wide, and 10 to 20 m high, 300 m from the Minkiang River and 65 km from the seacoast. Cultural remains are in the form of shellmounds, concentrated on the southern part of the hill and attaining a maximal depth of over 2 m. All specified shells are marine, including *Corbicula* sp., *Arca* sp., *Ostrea* sp., and *Auricula* sp., which must indicate that the coastline was closer to the site than it is at the present. Large numbers of animal bones and antlers occur. Stone implements, of "volcanic rock," slate, "flint," and schist, include axes, adzes, chisels, knives, and arrowheads, all polished. There are also bone awls, arrowheads, and chisels. Three human burials have been found; invariably the body lies on its back, stretched, and no grave-pit outline can be recognized. All these features recall the shellmound settlements of Fengpitou, but more striking similarities occur in the realm of ceramics.

According to the analysis of Chang and Lü (1965), the following wares occurred at the site.

Impressed hard pottery. This ware constitutes the majority of potsherds of the site, and includes two major varieties according to color. (1) *Impressed red:* no apparent tempering materials; fine and compact; orange-yellow-reddish in color, occasionally with gray reduced core; brown slip; a large variety of impressed designs, most of which are fine-cord and basket; appliqués; large pots with flat, round, or concave bases; no ring feet. (2) *Impressed gray:* hard and nonporous; tempered with a small amount of fine-grained sand; dark brown slip on the interior; impressed basket, check, and fine-cord designs; flaring rims; flat, round, or concave bases.

Fine polished ware. Very fine paste, gray or black skin and gray core, thin walled, polished, and not impressed, this ware includes a large number of ring feet with cutouts. Wheelmarks characterize all the sherds of this ware.

Sandy impressed ware. Sand-tempered, relatively soft, the sherds of this ware are gray or red in color. Cord-impressed and basket-impressed decorative patterns are common, and the manufacture was apparently by hand.

Painted ware. Some impressed hard pottery, either gray or red, has painted rims. The painting is executed in black or dark brown pigment, and the patterns are composed of short strokes in geometrical arrangement. The body impression of painted pottery is mostly in the form of checks.

Different kinds of pottery apparently occur at the site of T'an-shih-shan in a slightly different stratigraphical situation. Two strata are distinguished: an earlier one characterized by sandy impressed ware and fine polished ware, and a later stratum in which the predominant ceramics are impressed hard, impressed sandy, and painted wares. There are more forms in the earlier stratum, including a large

nostic features with the Ch'ing-lien-kang culture of Kiangsu; the shellmound cultures of southwestern Taiwan, with their sandy red ware and painted pottery, were definitely close affinities of the T'an-shih-shan culture of Fukien; and the Black Pottery Culture of central Taiwan must have been derived from the Liang-chu culture of Chekiang. The chronological sequence of these three cultural groups in Taiwan is parallel to the sequence of their ancestral cultures on the mainland, with Ch'ing-lien-kang culture the earliest, followed by the T'an-shih-shan and Liang-chu cultures which were probably largely contemporaneous.

The South China Seacoast and the Gulf of Tonkin

The Lungshanoid cultures of the southeastern coastal areas of China provide credible origins for the prehistoric cultures of central and southwestern Taiwan, as shown in the preceding section. The conclusions cannot be final until the prehistoric cultural sequences are better organized than at the present on the mainland, but the indications are clear and unequivocal. The Lungshanoid sites, however, do not provide a background under which to understand the derivation of the Yüan-shan culture of northern Taiwan.

In sharp contrast with the Lungshanoid cultures to the south, the Yüan-shan culture is characterized by a stone assemblage of stepped adz, shouldered ax, chipped and roughly polished hoe, and perforated triangular arrowhead—lacking the slate knives and stemmed arrowheads typifying the Lungshanoid—and by a pottery ware with coarse texture and slip and brushed and unpatterned red painting and some incisions (in completely different patterns from the southern cultures), but no impressed decorations of any kind but the small rings. The leading pottery form is a jar with lid, two vertical loop or strap handles on the neck, and a low ring foot, a form closely resembling the classical bronze *kui* of Shang and Chou China. This assemblage of stone and pottery characteristic of the Yüan-shan culture is not duplicated in any substantial way at Lungshanoid sites, even though isolated features (such as occasional handle forms, ring foot as a basic support, and stepped adzes) do occur here and there at Lungshanoid assemblages on the mainland. As an articulated culture the Yüan-shan apparently has a different major derivation from the Lungshanoid phases.

Despite the time difference and the basic demarcation of cultural types that separate the Yüan-shan culture from the much earlier Corded Ware culture of northern Taiwan, the two share a few characteristics. The only point of the Corded Ware culture, the perforated triangular type, is also the diagnostic type of arrowhead and spearpoint of the Yüan-shan culture, and slate was the common material. The *kui* is characteristic of both cultures, and both lack tripods. It can be said that Corded Ware culture continuities occurred in the Yüan-shan culture of a later period, but these continuities must not be the dominant elements of the new culture, which presumably derived its basic inspirations elsewhere. And, if there was such continuity, there were also important breaks, for cord marking no longer appeared on the Yüan-shan pottery.

As to where we must look for inspiration for the emergence of the new Yüan-shan culture, the stone implement types provide the only definite clues. The sole area in the Far East in the Formosa neighborhood where there is a combination of chipped and partially polished rectangular hoes, stepped adzes, and shouldered axes—a combination that characterizes the Yüan-shan culture and sets it apart from the southern Lungshanoid—is the northern coasts of the South China Sea and the Gulf of Tonkin, namely, the coastal areas of Kwangtung, Hainan Island, and the Gulf of Tonkin. Discussing the various ax and adz types of the Haifeng–Hong Kong area, Beyer (1948: 34) has arrived at the following conclusions:

  a. Rather typical oval adzes of Early Neolithic Type I are found in small numbers both at Hong Kong and at Hoifung [Hai-feng].
  b. There appear numerous transitional types, especially at Hoifung, between the oval adze and the shouldered adze, on the one hand; and between the plain-backed oval adze and the semi-ridged or tanged type, on the other. Also as between the round or oval shouldered-adze and the semi-ridged or tanged "stepped"-adze.
  c. In the same way there appear similar transitional types between the peculiar Hoifung rectangular or trapezoidal body—some of which closely resemble certain early Philippine stepped types.
  d. In Luzon—and, for the later types, also in Cebu and Mindanao—there appear almost exact duplicates of some of the Hoifung stepped and semi-ridged or tanged types.

Beyer further states, "Considering the above four items together, it is reasonable to assume that there was direct contact between the Hoifung–Hongkong areas and the Island of Luzon. Furthermore, that this contact occurred more than once." The same observations can be applied to the Haifeng–Hongkong and northern Taiwan interrelationship. It is on the basis of a study of stone implement types that Sung (1964: 99) suggests "the Yüan-shan Series is a local series of the Neolithic [rectangular] stone adz culture which is widely distributed along the southeast coast of China and in the South East Asia area. In conclusion, . . . if it was not diffused oppositely from Taiwan to the China mainland, the home of the Yüan-shan culture should be in the area between Haifeng and Canton."

A combination of stepped adz and shouldered ax, however, is not confined to the coastal region between Haifeng and Canton but is widely seen on the Kwangtung coasts, from the eastern end of the province (Jao 1951) to the island of Hainan (Mo 1960). On the island of Hainan there are, in addition to the stone ax-adz types, scattered findings of the double-grooved stone sinkers and the small loop handles of pottery applied to the neck of the jar, both characteristic of the Yüan-shan stratum at the site of Tapenkeng. The pottery of Hainan, furthermore, is a sandy brown-buff ware, singularly lacking the impressed geometric patterns (cord, mat, basket and check patterns) that are found on pottery of the Kwangtung coasts between Haifeng and Canton.

The Philippines

The northern end of Luzon is only a little over 200 statute miles south of the southern tip of Formosa, and the distance is further shortened by the Bataan and the Babuyan islands situated between the two regions. It is to be expected, therefore, that prehistoric cultures of Formosa and of the Philippines had much in common. Such interrelationships, however, have so far been examined only rarely and in cursory fashion. This is not the result of scholars' inattention but of insufficient study of the local prehistoric sequences on both sides.

Before the 1950s the local sequences of the Philippines had been constructed practically single-handedly by H. Otley Beyer, who, stimulated by Robert Heine-Geldern's (1932) cultural classifications for the western Pacific, formulated an elaborate sequence of prehistoric cultures solely on the basis of surface collections of stone and metal artifacts and porcelain of the Philippines, mainly of the southern part of Luzon. As pointed out by Wilhelm G. Solheim (1964a: 1), "prior to 1958, only two site reports written by trained archeologists had been published" for the entire area, and even up to the present "no reports on living sites, architectural sites, or stratified sites have been published." This makes inevitable the hypothetical nature of Beyer's cultural sequence for the Philippines and renders it difficult to explain whatever discrepancies may arise in comparing the Philippines data with the Formosa sequence which is firmly based on excavated material from stratified sites.

According to Beyer's scheme (1948) the so-called Neolithic period of the Philippines can be divided into three substages, *Early* (Round Ax), *Middle* (Shouldered Ax), and *Late* (Rectangular Ax). The period occupied by the Lungshanoid and Yüan-shan cultures of Formosa, namely the two and a half millennia before Christ, is filled in the Philippines, according to Beyer's chronology, by the Middle and Late Neolithic cultures:

Middle Neolithic

a. Early true shouldered axe-adze culture (*Schulterbeil*); probably from the West; found in Assam, Burma, Indo-China, South China, Japan, Formosa, and sparsely in Luzon and Celebes.

b. The ridged adze (*Riegelbeil*) culture, from the North . . . ; possible transitional forms in Formosa and the Hoifung–Hongkong area of South China, but true "Luzon ridged-adze" known only from the Philippines. . . .

c. Tanged Hawaiian and East-Polynesian adze culture, originating in Luzon (Bulakan to Batangas) and spreading to Eastern Pacific with northern type of early Polynesian (Indonesian A?) culture—*before true rectangular-adze culture reached Luzon.*

d. Early transitional "Hoifung" adze-type; from South China (Fukien or northern Kwang-tung) to Formosa and Luzon . . . b–d usually of andesites, porphyries or basalts; and spread into the Philippines, and beyond, between 2250 and 1750 B.C.

Late Neolithic

a. The true developed rectangular and trapezoidal adze (using very hard and highly polished stones) cultures; from the West, passing from Indo-China into Malaysia by probably three routes; probably reaching Philippines chiefly from south and west (through Borneo, or direct from Indo-China), between 1750 and 1250 B.C.

b. Characteristic early transitional forms of modified butt, ancestral to the early true "stepped"-adze (*Stufenbeil*), accompanied by a very limited number of bronze celts and weapons (and possibly ornaments?); from Indo-China ("Dongson culture" area?) or the Hongkong area, into Luzon and Formosa (c. 1250 to 800 B.C.). True early stepped adzes then developed rapidly in Luzon.

  c. True *Yangshao* and *Dongson* cultures, with developed "jade-cult" and with a special sawing and hole-boring technique, reached Luzon from Indo-China direct (about 800 to 500 B.C.)—and later spread from Luzon southeastward through Melanesia and on to parts of Central Polynesia and New Zealand.

  d. Final or "Philippine" form of the stepped adze; developed through the aid of the new sawing technique, and spread from Luzon southward through parts of the central and southern Philippines into northern Celebes; but the high point of development remained in the Batangas area of Luzon. (About 500 to 200 B.C.)

The assignment of absolute dates to the various Neolithic stages shows amazing insight on Beyer's part, and the grouping of stone implements is not in total disagreement with their distribution of types in today's light. But methodologically this scheme is a difficult one to apply for comparative purposes, for so many factors must be enumerated for the determination of stone ax-adz types that to plot cultural groupings and migrations according to them is manifestly unsafe.

Both the shouldered ax and the stepped adz occur in Formosa in the Yüan-shan culture without reference to stratigraphical order. There is no question that the Taiwan shouldered and stepped ax-adzes and their Philippine counterparts are culturally and historically related. The fact that they are separated in between by the Lungshanoid cultures of central and southern Taiwan, and also that the two types occur in association in Taiwan but apparently not in the Philippines, would make a direct connection difficult to assert. It is probable that they came to Formosa and the Philippines from a common source, perhaps the coasts of Kwangtung.

Direct connections between Taiwan and Luzon are indicated by the general category of rectangular adzes and also by the arrowheads and spearheads with broad stems found at Fengpitou and in the Batangas (Beyer 1948: his Figs. 22a,b, 23). The weapon heads are sufficiently specific for historic study, but the adzes are such a broad category of stone type that little specific information of cultural connections is revealed by them.

Neolithic interrelationship of Taiwan and the Philippines is made doubly difficult to ascertain on the basis of Beyer's scheme because of the apparent lack of pottery with Beyer's Neolithic stone implements in the Philippines. Beyer maintains (1948: 78) that "for some reason not easily explainable, the pottery-making art seems not to have accompanied the later Neolithic stone cultures into the tropical lands of the Philippines and Malaysia—and no positive evidence has yet been found that true Stone-Age pottery existed in these areas."

The nonexistence of pottery in Neolithic Philippines is being challenged, however, by recent archeological work of the area undertaken by Robert Fox, Alfredo Evangelista, and Wilhelm G. Solheim (Houston 1956; Solheim 1964a). In a significant contribution to the archeology of the central Philippines, Solheim (p. 192) recognizes three major prehistoric ceramic "complexes"—Kalanay, Bau, and Novaliches.

The sites with Kalanay complex pottery predominating are scattered through the Visayan

Islands, and in addition, are found in northwestern Palawan and the Calamianes Group. The Bau complex is found in Mindanao, northern Palawan, and northern Luzon. . . . The Novaliches sites are restricted to northwestern Palawan, the Calamianes Group, and Luzon in the neighborhood of Manila Bay.

Because of the fact that a small number of bronze ornaments and iron knives was found in association with the pottery and presumably influenced by Beyer's scheme of the Iron Age dating of the first pottery in this area, Solheim in his monograph refers to these three ceramic complexes as being of the Iron Age. More recent findings of the Kalanay pottery from "Late Neolithic" sites with carbon-14 dates of early first millennium B.C., however, has enabled Solheim (1961: 165) to conclude that "the Kalanay pottery complex entered the Philippines during Late Neolithic times, probably previous to 500 B.C. and remained as a distinctive pottery complex until Chinese porcelain of late T'ang or early Sung started coming in."

Apparently in the light of this fact, in a recent article Solheim (1964c: 376–7) discusses the prehistoric pottery of Southeast Asia under the general category of Neolithic and Iron Age, and raises the three complexes of the Philippines to the status of traditions for all of Southeast Asia:

a. The Sa-huynh–Kalanay Pottery Tradition

The pottery of this tradition is a sophisticated, technologically well-made pottery with variation in decoration and much variety in form. Usually the pottery was made with paddle and anvil with some of the forming done while turning on a slow wheel. The surface of the early pottery of this tradition was cord- or basket-marked from a cord-wrapped or basket-woven paddle . . . Later, polishing, incising, painting, and impressing with a dentate tool or Arca shell came into use. The patterns of decoration are commonly in horizontal bands, and include vertical or diagonal rectangular elements, curvilinear scrolls, rectangular scrolls or meanders, zigzags, triangles, and chevrons. The incised decoration is often emphasized by impressed punctations or circles, painting, or more rarely by a white inlay in the incised lines. The variety in form is the result of different combinations and proportions of three primary forms: the cylinder, truncated cone, and the sphere. There is often an angle, sometimes accentuated by a flange, at the line of change between two of these forms. Both high and low ring stands are used, though rounded bottoms are the most common with flat bottoms present . . . [The approximate date of this tradition, according to Solheim's latest estimate (see Solheim ms.), is between 2,000 B.C. and A.D. 1000].

b. The Bau–Malay Pottery Tradition

The pottery . . . has little variation in decoration and very little variation in form. It is made with a paddle and anvil. Usually a series of paddles is used, one or more of which have carved patterns on their surface . . . At first the carved patterns were simple, like those of the early Sa-huynh–Kalanay Tradition. These evolved into more complex patterns of considerable variety when examined closely but from a distance all have much the same appearance . . . Later in its development carved stamps were used . . . Forms are commonly spherical with rounded bottom and a short out-turned or straight rim.

c. The Novaliches Pottery Tradition

The diagnostic form is a shallow bowl with a high ring foot. In this form, the bowls are plain and the feet highly decorated. The decorations are cut-out triangles in the foot or several bands of repetitive decoration running around the foot. The majority of the pottery was extremely well polished. Circular forms are so symmetrical that they look as if they had been made on a potter's wheel. However, this was probably a slow wheel rather than a fast wheel. All sites with this pottery are of Early Iron Age (post 200 B.C.).

This categorization of prehistoric pottery in the Philippines offers a solid basis for comparison with the ceramic complexes of Southeast China in general and with Formosa in particular. Features of the Kalanay and Novaliches traditions are comparable in many instances with the Lungshanoid horizon of southeastern China—including Formosa, and the Bau–Malay tradition is without serious question an extension of the Geometric. As pointed out by Solheim (1964b: 255), some decoration of the Fengpitou pottery

> is very similar to the typical decoration on pottery of the Novaliches pottery complex in the Philippines, except for the *method* of decoration. The Philippine pottery is not painted but has an incised, impressed, or carved pattern. Also, the form of the vessels with this decoration is almost exactly the same as in the Novaliches pottery. The resemblances to the Kalanay pottery complex in the Philippines are less specific . . . The impressed decoration near the rims of the red pottery, illustrated by Tsuboi (1956: Figs. D28–30, 37), appears very similar to a style of impressed decoration found on rims, angles, or flanges of the Kalanay complex pottery. As to the similarity in form, the rim and body forms of the Painted pottery are all found in the Kalanay complex pottery.

When Solheim (1964b) made the preceding assessment he did not have the benefit of our new data from Fengpitou, for additional similarities can now be listed, such as the incised black pottery and the painted beakers with the greatest diameter at the lower part of the body, both of which find close affinities in the Kalanay varieties.

However, Solheim's conclusions for Formosa–Philippines relationships in prehistory pottery still hold: "Nearly all the artifact types found in Formosa can be matched with similar types in Southeast Asia, particularly in the Philippines and to a lesser degree in Celebes and northern Indochina. No complex of artifacts from a specific site in Formosa can be closely connected with a corresponding complex from a specific site in Southeast Asia" (1964b: 258).

Summary

The comparative studies undertaken in this chapter, admittedly preliminary in scope and tentative in nature, have made it abundantly clear that prehistoric Formosa was situated in a larger culture-historic sphere which included southeastern China and Southeast Asia. The Lungshanoid cultures of central and southwestern Taiwan, accounting for the bulk of the prehistoric remains of the west coast and probably the population ancestral to the present-day aborigines, can definitely be traced to the Lungshanoid cultures of the southeastern coastal areas of China. Furthermore, the various local Lungshanoid phases—now distinguishable into the fine red ware phase, the shellmound phase, and central black pottery phase—can be traced to their respective close relatives on the mainland, i.e. the

Ch'ing-lien-kang culture of Kiangsu, the T'an-shih-shan culture of Fukien, and the Liang-chu culture of Chekiang.

The Yüan-shan culture, on the other hand, cannot be identified as an integrated cultural entity anywhere in the vicinity. We maintain, however, that in addition to continuities from the aboriginal Corded Ware culture of the island the Yüan-shan culture owes its formation to inspiration from the direction of the South China sea-coast and the Gulf of Tonkin as well as to the Lungshanoid.

Comparisons with the Philippines do not seem to show that Formosa was a steppingstone for migrations of populations and culture *en masse* from the southeast Chinese mainland into the Pacific areas. Rather, the East and the South China Sea areas were in general large spheres of activity and communication, within which contacts and movements of small groups in successive waves and in all directions probably took place. This area includes the southeastern coasts of China, Taiwan, northern Indochina, and the Philippines. There is no question that the Kalanay and Novaliches pottery traditions of the Philippines were heavily influenced by the Lungshanoid pottery of southeastern China and Formosa, or that the Bau–Malay tradition was an extension of the Geometric horizon of the same area. But unless future explorations prove otherwise, southeast China on the whole, rather than Taiwan specifically, was the source of these ceramic traditions to the south.

This account omits the remains of the eastern coast of Taiwan and their significance. Available knowledge from this area indicates that additional information will be gained from the eastern Taiwan data when they are projected onto the larger picture, but that the main outline will not be altered.

Chapter 12. Interrelationship of Archeology and Ethnology in Taiwan

IN ADDITION to the twelve million Han Chinese there are on the island of Taiwan many Malayopolynesian-speaking aboriginal inhabitants. Among them, approximately 170,000, known as the *Kao-shan-tsu*, or Mountain Tribes, inhabit the central mountain range and the eastern coast, and unknown numbers of the remainder, referred to as *P'ing-p'u-fan*, or Plains Tribes, blend with the Han Chinese on the western and northern coasts. Aside from the Malayopolynesian languages they speak or are known to have spoken in the past, the aborigines are characterized by cultures decisively different from the Chinese but similar to the native cultures of the Philippines, Indonesia, and Malaysia, and are commonly thought to have come to the island long before the Chinese immigration more than three hundred years ago.

The archeologist is interested in Taiwan's ethnology for a number of obvious reasons. His research in the island's prehistory no doubt has a bearing upon the problem of derivation of the aboriginal population. The modern ethnographic situation presumably throws light on cultural classifications during the prehistoric period. Ethnohistoric information on migrations and settlements of peoples during the recent past helps interpret prehistoric movements and contacts of peoples and cultures. And ethnological knowledge of the aboriginal life would be of obvious use for prehistoric cultural reconstruction. To achieve most of these aims, however, the archeologist must first be able to demonstrate that cultural continuity or continuities exist from the prehistoric past to the present.

Moreover, the demonstration of cultural continuity in Formosa carries historic significance far beyond the borders of the island. For, as stated in the Introduction, to be able to demonstrate such continuity is to be able to demonstrate, at the same time, that the main stream of the culture of at least a portion of the modern Malayopolynesian speakers originated in southeast China. The implications of this for the studies of the culture history of the entire Pacific area are manifold and wide ranging. The author has elaborated on these implications repeatedly (K. C. Chang 1959, 1964a,b); it would be superfluous to reiterate them here.

There is no question that the study of Formosan prehistory as described in the preceding pages provides a hitherto lacking basis for the study of archeology–ethnology interrelationships. It is necessary, however, at the outset to distinguish the *general* and *specific* "continuities" that we deem it essential to demonstrate. Moreover, there are two kinds of specific continuity: cultural and ethnic. By general continuity we mean we can show that the modern aboriginal cultures, or some of them, can be classified with the same general cultural type or grouping as the prehistoric cultures, or some of them. By specific continuity we mean that continuity can be demonstrated from a prehistoric cultural phase all the way down to a modern ethnic group. If this can be demonstrated in terms of group identity, such specific continuity can be referred to as ethnic; if the continuity is specific only in the occurrence of a cluster of cultural items, then we can talk about nothing more than culturally specific continuities. These different kinds of continuities serve different purposes. On the problem of the Malayopolynesian culture history and the question of prehistoric cultural reconstructions, general continuities are sufficient. For ethnohistoric studies and for prehistoric cultural classifications, however, the continuities must be specific.

Both Kano (1955: 96–9) and Miyamoto (1956) have pointed up the fact that huge stones are being used for house construction among some eastern groups; that slab coffins are being used among the Ami of the eastern coast; that chipped stone hoes are known to have been used by some groups until recently; that some prehistoric pottery vessels have counterparts among the natives; and that some ornaments of the modern peoples have prototypes from archeological sites. On the basis of these common occurrences Miyamoto (1956: 334) concludes that he "cannot believe that the people who left such relics in all the islands had perished completely or migrated to other lands. It is probable that the descendants of the Stone Age man have survived in this island."

This conclusion is highly credible, and it can be reinforced by other items of both archeological and ethnological occurrence, such as head-hunting [both the Yüanshan culture (see K. C. Chang 1957) and the Lungshanoid (see the discussions in Chapter 9)], tooth extraction (Kanaseki 1951, 1952; K. C. Chang 1957), shell beads (K. C. Chang 1958), betel-chewing (Miyamoto 1956: 332), and pile buildings (see Chapter 4). All of these, plus the physical anthropological studies of prehistoric skeletons for whatever they are worth (Kanaseki 1952, 1956; T. M. Hsü in Appendix 2), suffice to show that there is *general* continuity from the prehistoric to the present, and that the prehistoric inhabitants belonged to the cultural type characterized as Ancient Southeast Asian, Indonesian, or Proto-Malay. The significance of this conclusion in the culture history of the western Pacific region is at once apparent (K. C. Chang 1964a). It also enables us to speculate upon the culture and society of the prehistoric inhabitants by means of a direct ethnological approach.

Specific ethnic continuities, however, are another matter. Which prehistoric phase was ancestral to which modern ethnic group? There must have been, during the interval, plenty of migrations, fissions, fusions, and extinctions, and it would be the exception rather than the rule that a one-to-one equation could ever be made. As I have pointed out before,

> An undertaking of great urgency would be to trace the routes of inland migrations of the various modern ethnic groups on the island, with all the historical methods at our disposal, and to identify the former settlement sites of each group along the general areas of such routes. Specific connections may eventually be pinned down between individual ethnic groups of today and the prehistoric cultural phases of various periods [K. C. Chang 1954a: 199].

Since such an undertaking has not even been started, we have at this point no more than faint clues in this area; they will be mentioned presently.

George Murdock (1964) subtitles his summary article in Isidore Dyen's recent study of the genetic classification of the Austronesian languages "a key to Oceanic culture history," and indeed the genetic classification of the Austronesian languages of Formosa is, in the absence of the kind of reliable and detailed ethnohistoric study characterized above, the *only* available key to the historical categorization of the speakers which in turn provides a useful basis for archeological correlation.

Various attempts have been made, since the beginning of modern ethnography in Taiwan, to classify the aboriginal population on the basis of culture in general and language in particular (Kano 1955: 121–66; Mabuchi 1953a). A common classification follows (Fig. 94). *Mountain tribes:* Atayal (Atayal, Sediq), Saisiat, Bunun, Tsou, Paiwan, Rukai, Puyuma, Ami, Yami. *Plains tribes:* Luilang, Ketangalan, Kavalan, Taokas, Pazeh, Papora, Babuza, Hoanya, Thao, Siraya. The contrast between the mountain tribes and the plains tribes is obviously both inaccurate and misleading, not only because some groups of the former (Ami, Puyuma, and Yami) in fact inhabit the plains and some of the latter (Thao) are found in the highlands but, more particularly, this contrast is based upon the respective extents of their sinicization but not upon their inherent genetic relationship. The relationship between two mountain tribes is not necessarily closer than one between a mountain tribe and a plains tribe. Inasmuch as the aboriginal cultural patterns of many of these groups—especially the plains group—are difficult or impossible to reconstruct, the only feasible approach for a historically meaningful hierarchy of their grouping is linguistic.

A recent lexicostatistical study undertaken by Dyen (1964) among the available Taiwan languages results in the comparisons in Table 32. According to Dyen (p. 263), "These results suggest that at the highest level there are three language groups in this comparison: F_1 containing Atayal and Seekik, F_2 containing Tsou, and F_3 containing the remaining languages." The components and the percentages of their shared cognates are:

F_1 : Atayalic (Atayal and Sediq)
   At_1–At_2 : 82.9 At_1 , At_2 , Se_1 , Se_2–all other languages: 06.0–15.8
   At_1–Se_1 : 37.7
   At_2–Se_2 : 32.7
   Se_1–Se_2 : 32.7
F_2 : Tsouic (Tsou, Kanabu, Saaroa)
                   TT–F_1 : 07.4–10.9
                   TT–F_3 : 13.1–16.7
F_3 : Paiwanic (Paiwan, Thao, Bunun, Pazeh, Ami, Kavalan, Puyuma, Rukai)
   Th–Bu_2 : 29.2 F_3–F_1 : 06.1–15.8
   Bu_2–Am_1 : 27.0 F_3–F_2 : 13.1–16.7
   Am_1–Kv : 24.7
   Am_1–Pa_1 : 27.3
   Pu_2–Pa_1 : 28.7
   Pu_2–R_2 : 25.6
   Pu_2–Pz   : 22.0

It is necessary for the interpretation of Formosa's place in the entire language

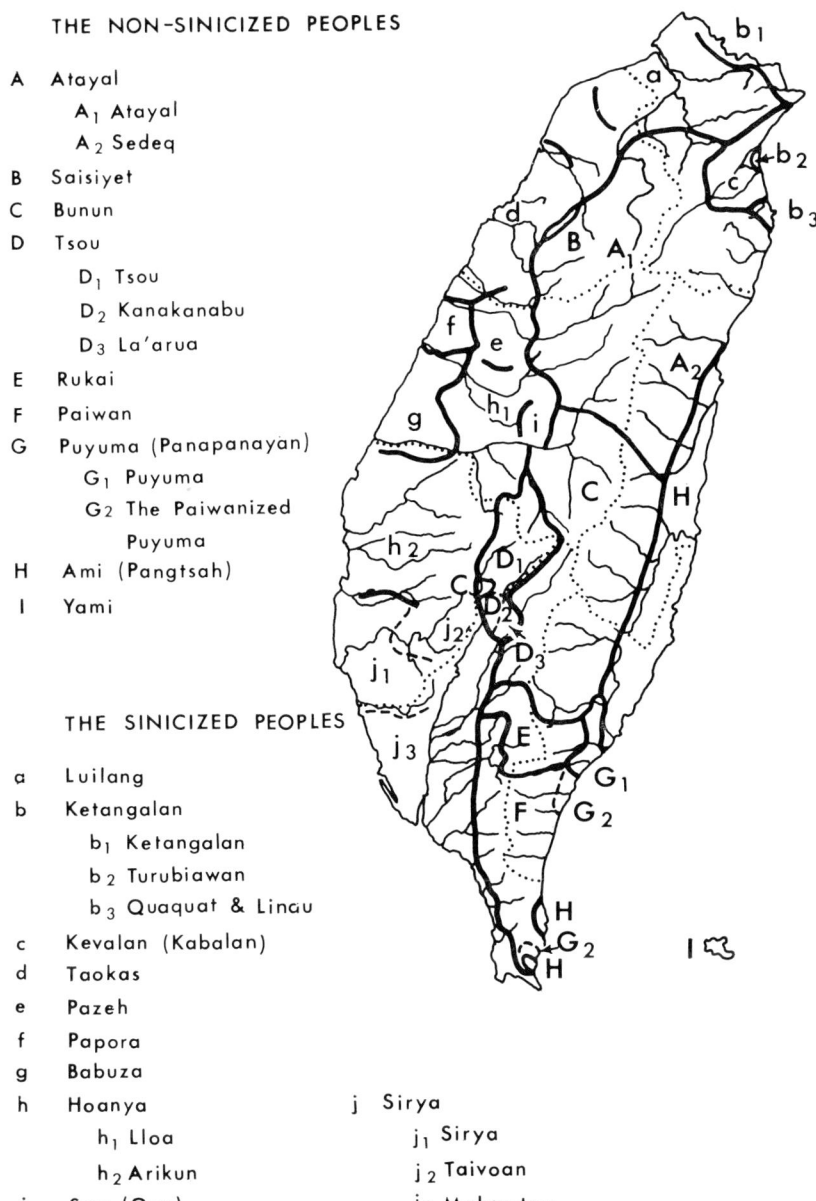

THE NON-SINICIZED PEOPLES

A   Atayal
    A_1 Atayal
    A_2 Sedeq
B   Saisiyet
C   Bunun
D   Tsou
    D_1 Tsou
    D_2 Kanakanabu
    D_3 La'arua
E   Rukai
F   Paiwan
G   Puyuma (Panapanayan)
    G_1 Puyuma
    G_2 The Paiwanized
        Puyuma
H   Ami (Pangtsah)
I   Yami

THE SINICIZED PEOPLES

a   Luilang
b   Ketangalan
    b_1 Ketangalan
    b_2 Turubiawan
    b_3 Quaquat & Linau
c   Kevalan (Kabalan)
d   Taokas
e   Pazeh
f   Papora
g   Babuza
h   Hoanya
    h_1 Lloa
    h_2 Arikun
i   Sau (Oau)

j   Sirya
    j_1 Sirya
    j_2 Taivoan
    j_3 Maka-tau

FIG. 94. Classification and Distribution of the Aborigines of Taiwan (*after* Mabuchi 1953a).

phylum and for the problem of its origin to carry out similar lexicostatistical comparisons between the Taiwan languages and extra-Taiwan Malayopolynesian languages. For our purposes, however, the above grouping of F_1–F_3 provides a linguistic hierarchy that is thought to be similar to one based on cultural assessment

TABLE 32. LEXICOSTATISTICAL COMPARISON OF MALAYOPOLYNESIAN LANGUAGES IN TAIWAN*

	Se₂	At₁	At₂	Se₁	TT	Th	Bu₁	Bu₂	Pz	Am₁	Am₂	Kv	Pu₂	R₂
At₁	59.0													
At₂	60.0	82.9												
Se₁	32.7	37.7	32.7											
TT	07.4	09.0	07.8	10.9										
Th	06.6	08.3	07.4	13.5	16.3									
Bu₁	07.8	07.6	06.8	12.2	15.2	28.8								
Bu₂	08.3	08.3	08.0	11.7	16.7	29.2	65.7							
Pz	10.3	18.9	08.6	14.6	14.3	23.0	20.0	16.1						
Am₁	09.7	08.9	08.7	12.9	15.7	25.9	25.4	27.0	19.9					
Am₂	08.7	08.9	08.4	13.2	14.6	25.5	24.0	23.5	20.7	75.1				
Kv	06.2	06.9	16.1	10.0	13.9	19.0	18.9	19.0	18.5	24.7	24.1			
Pu₂	08.7	07.5	07.8	12.9	14.7	22.5	21.2	21.2	22.0	29.8	28.3	19.9		
R₂	07.9	06.8	06.0	09.0	13.1	16.7	17.4	15.4	14.8	20.0	20.1	15.4	25.6	
Pa₁	09.4	09.3	08.0	15.8	16.7	24.4	23.7	24.5	23.5	27.3	27.4	20.3	28.7	23.8

Abbreviations: At₁–Atayal lexicostatistical list, Clare McGill
           At₂–Atayal list, Chen-Li
           Se₁–Sediq list, Ralph Covell
           Se₂–Sediq list, Chen-Li
           TT–Tsou, T. H. Tung
           Th–Thao, Chen-Li
           Bu₁–Bunun, Fu Wen-chih
           Bu₂–Bunun, Chen-Li
           Pz–Pazeh, Chen-Li
           Am₁–Ami, E. P. Torgesen
           Am₂–Ami, Chen-Li
           Kv–Kavalan, Chen-Li
           Pu₂–Puyuma, Chen-Li
           R₂–Rukai, Chen-Li

* After Dyen (1964: 263).

(Ferrell 1966) and relevant to purposes of archeological identification. It must be borne in mind, however, that although a critical percentage of 20 per cent cognates enables an F_1, F_2, F_3 grouping, a subhierarchy is again possible to formulate within F_3 itself, with the critical percentage of no other than 20 per cent. Thus,

1. Rukai stands out in a separate subcategory; its only +20 percentage occurs with Ami (20.0; 20.1) and Puyuma (25.6), its two neighboring groups with which it shares many cultural elements in common, while the cognates it shares with all other groups within F_3 are well below 20 per cent.

2. Kavalan also stands out by itself. Its percentages with the other groups are higher than that of Rukai; but only with its southern neighbors, the Ami, is it significantly above 20 (24.1; 24.7).

3. All others—Thao, Bunun, Pazeh, Ami, Puyuma, and Paiwan—can be comfortably placed together, invariably sharing cognates well above 20 per cent.

The significance of these subcategories within F_3 is not readily apparent, but this at least shows that group F_3 has itself had considerable time depth. As Ferrell (1966) maintains, it is possible that their arrival on Formosa "may have spread over a long period of time." On the basis of the most recent studies, Dyen (personal communication) thinks that the percentage of the Atayalic groups among themselves should be higher than it is in the table and he says also that he is not sure whether Tsouic should indeed be a group by itself or should be a subgroup within Paiwanic. Purely as a matter of interest, on the basis of the latest information, we can compute the theoretical times of separation of the three major language groups according to the glottochronological standard figures (Swadish 1952: 460),[1] arriving at the interesting result that both the Atayalic separation from Tsouic and Paiwanic and the beginning of the Paiwanic internal differentiation (lowest percentage being 14.8 between Pazeh and Rukai) could be placed at about 2500 B.C.[2] In other words, around 2500 B.C. both of the major events indicated by the lexicostatistical comparisons could have taken place: (1) separation of Atayalic from Paiwanic; and (2) the separation of the languages within the Paiwanic group, although they continued to stick together lexicostatistically. These results are certainly both interesting and instructive, and a comparison with similar results obtained elsewhere within the Malayopolynesian area would provide material for speculation about a number of historical problems concerning the Malayopolynesian culture history.

The precise figure of 2500 B.C. may well be highly suspect, but the low critical percentages involved in the lexicostatistical comparisons among the Taiwan languages suggest very strongly that the linguistic breakdown has been in train for millennia. The conclusion is thus inescapable that among the prehistoric cultures described in this study there were direct ancestors of the modern aborigines.

The attempt of an archeological identification with the ancestral groups of the three major Taiwan linguistic groups was initiated by Raleigh Ferrell (1966), whose identifications are marred, however, by the fact that the latest archeological information from the island was not available to him at the time of his writing. His general approach and many specific comparisons, nevertheless, show original insight to which the present discussions are greatly indebted.

Let us forget for a moment about specific cultural characteristics of the populations involved and concentrate on this logical fact: lexicostatistical study shows that at a period of considerable antiquity (ca. 2500 B.C.) glottochronologically speaking, the two major language groups on the island—Atayalic and Paiwanic—began to separate, and at approximately the same time the Paiwanic group began to

---

[1] Recent studies (Dyen, personal communication) have shown that these figures tend to give short results, especially when the time depth involved is great.

[2] In a personal communication Raleigh Ferrell arrived at a somewhat different set of figures by using Dyen's published percentages (Dyen 1964). Dyen's latest figures, raising the Atayalic percentages, do not alter the grouping of the languages but alter the glottochronological results considerably.

diversify within itself. The latter fact tends to suggest that the internal Paiwanic differentiation probably took place within the island after that group arrived.

At once we are struck by the remarkable coincidence of this with the archeological picture. At about 2500 B.C. two major cultures emerged in the Taiwan scene—the Yüan-shan in the north and the Lungshanoid in the south. At about the same time, moreover, the Lungshanoid culture had already experienced several divergent phases, each one of which could be traced to a cultural group on the mainland. Since the glottochronological results suggest that at exactly this same time the ancestral Atayalic and Paiwanic had just begun to separate, whereas the two pre-historic cultures already showed sharp contrasts, it would not be possible to identify the two ancestral linguistic groups with the two prehistoric cultures. It appears more likely that both Atayalic and Paiwanic split from a single prehistoric ancestor. Which—Yüan-shan or Lungshanoid—is the more likely?

There are many indications that the Lungshanoid–Paiwanic identification is entirely possible. The geographical spread of the Paiwanic languages—the southern half of the island plus the northern coasts—agrees with the spread of the Lungshanoid. The intrusion of check-impressed pottery into the Yüan-shan territory around 500 B.C. and the continuation of the geometric stamping tradition into the Ketanga-lan agrees with the linguistic positions of the Ketangalan and the Kavalan. Check-impressed wares are known to have been manufactured and used until recently among the Bununs, a Paiwanic member, and the pottery jars kept today among the Paiwans as heirlooms exhibit many features that are found in the fine red ware jars, such as the ridges on the exterior of the rim, the interior of the rim serving as a support for the lid, the low ring feet, and the decoration techniques (Jen 1960). The similarities between the Paiwan wood-carving motifs and some Kalanay ceramic decorations as pointed out by Solheim (ms.) serve as indirect supporting evidence in the same direction.

The present writer agrees with Ferrell (1966) that the Lungshanoid–Paiwanic correlation is the strongest archeological identification of ancestral groups with a modern population that can be made on the basis of available evidence. The archeo-logical picture shows that much of the island's prehistory was a succession of the different phases of the Lungshanoid cultures. This succession, as shown by the Ketangalan evidence, leads to the present. It would be surprising if the expansion and diversification of the Lungshanoid cultures in Taiwan did not directly reflect the expansion and diversification of the Paiwanic language group.

Then we are left with a major prehistoric culture, the Yüan-shan, and we ask what became of it? Geographically, the Atayalic group occupies the northern part of the mountainous area, overlapping the Yüan-shan distribution in the upper courses of the Tamsui River system. The customs of tooth extraction (K. C. Chang 1954a) and head-hunting (K. C. Chang 1957) that can be inferred for the Yüan-shan cul-ture are both prominent features of the Atayalic, even though they were also found among the other groups as well. If the southwest China affinities described above for the Yüan-shan culture suggest partial derivation of that culture and/or population from that direction, Ferrell's suggestion that the Atayalic group exhibits cultural and linguistic similarities with ethnic groups in southwest China and Assam is especially noteworthy (Ferrell 1966).

There is one thing that seems to point strongly in an opposite direction, however. According to the legendary traditions of the Atayal, their original homeland was in the southwestern corner of their present sphere of distribution rather than in the northern valleys required under a Yüan-shan identification hypothesis (Mabuchi 1953b). If the southwestern corner of their sphere of distribution is indeed their original homeland, this would point to the middle and upper Choshui River, where the prehistoric cultures were characterized by the central Taiwan Black Pottery culture. This would fit the glottochronological beginning better; that is, the ancestral Atayalic split from a Lungshanoid ancestor. The legendary tradition, however, has a time depth of no more than 300 years, as suggested by Mabuchi, and this evidence alone is insufficient to rule out an Atayalic–Yüan-shan identification. A more precise linguistic time depth for the Atayalic and a further effort in tracing the aboriginal legendary tradition would be necessary to decide among at least these two alternative possibilities.

In conclusion, the strong probability that the bulk of the modern Malayopolynesian speakers on the island descended from the two major prehistoric cultures, Lungshanoid and Yüan-shan, is of the utmost importance, not only for the reconstruction of culture history of Taiwan but also for the reconstruction of culture history of Oceanic regions and the prehistory of the Malayopolynesian speakers.

Summary and Conclusions

THE major contribution of the expedition to Taiwan during 1964 and 1965 is perhaps its experiments in methodology undertaken with an exploratory spirit and within an interdisciplinary framework. In a relatively brief span a little of everything was carried out, such as carbon-14 dating, natural stratigraphic excavation, the analysis of horizontal as well as vertical variations, close collaboration with geologists and geomorphologists, stress on the microenvironmental exploration, and the establishment of pollen profiles. Some of these approaches were carried out in Taiwan for the first time.

Methods can never be important by themselves and for their own sake; they must be employed to serve meaningful ends or they are wasted, and they must be evaluated according to the results that are obtained. Our excavations during relatively prolonged periods carried out intensively at a very few sites have established, above all, the associations of cultural remains of various types in natural stratigraphical units, and the formulation of prehistoric cultures and their time–space placement are thus of a scientific nature and verifiable reliability. An original contribution of this expedition was that the bulk of the prehistoric remains of Taiwan were shown to be attributable to three major groups: the Corded Ware culture, the Yüan-shan culture, and the Lungshanoid cultures. Within each of these and within each culture's developmental history, we were able to establish the organic association of various cultural elements, some aspects of their respective settlement and cultural patterns, a beginning of cultural ecology, and the most important features of cultural change. A comparison of the three major groups of culture with prehistoric data elsewhere in the Far East discloses interesting and instructive clues to many heretofore unsolved problems in the culture history of the wider area.

The Corded Ware culture apparently emerged on the island during great antiquity. Although the single carbon-14 date of 19,000 years B.P. means little if anything in determining the age of this culture, the main body of the culture is apparently separated from the later prehistoric cultures (Yüan-shan and Lungshanoid) by a *considerable* time interval. Tsukada's date of 11,000 B.P. for the beginning of the new vegetational phase of Jih-yüeh-t'an is highly significant in this regard, for there can be no other prehistoric culture at that early age on the island than the Corded Ware culture, but unfortunately, the remains of this culture have not been established in the central part of the island where the Jih-yüeh-t'an profile is worked out and to which its applicability must be initially confined.

Preliminary comparative studies of the Corded Ware culture remains suggest that, although cord marking as a ceramic feature in the broad sense has a wide distribution in East Asia, the closest affinities with such features of the Taiwan culture as the incised patterns and the associational stone artifacts occur in the southwestern part of China and the adjacent regions of Indochina. This is not saying that the Corded Ware culture of Taiwan originated in that direction, but it means that Taiwan was a part of the sphere of distribution of an ancient postglacial culture in Southeast Asia that is characterized above all by cord-marked pottery, chipped stone axes, and the group-instrument-incised decorations on pottery (wavy lines and cross-hatchings).

If the Jih-yüeh-t'an evidence can be stretched a bit it may be possible to say that some agricultural activities were carried out by the people of this Corded Ware culture. The total cultural assemblage does not give the impression of established village farmers engaged in intensive agriculture. Hunting, fishing, and collecting were probably the major subsistence means. We know that by the next stage— Lungshanoid—cereal agriculture became firmly established in southeast China, including Formosa, and it is commonly assumed that root and fruit crops were cultivated in Southeast Asia before the emergence of rice and millet. Recent ethnobotanical studies have convinced Jacques Barrau (1965a: 19) that "thousands of years ago, before cereals such as wheat and rice were domesticated, an horticultural revolution took place in the humid tropics of Indo-Oceania" (see also Barrau 1965b). It is therefore not surprising to find that potsherds of identical paste and decoration with the Taiwan remains have been collected in Melanesia (Shutler 1966). Although the possibility definitely exists, it is still much too early to say that the Corded Ware culture of Southeast Asia represents the early horticultural populations whence some of the Oceanic inhabitants were ultimately derived. A good deal more information from this cultural stratum will be necessary, not only from Taiwan but also from other regions where similar assemblages occur, before we can characterize the culture in more precise terms.

Events that took place after the middle of the third millennium B.C. are better known, and their significance in East Asian culture history is more appreciable, although not always obvious. The most important single event was probably the emergence of the Lungshanoid cultures in southwest Taiwan. Characterized by red and gray pottery with impressed and incised decorative patterns; thin, lustrous, wheel-touched black pottery; pottery tripods and lidded ring-footed *kui* jars; painted ceramic decoration; polished stone ax-hoes with rectangular cross sections; rectangular and semilunar slate knives; and a rich bone–antler–shell artifact inventory—the Taiwan Lungshanoid is without any serious doubt a regional facies of the widespread Lungshanoid horizon on the eastern coast of China from the Shantung Peninsula down to the delta of the Pearl River. Without ruling out two-way oscillations of the local phases of this horizon between the mainland of China and the island of Taiwan, we must nevertheless regard the Taiwan Lungshanoid as a derivative of the Chinese Lungshanoid in a broad sense. For the thesis for a Lungshanoid migration of millet-and-rice growing village farmers from the nuclear area of North China into the riverine, lacustrine, and coastal regions of eastern and southeastern China must be regarded as the most credible working hypothesis, according to the available evidence handled both comparatively and chronologically (K. C. Chang 1959, 1963, 1964b,d).

It has long been held by physical anthropologists (Birdsell 1951) that the explosive expansion of the Mongoloid populations in the eastern part of Asia was an event intimately related to the history of agriculture in this part of the world. When the Proto-Lungshan farmers emerged in the nuclear area of North China, the population pressure was presumably leading to territorial expansion, which by then was rendered possible by the advancement of cultivating techniques and the thorough domestication of the original cultigens. The vast low country in eastern North China and the coastal valleys of the southeast, sparsely populated if at all, presented the Proto-Lungshan people with a primeval land of alluring possibilities. The Ch'ing-lien-kang culture of Kiangsu, the Ch'ü-chia-ling culture of the lower Hanshui Valley in Hupei, the Liang-chu culture of northern Chekiang, the T'an-shih-shan culture of Fukien, and the Fengpitou and Ying-p'u cultures of central and southern Taiwan—these represent a series of cultures emerging at approximately the same broad range of time and exhibiting (albeit local divergences) a remarkably homogeneous pattern of material culture. If southeast China had a Corded Ware culture with an incipient horticulture, this culture was apparently overwhelmed by the successive and successful Lungshanoid immigrants who brought into this area the knowledge and techniques of cereal agriculture as the principal mode of subsistence. Whether or not and to what extent the aboriginal horticulturalists' way of life was absorbed by the newcomers, available evidence does not provide an answer.

If southeast China is the key to an understanding of the Lungshanoid cultures in Taiwan, the Taiwan cultures reciprocate by contributing essential information on the whole Lungshanoid horizon. Excavations at the Taiwan sites bring light to the problem of diversification of the Lungshanoid cultures. Classifiable into a single broad horizon, the archeological remains at the various localities nevertheless indicate a number of more or less different regional phases of culture having diversified cultural characters, centers of distribution, and periods of prevalence. The carbon-14 dates from the Taiwan Lungshanoid sites are the first and—so far—the only absolute age determinations within the entire Lungshanoid sphere, and they help estimate the probable time range of the horizon on the mainland and the relative order of its various local phases.

The striking coincidence in time range of the archeological Lungshanoid cultures in Taiwan and the reconstructed separation of the ancestral groups of the Taiwan Malayopolynesian languages carries significant implications for culture history of not only southeastern coastal China but also of much of the southwestern Pacific. For, if the Lungshanoid was ancestral to the culture of the modern Malayopolynesian speakers on the island, the traditional hypothesis for a Southeast Asian mainland origin of the Malayopolynesian culture would be archeologically substantiated, whereas the eastern New Guinea–Melanesia area, now favored by a growing number of linguists as an early center of Malayopolynesian dispersal, could only be a secondary (or even tertiary) center of such dispersal (e.g. Grace 1964). It would be foolish to insist, to be sure, that archeological cultures and reconstructed protolanguages must have complete identity, or that the great time depth involved in our archeological work would not allow for a multiplicity of ethnic and linguistic oscillations. But as an archeologist I regard the hypothesis of a Lungshanoid immigration of the ancestral Taiwan Malayopolynesians as the most probable of the alternatives, and the burden of proof that it is not must rest with those who can demonstrate a more acceptable hypothesis.

Contemporary with the initial Lungshanoid immigration was the emergence of the Yüan-shan culture in the northern part of the island. Our new carbon-14 dates elevate this culture to a status parallel to that of the Lungshanoid, thus raising at the same time the problems of its origin, its relationship with the Lungshanoid, and its posterity. Several alternative hypotheses can be formulated at this time. It could be descended from the Corded Ware culture, brought about by inspiration and influx from the Lungshanoid and from the cultures of southwest China and Indochina. It could also be a new culture coming, as it were, from the latter direction. It was a prosperous though highly isolated culture during the last two thousand years before Christ, but it was intruded into and partially absorbed by the Lungshanoid cultures ascending from the south during the last centuries before Christ. Perhaps it became extinct afterward as a cultural and linguistic entity, or it contributed to the formation of the ancestral Atayalic group.

The problems raised by these discussions must be tackled by more intensive work in linguistic comparisons, and more especially by a greater number of problem-oriented archeological projects that bridge the known archeological entities and the modern ethnological groups. The most serious gap in our current archeological knowledge is precisely the period of the late first and the early second millennium of our era, a period in which a number of important and presumably related changes must have occurred. For example, why did some aboriginal groups ascend into the hills while others remained in the foothills and on the plains? Why and how did pottery, a most conspicuous and dominant item of material culture throughout the island and throughout prehistory, all but disappear from the native cultural inventory? What was the role played in prehistoric cultural change by the introduction of iron technology? Why did rice cultivation, so prominent during the Lungshanoid period, shrink in importance until it had to be reintroduced into the island by the Han Chinese immigrants? What were the contact situations between the Han Chinese and the prehistoric cultures throughout the island? Before these and similar questions find their answers, archeologists in Formosa have little cause for complacency.

Indeed, culture history research of the island is only beginning. Too few sites have been excavated, and too few excavations have been intensive and interdisciplinary. A single core at Jih yüch-t'an has opened up tremendous possibilities in palynological research, and one can only imagine what sort of information can be brought to light when teams of scientists begin serious, competent, and extensive research. Perhaps archeological and environmental scientific research work could wait, and scholars could plan their projects on a long-term basis. But ethnohistoric research, essential for filling the gaps between archeology and ethnology, cannot be accomplished ever if it is not accomplished within our lifetimes, because ethnohistoric data are fast disappearing. The author cannot help but end this monograph with an urgent plea for meaningful and coordinated research. In some respects it is almost a matter of do it now or never.

Appendix 1
Mineralogical Notes on Prehistoric Potsherds from Taiwan

by Hsin-yüan Tu
Soil Survey Laboratory
SCS, USDA

Data

Twenty-seven prehistoric potsherds excavated from six archeological sites in Taiwan, provided by Kwang-chih Chang of Yale University, constitute the object of the present study. The following is a description and classification of these potsherds.

1. Ta-p'en-k'eng, Taipei Hsien (nine sherds, excavated in 1964 by the Yale–Taita expedition)

TPK-1a

Red Corded Ware. Inner color reddish-brown, outer color dark red; texture fine and not uniform. Thickness 7 mm. Corded Ware culture.

TPK-1b

Red Corded Ware. Inner and outer colors reddish-brown; texture fine and uniform. Thickness 1 cm. Corded Ware culture.

TPK-2

Buff Corded Ware. Inner and outer colors brownish-yellow; texture fine and uniform. Thickness 8 mm. Corded Ware culture.

TPK-3

Buff Corded Ware. Inner color dark gray, outer color very pale brown; texture coarser than TPK-2. Thickness 5–7 mm. Corded Ware culture.

TPK-4

Yüan-shan Ware. Inner and outer colors dark gray; texture coarse but compact. Thickness 4–7 mm. Yüan-shan culture.

TPK-5

TPK Brown Ware. Inner color dark gray, outer color reddish-brown; texture fine and compact. Thickness 3–4 mm. Yüan-shan culture.

TPK-6

TPK Red Ware. Inner color gray (only 1 mm thick), outer color reddish-yellow; texture fine and compact. Thickness 5–6 mm. Yüan-shan culture.

TPK-7

Botanical Garden Impressed Ware (red). Inner and outer colors reddish-yellow; texture medium fine and compact. Thickness 1 cm. Yüan-shan culture.

TPK-8

Botanical Garden Impressed Ware (buff). Inner color partly reddish-yellow, outer color partly pale gray; texture fine and compact. Thickness 13 mm. Yüan-shan culture.

2. Yüan-shan Shellmound, Taipei City (two sherds, excavated in 1952–53 by the Department of Archaeology and Anthropology, National Taiwan University)

YS-1

Red Corded Ware. Inner color dark brown, outer color light brown; texture coarse. Thickness 5–8 mm. Corded Ware culture.

253

YS-2

Yüan-shan Ware. Inner color gray, outer color light brown (only 1 mm); texture coarse. Thickness 5–10 mm. Yüan-shan culture.

3. Kou-t'i-shan, near Shu-lin, T'ao-yüan Hsien (one sherd, excavated in 1954 by the Department of Archaeology and Anthropology, National Taiwan University)

KTS-1

Botanical Garden Impressed Ware (buff). Inner and outer colors light gray; texture fine but not firm. Thickness 8 mm. Botanical Garden culture.

4. Ta-ma-lin, Nan-t'ou Hsien (two sherds, excavated in 1949 by the Department of Archaeology and Anthropology, National Taiwan University)

TML-1

Fine Gray Ware. Inner and outer colors dark gray; texture fine but soft. Thickness 4 mm. Ying-p'u ("First Black Pottery") culture.

TML-2

Coarse Gray Ware. Inner and outer colors dark gray; texture coarse and soft. Thickness 5 mm. Ying-p'u culture.

5. Ta-hu Shellmound, Tainan Hsien (one sherd, excavated by the staff of the Imperial Taihoku University before World War II)

TH-1

Black Pottery Ware. Inner and outer colors pale gray; texture fine, compact, but not firm. Thickness 5 mm. Lungshanoid culture.

6. Feng-pi-t'ou, Lin-yüan Hsiang, Kao-hsiung Hsien (twelve sherds, excavated in 1965 by the Yale–Taita expedition)

FPT-1a

Red Corded Ware. Inner color dark gray, outer color reddish-brown; texture fine. Thickness 6 mm. Corded Ware culture.

FPT-1b

Gray Corded Ware. Inner color black, outer color yellowish-brown; texture fine and compact. Thickness 5–8 mm. Corded Ware culture.

FPT-2

Fine Red Ware (burnished). Inner color pale red, outer color light red; texture fine and compact. Thickness 10–15 mm. Lungshanoid culture.

FPT-3

Fine Red Ware (porous). Inner color dark gray, outer color light red; texture very fine, compact, and hard. Thickness 4 mm. Lungshanoid culture.

FPT-4

Fine Red Ware (burnished). Inner color pale red, outer color light red; texture fine and compact. Thickness 3–5 mm. Lungshanoid culture.

FPT-5

Sandy Red Ware. Inner and outer colors reddish-brown; texture coarse. Thickness 5–6 mm. Lungshanoid culture.

FPT-6

Sandy Gray Ware. Inner and outer colors dark gray; texture coarse. Thickness 8 mm. Lungshanoid culture.

FPT-7

Black Ware. Inner and outer colors very dark gray; texture very fine, compact, and firm. Thickness 3 mm. Lungshanoid culture.

FPT-8

Black Ware. Inner and outer colors dark gray; texture very fine, compact, and firm. Thickness 3 mm. Lungshanoid culture.

FPT-9

Painted Ware. Two pieces. Inner and outer colors yellowish-red; texture fine but not firm. Thickness 3 mm. Lungshanoid culture.

FPT-10

Black Ware. Inner color dark gray (2 mm), outer color yellowish-brown (0.5 mm); texture very fine and firm. Thickness 3 mm. Lungshanoid culture.

FPT-11

Fine Red Ware (porous). Inner and outer colors reddish-yellow; texture very fine, compact, and firm. Thickness 5 mm. Lungshanoid culture.

Techniques

The temperature at which the pottery was fired may be determined by the changing phases of the minerals remaining in the sherd. By nature, each mineral has its own temperature of birth (crystallization) and its own temperature of destruction (decomposition or fusion). Under the temperature from 800 to 1,000°C, some minerals will be converted to other minerals (inversion or recrystallization). For example, quartz, which is the most abundant mineral on or in the earth's crust, begins to crystallize at about 573°C, according to Frondel. Then it will be converted to what is called the "high quartz" if the temperature is higher than 573°C. It will be destroyed at about 1,723°C (Frondel, 1962: 3–4). Other minerals such as stibnite and bismuth have their fusing points at 525°C and 271°C, respectively (Hurlbut, 1955: 180, 206). And both of them can be fused easily by candle flame (Kraus *et al.*, 1959: 217, 284). Many others, such as gibbsite and bayerite, with a decomposition point at 150°C (Brindley, 1951: Table X,4) can be destroyed by straw fire. Based on this principle, the temperature at which the pottery was fired may be estimated if the minerals contained in the pottery could be identified and their degree of destruction by fire could be measured.

The techniques used for this purpose are petrographic observation, chemical analysis, X-ray diffraction, and differential thermal analysis.

Under the polarized microscope, the minerals contained in the thin sections of the sherds will show signs of abnormality characterized by the effect of firing. In this case, most minerals will lose their natural color and clear appearance. Even the most resistant quartz will change its interference color from bright to dull and its extinction from distinct to wavy. So will the mica flakes. Also some burned organic material and minute plant roots are shown in many of these sherds.

The X-ray diffraction and the differential analysis (DTA) are both used for mineral identification. The DTA apparatus, however, is more sensitive in recording the low-temperature water, organic matter, and the amount of some clay minerals. Although the DTA method is generally used to supplement the results obtained by X-ray examination, it is now entering a new stage of evolution in that techniques are gradually being developed which may enable valid mineralogical analyses to be made by DTA method alone (Mackenzie 1957: 1).

The procedure of the DTA method in this study is as follows. First a DTA curve is obtained with the crushed powder of the sherd at room temperature. Its result will show the kinds of minerals, organic matter, etc. as they were, more or less, at the time the pottery was fired. (Except that some low-temperature water may be absorbed in a wet environment, most minerals remaining in the sherds will stay unchanged within a period of several thousand years.) Then the same sample is gradually heated, starting from 250°C, with an increment of 30°C every two hours. Comparisons are continuously made of the curve from gradual heating with the original DTA curve at room temperature, until a temperature is reached which shows a distinctive change or a positive difference from the original curve (whether the mineral remains are weakened or have completely disappeared); this temperature should be recognized, with no more than a 20°C error, as the original temperature at which the pottery was fired.

In addition, the color change of the sherd during gradual heating is a reliable indicator for temperature changes. An example here given is TPK-3. Its inside color is dark gray, its outside color is very pale brown, its texture is coarse, and its thickness is only 5 to 7 mm. The first impression is that the color of the outside layer might be caused by the slow process of oxidation. But after gradual heating up to 500°C, its color begins to change to reddish-brown both inside and out. The conclusion may be therefore reached, along with other data, that the color difference in the body of the pottery is not caused by oxidation but by the original heating temperature, which was too low, so that heat had not penetrated the thin layer of the pottery completely.

Again, take YS-1 sherd as an example. The color of the core is dark brown and the outer layer yellowish-brown, indicating the firing temperature was low and not uniform. The X-ray pattern shows the existence of quartz and some feldspar. The DTA curve indicates a high amount of low-temperature water at 50 to 250°C, some organic matter, and some aluminous clay mineral. Its color, both inside and out, begins to change at 500°C heating to an overall reddish-brown. After one more heating step (at 530°C), the DTA curve straightens out. Everything has been destroyed except quartz. The decomposition of the aluminous mineral, either diaspore or kaolinite, is at 450 to 500°C (Brindley 1951). Hence the original temperature at which YS-1 was fired should have been about 450°C (842°F).

Analytic Results

Sherds	Results of Analyses	Temperature °C	Remarks
TPK-1a	X-ray: Quartz (30%), feldspar (5%), trace of iron mineral DTA: Low-temp. H_2O, high content of organic matter, aluminous silicate or oxide mineral, probably kaolin or diaspore, quartz Reacts with H_2O_2 Magnetic	400–450	High organic or manganese content will react with H_2O_2
TPK-1b	Except for no low-temp. H_2O and lower content of aluminous minerals, results are same as above	450–500	
TPK-2	X-ray: Mostly quartz (35%), feldspar (15%), and mica. The mica peak becomes diffused at 300°C (mica can be completely destroyed at 800°C) DTA: Low-temp. H_2O, trace of aluminous mineral, quartz	450–500	Part of the low-temp. H_2O may be due to reabsorption
TPK-3	X-ray and DTA data are same as TPK-2 (30% quartz, 8% feldspar) Slightly magnetic Color change starts at 460°C heating	430–450	
TPK-4	X-ray: Mostly quartz (35%), feldspar (10%), trace of mica DTA: Quartz only Slightly magnetic Color change begins at 600°C		

Sherds	Results of Analyses	Temperature °C	Remarks
TPK-5	X-ray: Quartz (60%), feldspar (20%), some mica DTA: Low-temp. H_2O, organic matter, quartz, trace of aluminous mineral Weakly magnetic Reacts with H_2O_2	450–500	
TPK-6	X-ray: Quartz (65%), feldspar (10%), some mica DTA: Low-temp. H_2O, quartz, trace of aluminous mineral Slightly magnetic	450–500	
TPK-7	X-ray: Quartz (50%), feldspar (10%), mica DTA: Some organic matter, quartz Color changes to light red at 700°C heating Reacts weakly with H_2O_2	650–700	
TPK-8	X-ray: Quartz (6%), feldspar (3%), mica DTA: Organic matter, quartz Color begins to change at 720°C Slightly magnetic	700–750	
YS-1	X-ray: Quartz (40%), feldspar (12%), some mica DTA: Low-temp. H_2O, some organic matter, quartz Slightly magnetic Color changes to yellowish-red at 580°C	500–550	Contains fine quartz aggregates ground before mixing the paste
YS-2	X-ray: Quartz (55%), feldspar (5%) DTA: Some organic matter, quartz Slightly magnetic Color changes to yellowish-red at 580°C	500–560	Shows indications of fine quartz aggregates; contains many burned relics of organic matter
KTS-1	X-ray: Quartz (35%), feldspar (15%), trace of mica DTA: Some low-temp. H_2O, high amount of organic matter, quartz Color changes to grayish-yellow at 580°C Slightly magnetic	500–550	
TML-1	X-ray: Quartz (18%), some feldspar (3%) DTA: Lot of low-temp. H_2O, very high in organic matter, quartz Reacts with H_2O_2 Slightly magnetic Color changes to light brown at 500°C	400–450	

Sherds	Results of Analyses	Temperature °C	Remarks
TML-2	X-ray: Quartz (15%), some feldspar (2%) DTA: Lot of low-temp. H_2O, very high in organic matter, quartz Reacts with H_2O_2 Color changes to pale brown at 500°C	400–450	
TH-1	X-ray: Quartz (16%), some feldspar (3%), some mica DTA: High in low-temp. H_2O, some organic matter, quartz Reacts with KCl Reacts with H_2O_2 Slightly magnetic Color changes to yellowish-brown at 540°C	450–500	Lime reacts with KCl acid
FPT-1a	X-ray: Quartz (5%), feldspar, mica DTA: Some low-temp. H_2O, some aluminous mineral, quartz Slightly magnetic	450–500	
FPT-1b	X-ray: Quartz (25%), feldspar (6%), some mica DTA: Quartz Slightly magnetic Color changes to light red at 600°C	500–550	
FPT-2	X-ray: Quartz, feldspar, mica DTA: Quartz Slightly magnetic Color begins to change at 620°C	550–600	
FPT-3	X-ray: Quartz (5%), feldspar, some mica DTA: Quartz Slightly magnetic	550–600	Good quality
FPT-4	X-ray: Quartz (10%), feldspar (4%), some mica DTA: Quartz Slightly magnetic	550–600	Good quality
FPT-5	X-ray: Quartz (15%), feldspar (5%), mica DTA: Quartz Slightly magnetic	600–650	
FPT-6	X-ray: Quartz (25%), feldspar (10%), some mica DTA: Quartz Slightly magnetic Color changes to pale brown at 700°C	600–650	

Sherds	Results of Analysis	Temperature °C	Remarks
FPT-7	X-ray: Quartz (10%), feldspar (5%), mica DTA: Low-temp. H_2O, large amount of organic matter, quartz Color changes to light brown at 620°C Reacts with H_2O_2	550–600	
FPT-8	X-ray: Quartz, feldspar DTA: Quartz Color changes to pale brown at 600°C		
FPT-9	X-ray: Quartz (10%), feldspar (4%), some mica DTA: Quartz Color changes to pale red at 620°C Slightly magnetic	550–600	Dark red stripes and spots as decoration; material used may be red ocher or hematite
FPT-10	X-ray: Quartz (5%), feldspar, some mica DTA: Quartz Slightly magnetic Color changes to light brown at 600°C	550–580	
FPT-11	X-ray: Quartz (5%), feldspar, some mica DTA: Quartz Slightly magnetic Color changes to light red at 750°C	700–740	Very good quality

Discussion

X-Ray and DTA data show no sign of recrystallization in the sherds; that is, the temperature at which the wares were fired was below the 800–1,000°C inversion range. Based on these findings, the temperatures originally used were from 450° to 750°C, with TPK-1, TPK-3, TML-2 as the lowest and TPK-7 and TPK-8 as the highest.

Some of these sherds—TPK-5, FPT-6, FPT-7, YS-1, and TML-2—bear evidence of use as cooking utensils, most likely as baking pots, because the carbon layers, which react vigorously with H_2O_2, still adhere to the inside of these sherds.

The use of coal or charcoal as fuel for pottery making may be ruled out, since there is not enough evidence of such remains either in the soil samples that have been analyzed or from the thin sections of the sherds. The nonuniform color in the sherds and the low temperature for firing naturally lead to the inference that these pots were fired by straw and wood. The kilns used must have been poorly designed, since modern kilns for fine porcelain with wood as the main source of fuel can raise the temperature to as high as 1,500°C (Norton 1952: 141).

The technique of applying glaze to the pottery was still impracticable. A thorough study of these sherds has revealed that only two, FPT-7 and FPT-8, might have been glazed, although the material used was neither glass nor other metallic oxides.

Among the simple and rude decorations on the sherds, only one, FPT-9, was painted with dark red stripes and spots. The material used may have been red ocher (ferric oxide or hematite) or yellow ocher (limonite). Both will turn dull red when fired.

Appendix 2

A Study of the Neolithic Skeletal Remains from Fengpitou, Southwest Taiwan

by Tse-min Hsü
Division of Anthropology
Institute of History and Philology
Academia Sinica

The skeletal remains of a single burial, known as V-M1 and excavated in January, 1965, from a Lungshanoid stratum at the Fengpitou site in southwestern Formosa form the subject of this study.

The bones are poorly preserved. Most of the skull in norma basalis and norma facialis is damaged or missing, and the postcranials lack the sternum, the right fibula, the hipbone, the sacrum, most of the vertebrae, much of the scapula, some ribs, and most of the hand and foot bones. The principal long bones are also too fragile to be measured.

The skull is free from artificial deformation. The dental shows marked reduction in size. On the basis of the relatively massive skull and the related postcranials, although lacking comparative material, we tentatively conclude that this skeleton was of the male sex. The atrophy of the dental and the markedly lipped postcranial bones indicate a man of advanced age, but the unobliterated cranial sutures are at variance with this inference.

Cranial Observation

Norma verticalis (Pl. 104). The outline is nearly ovoid. A slightly sagittal elevation is noted between bregma and obelion. The coronal suture is obliterated ectocranially while the sagittal is very faintly closed. The suturation is medium in complexity.

Norma facialis (Pl. 103). A frontal crest is decidedly visible on the forehead. The metopic suture is absent. A somewhat V-shaped supraorbital ridge is noted. The nasal root intrudes slightly into the frontal bone, but the depression at nasion is medium. The orbits are rather low and nearly round in shape. The malar bone is slender, but the zygomatic process is prominent. The conspicuous feature is the tiny upper jaw and its related palate, showing nothing of the advanced age of the individual.

Norma lateralis (Pl. 104). The outline seems slightly asymmetrical from glabella to the occiput. The frontal eminence is only slightly depressed, and the occiput is rather prominent. The articular eminence and the postglenoid spine are in contrast to the glenoid cavity anterioposteriorly. On the left side, only a thin paperaceous lamina of bone separates the roof of the cavity from the temporal lobe of the brain. The temporal line and the supramastoid crest are well marked.

Norma occipitalis (Pl. 103). A nearly pentagonal outline is seen. The occipital torus is prominent, and the margin of the foramen magnum is extended downward and backward. The lambdoid suture is open—though possibly due in part to a certain amount of deformation caused by the earth's pressure—and is therefore very incongruent with the atrophy of the dental. Neither interparietal bone (Inca bone) nor Wormian bone is visible.

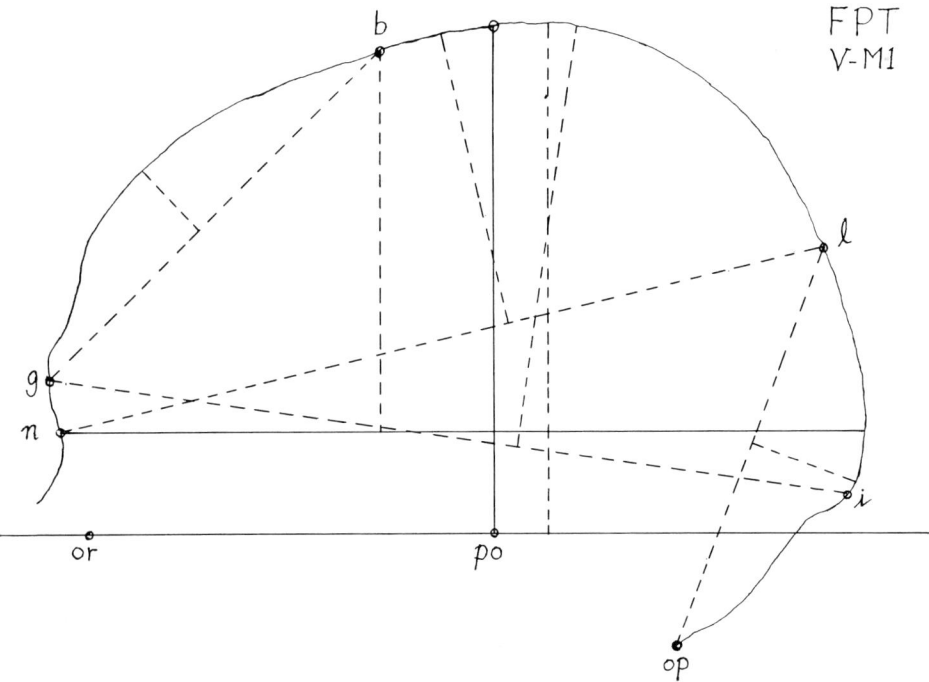

FIG. 95. Midsagittal Craniogram of the Fengpitou Skull.

Norma basalis. This is the most incomplete part of the skull. The jugular fossa is larger on the right and so is the digastric fossa. The foramen magnum is slightly shifted to the back of the skull, a primitive characteristic rarely found but not absent in modern man.

Mandibula. The mandibula is greatly reduced in size on account of the loss of all the teeth (except for the left lower third molar imbedded in the bone). The alveolar process is absorbed and the mental foramen is close to the alveolar border. All these features indicate the advanced age of the individual.

In summary, the skull is free from artificial deformation; nor is it informative about the mutilation of the teeth. The vertical and posterior aspects are ovoid and pentagonal. A somewhat V-shaped supraorbital ridge and a moderate sagittal crest are present. The low orbits, slender malar bones, and the small nasal aperture are largely responsible for the reduced size of the face. These morphological features resemble the Oceanic Mongoloids.

Cranial Measurements

Only the principal cranial measurements and especially those to be found in the comparative data will be given (Fig. 95). The method of measurement is mainly that of Hrdlicka (1947). The chart below shows the metric data of this skull together with the following comparative series:

K'en-ting-liao	Prehistoric	Formosa
Aeneolithic	3000–2000 B.C.	North China
Fu-shun	Prehistoric	North China
An-yang	Shang	North China
Atayal	Modern-aboriginal	Formosa

This shows that all metric items from all groups resemble each other in general characteristics but differ from each other only in detail. For instance, the tendency of the dolichocrany and the distinctively high skull vault are shared by all groups, whereas the usually long and narrow head of the Fengpitou skull is probably an individual variation. The relatively small face, low orbits, and slender malar bone of the Fengpitou skull, though closer to their adjacent series in Formosa than to the North China groups, are not extreme.

TABLE 33. MEASUREMENTS OF THE FENGPITOU (FPT) CRANIUM COMPARED WITH PREHISTORIC AND MODERN CRANIA*

	FPT (Hsü)	Atayal (Chang)	KTL (Kanaseki)	NC1 (Black)	NC2 (Black)	AY (Li)	FS (Shima)
Max. glabello-occipital length	191.00	178.31	184.30	178.50	181.60	181.27	180.80
	(1)	(74)	(10)	(86)	(25)	(136)	(76)
Max. head breadth	128.00	136.76	136.50	138.20	137.00	139.21	139.70
	(1)	(74)	(8)	(86)	(26)	(135)	(75)
Bas.-breg height	139.00	135.42	138.50	137.20	136.80	139.12	139.20
	(1)	(65)	(7)	(86)	(23)	(96)	(77)
Least frontal breadth	87.00			89.40	92.30		
	(1)			(85)	(24)		
Aur. vert. height	115.00			115.50	116.40		116.30
	(1)			(83)	(28)		(77)
Cranial index	66.49	77.02	75.00	77.56	74.96	76.96	76.90
	(1)	(72)	(7)	(86)	(25)	(135)	(49)
Cranial circumference	515.00	503.41	514.78			516.47	
	(1)	(71)	(7)			(134)	
Trans. cranial arc	310.00	309.62	310.84			319.54	
	(1)	(71)	(6)			(125)	
Med. sagittal cranial arc	369.00	365.84	377.36			375.62	
	(1)	(60)	(7)			(107)	
Upp. facial length	60.00	64.73	64.71	75.30	74.80		76.20
	(1)	(66)	(7)	(84)	(16)		(65)
Max. interzygomatic breadth	130.00	131.46	133.17	132.70	130.70		134.50
	(1)	(66)	(6)	(83)	(19)		(75)
Facial index	46.15	48.98	48.59	56.80	56.48		56.65
	(1)	(60)	(6)	(82)	(15)		(65)
Orbit breadth, mean	41.00	41.51	44.00	44.00	45.00		42.75
	(1)	(74)	(8)	(62)	(18)		(77)
Orbit height, mean	33.00	34.18	33.00	35.30	33.80		35.55
	(1)	(74)	(9)	(74)	(16)		(77)
Orbital index	80.40	82.16	76.72	80.66	75.02		83.35
	(1)	(74)	(7)	(62)	(19)		(77)
Nose breadth	25.00	26.36	26.83	25.00	25.60		25.70
	(1)	(71)	(6)	(86)	(17)		(75)
Nose length	52.00	50.14	50.00	55.30	55.00		55.10
	(1)	(72)	(7)	(86)	(20)		(76)
Nasal index	48.08	52.33	52.64	45.33	47.33		46.90
	(1)	(71)	(7)	(86)	(18)		(75)
Foramen magnum breadth	27.00	30.87	30.88		29.50		
	(1)	(63)	(7)		(16)		

TABLE 33 (Continued)

	FPT (Hsü)	Atayal (Chang)	KTL (Kanaseki)	NC1 (Black)	NC2 (Black)	AY (Li)	FS (Shima)
Foramen magnum length	34.00 (1)	36.31 (65)	36.88 (7)		35.50 (17)		
Foramen magnum index	79.41 (1)	84.78 (63)	83.23 (7)				
Length bas.-breg. ht. index	72.77 (1)	75.53 (64)	75.42 (7)	77.02 (86)	75.65 (23)	76.96 (96)	77.10 (76)
Breadth bas.-breg. ht. index	108.59 (1)	98.19 (64)	101.34 (6)			100.41 (95)	
Length aur. ht. index	60.21 (1)			64.87 (86)	63.85 (26)	64.71 (120)	
Breadth aur. ht. index	89.84 (1)					84.46 (119)	

* Atayal: Taiwan. KTL: K'en-ting-liao, prehistoric Taiwan, Fine Red Ware, Lungshanoid culture. NC1: Northern Chinese. NC2: North China Aeneolithic. AY: An-yang, Shang period. FS: Fu-shun, Manchuria, prehistoric. Sex, male. Measurements are in millimeters; number of individuals in parentheses.

Summary

On the basis of a single skeleton and concentrating on its cranial features, the following tentative conclusions can be made:

1. The cranium is unusually hyperdolichocranial, which is considered to indicate an individual variation.

2. The pronounced atrophy of the dentals is quite incongruent with the insignificant obliteration of the cranial sutures.

3. The high vault and the moderate elevation of the sagittal crest are shared by the Fengpitou specimen and the comparative Mongoloid series both in Formosa and in North China.

4. The slender facial part of the skull indicates agreement between this specimen and the Oceanic Mongoloids.

Appendix 3

Mollusks Recovered from the Shellmounds at Fengpitou, Kaohsiung Hsien, Taiwan

by C. C. Lin
Department of Geology
National Taiwan University

(Plates 105–107)

1. *Turbo (Olearia) marmoratus* Linné
2. *T. (Marmarostoma) setosus* Gmelin
3. *Nerita (Litena) lineata* Gmelin
4. *Turritella terebra cerea* Reeve
5. *Melanoides (Tarebia) crenulatus* Deshayes
6. *Cerithidea cingulata* Gmelin
7. *C. rhizoporarum* A. Adams
8. *Telescopium telescopium* Linné
9. *Terebralia semistriata* Bolten & Roding
10. *T. palustris* Linné
11. *Batillaria zonalis* Bruguiere
12. *Niso* sp.
13. *Strombus (Laevistrombus) isabella* Lamarck
14. *Thais mutabilis* Link
15. *Hemifusus* sp.
16. *Ganesella* sp.
17. *Anadara scapha* Meuschen
18. *A. (Tegillarca) granosa* Linné
19. *A. ehrenbergi* Dunker
20. *Placuna placenta* Linné
21. *Ostrea (Crassostrea) gigas* Thunberg
22. *O. (Saxostrea) vitrefacta* Sowerby
23. *Geloina fissidens* Pilsbry
24. *Tridachnes elongatus* Lamarck
25. *Gafrarium tumidum* Roding
26. *G. (Circe) scriptum tumefactum* Sowerby
27. *Meretrix petechialis* Lamarck
28. *Cyclina sinensis* Gmelin
29. *Chione (Anomalodiscus) squamosa* Linné
30. *C. (Clausinella) isabelina* Philippi
31. *Anomalocardia (Cryptonemella) producta* Kuroda & Habe
32. *Katelysia (Hemitapes) virginea* Linné

Appendix 4
Carbon-14 Dates from Taiwan[1]

1. North Taiwan

		B.P.
1. Tapenkeng, charcoal; Locus Q, Pit VI-1, layer 17 and Pit X-1, layers 13 and 14; Corded Ware culture	(Y-1552)	19,670 ± 450
2. Taipei peat, Hsin-sheng South Road, 2nd section, Taipei city; culturally sterile	(WR-1016)	4,880 ± 300
3. Taipei peat, Ying-chü Hsin-ts'un, Taipei city; culturally sterile		4,249 ± 281
4. Yüan-shan Shellmound, shell; 200 cm below surface; Yüan-shan culture	(Y-1547)	3,860 ± 80
5. Yüan-shan Shellmound, shell; 120 cm below surface; Yüan-shan culture	(Y-1548)	3,540 ± 80
6. Yüan-shan Shellmound, shell; 40 cm below surface; Yüan-shan culture	(Y-1549)	3,190 ± 80
7. Tapenkeng, charcoal; Locus Q, Pit VI-1, 142 cm below surface; Yüan-shan culture	(Y-1551)	2,850 ± 200
8. Tapenkeng, charcoal; Locus Q, Pit VI-1, 90 cm below surface, near kiln; Yüan-shan culture	(Y-1498)	2,030 ± 80
9. Shih-san-hang, shell; Shih-san-hang or Ketangalan culture	(NTU-7)	1,444 ± 209
10. Shih-san-hang, shell; Shih-san-hang or Ketangalan culture	(NTU-8)	1,145 ± 206

2. Central Taiwan

11. Ying-p'u, charcoal; T3PZE, R1, layer 10; Ying-p'u horizon, Lungshanoid culture	(Y-1630)	2,970 ± 80
12. Ying-p'u, charcoal; T3PZE, R1, layer 7; Ying-p'u horizon, Lungshanoid culture	(Y-1631)	2,810 ± 100
13. Ying-p'u, charred seeds; T1P3SW, R1, layer 3; Ying-p'u horizon, Lungshanoid culture	(Y-1632)	2,250 ± 60
14. Fan-tzu-yüan, shell; Fan-tzu-yüan horizon, Lungshanoid culture	(Y-1499)	1,100 ± 80

3. South Taiwan

15. Fengpitou, shell; V-section, lower horizon, Lower Shellmound segment, Lungshanoid culture	(Y-1580)	3,310 ± 80
16. Fengpitou, shell; V-section, upper horizon, Lower Shellmound segment, Lungshanoid culture	(Y-1581)	2,910 ± 80
17. Fengpitou, shell; Locus N, Pit A, layer 2e; Lower Shellmound segment, Lungshanoid culture	(Y-1649)	2,900 ± 120

[1] All dates reported by Minze Stuiver, Director of the Radiocarbon Laboratory, Yale University, except for the two NTU numbers, reported by the Carbon-14 Laboratory, National Taiwan University, and the two Taipei dates, one reported by National Taiwan University and the other by the United States Geological Survey.

18. Fengpitou, shell; Locus S, Pit E7, layer 3a; Lower Shellmound   (Y-1578)   2,780 ± 80
    segment, Lungshanoid culture
19. Fengpitou, shell; Locus K, Pit 1, layer 3. Lower Shellmound   (Y-1584)   2,670 ± 80
    segment, Lungshanoid culture
20. Fengpitou, shell; Locus K, Pit 3, layer 3d; Lower Shellmound   (Y-1648)   2,670 ± 60
    segment, Lungshanoid culture
21. Fengpitou, shell; Locus K, Pit 1, layer 2; Upper Shellmound   (Y-1577)   2,440 ± 100
    segment, Lungshanoid culture

4. Contaminated Samples

22. Tapenkeng, charcoal; Locus Q, Pit X-1, layer 14; bottom of   (Y-1496)   3,080 ± 350
    Corded Ware culture
23. Tapenkeng, seemingly charcoal; Locus Q, Pit VIII-1, layer 7   (Y-1553)   20,380 ± 400
    and Pit X-1, layer 7; Yüan-shan culture
24. Tapenkeng, charcoal; Locus L, Pit I-1, layer 5; Corded Ware   (Y-1497)   890 ± 80
    culture (ancient tree roots)
25. Fengpitou, charcoal; Locus V, Pit W3, layer 2; Lungshanoid   (Y-1600)   1,380 ± 160
    culture
26. Fengpitou, wood; Locus P, Pit E8, layer 2c, 100 cm below sur-   (Y-1601)   19th–20th
    face, near post mold of Lungshanoid culture, Fine Red   century,
    Ware settlement, probably from a modern wooden post   modern era

Appendix 5
Chinese Characters for Proper Names and Technical Terms

Only names and terms used in the text are included here. They are transliterated in the Wade-Giles system according to their Mandarin pronunciation (with less than half a dozen exceptions). All site names and site-derived cultural names are hyphenated, but major geological and geographical names are not hyphenated.

Akungtien 阿公店
An-p'ing 安平
An-tzu 鞍子
Ao-ti 澳底

Chang Ch'en Jui-li 張陳瑞麗
Chang Ch'eng-mei 張澄美
Chang-hua 彰化
Chang-yüan 樟原
Cheng Ch'eng-kung 鄭成功
Chia-yi 嘉義
Chiang Chia-chin 江家錦
Chiang Chin-p'ei 江金培
Chiang-t'ou 江頭
Chien-shan 尖山
Chih-shan-yen 芝山巖
Chihk'eng 直坑
Chin Chen-kuan 金貞觀
Chin-ning 晉寧
Chin-shan 金山
Choshui (R.) 濁水
Chou Ch'ung-teh 周崇德
Chu Shih-chün 竺士君
Chuang-pien-shan 莊邊山
Chün-kung-liao 軍功寮
Chung-chou 中洲
Chung-k'eng-men 中坑門
Chung-ts'u 中厝
Chungyangchienshan 中央尖山

Ch'ang-pin 長濱
Ch'ao-an 潮安
Ch'en Ching-yüan 陳靜遠
Ch'i-lai-shan 蕎萊山
Ch'ien Lung 乾隆

Ch'ien Ssu-liang 錢思亮
Ch'ien-shan-yang 錢山漾
Ch'ing-lien-kang 青蓮崗
Ch'ing-shui 清水
Ch'ing-yün-yen 青雲岩
Ch'üan-chou 泉州

Erh-ling 二苓

Fan-tzu-yüan 番仔園
Feng P'ing Shan 馮平山
Feng-ming 鳳鳴
Feng-pi-t'ou 鳳鼻頭
Fengkuitouhuk'eng 楓櫃斗湖坑
Fengshan 鳳山
Fu Meng-pi 傅夢羆
Fu-ch'ing 福清
Fu-ting-chin 覆鼎金
Fu-ts'un 浮村

Hai-feng 海豐
Hankiang 韓江
Hou-chin 後勁
Hou-lung-ti 後龍底
Hu Hung Hsiu-kui 胡洪秀桂
Hu-nei 湖內
Hu-wei 虎尾
Huai-an 淮安
Huang Shih-ch'iang 黃士強
Hungshuihsienk'eng 紅水仙坑
Hut'oupei 虎頭埤

267

Hsi-hsin-chuang-tzu 西新莊子
Hsi-t'ou-hsiang 西頭鄉
Hsia Tamsui (R.) 下淡水
Hsia-ku-ta-p'u 下罟大埔
Hsia-ma-ts'u 下馬厝
Hsia-p'u 下埔
Hsia-yüan 下園
Hsiang Ssu Shu 相思樹
Hsiao Yen-hsi 蕭延禧
Hsiao-kang 小港
Hsiao-kang-shan 小崗山
Hsiao-liu-ch'iu 小琉球
Hsiao-t'un 小屯
Hsiaopachienshan 小霸尖山
Hsien-jen-tung 仙人洞
Hsin-chu 新竹
Hsin-tien (R.) 新店
Hsü Tse-min 許澤民

Ichimura, I 市村毅

Jih-t'an 日潭
Jih-yüeh-t'an 日月潭
Jung-an 榮安

Kanaseki, Takeo 金關丈夫
Kaneko, Sueo 金子壽衛男
Kang-p'u 港埔
Kano, Tadao 鹿野忠雄
Kao 高
Kao-shan-tsu 高山族
Keelung (R.) 基隆
ko 戈
Kokubu, Naoichi 國分直一
Komalank'eng 噶瑪蘭坑
Kou-t'i-shan 狗蹄山
Kuan-tu 關渡
Kuanyinshan 觀音山
kui 毀
Kung-hsia 宮下

K'ang Hsi 康熙
K'en-ting 墾丁
K'o, Huan-yüeh 柯環月
K'o-k'o-tzu 蚵殼子

Lao-fo-san 流浮山
Lao-peng-shan 老崩山
Laoch'ienk'eng 老阡坑
li 禹
li 曆
Li-chia-ts'un 李家村
Liang-chu 良渚
Liang-wen-kang 良文港
Lin, Ch'ao-ch'i 林朝綮
Lin, Tsung-yüan 林宗源
Lin-chia 林家
Lin-yüan 林園
Ling, Shun-sheng 凌純聲
Ling-shan 靈山
Link'ou 林口
Liu, Pin-hsiung 劉斌雄
Liu-chia-ting 六甲頂
Liu-lin 劉林
Lo-ti 濕底
Lumolamolushan 魯牟拉莫魯山
Lu, Teng-fu 盧登福
Lü, Ch'eng-jui 呂承瑞
Lü, Yü-lin 呂宇霖
Lung-ch'üan-ssu 龍泉寺
Lung-shan 龍山

Ma-t'ou-lu 麻頭路
Mabuchi, Toichi 馬淵東一
Man-kok-tsui 萬角咀
Miao-hou 廟後
Mikouk'eng 米溝坑
Milun 米崙
Minkiang 閩江
Miyamoto, Nobuto 宮本延人

Nanhutashan 南湖大山
Neiyenk'eng 內岩坑
Niao-sung 鳥松
Niu-ch'ou-tzu 牛稠子
Niu-liao-p'u 牛寮埔
Niu-ma-t'ou 牛罵頭

Pa-chiao-chiao 芭蕉腳
Pa-hsien-tung 八仙洞
Pa-kua-shan 八卦山
Pa-li 八里
Pa-li-p'en 八里坌

Pai-sha　白沙
Pei-kang　北港
Pei-t'ou-ts'un　埤頭村
Pilushan　畢祿山

P'an, Hsiu-ying　潘秀英
P'ing-p'u-fan　平埔番
P'ing-ting　平頂
P'ing-ting-shan　平頂山
P'u-li　埔里

San-pen-mu　三本木
Su-ao　蘇澳
Sung, Wen-hsün　宋文薰
Sungshan　松山

Shen, Kang-po　沈剛伯
Sheng, Ch'ing-ch'i　盛清沂
sheng-wen　繩紋
Shih-chai-shan　石寨山
Shih-san-chia　十三甲
Shih-san-hang　十三行
Shih-shang-shan　誓尚山
Shou-shan　壽山
Shu-lin　樹林
Shui-yüan-ti　水源地
Shuiwei (R.)　水尾

Ta-chih　大直
Ta-hu　大湖
Ta-li　大理
Ta-ma-lin　大馬隣
Ta-mu-kung　大墓公
Ta-p'en-k'eng　大笨坑
Ta-p'ing　大平
Ta-p'u　大埔
Ta-tu　大肚
Ta-yüan　大園
Taan (R.)　大安
Tachia (R.)　大甲
Tahsüehshan　大雪山
Takok'an (R.)　大科崁
Tamsui (R.)　淡水
Tananwan　大南灣
Tapachienshan　大霸尖山
Tatu (R.)　大肚

Tat'un　大屯
ting　鼎
Ting-chieh　頂街
Ting-ku　頂罟
Ting-p'u　頂埔
Ting-yüan　頂園
Tingliaok'eng　頂寮坑
Torii, Ryuzō　鳥居龍藏
tou　豆
Tu-ch'uan-t'ou　渡船頭
Tung, P'eng-nien　董彭年
Tung-chang　東張
Tung-chiao　洞角
Tung-hsing　東興
Tung-men-wai　東門外
Tung-shan　東山
Tung-ting-shan　凍頂山
Tunghohuanshan　東合歡山

T'ai-yüan　泰源
T'an-shih-shan　曇石山
T'an-t'ou-shan　潭頭山
T'ao-tzu-yüan　桃子園
T'ao-yüan　桃園
T'ieh-chan-shan　鐵砧山
T'ientzup'uk'eng　田子埔坑
T'ouk'oshan　頭料山
T'u, Hsin-yüan　涂心園
T'u-ti-kung-shan　土地公山
t'ung　通
T'ung Chih　同治

Tsengwen (R.)　曾文
Tso-ying　左營
Tsuboi, Kiyotari　坪井清足
Tsukada, Matsuo　塚田松雄

Utsurikawa, Nenozo　移川子之藏

Wan Li　萬曆
Wan-nien　萬年
Wang-liao　網寮
Wang-t'ien　王田
Wu, Chi-jui　吳基瑞
Wu-shan-t'ing　烏山頂
Wu-shu-lin　烏樹林

Wukuk'eng 五股坑
Wushantingk'eng 烏山頂坑
Wung-yüan 甕源

Yen-hsing 鹽行
Yi Chou 夷州

Ying-p'an-li 營盤裏
Ying-p'u 營埔
Yü-shan 玉山
Yüan-li 苑裏
Yüan-shan 圓山
Yüng Li 永曆
Yüng Cheng 雍正

Bibliography

Abbreviations

BDAA   *Bulletin of the Department of Archaeology and Anthropology*, National Taiwan University, Taipei, Taiwan, China

BIE   *Bulletin of the Institute of Ethnology*, Academia Sinica, Taipei, Taiwan, China

BMFEA   *Bulletin of the Museum of Far Eastern Antiquities*, Stockholm, Sweden

CPCO   Commission for the Preservation of Cultural Objects

KK   *K'ao-ku*, Peking: Science Press

KKHP   *K'ao-ku Hsüeh Pao*, Peking: Science Press

VP   *Vertebrata Palasiatica*, Peking: Science Press

ANDERSSON, J. G.
> 1945   Researches into the Prehistory of the Chinese. *BMFEA*, no. 15. Stockholm.

BARRAU, JACQUES
> 1965a   Gardeners of Oceania. *Discovery*, vol. 1, no. 1, pp. 12–19, New Haven: Peabody Museum.
>
> 1965b   Witnesses of the Past: Notes on Some Food Plants of Oceania. *Ethnology*, vol. 4, pp. 282–94. Pittsburgh.

BEATH, S. S.
> 1939   Black Pottery of the Liang Chu Site Near Hangchow. *China Journal*, vol. 31, no. 6, pp. 262–6. Shanghai.

BEYER, H. O.
> 1948   Philippine and East Asian Archaeology, and Its Relation to the Origin of the Pacific Islands Population. *National Research Council of the Philippines Bulletin*, no. 29. Quezon City.
>
> 1956   Preliminary Notes to Eight Papers on Chinese Archaeology and Early History. *Proceedings of the Fourth Far-Eastern Prehistory and the Anthropological Division of the Eighth Pacific Science Congresses Combined*, part 1, fasc. 1, pp. 83–8. Quezon City.

BIRDSELL, JOSEPH B.
> 1951   The Problem of the Early Peopling of the Americas as Viewed from Asia. In *Papers on the Physical Anthropology of the American Indian*, ed. by. W. S. Laughlin, pp. 1–68. New York.

BLACK, DAVISON
> 1928   A Study of Kansu and Honan Aeneolithic Skulls and Specimens from Later Kansu Prehistoric Sites in Comparison with North China and Other Recent Crania. *Palaeontologia Sinica*, vol. 6, fasc. 1, ser. D. Peking.

BRINDLEY, G. W. (ed.)
> 1951   *X-ray Identification and Crystal Structures of Clay Minerals*. London.

CHANG, CH'I-HAI, AND LÜ JUNG-FANG
> 1965   Fu-chien Min-hou T'an-shih-shan Yi-chih T'ao-ch'i Fen-hsi. *KK*, vol. 1965, no. 4, pp. 192, 193–8. Peking.

CHANG, CH'I-YÜN
> 1953   *An Outline of History of Taiwan*. Taipei.

Chang, Chuan-shen
    1947 Anthropologische Untersuchungen über die Schadel von Atayal in Formosa. *Bulletin of the Anatomy Department, National Taiwan University*, fasc. 6. Taipei.

Chang, Hsiang
    1964 Shih Lun Chiang Che Hsin-shih-ch'i-shih-tai Yi-chih ti Lei-hsing. *KK*, vol. 1964, no. 9, pp. 468–71. Peking.

Chang, Kwang-chih
    1954a Yüan-shan Fa-chüeh tui T'ai-wan Shih-ch'ien-shih Yen-chiu chih Kung-hsien. *Ta-lu Tsa-chih*, vol. 9, no. 2, pp. 36–41. Taipei.
    1954b T'ai-pei P'en-ti ti Shih-ch'ien Wen-hua. *T'ai-wan Feng-t'u*, Literary Supplement to *Kung Lun Pao*, nos. 174 and 180 (May 24 and July 5). Taipei.
    1956 A Brief Survey of the Archaeology of Formosa. *Southwestern Journal of Anthropology*, vol. 12, pp. 371–86. Albuquerque.
    1957 Yüan-shan Ch'u-t'u ti Yi K'o Jen Ch'ih. *BDAA*, vols. 9/10, pp. 146–8. Taipei.
    1958 T'ai-wan T'u-chu Pei Chu Wen-hua Ts'ung chi ch'i Ch'i-yüan yü Ch'uan-po. *Bulletin of the Ethnological Society of China*, no. 2, pp. 53–133. Taipei.
    1959 A Working Hypothesis for the Early Cultural History of South China. *BIE*, no. 7, pp. 43–103. Taipei.
    1963 *The Archaeology of Ancient China*. New Haven and London.
    1964a Introduction to Special Section on the Prehistory of Taiwan. *Asian Perspectives*, vol. 7, nos. 1/2, pp. 195–203. Hong Kong.
    1964b Prehistoric Ceramic Horizons in Southeastern China and Their Extension into Formosa. *Asian Perspectives*, vol. 7, nos. 1/2, pp. 243–50. Hong Kong.
    1964c A Selected Bibliography of Taiwan Archaeology, 1953–62. *Asian Perspectives*, vol. 7, nos. 1/2, pp. 272–5. Hong Kong.
    1964d Prehistoric and Early Historic Culture Horizons and Traditions in South China. *Current Anthropology*, vol. 5, no. 9, pp. 359, 368–75, 399–400. Chicago.
    1967a *Rethinking Archaeology*. New York.
    1967b The Yale Expedition to Taiwan and the Southeast Asian Horticultural Evolution. *Discovery*, vol. 2, no. 2, pp. 3–10. New Haven: Peabody Museum.

Chekiang Province CPCO
    1960 Wu-hsing Ch'ien-shan-yang Yi-chih Ti Yi Erh ts'e Fa-chüeh Pao-kao. *KKHP*, vol. 1960, no. 2, pp. 73–91. Peking.

Ch'en, Chung-kuang, and Lin Teng-hsiang
    1961 Min-hou Chuang-pien-shan Hsin-shih-ch'i-shih-tai Yi-chih Shih Chüeh Chien Pao. *KK*, vol. 1961, no. 1, pp. 40–45. Peking.

Chiang, Tsuan-ch'u
    1959 Kuan-yü Chiang-su ti Yüan-shih Wen-hua Yi-chih. *KKHP*, vol. 1959, no. 4, pp. 35–45. Peking.

Davis, S. G., and Mary Tregear
    1961 Man Kok Tsui, Archaeological Site 30, Lantau Island, Hong Kong. *Asian Perspectives*, vol. 4, nos. 1/2, pp. 183–212. Hong Kong.

Dyen, Isidore
    1964 The Position of the Malayopolynesian Languages of Formosa. *Asian Perspectives*, vol. 7, nos. 1/2, 261–71. Hong Kong.

Ferrell, Raleigh
    1966 The Formosan Tribes: A Preliminary Linguistic, Archaeological, and Cultural Synthesis. *BIE*, no. 21, pp. 97–130. Taipei.

FRONDEL, CLIFFORD
    1962   *Silica Minerals*. The System of Mineralogy, vol. 3. New York and London.

FUKIEN PROVINCE CPCO
    1959   Fu-chien K'ao-ku Kung-tso Kai-k'uang. *KK*, vol. 1959, no. 11, pp. 619–21. Peking.

GRACE, GEORGE W.
    1964   The Linguistic Evidence. *Current Anthropology*, vol. 5, no. 5, pp. 361–8, 403–4. Chicago.

HAYASAKA, ICHIRO, AND C. C. RIN (LIN)
    1934   Taiwan Kōko Shiryō. *Taiwan Chigaku Kiji*, vol. 5, no. 1, pp. 1–6. Taihoku.

HEINE-GELDERN, ROBERT VON
    1932   Urheimat und früheste Wanderungen der Austronesier. *Anthropos*, vol. 27, nos. 3/4, pp. 543–619. Vienna.

HO, T'IEN-HSING
    1937   *Hang-hsien Liang-chu-chen chih Shih-ch'i yü Hei-t'ao*. Shanghai.

HOUSTON, CHARLES O., JR.
    1956   Progress in Philippine Archaeology: 1953–1957. *Journal of East Asiatic Studies*, vol. 5, no. 2, pp. 213–28. Quezon City.

HRDLICKA, ALES
    1947   *Practical Anthropometry*. Philadelphia.

HSIEH, CHIAO-MIN
    1964   *Taiwan—Ilha Formosa, A Geography in Perspective*. Washington.

HSÜ, CH'ING-CH'ÜAN
    1959   Fu-chien Ch'ung-an Hsin-shih-ch'i-shih-tai Yi-chih Tiao-ch'a. *KK*, vol. 1959, no. 11, pp. 601–3. Peking.
    1961   Min Pei Chien-ou ho Chien-yang Hsin-shih-ch'i-shih-tai Yi-chih Tiao-ch'a. *KK*, vol. 1961, no. 4, pp. 185, 192, 202. Peking.
    1965   Fu-chien Fu-ch'ing Tung-chang Hsin-shih-ch'i-shih-tai Yi-chih Fa-chüeh Pao-kao. *KK*, vol. 1965, no. 2, pp. 49–61, 79. Peking.

HURLBUT, CORNELIUS S., JR.
    1955   *Dana's Manual of Mineralogy*, 16th ed. New York and London.

ICHIMURA, TAKESHI
    1950   A Brief Geological Note on the Kuanyin Volcano, Formosa. *Journal of the Geological Society of Japan*, vol. 56, no. 66, pp. 493–8. Tokyo.

JAO, TSUNG-YI
    1951   *Han-chiang Liu-yü Shih-ch'ien Yi-chih chi ch'i Wen-hua*. Hong Kong: privately printed.

JEN, HSIEN-MIN
    1960   T'ai-wan P'ai-wan Tsu ti Ku T'ao-hu. *BIE*, no. 9, pp. 163–224. Taipei.

KANASEKI, TAKEO
    1943   Taiwan Senshijidai ni Okeru Hokuhō Bunka no Eikyō. *Taiwan Bunka Ronsō*, vol. 1. Taihoku.
    1951   Chugaku Kodai ni Okeru Basshi Rei. *Kaibōgaku Zasshi*, vol. 29, no. 2, p. 104. Tokyo.
    1952   Taiwan Kyujū Minzoku o Chūshin toshite Tōa Shominzoku no Jinruigaku. *Fukuoka Igaku Zasshi*, vol. 43, no. 2, pp. 1–13. Fukuoka.
    1956   On the Human Skulls Excavated from the Prehistoric Site K'entingliao, Hengch'un Prefecture, Formosa. *Proceedings of the Fourth Far-Eastern Prehistory*

and the *Anthropology Division of the Eighth Pacific Science Congresses Combined*, part 1, fasc. 2, sec. 1, pp. 303–8. Quezon City.

1957 Taiwan Niaosung kaizuka hakken no Ichi Kagankotsu ni Tsuite. *Jinruigaku Kipō*, vol. 18, pp. 347–54. Tokyo.

KANASEKI, TAKEO, AND KOKUBU NAOICHI

1949a T'ai-chung Hsien Ying-p'u Yi-chih Tiao-ch'a Yü Pao. *Tai-wan Wen-hua*, vol. 5, no. 1, pp. 29–34. Taipei.

1949b T'ai-wan Hsien-shih Shih-tai Hsüeh-hsing Shih-ch'i K'ao. *Jen-wen K'o-hsüeh Lun Ts'ung*, vol. 1, pp. 73–100. Taipei.

1950 T'ai-wan K'ao-ku-hsüeh Yen-chiu Chien Shih. *T'ai-wan Wen-hua*, vol. 6, no. 1, pp. 9–15. Taipei.

1953 Taiwan Senshi Kōkogaku Kinnen no Kōsaku. *Minzokugaku Kenkyū*, vol. 18, nos. 1/2, pp. 67–70. Tokyo.

KANEKO, ERIKA PURSE-STANEK

1953 Stone Implements and Their Use in the Agriculture of Taiwan. *Wiener Völkkundliche Mitteilungen*, vol. 1, no. 2, pp. 22–31. Vienna.

KANO, TADAO

1955 *T'ai-wan K'ao-ku-hsüeh Min-tsu-hsüeh Kai-kuan*, trans. from the Japanese by W. H. Sung. Taipei: Provincial Commission for Historic Research.

KKYCS (K'AO-KU YEN-CHIU SUO; Institute of Archaeology, Academia Sinica)

1962 *Hsin Chung-kuo ti K'ao-ku Shou-hu*. Peking.

KAPLAN, S.

1948/49 Early Pottery from the Liangchu Site, Chekiang Province. *Archives of the Chinese Art Society of America*, vol. 3, pp. 13–42. New York.

KIDDER, A. EDWARD, JR.

1957 *The Jomon Pottery of Japan*. Artibus Asiae, Suppl. 17. Ascona, Switzerland.

KOKUBU, NAOICHI

1941 Taiwan Nanbu ni Okeru Senshi Iseki to so no Ibutsu. *Nanpō Minzoku*, vol. 6, no. 3, pp. 179–96. Taihoku.

1943 Yuken sekifu Yudan sekifu oyobi Kokuto-bunka. *Taiwan Bunka Ronsō*, vol. 1, pp. 17–45. Taihoku.

1944 Hachiricho yori. *Minzoku Taiwan*, vol. 4, no. 9, pp. 30–31. Taihoku.

1960 Bōko Hontō ni Okeru Senshi Iseki to Ibutsu. *Journal of the Shimonoseki College of Fisheries (Civic Science)*, vol. 5, pp. 55–62. Shimonoseki.

1962a Taiwan Senshi Jidai no Kaizuka. *Journal of the Shimonoseki College of Fisheries (Civic Science)*, vol. 7, pp. 52–72. Shimonoseki.

1962b Ko-bunken ni Arawareta Taiwan Senshi Jidai. *Journal of the Shimonoseki College of Fisheries (Civic Science)*, vol. 7, pp. 41–51. Shimonoseki.

1964a Taiwan Takao-shi Jusan Sanzō no Senshi Iseki. *Journal of the Shimonoseki University of Fisheries (Civic Science)*, vol. 8, pp. 1–10. Shimonoseki.

1964b The Prehistoric Southern Islands and East China Sea Areas. *Asian Perspectives*, vol. 7, nos. 1/2, pp. 224–42. Hong Kong.

KOKUBU, NAOICHI, *et al.*

1949 Kuan-yü Tsui-chin T'a-ch'a chih Hsin-chu Hsien chi T'ai-pei Hsien chih Hai Pien Yi-chi. *T'ai-wan Wen-hua*, vol. 5, no. 1, pp. 35–40. Taipei.

KRAUS, EDWARD H., WALTER F. HUNT, AND L. S. RAMSDELL

1959 *Mineralogy*, 5th ed. New York, Toronto, and London.

Ku, Yü-min
1962 Kuang-tung Ling-shan Tung-hsüeh Tiao-ch'a Pao-kao. *VP*, vol. 6, no. 2, pp. 193–9. Peking.

Kuo, Yüan-wei, and Li Chia-ho
1963 Chiang-hsi Wan-nien Ta-yüan Hsien-jen-tung Tung-hsüeh Yi-chih Shih Chüeh. *KKHP*, vol. 1963, no. 1, pp. 1–16. Peking.

Li, Chi
1954 Notes on Some Metrical Characters of Calvaria of the Shang Dynasty Excavated from Houchiachuang, Anyang. *Annals of Academia Sinica*, no. 1, Taipei.

Lin, Chao
1955 Min-hou T'an-shih-shan Hsin-shih-ch'i-shih-tai Yi-chih T'an-chüeh Pao-kao. *KKHP*, vol. 10, pp. 53–68. Peking.
1957 Fu-chien Kuang-tse Hsin-shih-ch'i-shih-tai Yi-chih ti Tiao-ch'a. *KKHP*, vol. 1957, no 1, pp. 31–5. Peking.
1961 Min-hou T'an-shih-shan Hsin-shih-ch'i-shih-tai Yi-chih Ti Erh chih Ssu Ts'e Fa-chüeh Chien Pao. *KK*, vol. 1961, no. 12, pp. 669–72, 696. Peking.

Lin, Ch'ao-ch'i
1957 Ti-hsing (Topography). *T'ai-wan Sheng T'ung Chih Kao*, vol. 1, no. 1. Taipei: Provincial Commission for Historic Research.
1960 T'ai-wan Hsi-nan-pu chih Pei-chung chi ch'i Ti-shih-hsüeh Yi-yi. *BDAA*, nos. 15/16, pp. 49–94. Taipei.
1963 T'ai-wan chih Ti-ssu-chi. *T'ai-wan Wen-hsien*, vol. 14, nos. 1/2, pp. 1–92. Taipei.
1964 Geology and Ecology of Taiwan Prehistory. *Asian Perspectives*, vol. 7, nos. 1/2, pp. 203–13. Hong Kong.
1965 T'ai-wan Ketangalan-tsu chih K'uang-yieh. *T'ai-wan K'uang-yieh*, vol. 17, nos. 2/3, pp. 1–21. Taipei.
1966 An Outline of Taiwan's Quaternary Geohistory with Special Discussion of the Relation between Natural History and Cultural History in Taiwan. *BDAA*, no. 28, pp. 7–44. Taipei.

Ling, Shun-sheng
1951 Ku-tai Min-Yüeh-jen yü T'ai-wan T'u-chu-tsu. *Hsüeh-shu Chi K'an*, vol. 1, no. 2, pp. 1–17. Taipei.

Liu, Chih-wan
1956a Nan-t'ou Hsien K'ao-ku Chih-yao. *Nan-t'ou Wen-hsien Tsung Chi*, vol. 4, pp. 7–89. Nan-t'ou.
1956b Nan-t'ou Hsien Cho-shui-hsi Nan-an She-liao T'ai-ti Shih-ch'ien Yi-chih. *Nan-t'ou Wen-hsien Ts'ung Chi*, vol. 4, pp. 91–113. Nan-t'ou.
1960a Nan-t'ou Hsien Chün-kung-liao Yi-chih Tiao-ch'a Pao-kao. *T'ai-wan Wen-hsien*, vol. 11, no. 3, Special Supplement. Taipei.
1960b T'ai-chung Hsien Ku-kuan Yi-chih. *K'o-hsüeh Nien K'an*, vol. 3, pp. 7–22. Taipei.

Liu, Pin-hsiung
1954 Tung-chiao Yi-chih Fa-chüeh Chien Pao. *Nan-t'ou Wen-hsien Ts'ung Chi*, vol. 1, pp. 3–4. Nan-t'ou.
1955 T'ai-chung Hsien Ch'ing-shui Chen Niu-ma-t'ou Yi-chih Tiao-ch'a Pao-kao. *T'ai-wan Wen-hsien*, vol. 6, no. 4, pp. 69–83. Taipei.
1964 Excavations and Discoveries at Ta p'en-k'eng and Other Prehistoric Sites of Pali District. *Asian Perspectives*, vol. 7, nos. 1/2, pp. 214–23. Hong Kong.

Liu, Pin-hsiung, and Liu Chih-wan
    1957   Jih-yüeh-t'an K'ao-ku Pao-kao. *Nan-t'ou Wen-hsien Ts'ung Chi*, vol. 5, pp. 1–64.
        Nan-t'ou.
Lü, Jung-fang, Tseng Fan, and Yieh Wen-ch'eng
    1964   Fu-chien Min-hou T'an-shih-shan Hsin-shih-ch'i-shih-tai Yi-chih Ti Wu Ts'e
        Fa-chüeh Chien Pao. *KK*, vol. 1964, no. 12, pp. 601-2, 618. Peking.
Mabuchi, Toichi
    1953a   Takasagozoku no Benrui—Gakushi teki Kaiko. *Minzokugaku Kenkyū*, vol. 18,
        nos. 1/2, pp. 1–11. Tokyo.
    1953b   Takasagozoku no Idō oyobi Bunpu. *Minzokugaku Kenkyū*, vol. 18, nos. 1/2, pp.
        123–54. Tokyo.
Mackenzie, Robert C. (ed.)
    1957   *The Differential Thermal Investigation of Clays*. London.
Maglioni, Raphael
    1938   Archaeological Finds in Hoifung, Part 1. *Hong Kong Naturalist*, vol. 8, nos. 3/4,
        pp. 208–44. Hong Kong.
    1952   Archaeology in South China. *Journal of East Asiatic Studies*, vol. 2, no. 1, pp.
        1–20. Quezon City.
Mansuy, Henri
    1924   Stations préhistoriques dans les cavernes du massif calcaire de Bac-Son (Tonkin).
        Mémoire, Service Geologique de l'Indochine, vol. 11. Hanoi.
    1925   Nouvelles découvertes dans les cavernes du massif calcaire de Bac-Son (Tonkin).
        Mémoire, Service Geologique de l'Indochine, vol. 12. Hanoi.
Miyamoto, Nobuto
    1956   A Study of the Relation between the Existing Formosan Aborigines and Stone
        Age Remains in Formosa. *Proceedings of the Fourth Far-Eastern Prehistory and the
        Anthropology Division of the Eighth Pacific Science Congresses Combined*, part 1,
        fasc. 2, sec. 1, pp. 329–34. Quezon City.
Mo, Chih
    1959   Kuang-tung Nan-hai Hsi-chiao-shan Ch'u-t'u ti Shih Ch'i. *KKHP*, vol. 1959, no.
        4, pp. 1–15. Peking.
    1960   Kuang-tung Hai-nan-tao Yüan-shih Wen-hua Yi-chih. *KKHP*, vol. 1960, no.
        2, pp. 121–31. Peking.
    1961a   Kuang-tung Ch'ao-an ti Pei-ch'iu Yi-chih. *KK*, vol. 1961, no. 11, pp. 577–84.
        Peking.
    1961b   Kuang-tung K'ao-ku Tiao-ch'a Fa-chüeh ti Hsin Shou-hu. *KK*, vol. 1961, no. 12,
        pp. 666–8. Peking.
Mo, Chih, and Ch'en Chih-liang
    1961   Kuang-tung Tung-hsing Hsin-shih-ch'i-shih-tai Pei-ch'iu Yi-chih. *KK*, vol. 1961,
        no. 12, pp. 644–9, 688. Peking.
Mo, Chih, and Li Shih-wen
    1960   Kuang-tung Chung-pu Ti Ti-ch'ü Hsin-shih-ch'i-shih-tai Yi-ts'un. *KKHP*, vol.
        1960, no. 2, pp. 107–19. Peking.
Mo, Chih, Li Shih-wen, and Huang Pao-ch'üan
    1964   Kuang-tung Ch'ü-chiang Nien-yü-chuan Ma-t'i-p'ing ho Shao-kuan Tsou-ma-
        kang Yi-chih. *KK*, vol. 1964, no. 7, pp. 323–32, 345. Peking.

MURDOCK, GEORGE P.
    1964   Genetic Classification of the Austronesian Languages: A Key to Oceanic Culture History. *Ethnology*, vol. 3, no. 2, pp. 117–26. Pittsburgh.

NORTON, F. H.
    1952   *Elements of Ceramics*. Cambridge, Mass.

OBA, TOSHIO, AND CHESTER S. CHARD
    1963   New Dates for Early Pottery in Japan. *Asian Perspectives*, vol. 6, pp. 75–76. Hong Kong.

PEARSON, RICHARD J.
    1966   "The Spatial and Temporal Variation in Ryukyu Prehistory." Unpublished Ph.D. Thesis, Yale University.

P'ENG, JU-TS'E
    1961   Kuang-tung Wung-yüan Hsien Ch'ing-t'ang Hsin-shih-ch'i-shih-tai Yi-chih. *KK*, vol. 1961, no. 11, pp. 585–8. Peking.

SAURIN, EDMOND
    1940   Stations préhistoriques du Qui-Chan et de Thuong-Xuan (Nord Annam). *Proceedings of the Third Congress of Prehistorians of the Far East, Singapore, 1938*, pp. 71–90. Singapore.

SCHOFIELD, W.
    1940   The Proto-historic Site of the Hong Kong Culture at Shek Pek, Lantau, Hong Kong. *Proceedings of the Third Congress of Prehistorians of the Far East, Singapore, 1938*, pp. 235–305. Singapore.

SHENG, CH'ING-CH'I
    1960   Shih Ch'ien Chih. *T'ai-pei Hsien Chih*, vol. 4. Pan-ch'iao: Commission for Historic Research of Taipei Hsien.
    1962a T'ai-wan-sheng Pei Hai An Shih-ch'ien Yi-chih Tiao-ch'a Pao-kao. *T'ai-wan Wen-hsien*, vol. 13, no. 3, pp. 1–93. Taipei.
    1962b Tan-shui-ho Shang-yu Shih-ch'ien Yi-chih Tiao-ch'a Pao-kao. *T'ai-wan Wen-hsien Chuan-k'an*, vol. 13, no. 4, pp. 111–91. Taipei.
    1963a T'ao-yüan Hsien Yen Hai chi T'ai-ti Ti-ch'ü Shih-ch'ien Yi-chih Tiao-ch'a Pao-kao. *T'ai-wan Wen-hsien*, vol. 14, no. 2, pp. 117–38. Taipei.
    1963b Yi-lan P'ing-yüan Pien-yüan Shih-ch'ien Yi-chih Tiao-ch'a Pao-kao. *T'ai-wan Wen-hsien*, vol. 14, no. 1, pp. 1–60. Taipei.
    1965   Miao-li Hsien Ti-ch'ü Shih-ch'ien Yi-chih Tiao-ch'a Pao-kao. *T'ai-wan Wen-hsien*, vol. 16, no. 3, pp. 91–156. Taipei.

SHENG, CH'ING-CH'I, LIU PIN-HSIUNG, AND WU CHI-JUI
    1961   *T'ai-pei Hsien Ta-an-liao T'u-ti-kung-shan Yi-chih Fa-chüeh Pao-kao*. Taipei: Commission for Historic Research of Taipei Hsien.

SHIH, CHANG-JU
    1953   T'ai-wan Ta-ma-lin Yi-chih Fa-chüeh Chien Pao. *BDAA*, no. 1, pp. 13–15. Taipei.

SHIH, CHANG-JU, AND SUNG WEN-HSÜN
    1956   T'ieh-chan-shan Shih-ch'ien Yi-chih Shih Chüeh Pao-kao. *BDAA*, no. 8, pp. 35–92. Taipei.

SHIH, HSIN-KENG
    1938   *Liang-chu: Hang Hsien Ti-erh Ch'ü Hei-t'ao Wen-hua Yi-chih Ch'u-pu Pao-kao*. Hangchow: Hsihu Museum.

SHIMA, GORO
1933 Anthropological Study of the Chinese Skulls Obtained from the Suburbs of Fu-shun, Manchuria. *Journal of the Anthropological Society of Tokyo*, vol. 40, no. 8. Tokyo.

SHUTLER, RICHARD, JR., AND MARY E.
1966 Potsherds from Bougainville Island. *Asian Perspectives*, vol. 8, no. 1, pp. 181–3. Hong Kong.

SOLHEIM, WILHELM G., II
1961 Further Notes on the Kalanay Pottery Complex in the Philippines. *Asian Perspectives*, vol. 3, no. 2, pp. 157–65. Hong Kong.

1964a *The Archaeology of Central Philippines*, Monograph 10. Manila: The National Institute of Science and Technology.

1964b Formosan Relationships with Southeast Asia. *Asian Perspectives*, vol. 7, nos. 1/2, pp. 251–60. Hong Kong.

1964c Pottery and the Malayo-Polynesians. *Current Anthropology*, vol. 5, no. 5, pp. 360, 376–84. Chicago.

ms. "The Sa-Huynh-Kalanay Pottery Tradition: Past and Future Research." (Undated.)

SU, CHAO-K'AI
1959 Taiwan Senshi Jidai Iseki Shitsudo Dōbutsu-kotsu no Kenkyū. *Jinruigaku Kenkyū*, vol. 6, no. 1, pp. 133–70. Tokyo.

SU, PING-CH'I
1965 Kuan-yü Yang-shao Wen-hua ti Jo-kan Wen-t'i. *KKHP*, vol. 1965, no. 1, pp. 51–82. Peking.

SUNG, WEN-HSÜN
1953/54 Books and Articles Relating to the Archaeology of Taiwan. *BDAA*, no. 1, pp. 39–42; no. 2, pp. 46–9; no. 3, pp. 57–60. Taipei.

1957 T'ai-wan Shih-ch'ien Yi-chih Ch'u-t'u ti T'ao Chih-chiao. *BDAA*, nos. 9/10, pp. 137–45. Taipei.

1958 Ōseki no Yōto. *Minzokugaku Kenkyū*, vol. 22, nos. 1/2, pp. 120–2. Tokyo.

1962 T'ai-chung-hsien Fan-tzu-yüan Pei-chung chih Mu-tsang. *BDAA*, nos. 19/20, pp. 83–90. Taipei.

1964 The Stone, Bone, and Horn Industries of the Yüan-shan Shellmound. *Bulletin of the China Council for East Asian Studies*, vol. 3, pp. 98–9. Taipei.

1965 T'ai-wan Hsi-pu Shih-ch'ien Wen-hua ti Nien-tai. *T'ai-wan Wen-hsien*, vol. 16, no. 4, pp. 144–55. Taipei.

SUNG, WEN-HSÜN, AND CHANG KWANG-CHIH
1954 T'ai-chung Hsien Shui-wei-hsi p'an Shih-ch'ien Yi-chih Shih Chüeh Pao-kao. *BDAA*, no. 3, pp. 26–38. Taipei.

1964 Yüan-shan Wen-hua ti Nien-tai. *BDAA*, nos. 23/24, pp. 1–11. Taipei.

SWADISH, MORRIS
1952 Lexicostatistical Dating of Prehistoric Ethnic Contact. *Proceedings of the American Philosophical Society*, no. 96, pp. 452–63, Philadelphia.

TAN, KEINOSUKE
1934 *Corbibula maxima* Prime no gensei hyōhon to Kaizuka hyōhon to ni Arawa-reru heni ni tsuite. *Kairui Kenkyū Zasshi, The Venus*, vol. 4, no. 5, pp. 289–302. Kyoto.

Torii, Ryūzō
   1897   Enzan Kaizuka ni Kansuru Tsūshin. *Jinruigaku Zasshi*, vol. 13, no. 141, pp. 116–18. Tokyo.
   1900   Shinkōzan Chihō ni Okeru Kako Oyobi Genzai no Jūmin. *Jinruigaku Zasshi*, vol. 15, no. 170. Tokyo.
   1925   *Yūshi Izen no Nippon*. Tokyo.
Tseng, Chao-yüeh, *et al.*
   1963   *Chiang-su-sheng Ch'u-t'u Wen-wu Hsüan Chi*. Peking.
Tseng, Fan
   1958   Fu-chou Fu-ts'un Yi-chih ti Fa-chüeh. *KKHP*, vol. 1958, no. 2, pp. 17–27. Peking.
   1959   Fu-chien Chang-p'u Hsin-shih-ch'i-shih-tai Yi-chih Tiao-ch'a. *KK*, vol. 1958, no. 6, pp. 273–5. Peking.
Tseng, Fan, and Huang Ping-yüan
   1961   Min Nan Hsin-shih-ch'i-shih-tai Yi-chih ti Tiao-ch'a. *KK*, vol. 1961, no. 5, pp. 237–44. Peking.
Tsuboi, Kiyotari
   1956   Fengpit'ou—A Prehistoric Site in Southern Formosa that Yielded Painted and Black Pottery. *Proceedings of the Fourth Far-Eastern Prehistory and the Anthropology Division of the Eighth Pacific Science Congresses Combined*, part 1, fasc. 2, sec. 1, pp. 277–302. Quezon City.
Tsukada, Matsuo
   1966   Late Pleistocene Vegetation and Climate in Taiwan (Formosa). *Proceedings of the National Academy of Sciences*, vol. 55, pp. 543–8. Washington.
   1967   Vegetation in Subtropical Formosa during the Pleistocene Glaciations and the Holocene. *Palaeography, Palaeoclimatology, Palaeecology*, vol. 3, pp. 49–64. Amsterdam.
T'ung, Chu-ch'en
   1957   Huang-ho Ch'ang-chiang Chung Hsia Yu Hsin-shih-ch'i Wen-hua ti Fen-pu yü Fen-ch'i. *KKHP*, vol. 1957, no. 2, pp. 7–21. Peking.
Utsurikawa, Nenozō
   1934   Patsu o Meguru Taiheiyō Bunka Kōshō Neidai to Taiwan Hakken no Ruiji Sekki. *Taihoku Teikoku Daigaku Bunshigakubu Kenyū Nenpō*, no. 1. Taihoku.
   1936   Nenteiryu Sekki Jidai Iseki. *Taiwan Sōtokufu Shiseki Chōsa Hōkoku*, no. 2, pp. 1–4. Taihoku.
Utsurikawa Nenozō, and Miyamoto Nobuto
   1937   Sōogun Shinjō Sekki Jidai Iseki. *Nanpō Dozohu*, vol. 2, no. 3, pp. 1–10. Taihoku.
Ward, Lauriston
   1954   The Relative Chronology of China Through the Han Period. In *Relative Chronologies in Old World Archaeology*, ed. by Robert Ehrich. Chicago.
Yang, Chün-shih
   1961   T'ai-pei Hsien Pa-li-hsiang Shih-san-hang chi Ta-p'en-k'eng Liang Shih Ch'ien Yi-chih Tiao-ch'a Pao-kao. *BDAA*, nos. 17/18, pp. 45–70. Taipei.

Plates

PLATE 1

The Site of Fengpitou

A, The Fengpitou terrace, view from east. *B*, The coastal plain and the Islet of Hsiao-liu-ch'iu; view from top of site to south.

The Site of Fengpitou

PLATE 2

THE EXCAVATION OF FENGPITOU

A, Excavation at Locus P. *B*, Quadrants of Square E3 at Locus P.

The Excavation of Fengpitou

PLATE 3

Stratigraphy of Fengpitou

A, North wall of K-3. from top to bottom, approximately 4 m. *B*, K-2 column for midden analysis.

Stratigraphy of Fengpitou

PLATE 4

A, East wall, square E-10, Locus V. Fine red pottery layer below, sandy gray pottery layer above. *B*, North wall, Locus N. Fine red pottery layer below, sandy gray and red pottery layer above.

Stratigraphy of Fengpitou

Human Burial and Pottery Remains at Fengpitou

PLATE 6

Post Molds of House, Locus P, Fengpitou

A, View from northeast. *B*, View from south.

Post Molds of House, Locus P, Fengpitou

PLATE 7

POST MOLDS OF HOUSE, LOCUS P, FENGPITOU
SOUTH WALL

Post Molds of House, Locus P, Fengpitou, South Wall

PLATE 8

A, View from north of site at foothill of Kuanyin volcano. *B*, View of Tamsui estuary to the north from Locus N.

The Site of Tapenkeng

PLATE 9

The Excavation of Tapenkeng

A, Excavation of Locus L, view from north. *B*, Microstratigraphical excavation of pit IX-2, Locus L.

The Excavation of Tapenkeng

PLATE 10

STRATIGRAPHY OF TAPENKENG

A, West wall, pit VI-1, Locus Q. Column of depressions on wall was produced by removal of soil samples at 20-cm intervals. *B*, Lower portions of east wall, pit VI-1, Locus Q, showing layer of andesite slabs below which cord-marked pottery occurs. *C*, South wall of pit in *B*.

Stratigraphy of Tapenkeng

PLATE 11

STRATIGRAPHY OF TAPENKENG

A, North wall, pit VII-2, Locus L. *B*, North wall, pit V-7, Locus P.

Stratigraphy of Tapenkeng

PLATE 12

KILN, PIT VI-1, LOCUS Q, TAPENKENG. VIEW FROM
NORTHWEST

Kiln, Pit VI-1, Locus Q, Tapenkeng, View from Northwest

PLATE 13

A, Post hole surrounded by rocks, pit IV-2, Locus N. *B*, Modern mud-brick house with stone foundations, at Pei-t'ou-ts'un. *C*, Remains of clay plaster adhering to stone base, pit V-8, Locus P. *D* and *E*, Reed impressions on burned clay fragments in kiln.

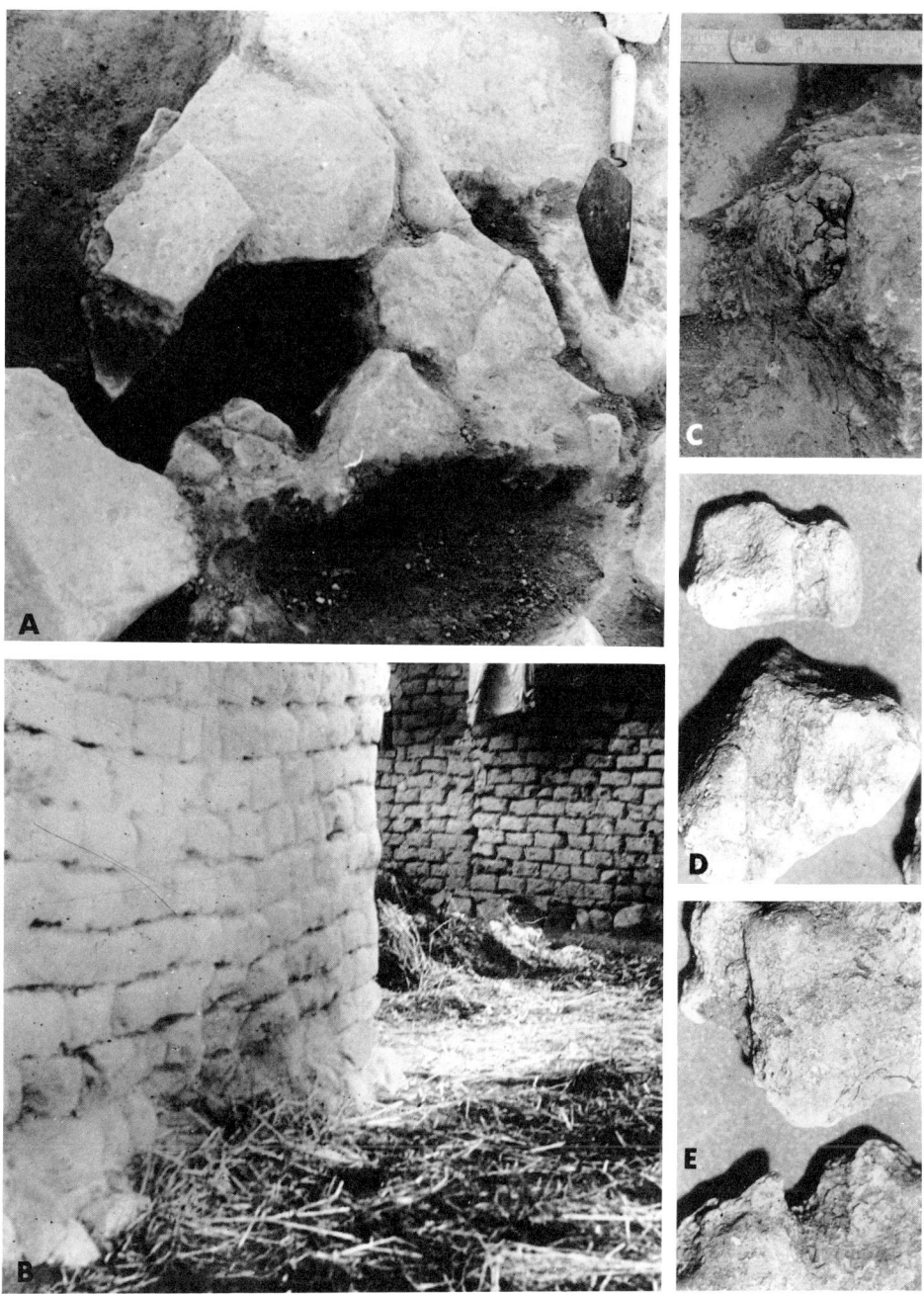

Architectural Remains at Tapenkeng

PLATE 14

CORD-MARKED POTTERY, FENGPITOU

A, P-E3-Ditch 2, *B*, *D*, *E*, *H*, *J*, *K*: K-3-L4. *C*, *F*, *I*, *L*: P-E9-L3. *G*, P-E9-B1-L3. *M*, P-E9-B2-L3.

Cord-marked Pottery, Fengpitou

PLATE 15

CORD-MARKED POTTERY, FENGPITOU

A–P, Rim sherds. *Q* and *R*, Ring-feet fragments. *A*, *B*, *H*, *L*, *M*, *R:* P-E0-L3. *C*, *G*, *J*, *K*, *O*, *P:* K-3-L4. *D*, P-E8-A2-L3. *E*, P-E3-B2-L2f. *F*, K-3-L1b. *I*, N-B-L2c. *N*, P-E8-A1-L3. *Q*, P-E9-B1-L3.

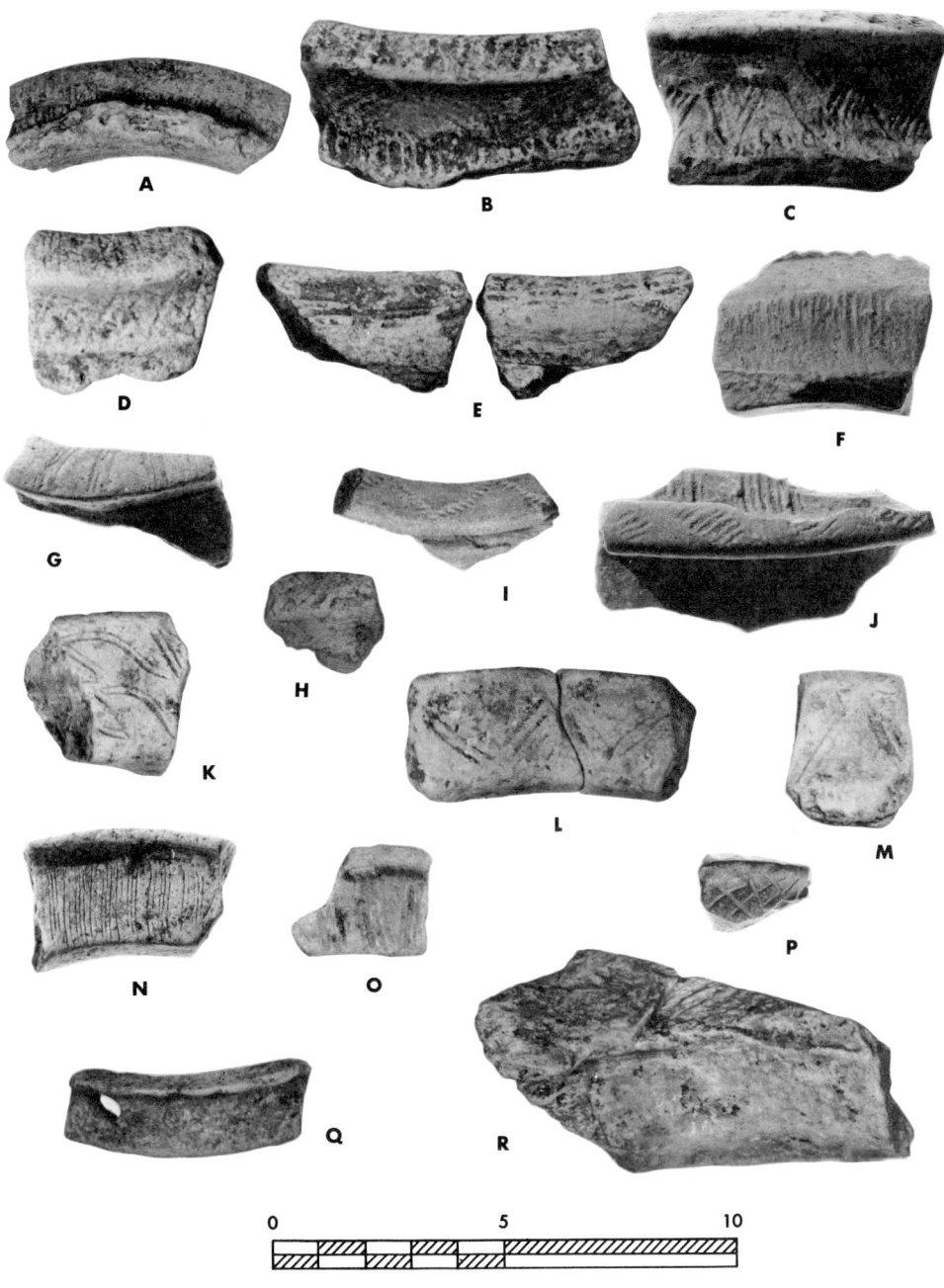

Cord-marked Pottery, Fengpitou

PLATE 16

Stone, Bone, and Clay Artifacts Associated with Cord-Marked Pottery, Fengpitou

A, Pebble with two side notches, P-W4-A2-L3a. *B*, Fragment of worked stone, P-E4-B2-L3. *C*, Slate arrowhead, K-3-L4. *D*, Perforated slate arrowhead, views of both sides, P-E8-B1-L3. *E*, Fragment of worked stone, P-E4-B2-L3. *F*, Clay rectangle, with two holes, P-E9-L3. *G*, Fragment of worked bone, P-E4-B2-L3.

A

B

C

D

E

F

G

0   5   10

Stone, Bone, and Clay Artifacts Associated with Cord-marked Pottery, Fengpitou

Cord-marked Pottery, Tapenkeng

PLATE 18

CORD-MARKED POTTERY, TAPENKENG

A–E, rim sherds; *H*, base sherd; *F, G, I, J*, fragments of ring feet. *A*, VI-1-A2-17. *B*, X-1-b1-14. *C*, X-1-d2-11. *D*, X-1-a2-15. *E*, X-1-b1-10. *F*, X-1-b2-12. *G*, X-1-b1-12. *H*, X-1-d1-10. *I*, I-1-c1-6. *J*, X-1-a1-12.

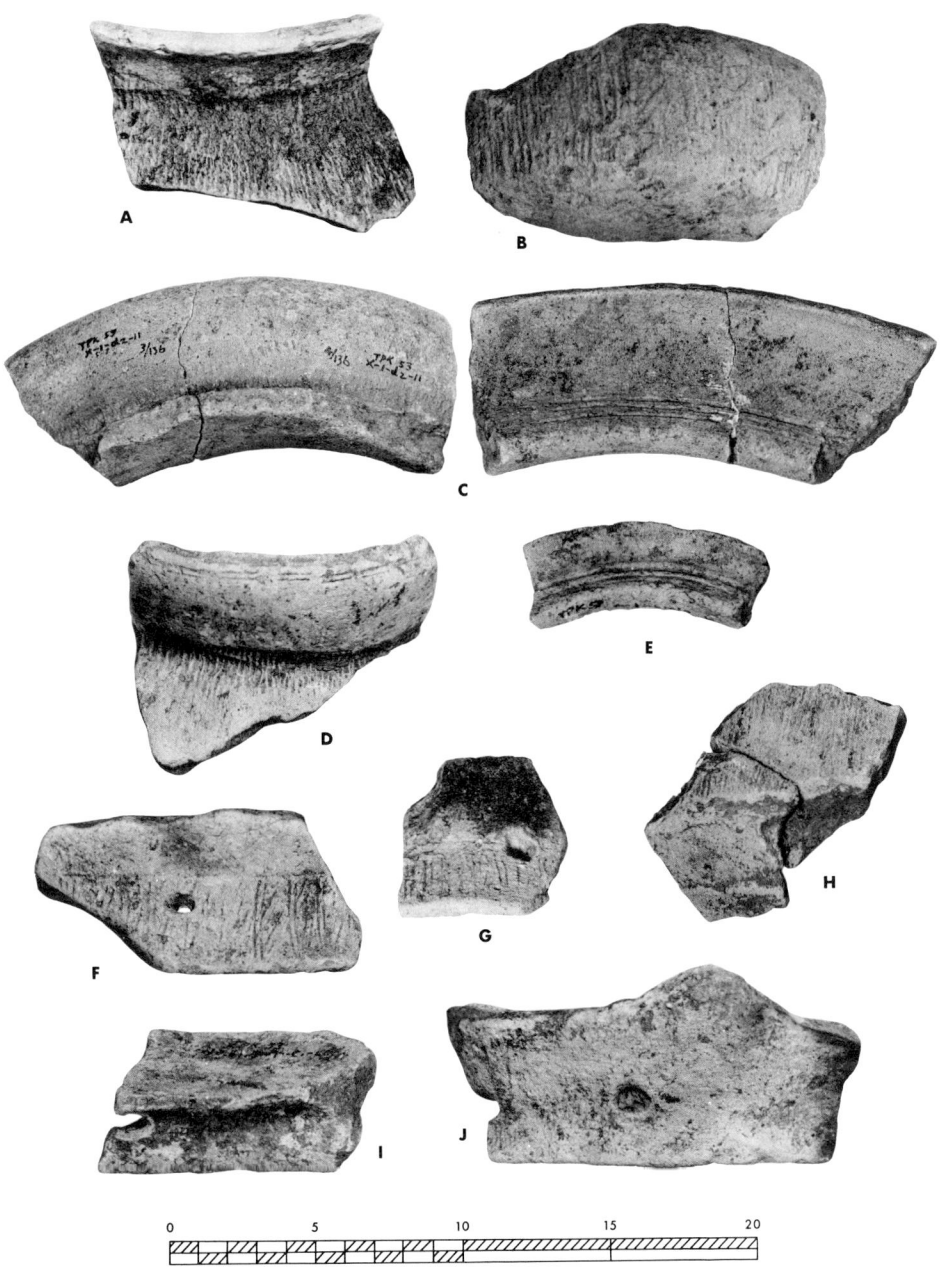

Cord-marked Pottery, Tapenkeng

PLATE 19

CORD-MARKED POTTERY (INCISED RIM SHERDS),
TAPENKENG

A, X-1-d1-9. *B*, X-1-b4-7. *C*, X-1-d2-11. *D*, X-1-b1-12. *E*, V-8-c2-2. *F*, X-1-d2-11. *G*, X-1-d2-11.

Cord-marked Pottery (Incised Rim Sherds), Tapenkeng

PLATE 20

CORD-MARKED POTTERY (INCISED RIM SHERDS), TA-
PENKENG

A, X-1-d1-9. *B*, X-1-c4-13. *C*, V-7-c3-13. *D*, VI-1-a3-
13. *E*, VI-1-A2-18. *F*, X-1-a1-11. *G*, X-1-d-12.

Cord-marked Pottery (Incised Rim Sherds), Tapenkeng

Cord-marked Pottery (Incised Rim Sherds), Tapenkeng

PLATE 22

CORD-MARKED POTTERY, TAPENKENG

D, *E*, body sherds with incised patterns; *J*, lug; all others, rim sherds with incisions.

A, X-1-b1-11. *B*, VI-1-A2-17. *C*, X-1-c1-9. *D*, VI-1-A1-17. *E*, X-1-b3-13. *F*, X-1-d1-9. *G*, VII-2-b2-6. *H*, X-1-b2-12. *I*, X-1-b1-10. *J*, IX-2-d4-7. *K*, VI-1-a3-15. *L*, V-7-c4-14. *M*, X-1-c1-4. *N*, X-1-b1-14. *O*, VI-1-A2-18.

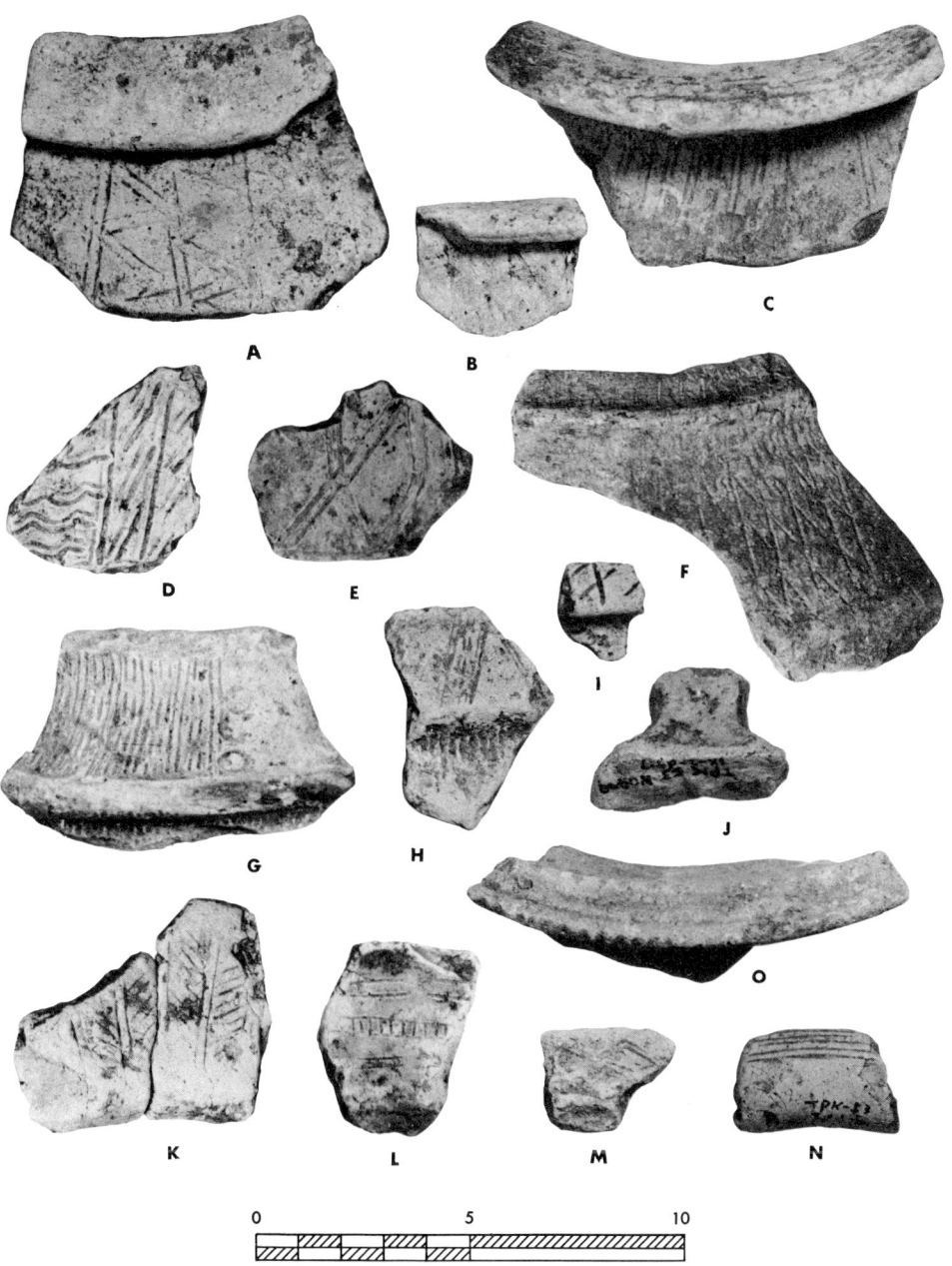

Cord-marked Pottery, Tapenkeng

PLATE 23

A, Chipped stone ax, VI-1-b2-17. *B*, Polished adz with step-like feature, X-1-d3-12. *C*, Polished ax, views of both sides, X-1-b1-15. *D*, Polished ax, views of both sides, X-1-c1-11. *E*, Polished adz, views of both sides, X-1-c1-11. *F*, Fragment of polished ax-adz, VII-2-d2-8. *G*, Fragment of polished ax-adz, IX-2-a1-8. *H*, Perforated arrowhead, views of both sides, X-1-b1-12. *I*, Perforated stone disk, X-1-c4-11. *J–M*, Perforated slate arrowheads, views of both sides. *J*, I-1-d1-6. *K*, VI-2-a1-8. *L*, X-1-d4-14. *M*, VII-2-d2-8.

Stone Artifacts Associated with Cord-Marked Pottery, Tapenkeng

PLATE 24

ARTIFACTS OF THE CORDED WARE CULTURE, VARIOUS
LOCALITIES, TAIWAN

A, Half fragment of clay cylinder with central hole,
X-1-d3-11, Tapenkeng. *B*, Pitted pebble, V1-1-a3-15,
Tapenkeng. *C*, Rim sherd with incised design, Hsia-ku-
ta-p'u, Taipei Prefecture; Yale–Taita Expedition collection. *D*, Polished serpentine adz, Hsia-ku-ta-p'u;
Yale–Taita Expedition collection. *E*, *F*, Rim sherds
with incised designs, Chih-shan-yen, Taipei City; Taita
collection. *G*, *H*, Incised sherds, Ta-p'ing site, Ch'ang-
pin, Taitung Prefecture; Taita collection. *I*, Incised
sherd, Erh-ling site, Kao-hsiung Prefecture; Taita collection.

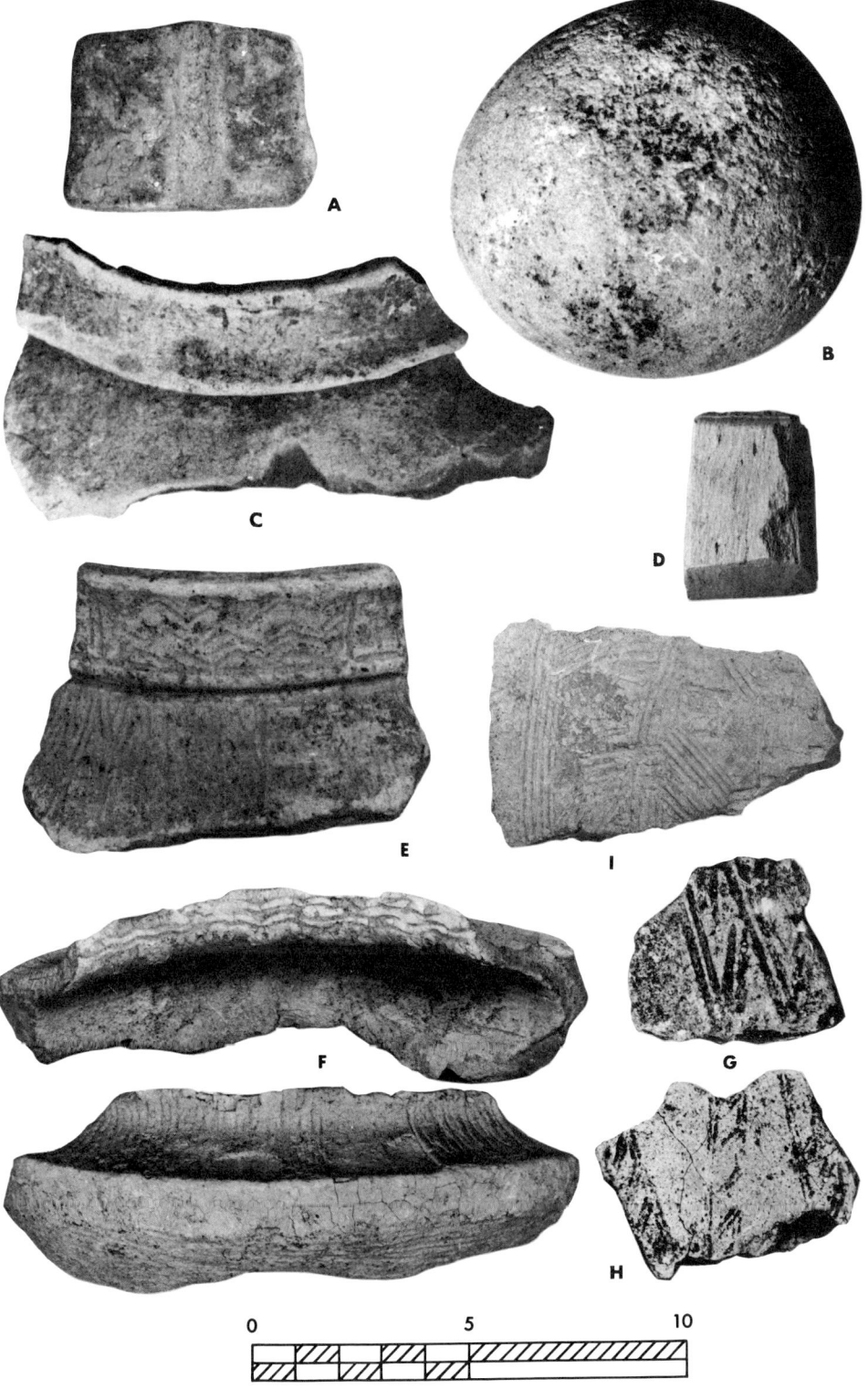

Artifacts of the Corded Ware Culture, Various Localities, Taiwan

PLATE 25

POTSHERDS OF THE FINE RED WARE, FENGPITOU:
MANUFACTURE

A, Body sherd with coarse cord marks, V-W3-A1-L3a. *B*, Body sherd with fine cord marks, N-B-L2gs. *C*, Interior of painted body sherd, showing coils, K-1-L1. *D*, Rim of bowl with mat impression, V-W3-A1-L3a. *E*, Interior of painted bowl rim sherd, showing impression of interior mold, V-W3-A1-L2a. *F*, Bottom of bowl, showing impression of modeling stand, P-E4-B1-L2a. *G*, Interior of ring foot, showing impression of interior mold, V-sc.

Sherds of the Fine Red Ware, Fengpitou: Manufacture

PLATE 26

SHERDS OF FINE RED WARE BOWLS, FENGPITOU

A, V-W3-B1-L2b. *B*, N-B-L3a. *C*, N-A-L2f. *D*, V-W3-B1-L3a. *E*, N-B-L3a.

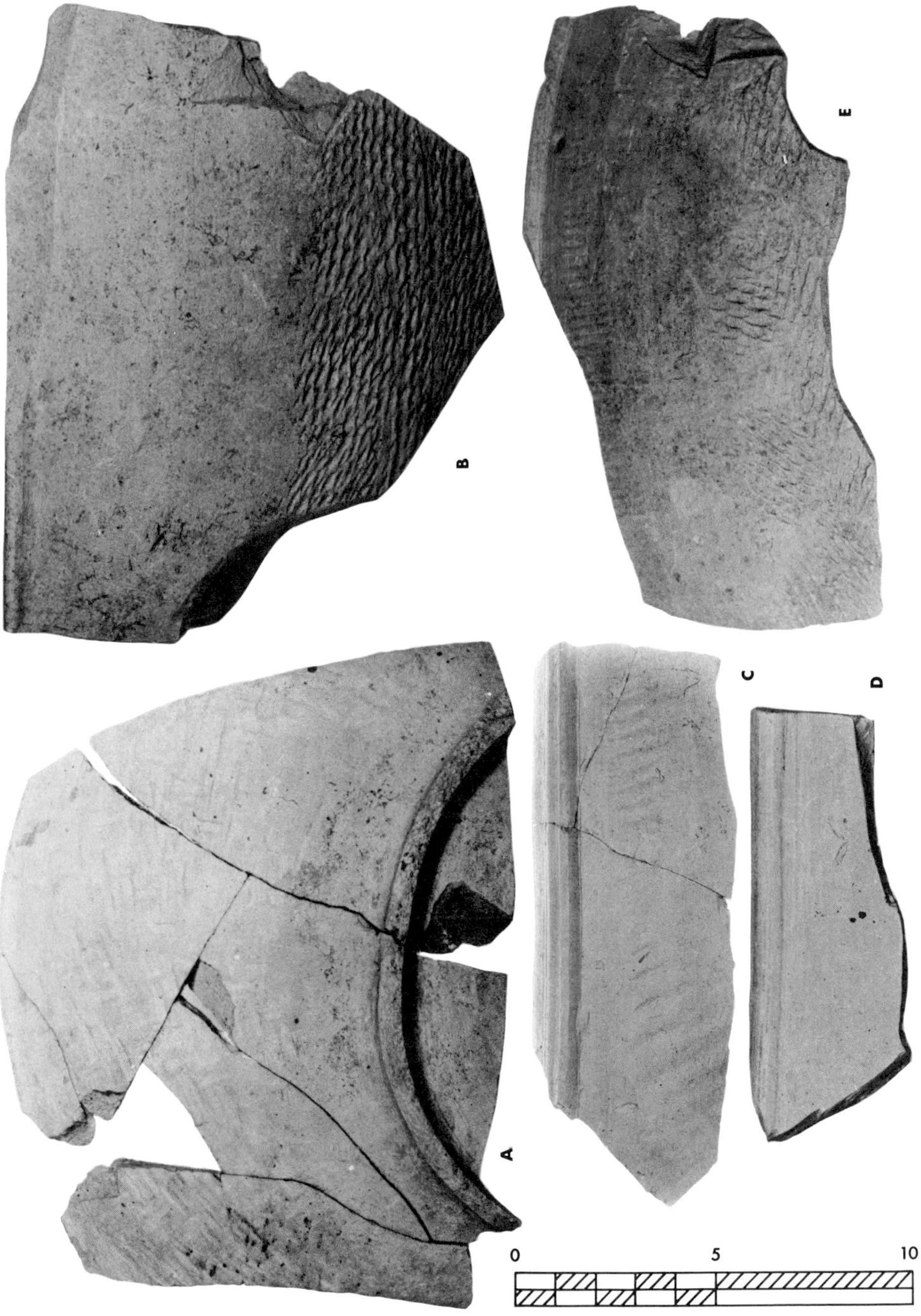

Sherds of Fine Red Ware Bowls, Fengpitou

PLATE 27

SHERDS OF FINE RED WARE JARS, FENGPITOU

A, P-E8-A2-L2c. *B*, V-W3-B2-L3a. *C*, N-A-L2f. *D*, V-W3-B1-L3a. *E*, V-sc. *F*, P-W3-A1-L2c.

Sherds of Fine Red Ware Jars, Fengpitou

PLATE 28

SHERDS OF FINE RED WARE PEDESTALS, FENGPITOU

A, P-E8-B1-L2e. *B*, P-W1-B2-L2b.

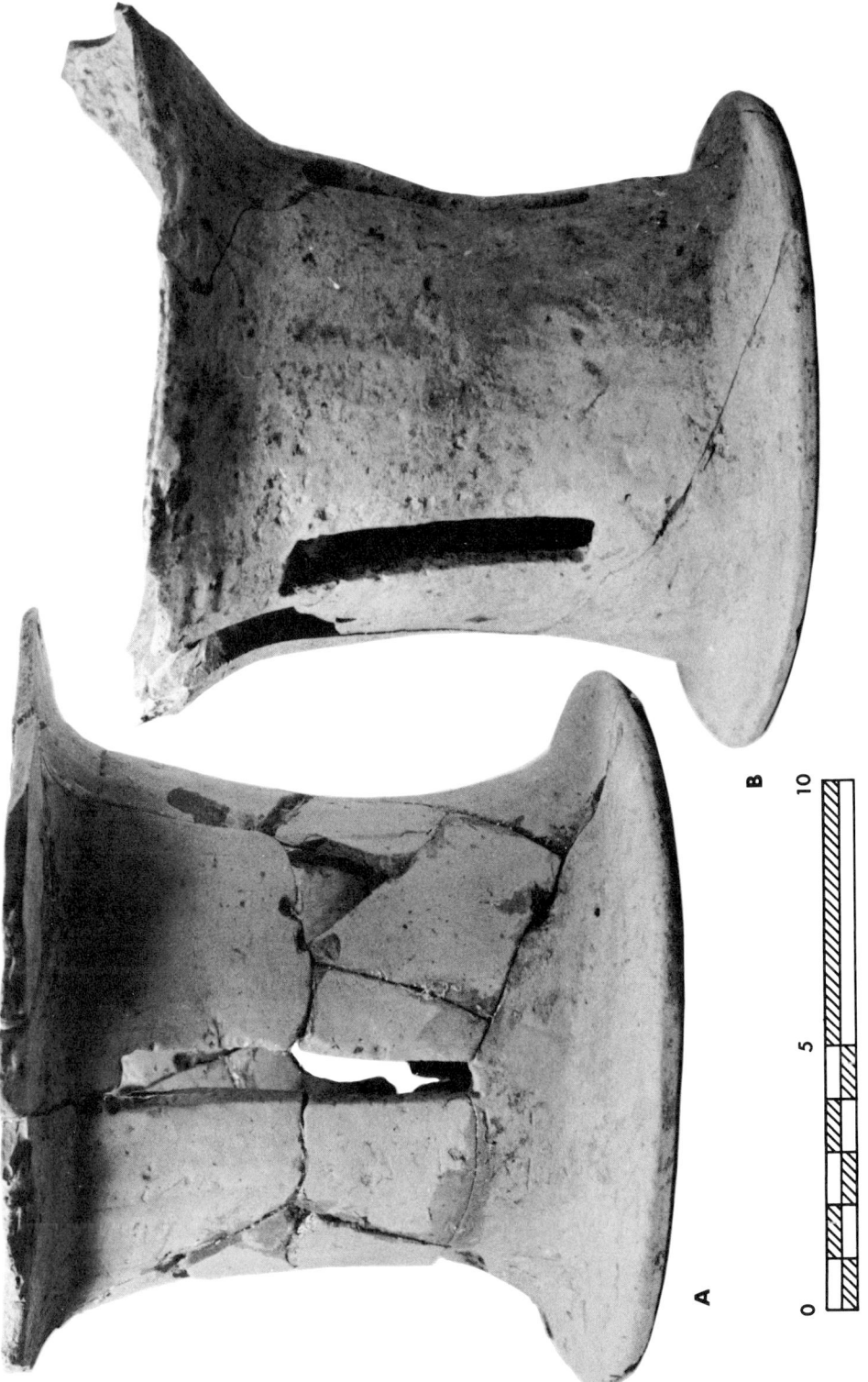

Sherds of Fine Red Ware Pedestals, Fengpitou

PLATE 29

SHERDS OF FINE RED WARE TOUS, FENGPITOU

A, P-W1-B2-L2c. *B*, P-E9-A2-L1f. *C*, P-W1-A1-L2b.
D, P-E8-A2-L2e. *E*, P-E3-B2-L2d. *F*, P-W1-A1-L2a.

Sherds of Fine Red Ware Tous, Fengpitou

PLATE 30

MISCELLANEOUS POTSHERDS OF THE FINE RED WARE,
FENGPITOU

A, Small bowl, P-E4-B1-L2a. *B*, Neck of jar, P-E9-
A2-198-cm below surface. *C*, Neck of jar, P-E3-B2-L2e.
D, Strap handle, V-W7-B2-L3a. *E*, *Ting* foot, V-E10-
B2-L1c. *F*, Loop handle, V-W3-A1-L3a. *G*, Figurine
with punctated design, top and side views, V-E10-B2-
L1c.

Miscellaneous Potsherds of the Fine Red Ware, Fengpitou

PLATE 31

Painted Pottery of Fengpitou: Bowls and Dishes

A, K-3-L1e. *B*, V-E10-B2-L1b. *C*, K-2-L3b. *D*, V-E4-A1A2-L1c. *E*, N-A-L2b. *F*, N-A-L2c. *G*, N-A-L2f. *H*, N-A-L2b. *I*, N-B-L2d. *J*, V-E10-A1-L1b. *K*, V-E10-A2-L1b. *L*, N-B-L2d. *M*, K-3-L3c. *N*, N-A-L2f. (*A*, *B*, *E*, *G*, *H*, *N*, views of both exterior, *left*, and interior, *right*; *C*, *D*, *F*, *I*, *J*, *K*, interior view; *L*, *M*, exterior view.)

Painted Pottery of Fengpitou: Bowls and Dishes

PLATE 32

Painted Pottery of Fengpitou: Beakers

A, N-A-L2f. *B*, N-A-L2f. *C*, K-3-L3i. *D*, K-3-L3e.
E, N-A-L2f. *F*, K-1-L1a. *G*, N-B-L2d. (*A*, *B*, *F*, *G*,
rim sherds; *C*, *D*, *E*, body sherds.)

Painted Pottery of Fengpitou: Beakers

PLATE 33

PAINTED POTTERY OF FENGPITOU: JARS

A, V-W7-B2-L2a. *B*, V-W3-B2-L2a. *C*, K-2-L3c.
D, V-E10-B2-L1b (views from top, *left*, and bottom,
right).

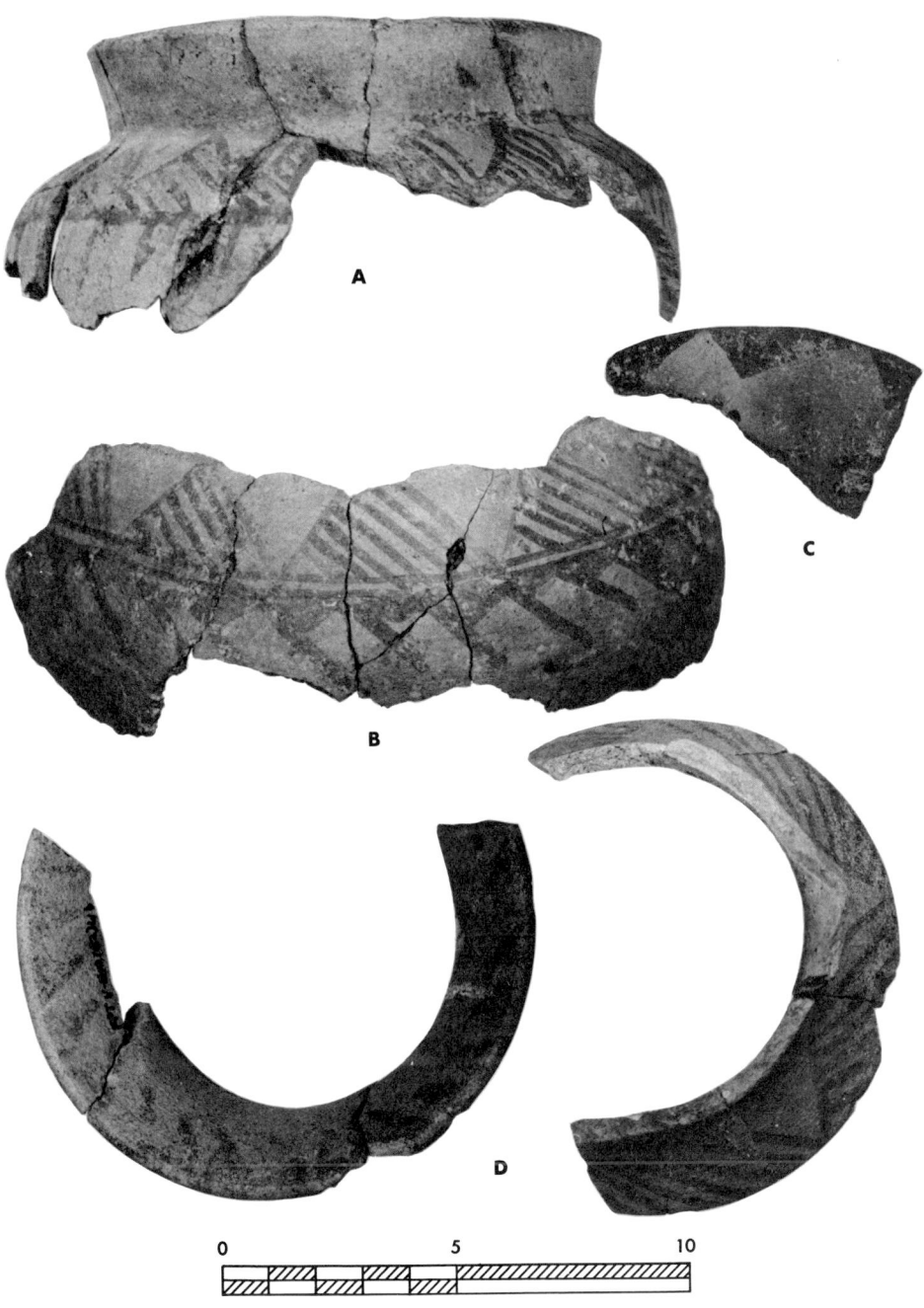

Painted Pottery of Fengpitou: Jars

PLATE 34

PAINTED POTTERY OF FENGPITOU: RIM SHERDS

A, N-A-L2b. *B*, N-sc. *C*, K-3-L2. *D*, K-3-L1d. *E*, N-sc. *F*, K-3-L2. *G*, K-3-L3c. (*A*, *B*, *D*, both exterior, *left*, and interior, *right; E*, exterior; *C*, *F*, *G*, interior.)

Painted Pottery of Fengpitou: Rim Sherds

PLATE 35

PAINTED POTTERY OF FENGPITOU: RIM SHERDS

A, K-3-L3a. *B*, K-3-L3c. *C*, K-3-L1e. *D*, K-3-L2. *E*, K-3-L1d. *F*, K-3-L3b. (*A*, *B*, *E*, *F*, both exterior, *left*, and interior, *right*; *C*, *D*, exterior.)

Painted Pottery of Fengpitou: Rim Sherds

PLATE 36

Painted Pottery of Fengpitou: Body Sherds

A, V-E10-A2-L1b (*two sherds on left*) and V-W7-B2-L2a (*sherd on right*). *B*, V-E10-A2-L1b. *C*, V-E10-B2-L1b. *D*, V-E10-A2-L1b. *E*, V-E10-A2-L1b. *F*, K-3-L3c. *G*, K-3-L3a. *H*, K-3-L3g.

Painted Pottery of Fengpitou: Body Sherds

PLATE 37

PAINTED POTTERY OF FENGPITOU: BODY SHERDS

A, K-3-L1b. *B*, K-3-L1c. *C*, K-3-L3a. *D*, K-3-L2. *E*, K-3-L2. *F*, K-3-L1e. *G*, K-3-L1e. *H*, K-3-L1c. *I*, K-3-L2. *J*, K-3-L1e. *K*, K-3-L2. *L*, N-B-L1d. *M*, K-3-L3a. *N*, K-3-L1. *O*, K-3-L1e.

Painted Pottery of Fengpitou: Body Sherds

PLATE 38

PAINTED POTTERY OF FENGPITOU: BODY SHERDS

A, V-W3-A2-L2b. *B*, N-sc. *C*, N-A-L2e. *D*, K-3-L1e.
E, N-sc. *F*, K-3-L2. *G*, K-3-L1f.

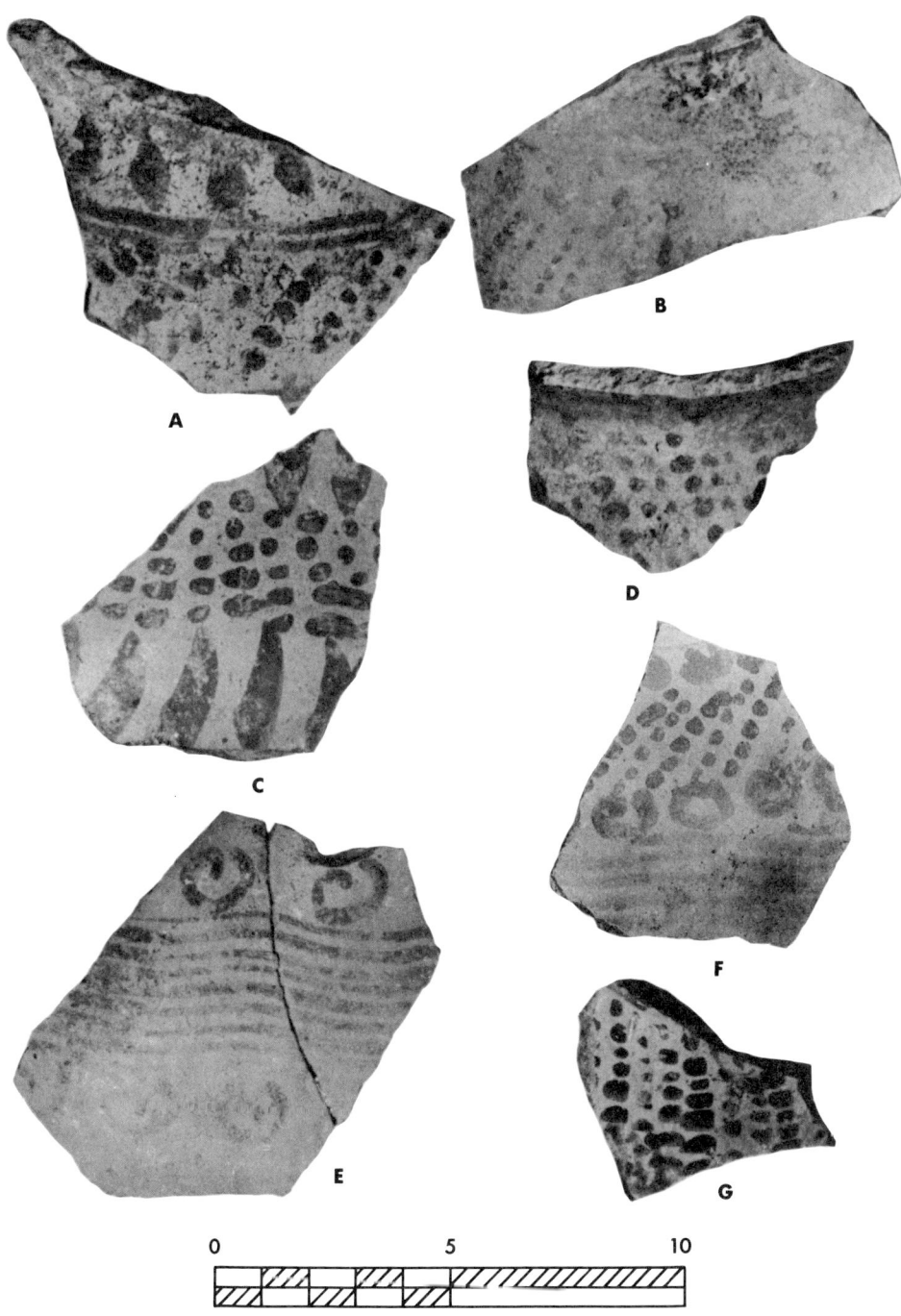

Painted Pottery of Fengpitou: Body Sherds

PLATE 39

PAINTED POTTERY OF FENGPITOU: BODY SHERDS

A, *B*, *D*, V-E10-A2-L1b. *C*, V-E10-A1-L1b. *E*, V-W7-B2-L2a. *F*, K-1-L3. *G*, *H*, K-3-L3b.

Painted Pottery of Fengpitou: Body Sherds

PLATE 40

PAINTED POTTERY OF FENGPITOU: BODY SHERDS

A, N-B-L2a. *B*, *D*, *E*, N-B-L2c. *C*, N-B-L2f. *F*, K-3-L3a. *G*, V-E10-A2-L1b. *H*, V-W3-B2-L2a. *I*, V-E10-B2-L1b.

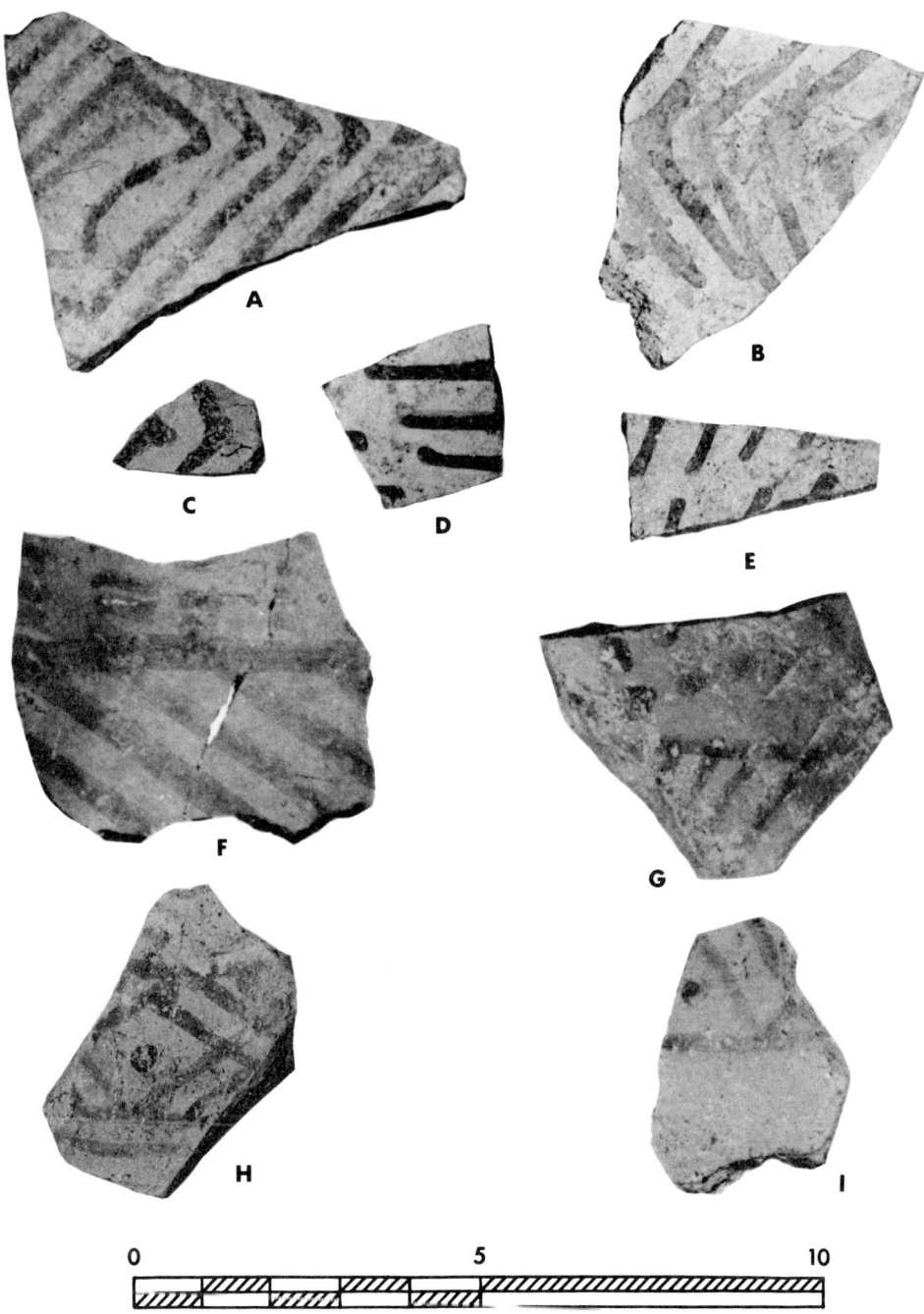

Painted Pottery of Fengpitou: Body Sherds

PLATE 41

PAINTED POTTERY OF FENGPITOU: RING FEET

A, *B*, V-E10-A2-L1b. *C*, K-1-L3a. *D*, K-1-L3. *E*, K-1-L3e.

Painted Pottery of Fengpitou: Ring Feet

PLATE 42

<small>Painted Pottery of Fengpitou: Ring Feet</small>

A, V-E4-A1A2-L1c. *B*, V-E4-A1-L1b. *C*, N-B-L2f.
D, V-W3-B2-L2a. *E*, K-3-L3d. *F*, V-W7-L1b.

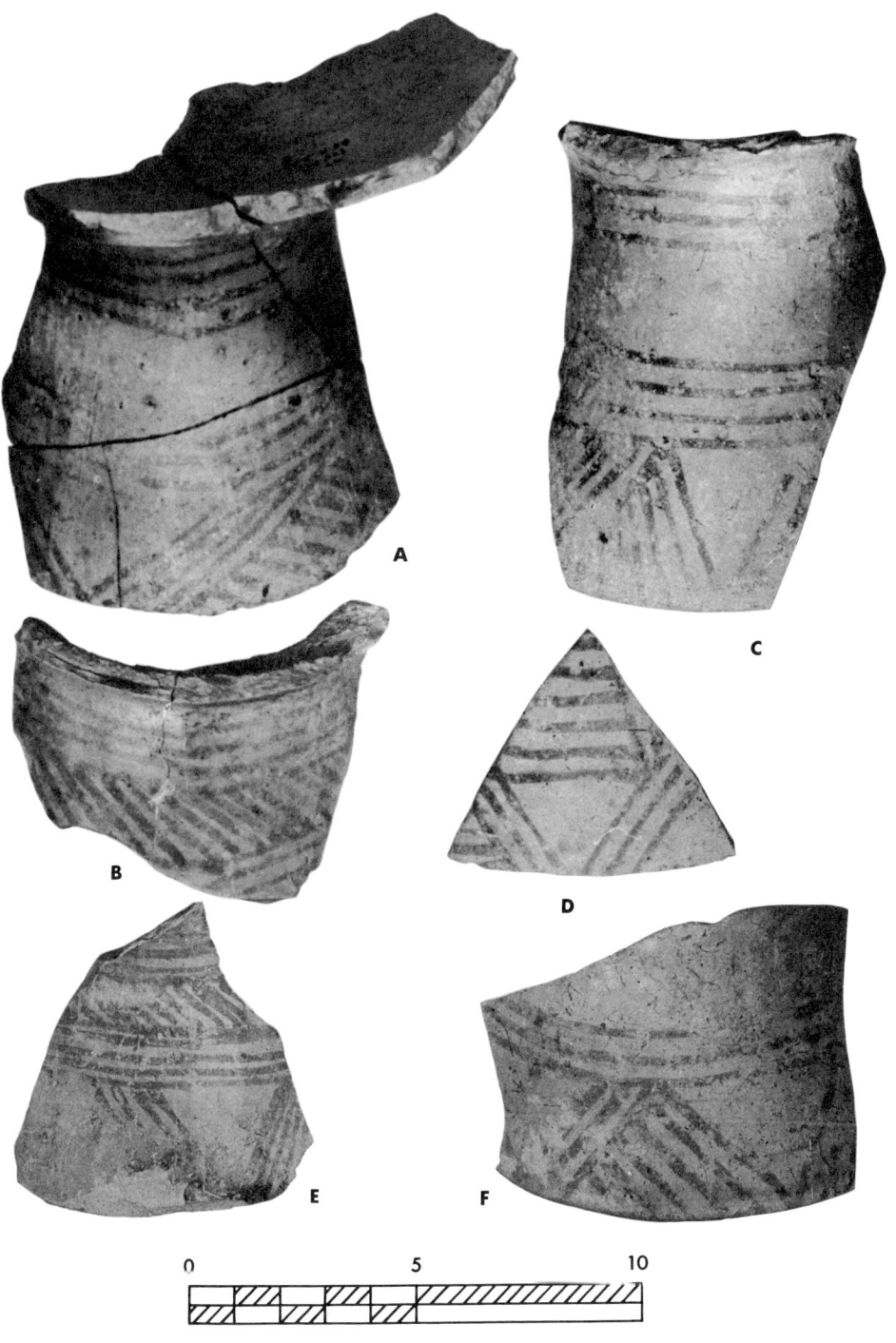

Painted Pottery of Fengpitou: Ring Feet

PLATE 43

PAINTED POTTERY OF FENGPITOU: RING FEET

A, V-W7-B1-L2a. *B*, N-A-L2e. *C*, K-3-L3c. *D*, N-A-L2c. *E*, N-sc. *F*, V-W3-B2-L2a. *G*, V-E10-A2-L1b. *H*, N-C-L1d.

Painted Pottery of Fengpitou: Ring Feet

PLATE 44

BLACK POTTERY OF FENGPITOU: POTS AND JARS

A, K-3-L3b. *B*, E-sc. *C*, M-sc. *D*, V-W3-A1-L2a.

Black Pottery of Fengpitou: Pots and Jars

PLATE 45

Black Pottery of Fengpitou: Bowls

A, K-3-L1f. *B*, K-3-L1b. *C*, E-sc. *D*, K-1-L1c. *E*, K-1-CL. *F*, N-B-L1d. *G*, K-3-L3f. *H*, K-1-L3a.

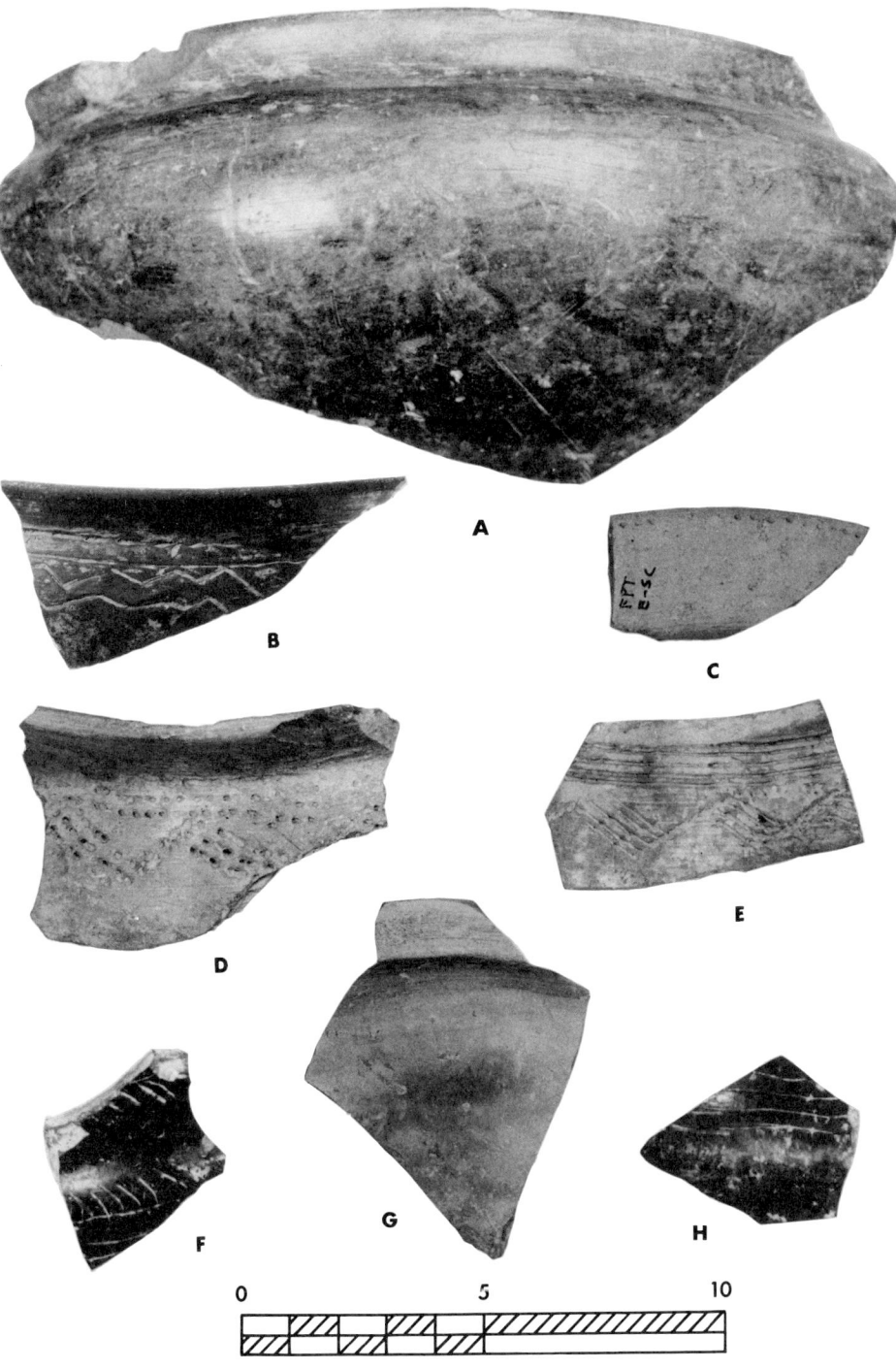

Black Pottery of Fengpitou: Bowls

PLATE 46

BLACK POTTERY OF FENGPITOU: BOWLS

A, N-B-L1d. *B*, N-C-L1d. *C*, K-1-L1a. *D*, K-3-L1c.
E, K-3-L1b. *F*, K-3-L3a. *G*, K-3-L3b. *H*, K-3-L3a.

Black Pottery of Fengpitou: Bowls

PLATE 47

A, V-E4-A1A2-L1c. *B*, V-E4-A2-L1c. *C*, V-W3-A1-L2a. *D*, V-E10-A2-L1b. *E*, V-E10-A2-L1b. *F*, K-3-L3b.

Black Pottery of Fengpitou: Beakers

PLATE 48

BLACK POTTERY OF FENGPITOU: BEAKERS WITH HORIZONTAL INCISIONS AND ENGRAVINGS

A, K-3-L3e. *B*, K-3-L3e. *C*, K-3-L2. *D*, N-B-L3b. *E*, K-3-L2. *F*, K-3-L3g.

Black Pottery of Fengpitou: Beakers with Horizontal Incisions and Engravings

PLATE 49

BLACK POTTERY OF FENGPITOU: BEAKERS WITH ZONAL
INCISIONS

A, B, C, H, M, K-1-L2. *D, L*, K-3-L1e. *E*, N-C-L1d.
F, N-B-L1d. *G*, K-3-L3a. *I*, P-sc. *J*, K-3-L1d. *K*, K-
1-L3b.

Black Pottery of Fengpitou: Beakers with Zonal Incisions

Black Pottery of Fengpitou: Feet

PLATE 51

SANDY RED WARE OF FENGPITOU: LIDS

A, K-3-L2. *B*, N-B-L2e. *C*, K-3-L3d. *D*, K-3-L3e.
E, K-3-L3d. *F*, K-3-L3b. *G*, K-3-L3c. *H*, P-E4-B2-L2c.

Sandy Red Ware of Fengpitou: Lids

PLATE 52

SANDY RED WARE OF FENGPITOU: JAR K-3.

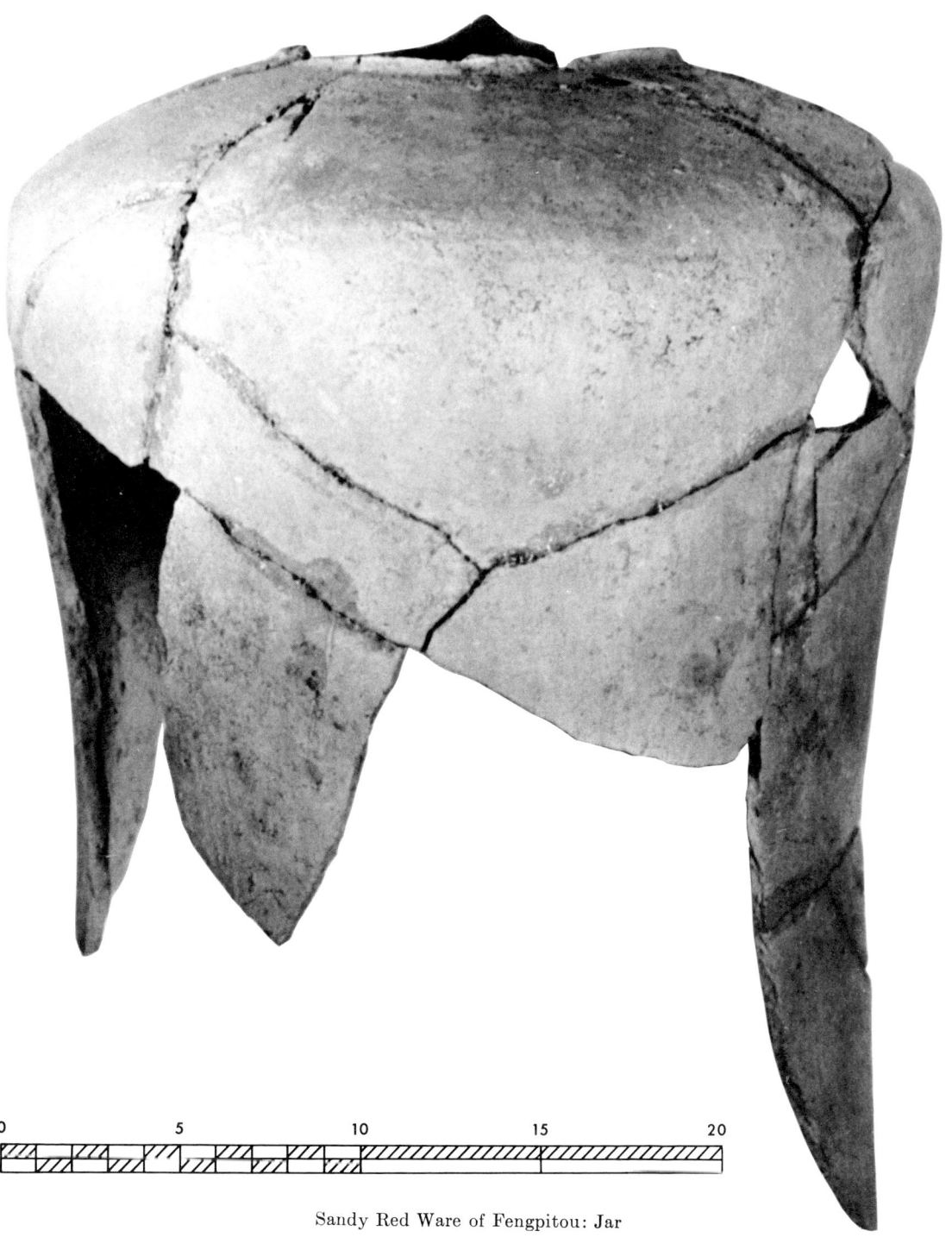

Sandy Red Ware of Fengpitou: Jar

PLATE 53

SANDY RED WARE OF FENGPITOU: INCISED RIMS OF
BOWLS, JARS, AND POTS

A, K-3-L1b. *B*, N-A-L1c. *C*, K-3-L1b. *D*, N-B-L1c.
E, K-2-CL. *F*, K-2-CL. *G*, K-3-L1b. *H*, K-2-L2c. *I*,
K-2-L2. *J*, N-B-L1d (exterior, *left*, and interior, *right*).
K, K-3-L1b (interior). *L*, K-3-L1b (interior). *M*, K-3-
L1b. *N*, K-3-CL (interior). *O*, K-3-L3b. *P*, K-1-L1a.
Q, N-AB-L1b. *R*, K-3-L3c. (*A-I* bowls; *J-R* jars and
pots.)

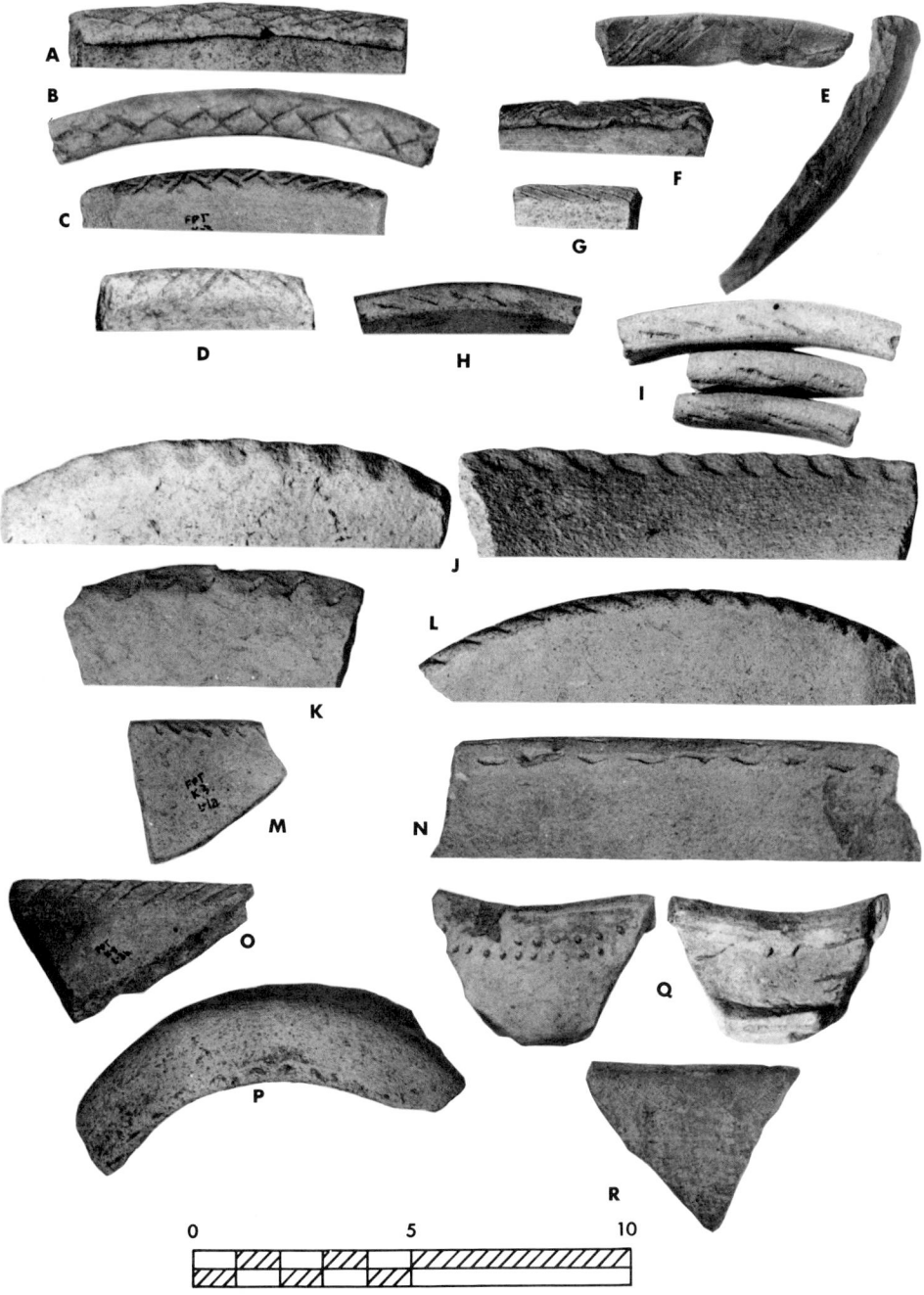

Sandy Red Ware of Fengpitou: Incised Rims of Bowls, Jars, and Pots

PLATE 54

SANDY RED WARE OF FENGPITOU: RIM SHERDS WITH
INCISED SIGNS

A, K-3-L1b. *B*, K-3-L1b. *C*, K-1-L1. *D*, K-3-L3b.
E, K-3-CL. *F*, K-3-L3b. *G*, K-2-L2a. *H*, E-sc. *I*, N-A-
L2b. *J*, K-3-L3b. *K*, K-3-L1b. (*F*, *H*, *J*, signs on the
exterior of rim; all others on the interior of rim.)

Sandy Red Ware of Fengpitou: Rim Sherds with Incised Signs

PLATE 55

SANDY RED WARE OF FENGPITOU: BOWLS

A, K-3-L1c. *B*, E-sc. *C*, K-3-L1c.

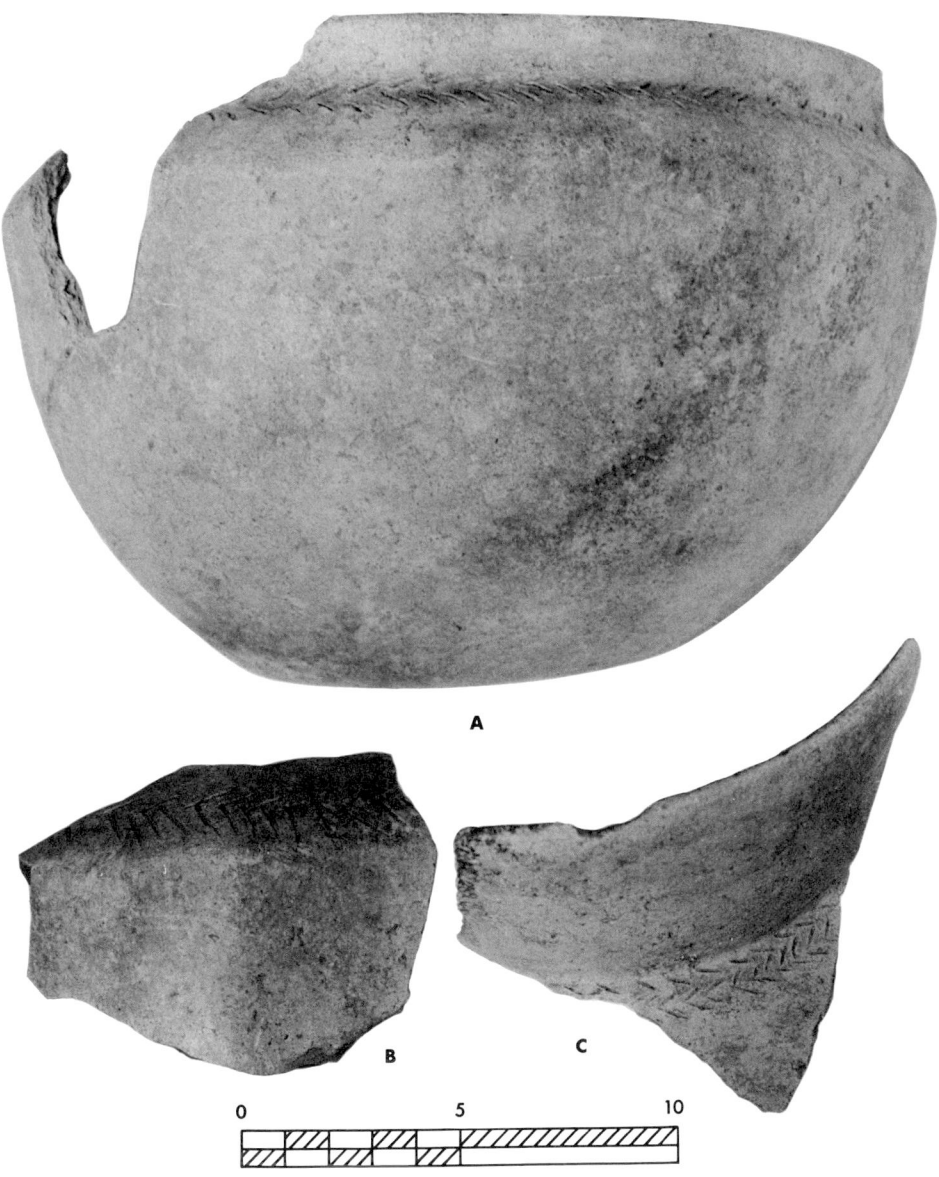

Sandy Red Ware of Fengpitou: Bowls

PLATE 56

SANDY RED WARE OF FENGPITOU: INCISED AND IMPRESSED SHERDS

A, K-3-L1b. *B*, K-3-L1d. *C*, V-W3-A1-L3a (check impressed). *D*, K-3-L3c. *E*, K-2-L2b. *F*, K-3-L1b. *G*, K-3-CL. *H*, K-3-L1e. *I*, K-3-L1b. *J*, K-3-L1b. *K*, E-sc. *L*, K-3-L1b.

Sandy Red Ware of Fengpitou: Incised and Impressed Sherds

PLATE 57

Sandy Red Ware of Fengpitou: Beakers, Handle, and Legs

A, U-sc. *B*, K-3-L3b. *C*, K-3-L1e. *D*, N-A-L1c. *E*, N-B-L1c. *F*, N-B-L1c. *G*, U-sc. *H*, K-3-L3e. *I*, K-1-L1b. *J*, K-1-L1.

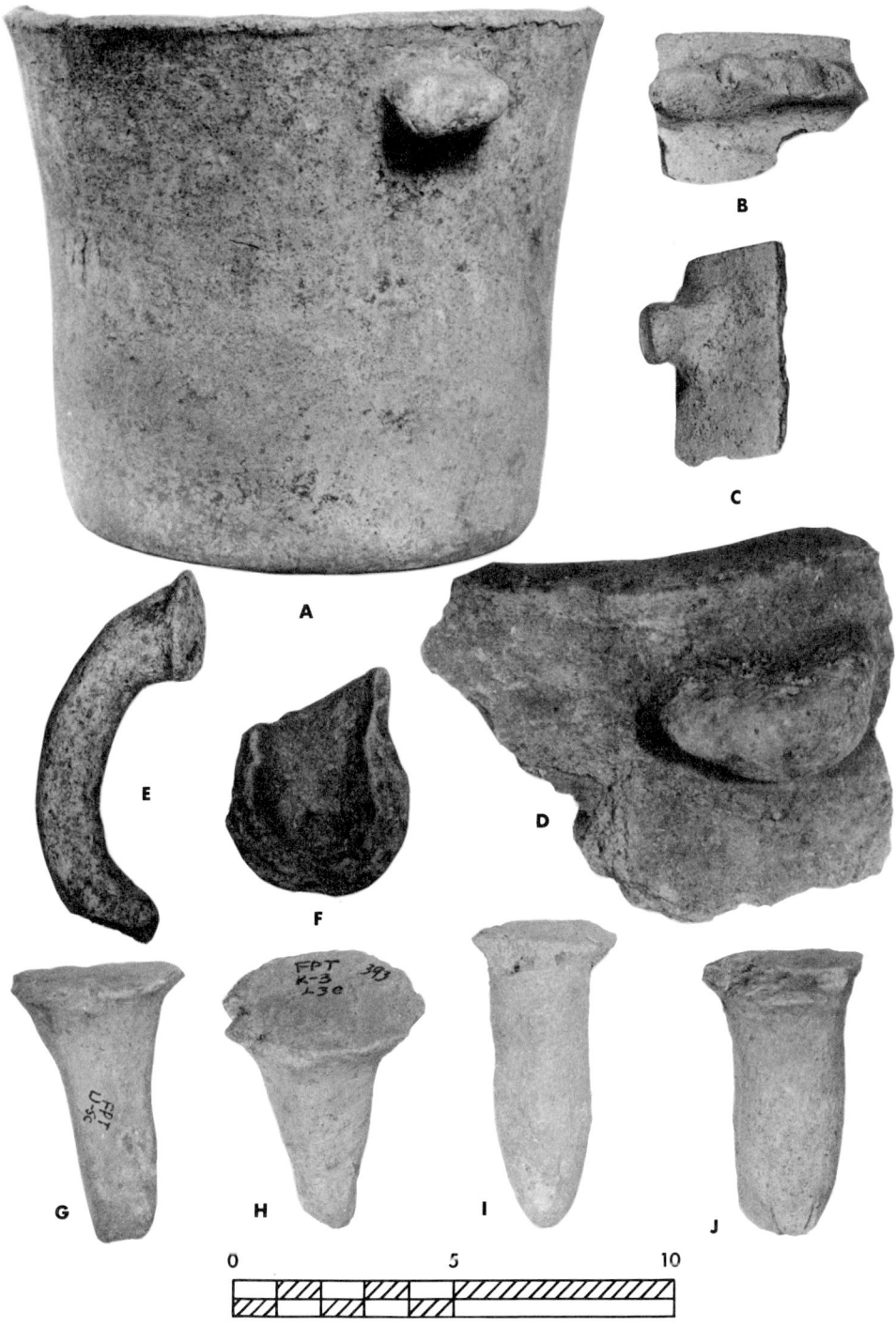

Sandy Red Ware of Fengpitou: Beakers, Handle, and Legs

PLATE 58

SANDY GRAY WARE OF FENGPITOU: LIDS

A, N-A-L2b. *B*, P-sc. *C*, N-B-L2b. *D*, K-3-L3e.

Sandy Gray Ware of Fengpitou: Lids

PLATE 59

A, N-B-L3a. *B*, V-W7-B1-L2a. *C*, E-sc. *D*, K-1-CL.
E, N-B-L2gs.

Sandy Gray Ware of Fengpitou: Impressed Pottery

PLATE 60

SANDY GRAY WARE OF FENGPITOU: PLAIN POTTERY

A. V-W7-B1-L2a. *B.* V-W3-L2.

Sandy Gray Ware of Fengpitou: Plain Pottery

PLATE 61

SANDY GRAY WARE OF FENGPITOU: POTS, JARS, AND BOWLS

A, E-sc. *B*, sc. *C*, K-1-CL. *D*, K-3-L3c. *E*, sc. *F*, K-3-L1e. *G*, K-3-L2. *H*, K-3-L1e.

Sandy Gray Ware of Fengpitou: Pots, Jars, and Bowls

PLATE 62

SANDY GRAY WARE OF FENGPITOU: INCISED POTTERY

A–E, *G*, E-sc. *F*, K-3-L1d. *H*, *L*, K-3-L1e. *I*, K-1-L1a.
J, sc. *K*, K-3-CL.

Sandy Gray Ware of Fengpitou: Incised Pottery

PLATE 63

A, V-W3-A2-L3a. *B*, U-sc. *C*, K-3-L3a. *D*, V-sc. *E*, V-E10-B2-L1c. *F*, S-E7-A1-L2b. *G*, K-3-L3b. *H*, V-E10-A2-L1b. *I*, P-E3-L2. *J*, V-W3-B2-L3a. *K*, S-W6-1. *L*, S-W6-B1-L2. *M*, V-E10-A1-L1b. *N*, S-W6-A2-L2. *O*, V-sc. *P*, N-A-L2a. *Q*, U-sc. *R*, V-E10-B1-L1b. *S*, U-sc. *T*, V-E10-B2-L1b. *U*, K-3-L3a. *V*, K-3-L3b. *W*, P-E4-B2-L2c. *X*, K-2-L3. *Y*, P-W3-A2-L2b. *Z*, V-W9-A2B2-L1b. (*A-D*, spindle whorls; *E*, clay object; *Q*, clay tube; *F*, *G*, shell rings; *H*, bone ring; *I-L*, stone rings; *M-P*, *R-Z*, clay rings.)

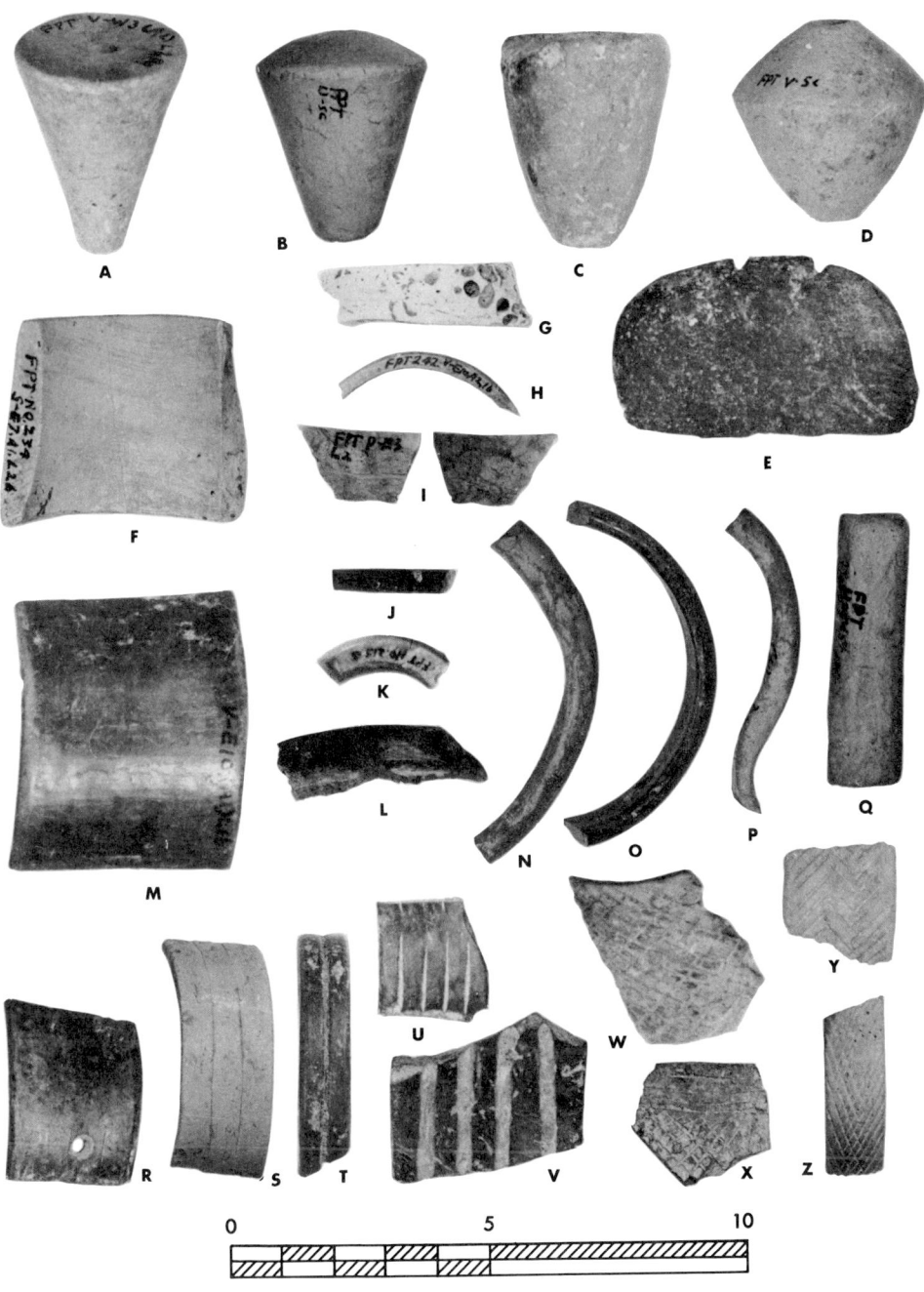

Clay Spindle Whorls, Bracelets, and Other Objects, Fengpitou

PLATE 64

A, Clay tube, probably bracelet, K-3-L1b. *B*, Clay tube, K-1-L1a. *C*, Clay spindle whorl with pierced design, P-E4-B2-L2c. *D*, Perforated shell disk, V-E10-A2-L1b. *E*, *F*, Worked antlers (*E*, S-sc; F, V-E9-A1-L1b).

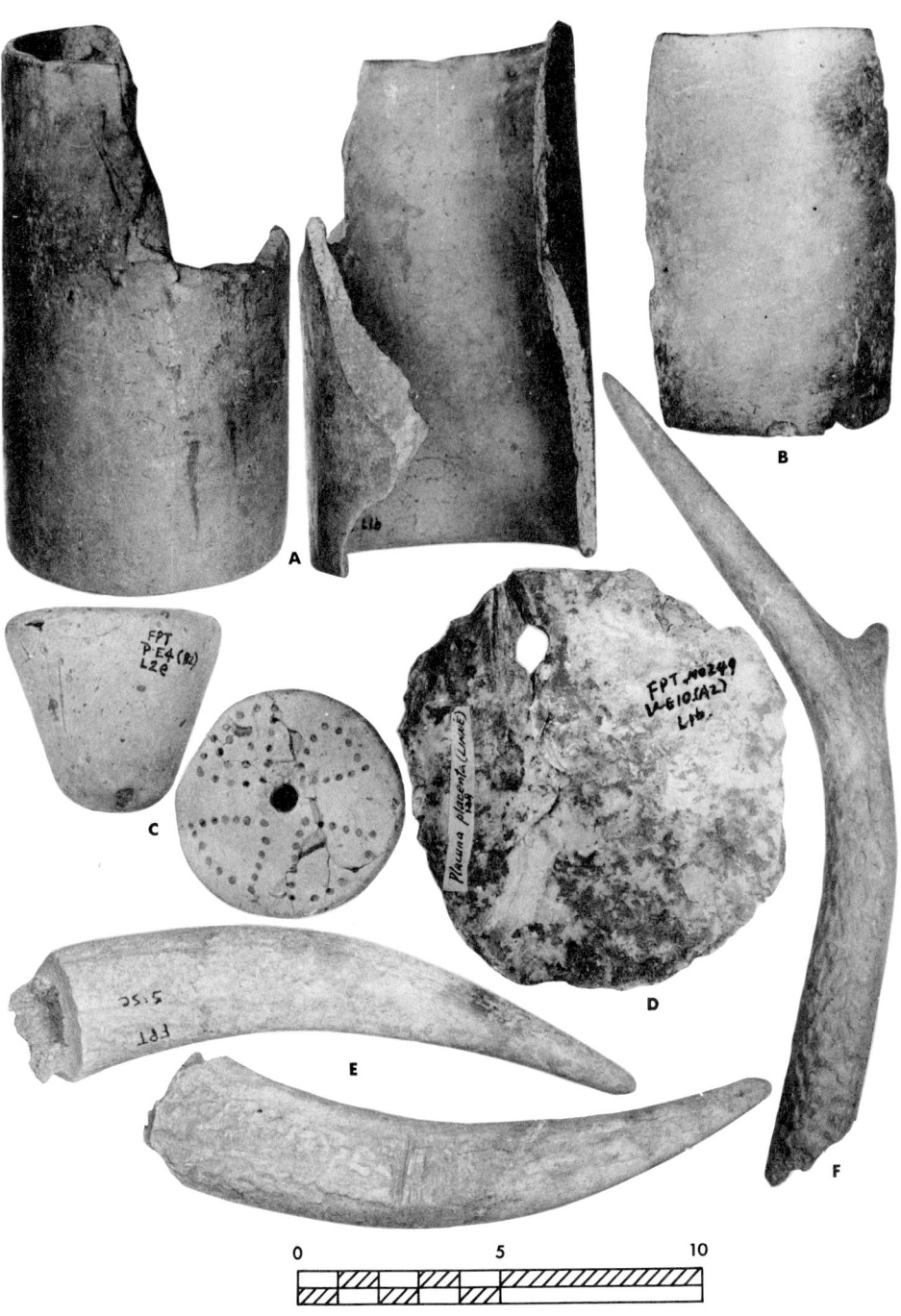

Clay, Bone, Shell, and Antler Objects, Fengpitou

PLATE 65

PENDANTS AND DISKS, FENGPITOU

A, V-E10-B2-L1b. *B*, K-1-L2. *C*, Clay, V-E10-A2-L1c. *D*, Clay, P-E8-A2-L1. *E*, Shell, S-E7-A2-L2a. *F*, Shell, K-sc. *G*, V-E4-A1-L1b. *H*, V-E4-A1-L1c. *I*, P-E8-B2-L1. *J*, V-E9-A1-L1b. *K*, P-E8-A1-L2e. *L*, P-E3-L2. *M*, P-E9-A1B1-L2b.

Pendants and Disks, Fengpitou

PLATE 66

A, K-1-L3. *B*, K-2-L1c. *C*, K-2-L2a. *D*, K-1-L1a. *E*, K-2-L1e. *F*, K-1-L3. *G*, V-W3-L1a. *H*, S-E7-L1.

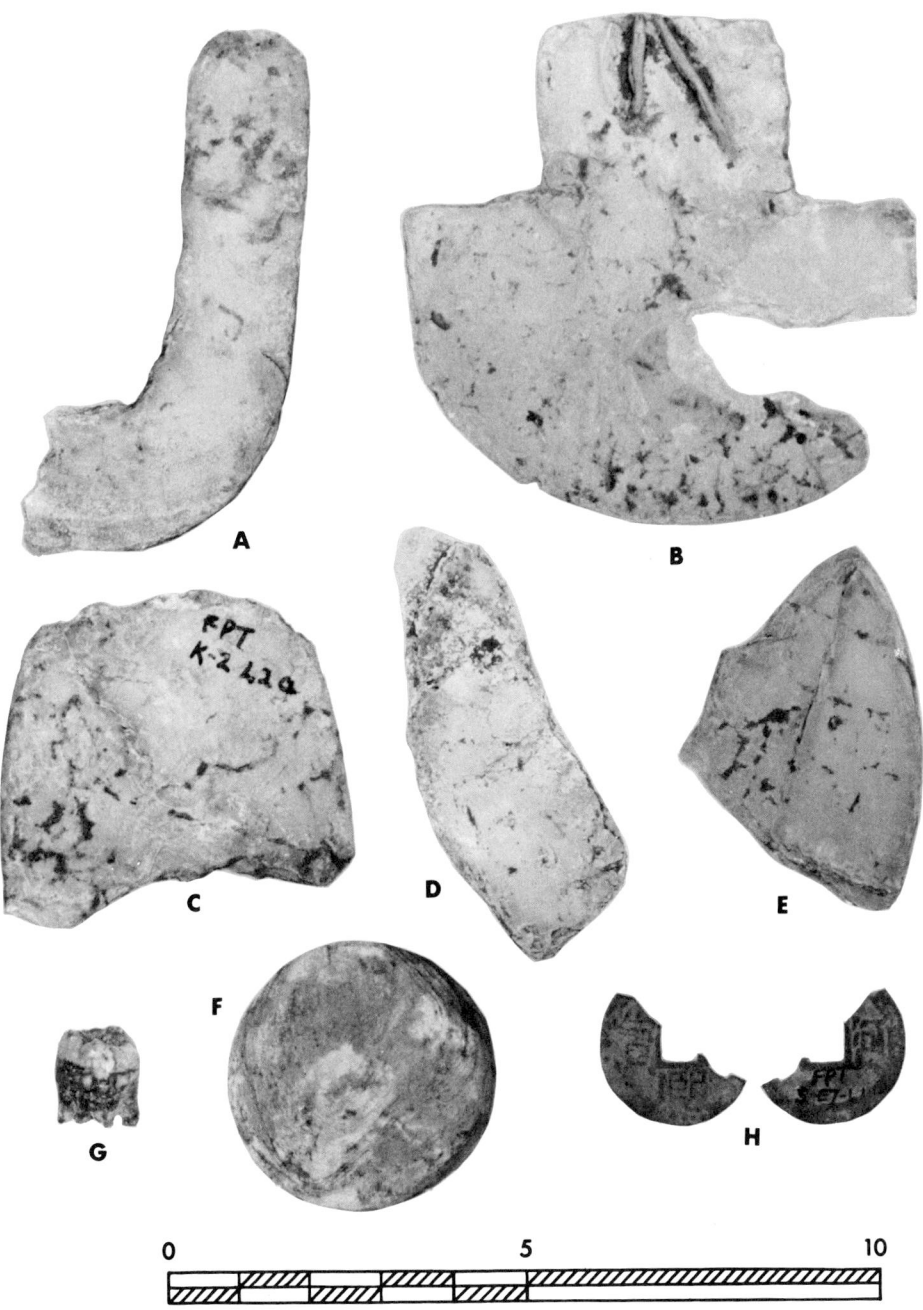

Shell Objects, Human Tooth, and Coin, Fengpitou

PLATE 67

Bone Points, Fengpitou

A, S-E7-B2-L2b. *B*, K-1-L1a. *C*, N-A-L2f. *D*, V-E10-B2-L1c. *E*, V-sc. *F*, K-1-L1. *G*, K-3-L1e. *H*, K-sc. *I*, K-1-L3. *J*, V-E4-A2-L1b. *K*, V-E10-A2-L1b. *L*, S-E7-B2-L2a. *M*, S-E1-B2-L2. *N*, K-1-L3b. *O*, K-3-L1d. *P*, V-E10-A2-L1b. *Q*, N-A-L1d. *R*, V-E4-B1-L1b.

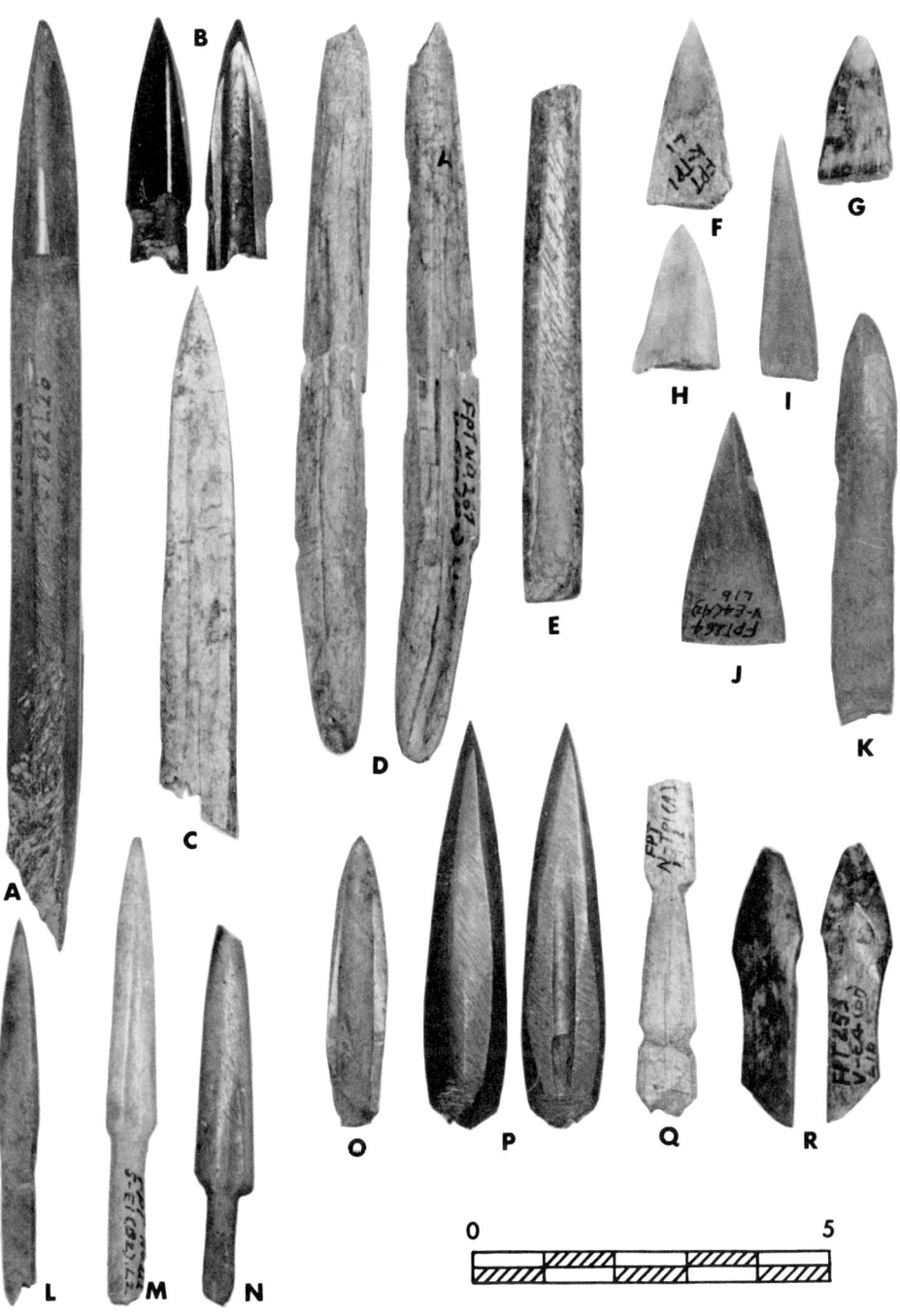

Bone Points, Fengpitou

PLATE 68

BONE AND ANTLER WEDGES, NEEDLES, AND AWLS,
FENGPITOU

A, S-E1-B1-L2a. *B*, B-E10-B1-L1c. *C*, N-A-L1d. *D*,
K-2-L2b. *E*, S-E7-A1-L2a. *F*, K-1-L3b. *G*, S-E7-B2-L2b
H, K-1-L1. *I*, N-A-L1c. *J*, S-E1-L2. *K*, K-1-L1a. *L*,
K-1-L2a. *M*, K-1-L1. *N*, K-1-L1. *O*, S-sc. *P*, K-3-L3f.
Q, K-1-CL. *R*, K-3-L1f. *S*, V-E9-A1-L1b. *T*, V-E4-A1-
L1b. *U*, V-E10-A2-L1b. *V*, N-B-L1c. *W*, S-E7-A1-L2.
X, S-E7-A1-L2a. *Y*, V-E10-A2-L1b. *Z*, N-A-L1c. *a*,
S-sc. *b*, V-E4-A2-L1b. *c*, V-W7-B1-L2a. *d*, N-B-L2a.
e, N-B-L2d. *f*, N-B-L2bs. *g*, V-E9-B1-L1b. *h*, V-E9-
A1-L1b. *i*, S-E1-L1. *j*, V-E10-A2-L1b. *k*, V-W3-A1-L3a.
l, S-E1-B2-L2. *m*, V-E10-A2-L1b. *n*, K-3-L2. *o*, K-1-L1.
p, U-sc. *q*, K-3-L3c. *r*, S-sc. *s*, S-E7-A1-L2.

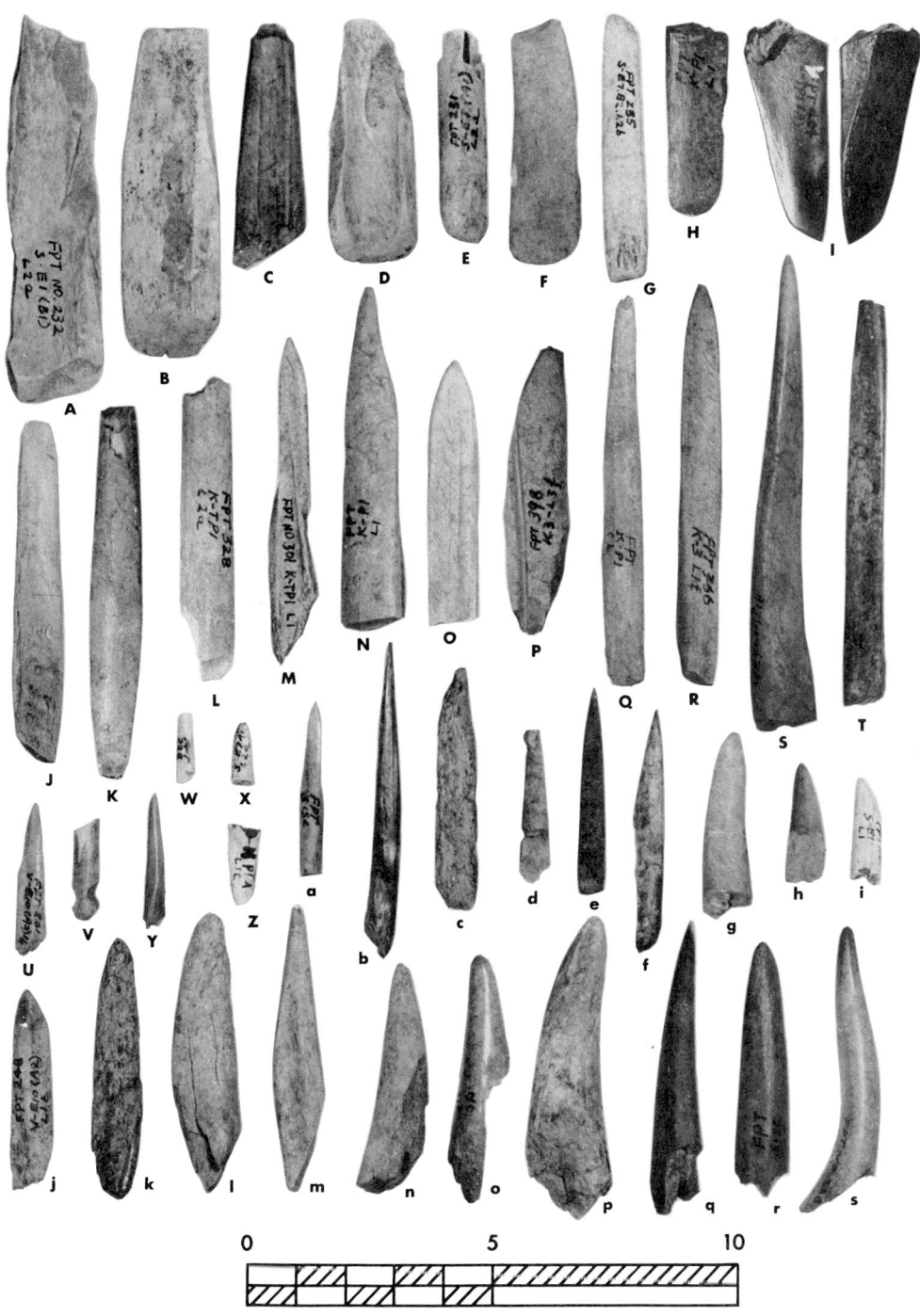

Bone and Antler Wedges, Needles, and Awls, Fengpitou

PLATE 69

Stone Hoe-Axes of Fengpitou: Spatula-Shaped

A, E-sc. *B*, K-1-L2b. *C*, N-sc. *D*, K-3-L1f. *E*, P-E9-A1-L2d.

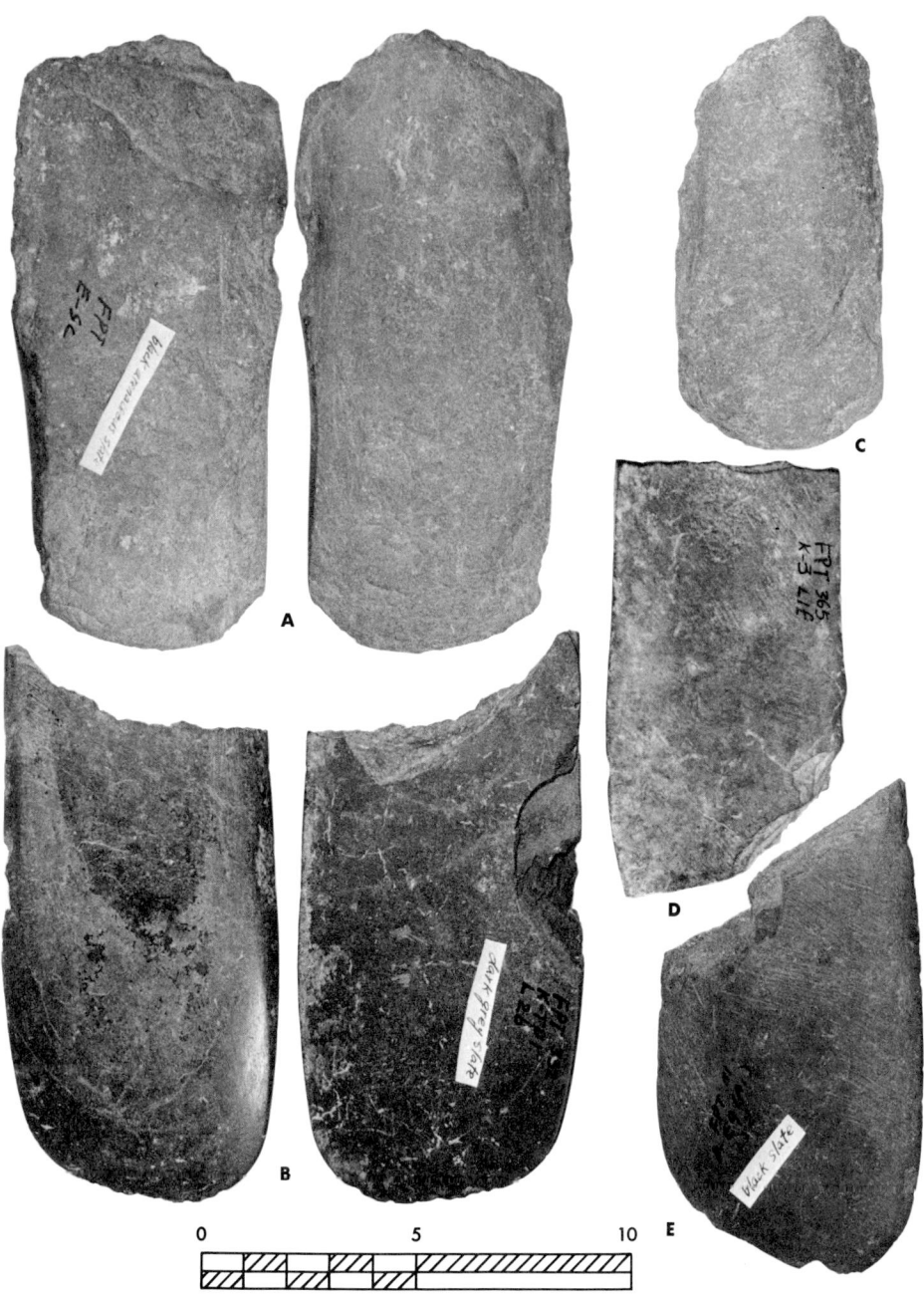

Stone Hoe-axes of Fengpitou: Spatula-shaped

PLATE 70

STONE HOE-AXES OF FENGPITOU: CHIPPED, LARGE, AND
PERFORATED TYPES

A, E-sc. *B*, V-E5-A2-L1a. *C*, P-E3-L2a. *D*, P-W4-A2-
L2b. *E*, N-A-L1b. *F*, U-sc.

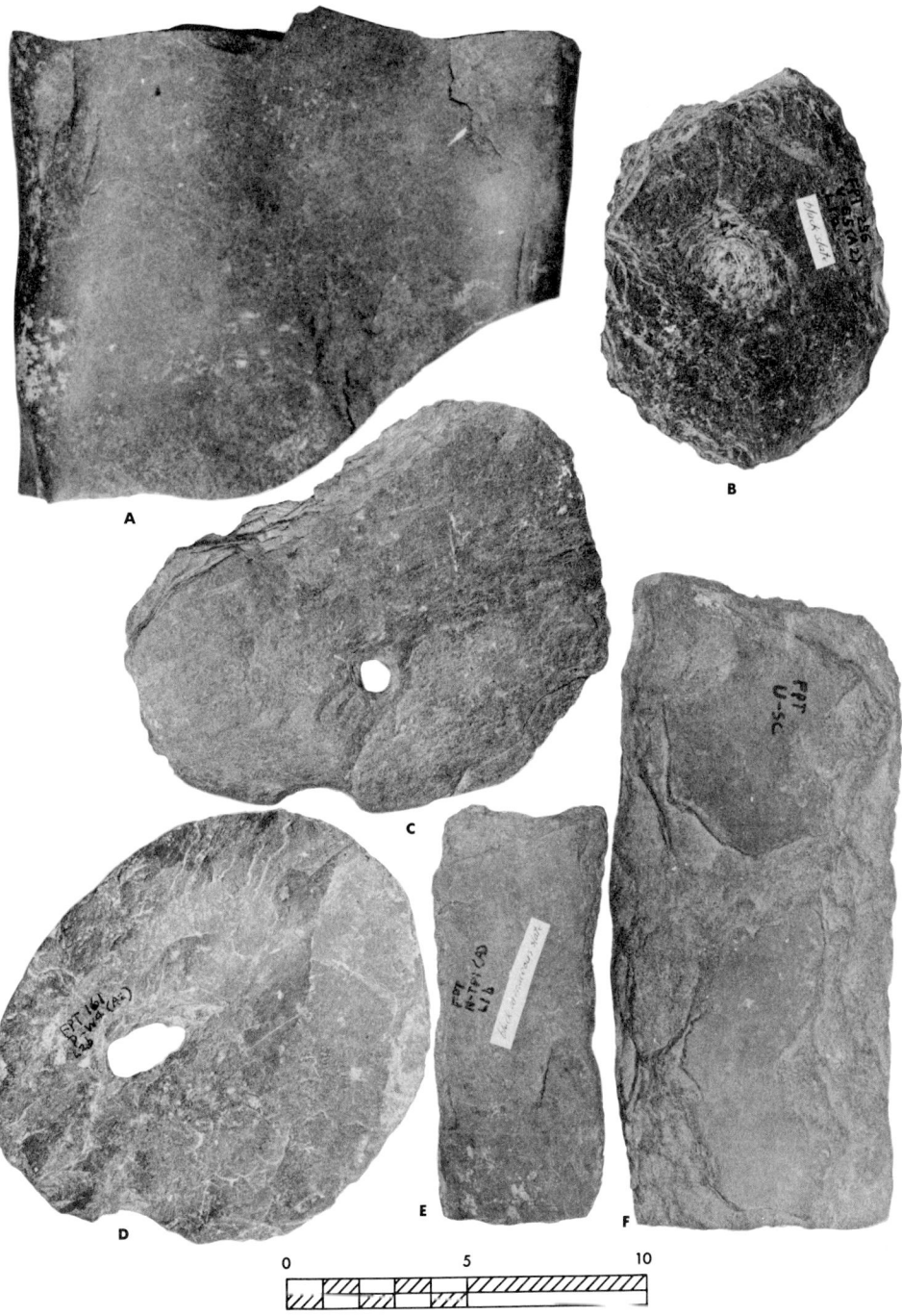

Stone Hoe-axes of Fengpitou: Chipped, Large, and Perforated Types

PLATE 71

Basalt Hoe-Axes, Fengpitou

A, sc. *B*, P-E3-L2a. *C*, V-W7-B1-L2c. *D*, P-E2-L2.
E, P-E9-A1-L2a. *F*, P-W3-A2-L2b. *G*, P-E2-B2-L2a.
H, E-sc.

Basalt Hoe-axes, Fengpitou

PLATE 72

SLATE AND BASALT HOE-AXES, FENGPITOU

A, V-E4-A2-L1d. *B*, P-E4-B1-L2b. *C*, V-W7-A2-L3a. *D*, N-B-L2b. *E*, K-1-L3b. *F*, K-3-L3d. *G*, P-E3-L1. *H*, U-sc.

Slate and Basalt Hoe-axes, Fengpitou

PLATE 73

BOOT-SHAPED KNIFE, FENGPITOU

A, Possible mounting device for the boot-shaped knife, Taiwan University collection, no. 2618. *B*, P-E4-B2-L2b (shaft) and P-E5-A2-L2c (blade).

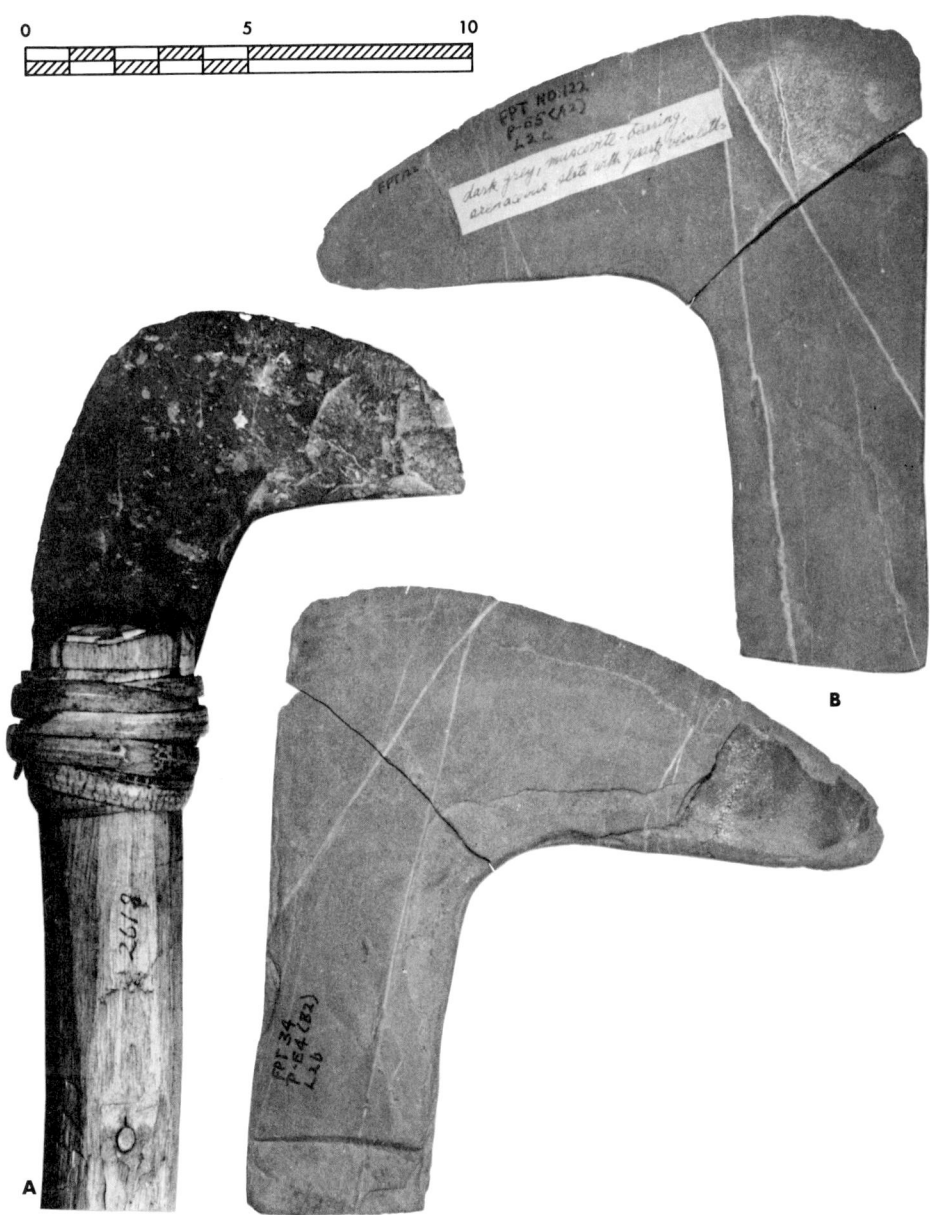

Boot-shaped Knife, Fengpitou

PLATE 74

Stone Adzes, Fengpitou

A, P-E5-B1-L2a. *B*, S-sc. *C*, K-1-L3. *D*, K-1-L3b.
E, U-sc. *F*, U-sc. *G*, P-E8-A1-L2c. *H*, P-W3-B2-L2c.
I, P-W3-A1-L2c. *J*, V-W7-B2-L3a. *K*, K-1-L1a.

Stone Adzes, Fengpitou

PLATE 75

A, P-E3-A2-L2d. *B*, P-E5-A2-L2d. *C*, V-E10-A2-L1c. *D*, P-E5-B1-L2a. *E*, K-3-L3b. *F*, P-W3-B1-L2b. *G*, N-B-L2d. *H*, K-3-L3b. *I*, U-sc. *J*, N-B-L3b. *K*, K-3-L1e. *L*, S-W6-B1-L2. *M*, P-E4-B2-L2a.

Small Stone Adzes and Chisels, Fengpitou

PLATE 76

Stone Knives, Fengpitou

A, V-E10-A2-L1d. *B*, K-3-L1e. *C*, P-W3-A1-L2c. *D*, P-E8-B1-L2c. *E*, P-E3-A2-L2e. *F*, S-sc. *G*, V-sc. *H*, N-B-L1c. *I*, U-sc. *J*, N-B-L1b. *K*, P-E2-B2-L1b. *L*, V-W3-B2-L2a. *M*, P-W3-B2-L2b. *N*, V-W7-B1-L3a. *O*, R-sc. P, U-sc. *Q*, V-W7-L1a.

Stone Knives, Fengpitou

PLATE 77

Stone Arrowheads, Fengpitou

A, P-E4-B1-L2c. *B*, N-B-L3b. *C*, B-1. *D*, Q-sc. *E*, P-E4-B2-L2c. *F*, S-E7-A1-L2. *G*, P-E3-L2. *H*, K-3-L1d. *I*, B-1-L8. *J*, S-E7-B1-L2a. *K*, B-1. *L*, P-E4-B1-L2a. *M*, K-3-L1. *N*, K-sc. *O*, K-3-L1d. *P*, P-W7-A2-L2b. *Q*, K-3-L1d. *R*, sc. *S*, P-E9-A1-L2bn. *T*, K-3-L1e. *U*, U-sc. *V*, P-W1-B1-L2c. *W*, S-sc. *X*, S-W6-L1. *Y*, V-sc. *Z*, N-B-L2d. *a*, N-B-L1d. *b*, S-E-L1. *c*, P-sc. *d*, K-1-L1a. *e*, S-W6-L2.

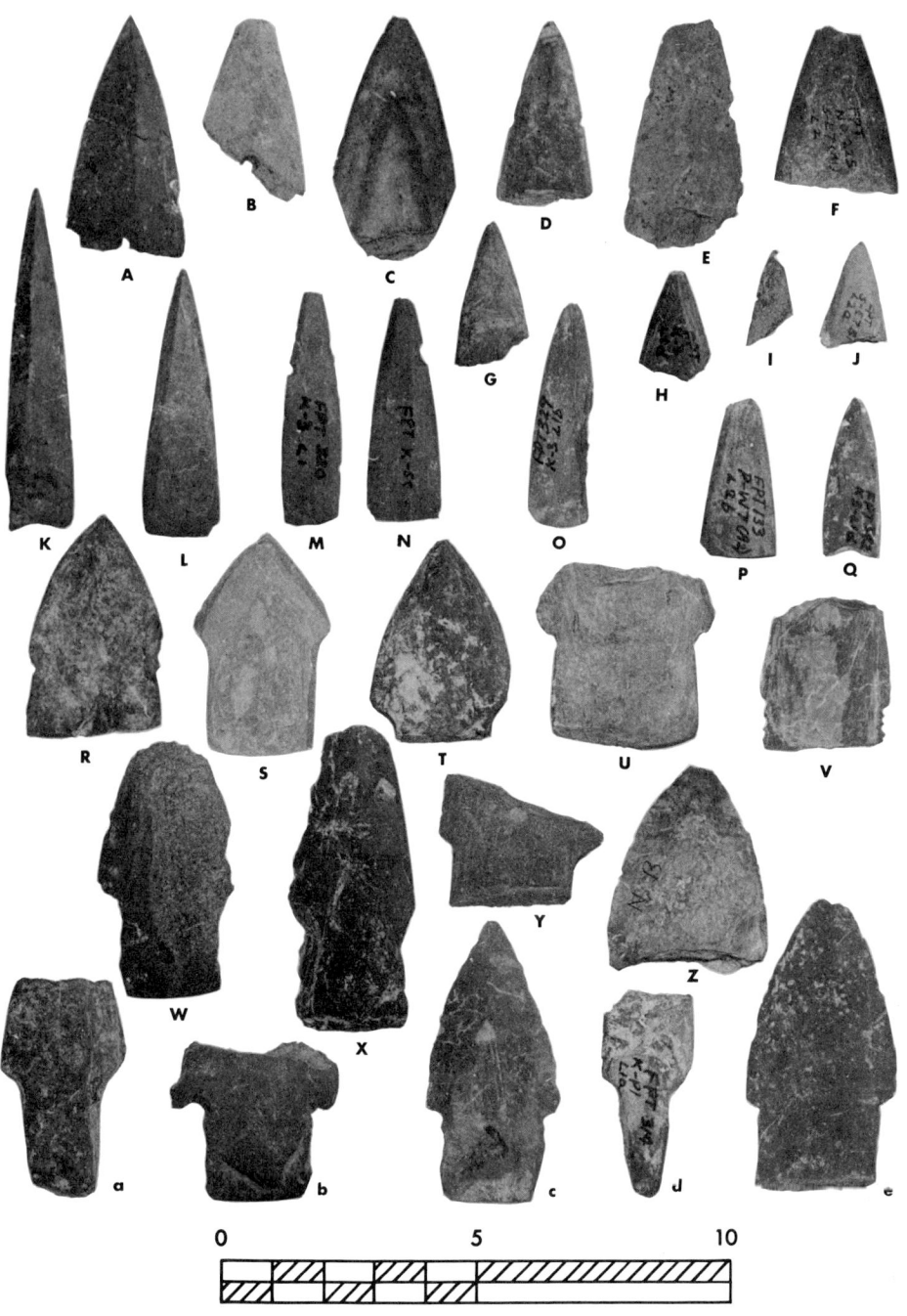

Stone Arrowheads, Fengpitou

PLATE 78

STONE DAGGERS AND HALBERDS, FENGPITOU

A, N-sc. *B*, K-3-L1e. *C*, K-1-L2b. *D*, V-W3-A2-L3a.
E, K-3-L1. *F*, V-W3-B2-L2a. *G*, K-1-L1.

Stone Daggers and Halberds, Fengpitou

PLATE 79

STONE SPEARHEADS, GRINDING STONE, AND WAISTED
PEBBLES, FENGPITOU

A, V-E10-B2-L1e. *B*, B-1. *C*, E-sc. *D*, K-1-L1. *E*, N-B-L2d. *F*, P-W4-A2-L1. *G*, Q-sc. *H*, V-sc. *I*, P-sc. *J*, U-sc. *K*, E-sc.

Stone Spearheads, Grinding Stone, and Waisted Pebbles, Fengpitou

PLATE 80

YÜAN-SHAN WARE OF TAPENKENG: LIDS

A, Stone lid, V-7-d1-6. *B*, X-1-aO-7. *C*, VIII-1-a1-6.
D, VIII-1-d4-6. *E*, X-1-b4-5. *F*, X-1-c4-7. *G*, VIII-1-
a2-8.

Yüan-shan Ware of Tapenkeng: Lids

PLATE 81

YÜAN-SHAN WARE OF TAPENKENG AND YÜAN-SHAN
SHELLMOUND: RIM SHERDS

A, Yüan-shan Shellmound, Taita collection. *B*, V-9-2. *C*, VI-2-c6-4. *D*, VI-2-b3-5. *E*, V-7-c2-11. *F*, VIII-1-c2-7. *G*, X-1-a4-3.

Yüan-shan Ware of Tapenkeng and Yüan-shan Shellmound: Rim Sherds

PLATE 82

Yüan-shan Ware of Tapenkeng: Decorated Rim
Sherds

A, VIII-1-d4-5. *B*, VI-1-a4-12. *C*, VI-1-c3-11. *D*, X-1-b4-5. *E*, VI-2-a1-6. *F*, VI-2-a1-6. *G*, X-1-a1-4. *H*, V-9-2. *I*, V-7-1. *J*, X-1-b3-9. *K*, VI-1-c1-13.

Yüan-shan Ware of Tapenkeng: Decorated Rim Sherds

PLATE 83

A, V-7-b1-3. *B*, IX-2-c1-5. *C*, VI-1-b2-9. *D*, VI-1-d3-10. *E*, VIII-1-b1-5. *F*, Hsia-p'u, sc. *G*, VI-2-a3-4. *H*, sc. *I*, IV-8-d4-2. *J*, VI-1-c5-7. *K*, IV-9-b4-8. *L*, VI-1-b2-1. *M*, VI-1-b1-13. *N*, V-7-4.

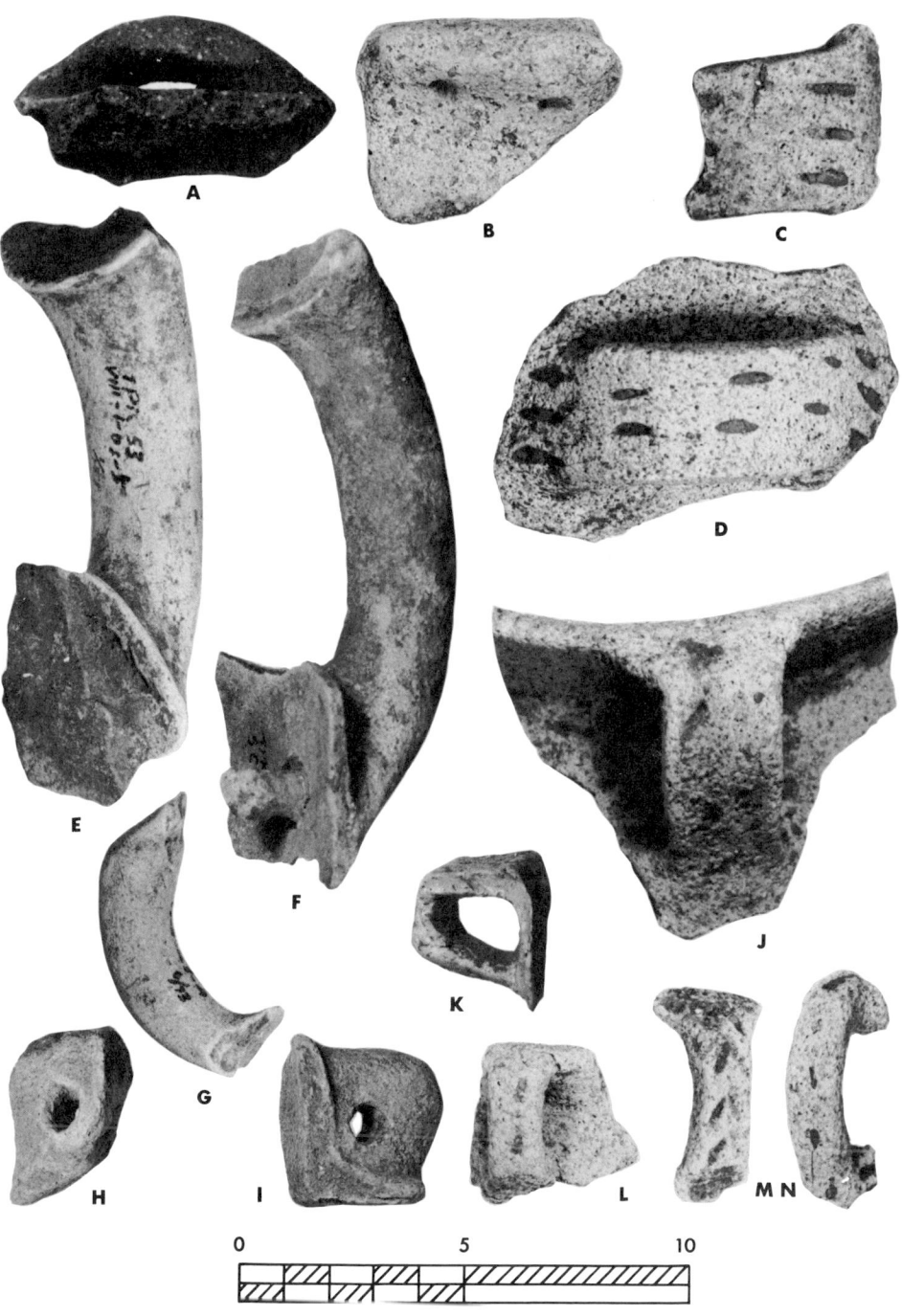

Yüan-shan Ware of Tapenkeng: Handles

PLATE 84

Yüan-shan Ware of Tapenkeng: Decorated Sherds

A, *B*, *D*, *E*, *G*, *J*, Yüan-shan Shellmound, Taita collection. *C*, VI-1-a3-13. *F*, VI-1-?. *H*, V-9-c1-3. *I*, V-9-c4-7.

Yüan-shan Ware of Tapenkeng: Decorated Sherds

Yüan-shan Ware of Tapenkeng: Ring Feet

PLATE 86

YÜAN-SHAN AND TPK RED WARES OF TAPENKENG

A, *D*, *E*, gritty Yüan-shan ware; *B*, *C*, Red. *A*, VII-1-c3-6. *B*, VI-2-a2-5. *C*, VI-2-d3-9. *D*, VI-2-a4-4. *E*, VI-2-3, VI-2-b3-4.

Yüan-shan and TPK Red Wares of Tapenkeng

PLATE 87

BOTANICAL GARDEN IMPRESSED WARE OF TAPENKENG

A, VI-1-c2-6. *B*, VI-1-d1-7. *C*, VI-1-a4-6. *D*, VI-1-b2-6. *E*, X-1-d2-7. *F*, V-7-c3-13. *G*, VI-1-b2-4. *H*, VI-1-d2-4.

Botanical Garden Impressed Ware of Tapenkeng

PLATE 88

IMPRESSED POTTERY OF KOU-T'I-SHAN, SHU-LIN, TAIPEI
PREFECTURE: TAITA COLLECTION

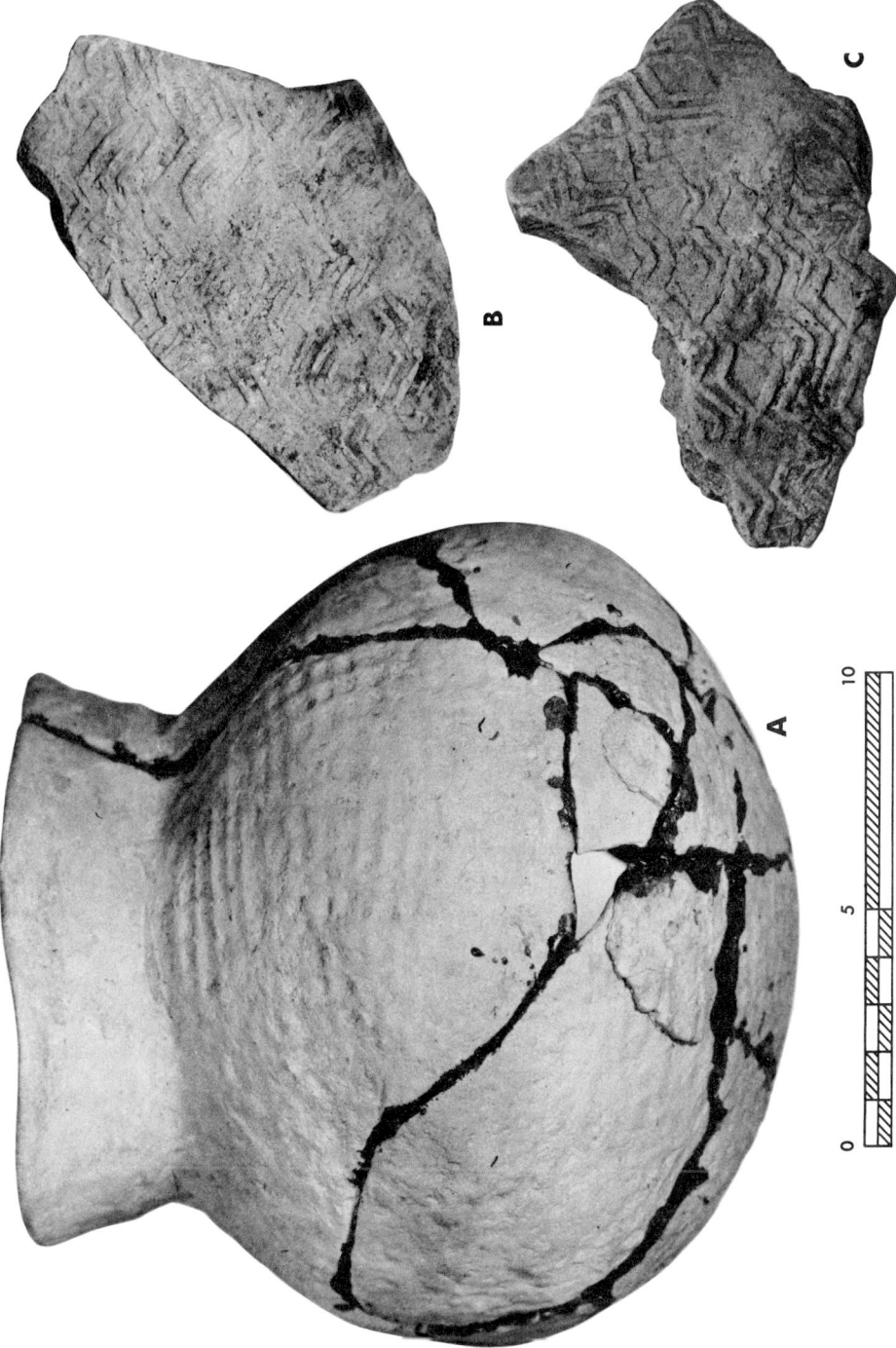

Impressed Pottery of Kou-t'i-shan, Shu-lin, Taipei Prefecture: Taita Collection

PLATE 89

Stone Manufacture at Tapenkeng

A, *B*, polishing stones; *C*, chipped pebbles; *D*, *E*, stone polishers; *F*, *G*, materials of slate. *A*, V-7-d1-13. *B*, IV-2-b1-2. *C*, IV-2-3. *D*, VIII-1-b4-2. *E*, VIII-1-b3-3. *F*, IV-8-c1-2. *G*, VIII-1-bO-4.

Stone Manufacture at Tapenkeng

PLATE 90

STONE HOES OF TAPENKENG: POLISHED

A, I-1-b2-2. *B*, Hsia-p'u, sc. *C*, V-8-c4-4. *D*, Possible mounting device, Taita collection, no 2617. *E*, V-8-a2-2. *F*, VI-1-b5-4. *G*, VIII-1-b4-4. *H*, I-2-d1-2.

Stone Hoes of Tapenkeng: Polished

PLATE 91

STONE HOES OF TAPENKENG: CHIPPED

A, sc. *B*, Hsia-p'u, sc. *C*, Hsia-yüan, sc. *D*, Hsia-p'u, sc. *E*, III-2. *F*, IV-1-c4-3. *G*, I-2-d4-2. *H*, Ting-p'u, sc. *I*, V-7-d1-4.

Stone Hoes of Tapenking: Chipped

PLATE 92

GROOVED PEBBLES, NET SINKERS, AWL, AND STONE
KNIVES OF TAPENKENG

A, X-1-d1-7. *B*, IV-2-b3-2. *C*, IV-2. *D*, X-1-c4-7. *E*,
VI-1-d2-8. *F*, VIII-1-c3-5. *G*, X-1-a2-9. *H*, Ting-p'u,
sc. *I*, Ting-p'u, sc. *J*, *K*, Kou-t'i-shan site, Taita collection. *L*, V-7-a1-10. *M*, I-2-c4-2. *N*, III-1-a2-2. *O*,
IV-8-sc. *P*, III-1-c4-1.

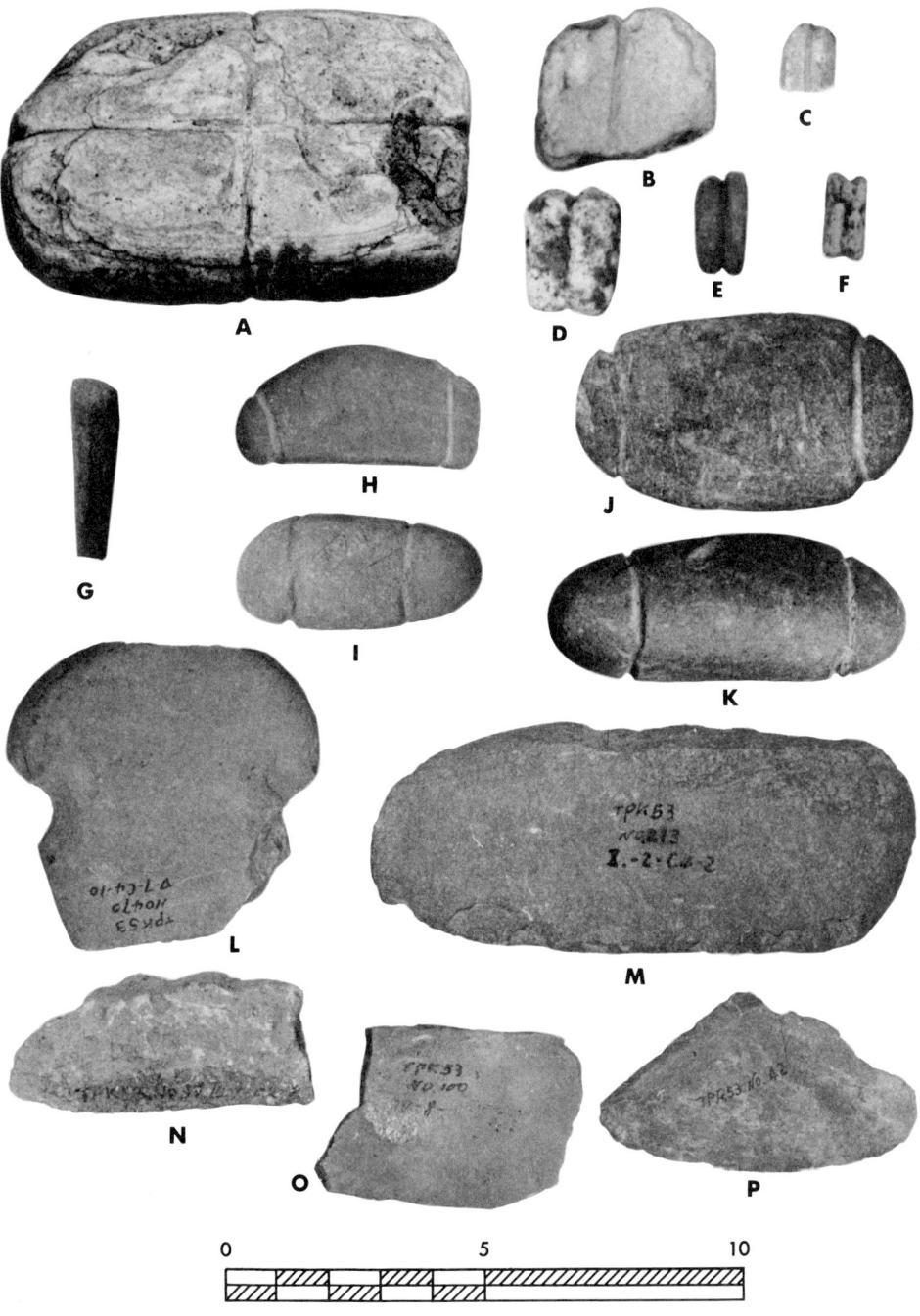

Grooved Pebbles, Net Sinkers, Awl, and Stone Knives of Tapenkeng

PLATE 93

<small>SHOULDERED AXES, TAPENKENG</small>

A, Hsia-p'u, sc. *B*, I-3-a4-1. *C*, VII-2-a2-1. *D*, Hsia-p'u, sc. *E*, V-8-a3-2. *F*, sc. *G*, V-7-c4-4. *H*, I-4-sc. *I*; I-2-a4-2. *J*, Ta-chih, Taipei City, Taita collection.

Shouldered Axes, Tapenkeng

PLATE 94

STEPPED ADZES, TAPENKENG

A, V-9-c2-2. *B*, V-7-c2-10. *C*, V-7-c3-2. *D*, V-8-d4-4.
E, VIII-1-b1-6. *F*, V-9-d1-3. *G*, VIII-1-b0-8. *H*, IV-7-
c3-1. *I*, III-2-c2-2. *J*, VI-1-a1-12. *K*, I-3-b4-3.

Stepped Adzes, Tapenkeng

PLATE 95

STEPPED ADZES, TAPENKENG

A, V-8-c3-6. *B*, IV-8-c-1. *C*, X-1-c3-7. *D*, V-8-c2-5.
E, Ting-p'u, western part, sc. *F*, V-7-c1-2. *G*, III-2-c2-5.
H, VI-2-d2-1. *I*, V-8-a3-1. *J*, VI-1-b3-4. *K*, X-1-b3-7.
L, I-1-a1-4. *M*, IV-8-b4-2. *N*, V-7-c1-4. *O*, I-2-a2-1. *P*,
Ting-p'u, sc. *Q*, VIII-1-b2-4. *R*, Test Pit 7, layer 5. *S*,
IV-8-b4-2. *T*, VIII-1-c3-2.

Stepped Adzes, Tapenkeng

PLATE 96

A, Hsia-yüan, sc. *B*, Ting-p'u, sc. *C*, Ting-p'u, sc. *D*,
VIII-1-4. *E*, Ting-p'u, sc. *F*, Ting-p'u, sc. *G*, Ting-p'u,
western part, sc. *H*, Hsia-p'u, sc. *I*, III-2-c2-1. *J*, VII-
1-b0-4. *K*, *L*, Yüan-shan Shellmound, Taita collection.
M, Kou-t'i-shan, Taita collection.

Stone Adzes, Tapenkeng

PLATE 97

STONE HOES OF KOU-T'I-SHAN: TAITA COLLECTION

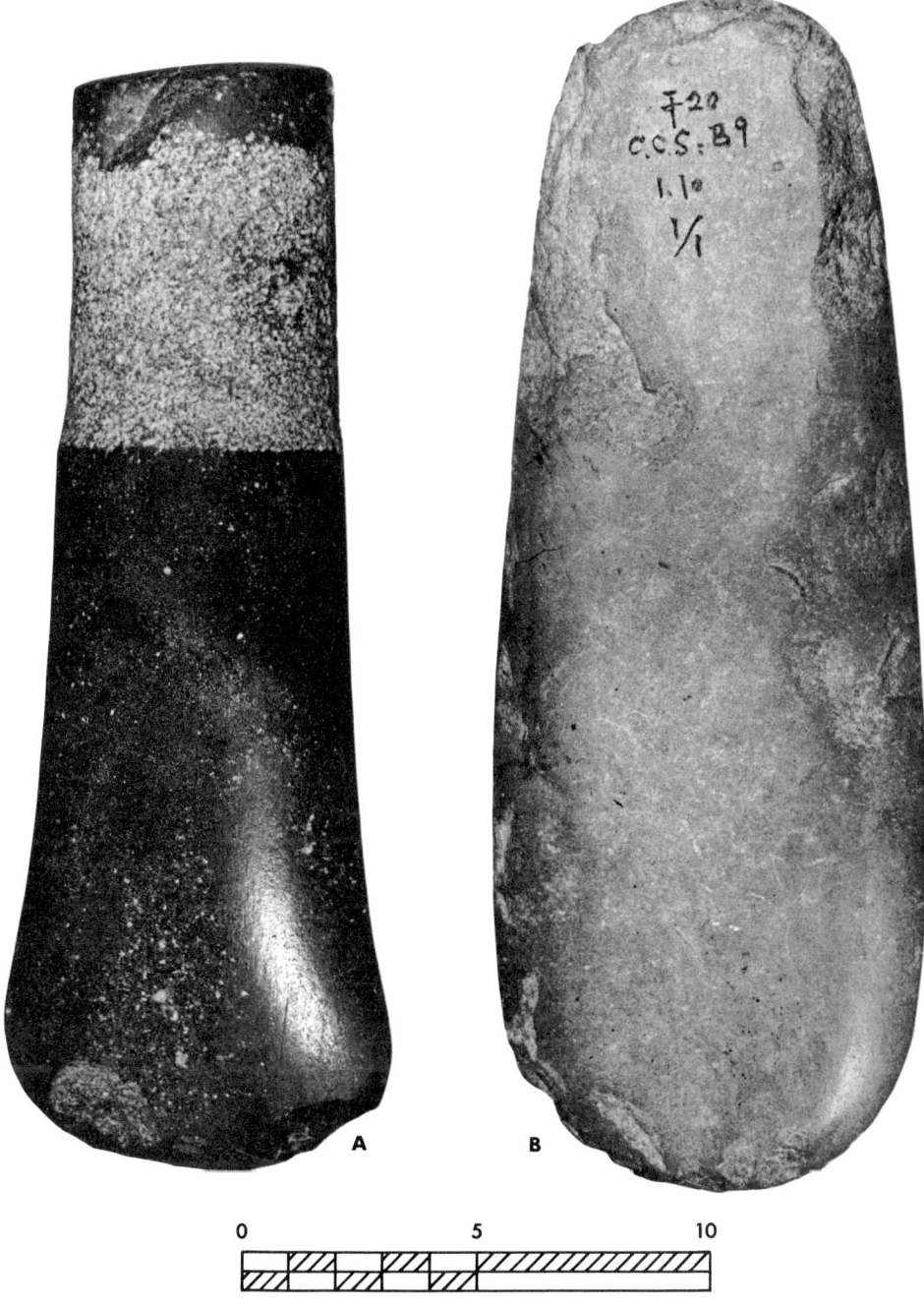

Stone Hoes of Kou-t'i-shan: Taita Collection

PLATE 98

A, V-8-d4-3. *B*, IV-8-d0-7. *C*, IV-2-d1-4. *D*, Ting-p'u, sc. *E*, sc. *F*, VI-1-a5-4. *G*, V-7-c1-2. *H*, I-3-d2-2. *I*, IV-8-1. *J*, IV-2-d2-4. *K*, VI-1-b1-9. *L*, VIII-1-b0-8. *M*, III-2-a4-1. *N*, V-8-c4-3. *O*, VI-1-a3-4. *P*, VI-1-b5-6. *Q*, VI-2-a2-4. *R*, I-1-1. *S*, VI-2-a2-2. *T*, Ting-p'u, sc. *U*, IV-3-d3-7. *V*, Test Pit 5, −26 cm. *W*, Ting-p'u, sc. *X*, III-1-c4-2. *Y*, VI-1-d2-10. *Z*, V-7-d4-4.

Stone Arrowheads, Tapenkeng

PLATE 99

Pot Supporters of the Yüan-shan Culture

A, Clay, Yüan-shan Shellmound; Taita collection.
B, Stone, Tapenkeng, I-1-d1-4.

Pot Supporters of the Yüan-shan Culture

PLATE 100

SPINDLE WHORLS, POTTERY DISKS, AND ORNAMENTS,
TAPENKENG

A, VI-1-c3-2. *B*, V-8-d2-3. *C*, V-8-c4-3. *D*, Yüan-shan
Shellmound, Taita collection. *E*, X-1-a4-4. *F*, Yüan-shan
Shellmound, Taita collection. *G*, VI-1-c2-2 (stone). *H*,
Hsia-p'u, sc. *I*, X-1-d2-7. *J*, X-1-d1-9. *K*, X-1-d4-9. *L*,
VI-1-d4-8. *M*, III-1-b2-?. *N*, VI-1-a1-7. *O*, IX-2-d1-3
(bronze). *P*, VIII-1-a0-1/3. *Q*, VI-2-a4-2. *R*, VIII-1-a1-
7. *S*, IV-1-d4-2. *T*, III-1-a4-2. *U*, IV-2-c2-3. *V*, V-8-
a1-5. *W*, V-7-c2-5. *X*, VI-1-d3-8. *Y*, sc. *Z*, IX-2-d1-3.
a, V-7-b2-5. *b*, X-1-a1-4. *c*, Ting-p'u, sc. *d*, V-8-d-4. *e*,
sc.

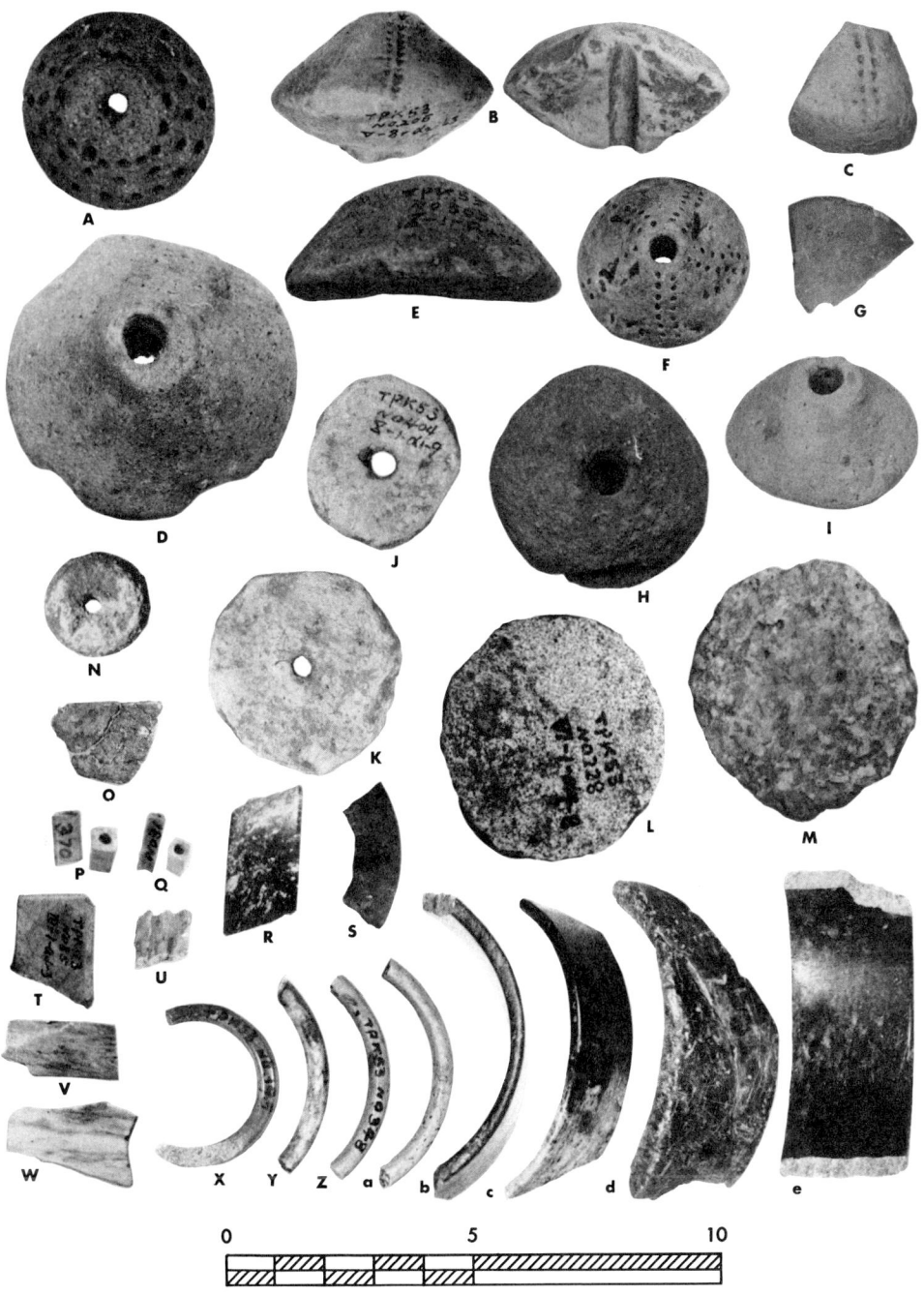

Spindle Whorls; Pottery Disks, and Ornaments, Tapenkeng

PLATE 101

ARTIFACTS OF THE SHIH-SAN-HANG CULTURE AT TAPEN-
KENG

A–E, iron objects; *F*, iron slug; *G–J*, impressed pottery; *K–M*, Chinese procelain sherds.

A, VI-2-a1-1. *B*, VIII-1-a2-4. *C*, X-1-c2-3. *D*, V-7-a4-
5. *E*, VI-1-a1-?. *F*, VI-1-a2-3. *G*, Eastern shellmound
on top of terrace. *H*, VI-1-b4-4. *I*, X-1-a4-5. *J*, Test
Pit 7, layers 3 and 4. *K*, X-1-c2. *L*, X-1-2. *M*, X-1-2.

Artifacts of the Shih-san-hang Culture of Tapenkeng

PLATE 102

POTSHERDS FROM THE SITE OF MAN-KOK-TSUI, LANTAU
ISLAND, HONG KONG

A, Coarse cord-marked pottery. *B*, "Soft" geometric-
impressed pottery. *C*, "Hard" geometric-impressed pottery.

Potsherds from the Site of Man-kok-tsui, Lantau Island, Hong Kong

PLATE 103

HUMAN SKULL FROM THE LUNGSHANOID BURIAL AT
FENGPITOU

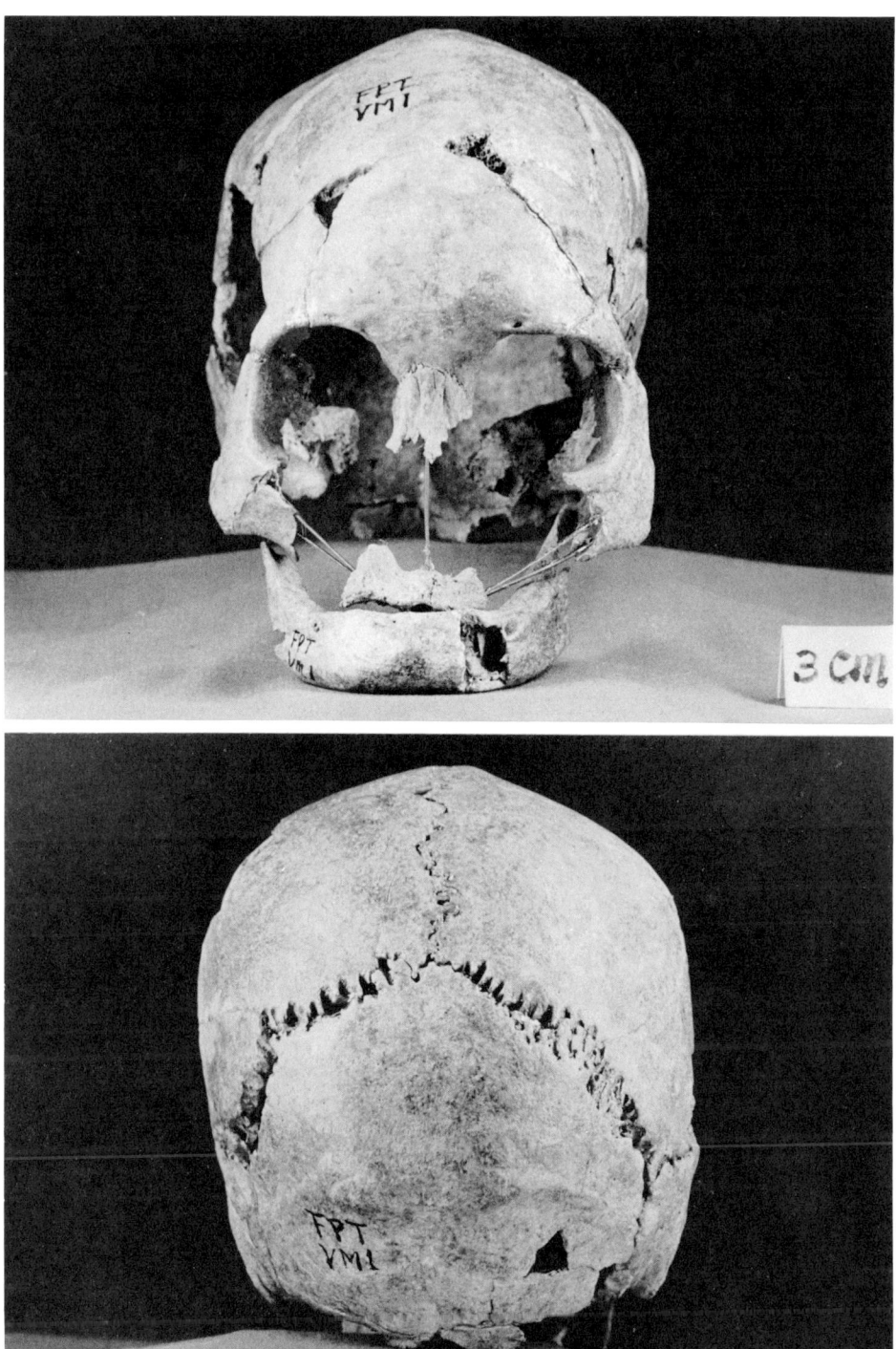

Human Skull from the Lungshanoid Burial at Fengpitou

PLATE 104

HUMAN SKULL FROM THE LUNGSHANOID BURIAL AT
FENGPITOU

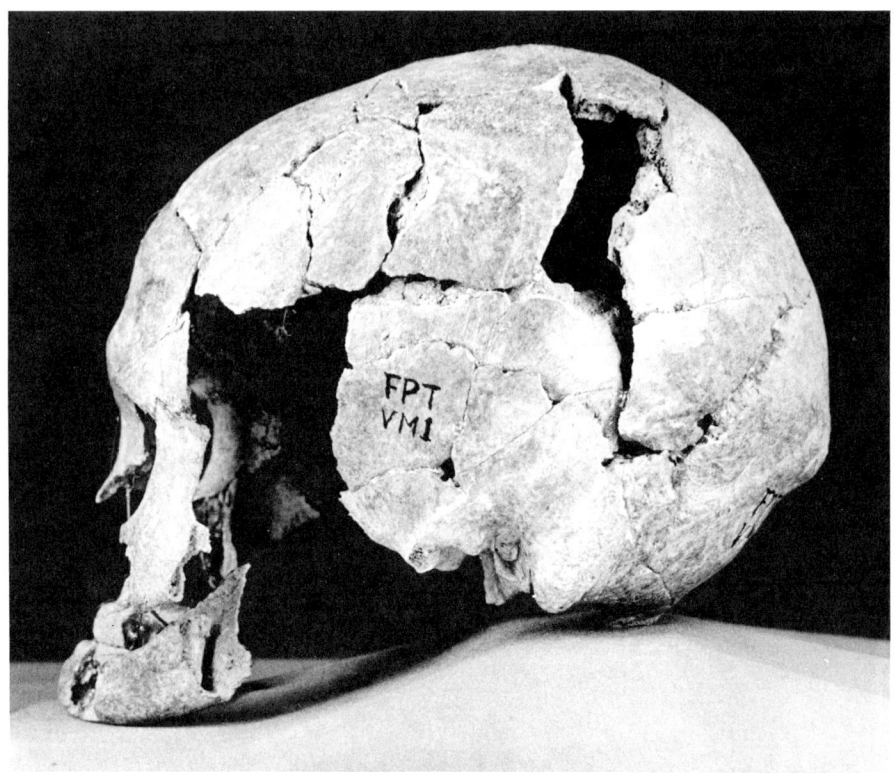

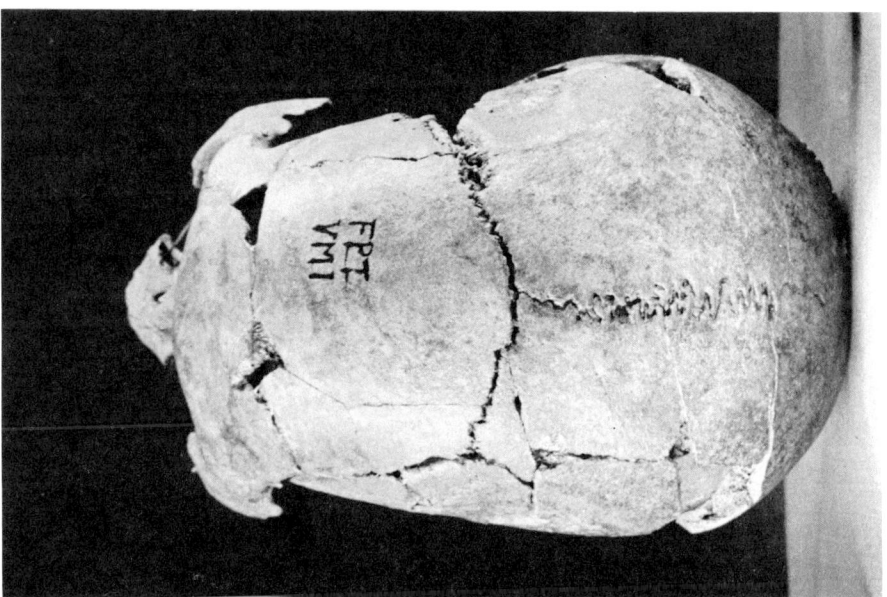

Human Skull from the Lungshanoid Burial at Fengpitou

PLATE 105

Mollusk Shells from Fengpitou

1, Gafrarium tumidum Boding. *2, Anomalocardia (Cryptonemella) producta* Kuroda & Habe. *3, Gafrarium (Circe) scriptum tumefactum* Sowerby. *4, Chione (Anomalodiscus) squamosa* Linné. *5, Anadara ehrembergi* Dubker. *6, Chione (Clausinella) isabellina* Philippi. *7, Thais mutabilis* Link. *8, Telescopium telescopium* Linné. *9, Terebralia semistriata* Bolten & Roding. *10, Niso?* sp. *11, Turritella terebra cerea* Reeve. *12, Nerita (Ritena) lineata* Gmelin. *13, Terebralia palustris* Linné. *14, Melanoides (Tarebia) crenulatus* Deshayes. *15, Cerithidea (Cerithideopsilla) cingulata* Gmelin. *16, Cerithidea (Cerithidea) rhizoporarum* A. Adams. *17, Balillaria zonalis* Bruguiere.

Mollusk Shells from Fengpitou

PLATE 106

MOLLUSK SHELLS FROM FENGPITOU

1, Terebralia palustris Linné. *2, Strombus isabella* Lamarck. *3, Anadara granosa* Linné. *4, Geloina fissidens* Pilsbry. *5, Katelysia (Hemitapes) virginea* Linné. *6, Ostrea (Saxostrea) vitrefacta* Sowerby. *7, Cyclina sinensis* Gmelin.

Mollusk Shells from Fengpitou

PLATE 107

Mollusk Shells from Fengpitou

1, Hemifusus sp. *2, Turbo (Olearia) marmoratus* Linné. *3, Placuna placenta* Linné. *4, Tridachnes (Vulgodacna) elongatus* Lamarck. *5, Meretrix petechialis* Lamarck. *6. Ostrea (Crassostrea) gigas* Thunberg.

Mollusk Shells from Fengpitou